AUTONOMY AN
Negotiating Comp
Multi-ethnic States

This book deals with one of the most urgent problems of contemporary times: the political organisation of multi-ethnic states. Most major conflicts of our time are internal to the state and revolve around the claims of access to or the redesign of the state. Responses to ethnic conflicts have ranged from oppression and ethnic cleansing to accommodations of ethnic claims through affirmative policies, special forms of representation, power sharing, and the integration of minorities. One of the most sought after, and resisted, devices for conflict management is autonomy. Within an overarching framework that explores different understandings of ethnic consciousness and the variety of territorial autonomies, the authors examine the experiences of spatial distribution of power in Canada, India, China, South Africa, Spain, the former Yugoslavia, Ethiopia and Eritrea, Sri Lanka, Cyprus, Papua New Guinea and Australia.

YASH GHAI is the Sir Y. K. Pao Professor of Public Law at the University of Hong Kong, before which he was Professor of Law at the University of Warwick, Dean of Law at the University of East Africa, and visiting professor at Yale University, Harvard University, University of Toronto, National University of Singapore and University of Wisconsin. His previous books include *Public Law and Political Change in Kenya* (1970); *Political Economy of Law* (1987); *Law, Administration and the Politics of Decentralisation in Papua New Guinea* (1993); *Law, Government and Politics in Pacific Island States* (1988); *Hong Kong's New Constitutional Order* (1997, 2nd edn 1998); *Hong Kong's Constitutional Debate* (2000). He has published articles in the *Journal of Modern African Studies, International Journal of the Sociology of Law, International and Comparative Law Quarterly, Pacifica Review,* and *Development and Change.* He has also been a constitutional and legal adviser to several governments, political parties, international organisations and non-governmental organisations.

CAMBRIDGE STUDIES IN LAW AND SOCIETY

Series editors:
Chris Arup, Martin Chanock, Pat O'Malley
School of Law and Legal Studies, La Trobe University
Sally Engle Merry, Susan Silbey
Departments of Anthropology and Sociology, Wellesley College

Editorial board:
Richard Abel, Harry Arthurs, Sandra Burman, Peter Fitzpatrick, Marc Galanter,
Yash Ghai, Nicola Lacey, Bonaventura da Sousa Santos, Sol Picciotto, Jonathan
Simon, Frank Snyder

The broad area of law and society has become a remarkably rich and dynamic
field of study. At the same time, the social sciences have increasingly engaged
with questions of law. In this process, the borders between legal scholarship and
the social, political and cultural sciences have been transcended, and the result
is a time of fundamental re-thinking both within and about law. In this vital
period, Cambridge Studies in Law and Society provides a significant new book
series with an international focus and a concern with the global transformation
of the legal arena. The series aims to publish the best scholarly work on legal
discourse and practice in social context, combining theoretical insights and
empirical research.

Already published:
Anthony Woodiwiss *Globalisation, Human Rights and Labour Law in Pacific Asia*
     0 521 62144 5 hardback 0 521 62883 0 paperback
Mariana Valverde *Diseases of the Will: Alcoholism and the Dilemmas of Freedom*
     0 521 62300 6 hardback 0 521 64469 0 paperback
Alan Hunt *Governing Morals: A Social History of Moral Regulation*
     0 521 64071 7 hardback 0 521 64689 8 paperback
Ronen Shamir *The Colonies of Law: Colonialism, Zionism and Law in Early
     Mandate Palestine*
     0 521 63183 1 hardback
John Torpey *The Invention of the Passport: Surveillance, Citizenship and the State*
     0 521 63249 8 hardback 0 521 63493 8 paperback
William Walters *Unemployment and Government: Genealogies of the Social*
     0 521 64333 3 hardback
Christopher Arup *The New World Trade Organization Agreements: Globalizing Law
     Through Services and Intellectual Property*
     0 521 77355 5 hardback
Heinz Klug *Constituting Democracy: Law, Globalism and South Africa's Political
     Reconstruction*
     0 521 78113 2 hardback 0 521 78643 6 paperback
Eric Feldman *The Ritual of Rights in Japan: Law, Society, and Health Policy*
     0 521 77040 8 hardback 0 521 77964 2 paperback

DEDICATION

We dedicate this book to Neelan Tiruchelvam with pride and gratitude, and sadness. Neelan, then director of the International Centre for Ethnic Studies, was the inspiration behind the project which has resulted in this book; his ideas, enthusiasm and energy ensured its completion. He dedicated his life to the cause of ethnic harmony and inter-ethnicity equity, and grappled intellectually and practically with constitutional forms that would promote this cause. One of the forms that particularly interested him was federalism. We are sad that he did not live to see the results of the research and reflections of his collaborators on the experience and potential of autonomy to accommodate competing ethnic claims. The life of this gentle and modest person, bursting with vitality and imagination, was brought to an untimely end by a suicide bomber on 29 July 1999.

AUTONOMY AND ETHNICITY

Negotiating Competing Claims in Multi-ethnic States

EDITED BY

Yash Ghai
University of Hong Kong

CAMBRIDGE
UNIVERSITY PRESS

PUBLISHED BY THE PRESS SYNDICATE OF THE UNIVERSITY OF CAMBRIDGE
The Pitt Building, Trumpington Street, Cambridge, United Kingdom

CAMBRIDGE UNIVERSITY PRESS
The Edinburgh Building, Cambridge CB2 2RU, UK
40 West 20th Street, New York, NY 10011–4211, USA
10 Stamford Road, Oakleigh, VIC 3166, Australia
Ruiz de Alarcón 13, 28014 Madrid, Spain
Dock House, The Waterfront, Cape Town 8001, South Africa

http://www.cambridge.org

First published 2000

Printed in Singapore by Green Giant Press Pte Ltd

Typeface New Baskerville (Adobe) 10/12 pt.   *System* QuarkXPress®   [PK]

A catalogue record for this book is available from the British Library

National Library of Australia Cataloguing in Publication data
Autonomy and ethnicity: negotiating competing claims in
multi-ethnic states.
Includes index.
ISBN 0 521 78112 4.
ISBN 0 521 78642 8 (pbk).
1. Autonomy. 2. Ethnicity. I. Ghai, Yash P., 1938– .
305.8

ISBN 0 521 78112 4 hardback
ISBN 0 521 78642 8 paperback

CONTENTS

ACKNOWLEDGEMENTS

I would like to record my gratitude to Neelan Tiruchelvam for initiating the project for this book and for asking me to direct it. Neelan was a close and affectionate friend from whom I learnt much about the complexity of ethnic relations and its interaction with constitutionalism.

I thank the staff of the International Centre for Ethnic Studies in Colombo for the administrative assistance they have provided throughout the duration of the project.

I am grateful to my colleague Jill Cottrell for valuable editorial assistance and for preparing the index.

The International Centre for Ethnic Studies would like to thank the Ford Foundation for a generous grant which facilitated the project.

CONTRIBUTORS

DANIELE CONVERSI is a Senior Lecturer in politics and sociology at the University of Lincolnshire and Humberside. He has taught at the Central European University, Budapest, University of Barcelona, and Cornell University. His publications include *The Basques, the Catalans, and Spain: Alternative Routes to Nationalist Mobilization* (1997), and *German Foreign Policy and the Breakup of Yugoslavia* (1998), as well as numerous journal articles. He is currently working on a book on theories of nationalism.

REED COUGHLAN is Professor of Sociology at Empire State, State University of New York. He has published work on ethnicity and the state, theories of ethnic identity and conflict, and the conflicts in Northern Ireland and Cyprus. He co-edited *The Economic Dimensions of Ethnic Conflict* (1991). The recent recipient of the Imperatore Fellowship, he is currently working on a study of the breakup of Yugoslavia as well as on a project which focuses on the Bosnian communities of upstate New York.

YASH GHAI is Sir Y. K. Pao Professor of Public Law at the University of Hong Kong, before which he was Professor of Law at the University of Warwick, Dean of Law at the University of East Africa, and visiting professor at Yale University, Harvard University, University of Toronto, National University of Singapore, and University of Wisconsin. His previous books include *Public Law and Political Change in Kenya* (1970); *Political Economy of Law* (1987); *Law, Administration and the Politics of Decentralisation in Papua New Guinea* (1993); *Law, Government and Politics in Pacific Island States* (1988); *Hong Kong's New Constitutional Order* (1997, 2nd edn 1998); and *Hong Kong's Constitutional Debate* (2000). He has published articles in the *Journal of Modern African Studies, International Journal of the Sociology of Law, International and Comparative Law Quarterly, Pacifica Review,* and *Development and Change.* He has also been a constitutional and legal adviser to several governments, political parties, international organisations and non-government organisations.

HEINZ KLUG is Assistant Professor in the Law School at the University of Wisconsin, Madison and Honorary Research Associate, Law School, University of Witwatersrand. Growing up in Durban, South Africa, he participated in the anti-apartheid struggle, serving as an activist in the African National Congress and spending eleven years in exile. He first taught law at the University of the Witwatersrand, and has worked in various South African government ministries and ANC commissions since 1990. Throughout his career he has published widely in such journals as *South African Journal on Human Rights, Review of Constitutional Studies, Journal of Legal Pluralism, Verfassung und Recht in Übersee, Hastings International and Comparative Law Journal, Wisconsin International Law Journal, Contemporary Sociology, American Journal of International Law* and *South African Law Journal.*

SINIŠA MALEŠEVIĆ is a Lecturer in the Department of Political Science and Sociology, National University of Ireland, Galway. He has published extensively on ethnic relations, nationalism, culture and ideology. His articles have appeared in *Nations and Nationalism, Europa Ethnica, East European Quarterly, Development in Practice* and other journals. He is also editor of *Culture in Central and Eastern Europe: Institutional and Value Changes* (1997).

VASUKI NESIAH completed her JD (1993) and doctoral degree (2000) at Harvard Law School. Her doctoral dissertation examined how territory was conceptualised in public international law. She has taught in varying capacities at Syracuse University, Harvard Law School and the University of Puerto Rico. Her research interests include international law, property law, legal history, jurisprudence, feminism and comparative federalism.

JAMES C.N. PAUL has served as Legal Secretary to the Chief Justice of the United States, and has taught law at the University of North Carolina, University of Pennsylvania, and Rutgers, the State University of New Jersey. He has also served as Adjunct Professor at Columbia University, where he gave seminars on Law and Social Change in Africa for many years. He served as founding Dean of the Law School of Haile Selassie University (now the University of Addis Ababa) during 1962–67 and as Academic Vice-President of that university during 1967–69 and as a sometime consultant to its President during 1973–74. He returned to Ethiopia on a number of occasions during 1991–95 as a guest of the Constitutional Commission and a consultant to the Special Prosecutor appointed to investigate crimes against humanity committed during the military dictatorship (1979–91). He also participated in the international seminar organised by the Constitutional Commission of Eritrea in 1995. He is presently William J. Brennan Professor of Law (Emeritus) at Rutgers, and Trustee and Secretary of the International Center for Law in Development which is based in New York. Over the past four decades he has written a number of pieces on law and development, human rights, and constitutional ordering in sub-Saharan Africa.

ANTHONY REGAN works in the Research School of Pacific and Asian Studies at the Australian National University, Canberra, in a project on the State, Society and Governance in Melanesia. He is a lawyer who has worked in Papua New Guinea (13 years) and Uganda (3 years) from 1981 to 1996. His research focuses on the relations of state and society in post-colonial states, with particular reference to the role of constitutions, decentralisation policies and conflict resolution. He has done work in Bougainville since 1981, first for the North Solomons Provincial Government, and since 1995 for the Bougainville Transitional Government and the Bougainville People's Congress. He has been involved as a technical adviser in several phases of processes directed towards resolving the conflict that has divided Bougainville since 1988.

CHERYL SAUNDERS is Professor of Law at the University of Melbourne, where she is also the Director of its Centre for Comparative Constitutional Studies, and Deputy Chair of the Constitutional Centenary Foundation. She has written extensively on both federalism and Australian constitutional reform. She has also been a consultant both on federalism and Australian constitutional aspects of Aboriginal reconciliation, and on other constitutional issues affecting the indigenous peoples of Australia.

NEELAN TIRUCHELVAM had masters and doctoral degrees in law from Harvard Law School. He was a Fellow in Law and Modernisation at Yale Law School, and an Edward Smith Visiting Fellow and Lecturer at Harvard Law School. He was a director of both the International Centre for Ethnic Studies and the Law and Society Trust in Colombo. Dr Tiruchelvam took part in a number of international election observation missions, assisted in an evaluation of the draft constitution of Kazakhstan in September 1999 and also participated in an early review of the constitution-making process in Ethiopia. He also worked on the Nepal constitution. He was a co-chairman of an international evaluation team on the peace structures in South Africa, constituted by the National Peace Secretariat and International Alert. Tiruchelvam was a member of the Sri Lankan parliament and a constitutional lawyer. He was appointed a President's Counsel in March 1998. He was elected chairman of the London-based Minority Rights Group International in April 1999.

RONALD L. WATTS is Principal Emeritus, Professor Emeritus of Political Studies and Fellow of the Institute of Intergovernmental Relations at Queen's University at Kingston, Canada, where he has been a member of the academic staff since 1955 and was Principal and Vice-Chancellor 1974–84. From 1988 to 1993 he was Director of the Institute of Inter-governmental Relations. He was President of the International Association of Centres for Federal Studies 1991–98. He is currently a member of the board of the Forum of Federations. On several occasions he has been a consultant to the Government of Canada during constitutional deliberations, most notably 1980–81 and 1991–92, and has been a consultant for governments in several other countries. As a political scientist he has worked for over forty years on the comparative study of federal systems, and has written or edited more than twenty books and monographs and over forty-five chapters in books and articles. He has received five honorary degrees, and became an Officer of the Order of Canada in 1979. His most recent books are *Comparing Federal Systems*, of which the second edition was published in 1999, and *The Spending Power in Federal Systems: A Comparative Study* (1999).

CHAPTER 1

ETHNICITY AND AUTONOMY:
A FRAMEWORK FOR ANALYSIS

YASH GHAI

More than any previous age, ours is marked by ethnic conflicts. In recent decades, domestic conflicts and wars have greatly exceeded interstate conflicts. Most internal conflicts are about the role, structure and policies of the state, and about social justice. Responses to ethnic conflicts have ranged from oppression and ethnic cleansing to accommodations of ethnic claims through affirmative policies, special forms of representation, power sharing, and the integration of minorities. One of the most sought after, and resisted, devices for conflict management is autonomy.

Despite its popularity, autonomy is controversial, and many conflicts are themselves about the demand for and resistance to autonomy. At other times, autonomy seems to offer a way out of conflict or the transformation of the conflict. The promise to consider or negotiate autonomy has been used successfully to bring about truces between warring parties. Autonomy has sometimes secured a breathing space as an interim, or even ambiguous, expedient while longer-term solutions are explored and negotiated. Autonomy has been used to separate as well as to bring people together. In recent years it has been seen as a panacea for cultural diversity, and as, under the influence of identity politics, the realisation of the extreme heterogeneity of states dawns on us, autonomy seems to provide the path to maintaining unity of a kind while conceding claims to self-government. But autonomy can also be used to marginalise communities, as in apartheid Bantustans; and in contemporary times it can constitute subtle forms of control or isolation, as is claimed here by the authors of chapters on Ethiopia, China, Yugoslavia and even India.

This book explores the dialectics of ethnicity and territoriality as mediated by a variety of forms of autonomy. The countries chosen for study are marked by ethnic distinctions and conflicts, but they do not tell

1

a similar story. Some have basically two ethnic groups, others comprise great heterogeneity. In some cases the distance between groups is aggravated by an accumulation of cleavages, while in others the cleavages overlap, moderating the salience of particular distinctions. What they have in common, as with so many other countries, is the search for some kind of accommodation through the political reorganisation of space. We have examples of relative stability through autonomy (Canada, India and Spain), of states which collapsed, allegedly, under the weight of autonomy (the former Yugoslavia) and some which are still engaged in its pursuit (Cyprus and Sri Lanka). The states which emerged from the fall-out of Yugoslavia, particularly Bosnia–Herzegovina, are pursuing autonomy in their own fashion, while NATO has reimposed it on Serbia through its restoration in Kosovo. South Africa has warded off ethnic autonomy by modifying its claims, providing through regionalism wider participation in national policy and law making. A 'high degree of autonomy' is China's preferred formula for the reunification of Greater China, motivated by recognition of economic, not ethnic, differences; for ethnic minorities, not ensconced in market economies, are only entitled to a lower and uncertain form of autonomy. Bougainville, having successfully negotiated autonomy from Papua New Guinea in 1976, is renegotiating a new status, more like association than the traditional sharing of sovereignty. Australia is redefining its relationship to the Aboriginal peoples but, unlike for Canada's First Nations, the territorial arrangements do not have an important role. The fact that states which already have some form of autonomy or where autonomy has failed are still engaged in new forms of autonomy shows both the dynamic nature of ethnicity and the appeal of autonomy.

The use of autonomy as a species of group rights has changed the character of international law. Under the impetus of the human rights movement, individuals have secured a status in international law hitherto denied them. Under the autonomy movement, groups also have obtained recognition, which has given new impetus to the currency of self-determination. At the domestic level, autonomy is beginning to transform our notions of the organisation of state, the rationalisation of public power and the homogenising mission of the state (Parekh 1993; Tully 1995; Walker 1997). Both domestic and international developments challenge the liberal theory of state and power. New configurations of power, fresh claims for recognition, and imaginative layerings of territories constantly press against established principles and practice, offering accommodation to identity claims within the interstices of the state or threatening to break it apart. Autonomy is increasingly becoming the metaphor of our times.

In recent years, significant developments in international law have served to provide legal foundations for autonomy, although its legal basis is still unclear (Hannum 1990; Thornberry 1998). Legal bases are relevant to the possibilities of intervention by the international community in the dispute and its role in supervising and guaranteeing the outcome. The presence or absence of an entitlement in either international or national law to autonomy, as well as provisions limiting its scope, can play an important role in the conduct of negotiations and the relative bargaining position of parties, especially when there is international or third-party mediation. The case for autonomy rests on three major principles: minority rights, indigenous rights and, more controversially, the right to self-determination. On the first, the UN Committee on Human Rights has given a broad interpretation, encompassing the notion of collective rights and positive duties on the state, to the parsimonious provision on minorities in the International Covenant on Civil and Political Rights (art. 27). This approach is taken further in the 1992 UN Declaration on the Rights of Minorities. On indigenous peoples, the 1959 paternalistic and assimilationist convention was replaced in 1989 by another which adopts a more robust attitude towards the value of their traditional cultures and land rights. The Draft Declaration on the Rights of Indigenous People (1994) proclaims their right to self-determination, including an entitlement to autonomy. These ideas have influenced state policies in Canada and Australia, and have led to negotiations on autonomy and collective rights. Finally, the right to self-determination has increasingly been reinterpreted in terms of internal constitutional arrangements for the political and autonomy rights of minorities. The Canadian Supreme Court has given a new twist to the right to secession in its answer to the reference from the federal government as to whether Quebec has a right to unilateral secession. The court held that under neither the Canadian constitution nor international law did Quebec have that right but that, once a part of Canada declared emphatically that it wished to secede, all parties had to enter into negotiations over this claim (Quebec Secession Reference (1998) 161 DLR (4th) 385).

Such a view of self-determination has some support in certain national constitutions, indicating no more than a trend at this stage. A number of constitutions now recognise an entitlement to self-government, such as the Philippines in relation to its indigenous peoples and the Muslim minority; Spain, which guarantees autonomy to three regions and invites others to negotiate with the centre for autonomy; Papua New Guinea, which authorises provinces to negotiate with the central government for substantial devolution of power; and Ethiopia, which gives its 'nations, nationalities and peoples' the right to seek wide-ranging powers as states within a federation and even guarantees their right to secession. The Russian constitution of 1993, in the wake of the break-up of the Soviet Union, provides for extensive autonomy to its constituent parts, whether republics or autonomous areas (Agnew 1995; Lynn and Novikov 1997; Smith 1996).The Chinese constitution entrenches the rights of ethnic minorities to substantial self-government, although in practice the dominance of the Communist Party negates their autonomy. In other instances, the constitution authorises, but does not require, the setting up of autonomous areas, with China again an interesting example, in order to provide a constitutional basis for the 'One Country, Two Systems' policy for the reunification of Hong Kong, Macau and Taiwan. It should also be noted, on the other hand, that some constitutions prohibit or restrict the scope of autonomy by requiring that the state be 'unitary' or some similar expression; such a provision has retarded the acceptance or the implementation of meaningful devolution in, for example, Sri Lanka, Papua New Guinea and China.

There is no developed or reliable theory of autonomy; modern but contested justifications revolve around the notion of identity. We are, for the most part, hazy about its structures or the mechanisms to capture its potential. We have yet to find a balance between the common and the particular which lies at the heart of autonomy. Our increasing preoccupation with autonomy has made us opportunistic in its use, over-ambitious in our expectations, and excited by the variations and flexibility to which it will lend itself. Our purpose in this book is to try to gain some insight into the potential – and pitfalls – of autonomy by comparing different national experiences. There are limits to generalisations and comparisons, for the concession and operation of autonomy are contingent on several factors – such as history, traditions of governance, the size of territory, the size and number of communities, and internal and external pressures. But the diversity of circumstances can also provide insights into the feasibility and viability of autonomy, these differences serving as variables.

ETHNICITY

Ethnicity is used here as a broad concept, covering a variety of factors which distinguish one group of people from others. Important contemporary distinctions are language, race, religion, and colour. When these markers cease to be mere means of social distinctions, and become the basis of political identity and claims to a specific role in the political process or power, ethnic distinctions are transformed into ethnicity. There is now considerable literature on why and how the transformation takes place – varying from theories of primordialism and socio-biology to the deliberate mobilisation and manipulation of differences for political

4

and economic reasons (Brass 1991; Eriksen 1993; Horowitz 1985; Kothari 1988; Rex and Mason 1986). The position of most authors in this book is that ethnicity is not primordial, in the sense that the emotive power of ethnic distinctions inevitably leads to political conflict and demands. On the contrary, the ebb and flow of ethnicity, its assertiveness or decline, are explicable on a variety of social and economic factors, of which a particular concern of ours is the effect of the design and orientation of the state itself. Most authors provide fascinating accounts of manipulation, when intellectuals and grammarians invoke distorted versions of history or phonetics. But many studies in this volume show that ethnicity is not simply a matter of manipulation. Economic and social developments can disrupt traditional patterns and cause dislocations, on which ethnic resentment can feed, as in Bougainville. Modernity is a potent cause of ethnicity, as China may soon discover. Studies of Sri Lanka, Bougainville and the Balkans show that ethnic consciousness – and resentment – is a frequent result of oppression by the state or the majority community. There is also a tendency to label conflicts as 'ethnic', both by members of minority groups and by the media, the former because they consider such categorisation strengthens their case and the latter because of laziness. Once such a categorisation is accepted, it can change the focus of attention – from the analysis of underlying economic and social problems to the accommodation of competing ethnic claims – and thus both simplify the problem and render its solution complex.

Our case studies also show that identities may also be forced upon the people by the state. The colonial experience provides many examples of how the formation of identities was facilitated by the way in which the government drew administrative boundaries or categorised people, for example for the purpose of the census. The Spanish constitution stimulated new identities by its provisions for autonomy for groups additional to the 'historic communities'. During apartheid, the South African government tried to break up the blacks into different communities through Bantustans, and divided other groups too by particularising representation and participation by race. China, following the nationality policies of Lenin and Stalin, has imposed ethnic categories on the people, sometimes arbitrarily. More recently, Paul argues, the Ethiopian constitution imposes 'nationality' on people. Many of these 'impositions' are intended to replace class politics with ethnic politics. In the course of time, the communities concerned may begin to accept these categories as their own perception of identity – and turn it to political purpose. We examine the political demands of ethnic groups, especially when they relate to autonomy, and the consequences of autonomy arrangements on ethnicity, particularly its articulations with the ideology, organisation and apparatus of the state. We are also interested in the relationship of ethnic groups among themselves, for ethnic consciousness arises only in the presence of other groups, and the state is frequently perceived as being under the domination of one or associated ethnic groups. Because ethnicity is fluid and changing, it is necessary to decide what the appropriate constitutional response to ethnic demands should be. The response could have a major impact on ethnicity, particularly on whether it is mitigated or intensified. There may be differences of view as to the effect of a particular concession to ethnic demands, between those who consider that the concession would lead to integration of the group and others who believe that it would reinforce both its desire and capacity for separation. And because ethnicity itself is regarded as the result of manipulation, the response of the state or groups which dominate the state may be less to engage in constitutional engineering than to combat the manipulation through political or military means.

We make no sharp distinction between different markers. But clearly the differences in markers matter. Some forms of ethnicity are more malleable than others (religion is losing some salience in Europe, even in Ireland, while language is still a divisive force, but religion is fundamental in Asia). In Cyprus, we see the shift from religion to language as the basis of distinction between its Greek and Turkish populations. The original Canadian diversity revolved around language and law; subsequently, it extended more broadly to culture and way of life, to the claims of being a 'distinct society' (we see a similar progression in relation to Sri Lanka Tamils). The simple duality has been challenged by other ethnically related claims, producing a complexity which is at the heart of Canada's political and constitutional difficulties, so well explored by Watts in this volume. It has been suggested that had the British in India not privileged religion over language, the course of history would have been different, and with no partition or a different kind of partition. India today seems to be able to handle linguistic differences and claims better than religious ones. The new Ethiopian constitution is all-embracing – it gives the right of self-determination to all 'nations, nationalities and peoples', who are defined as a 'group of people who have or share a large measure of a common culture or similar customs, mutual intelligibility of language, belief in a common or related identities, a common psychological make-up, and who inhabit an identifiable, predominantly contiguous territory' (art. 39(5)). Conversi discusses the differential impact of cultural and other markers, culture being more open and less exclusionary than other markers. On the other hand, culture is the foundation of many identity claims and more morally compelling than distinctions of colour or race.

The occupation with identity politics means growing complexity and fuzziness in acceptable markers, as the extract from the Ethiopian constitution demonstrates. There is increasing emphasis on self-identity.

Politically, ethnic groups can be and are defined (or define themselves) by their political aims. They are content to be called minorities if their aspirations do not extend beyond special linguistic or educational or religious facilities. They proclaim their ethnicity if the goal is some form of autonomy. Further along the line, they may designate themselves 'nation' or 'nationality' if they aim to set up a separate state of their own. Although the state may respond to them in terms of these distinctions, the utility of the distinctions is doubtful since there is an easy progression from one to another. But the state may also impose markers, as China has with 'nationality' but not 'nation' as the latter might imply extensive autonomy with the right to secede.

Some markers get more recognition than others under international law. The most obvious example is the distinction based on indigenousness, a category grounded in a combination of cultural and ethnic features. Until recently, neither international nor domestic systems provided any protection for them. Although federations are well placed to deal with indigenous people generously, because they have already come to terms with divided sovereignty, and the indigenous people are geographically concentrated, in few federations have indigenous people fared well. The institution of 'reserves', invented in the United States and carried to other colonial places, was used to segregate and subjugate them. Now, under the influence of international conventions for indigenous peoples, national systems are providing a constitutional framework for autonomy for them. Because of their small size and distance from urban centres, indigenous people are unlikely to have influence on national institutions and policies, even if they are enfranchised, which they have not always been. Autonomy for indigenous peoples is less contested than for other groups; they do not raise the same kinds of problems as the coexistence of other ethnic groups who are in competition in modern politics and economy – at least, not until the moving frontier of the market chances upon natural resources on their land. Australia is considerably behind Canada in questions of autonomy for indigenous peoples, as appears from Watts' account; there is much discussion in Canada of 'treaty' rather than provincial autonomy, drawing upon assurances given by the Crown to them. Saunders notes how the debates on Aboriginal rights in Australia are confused and unproductive.

The incorporation of territorial and cultural autonomy for indigenous peoples has posed various difficulties. They invariably create asymmetry and are hard to fit within national norms of human rights. This is because the autonomy they seek preserves customary law and practices, which imply unequal rights or discrimination against outsiders as well as insiders. Their demands can have a major effect on other federal arrangements; the Aboriginals in Quebec, a minority within a minority, have resisted Quebecan independence. They can also raise difficult sovereignty issues – just as the Canadian francophones want an acknowledgement of their 'distinct society', indigenous peoples want a recognition of their prior sovereignty. Yet the exercise of this sovereignty is difficult in the modern context, not only for the reasons mentioned above but also because of the lack of technical resources and expertise and the size of the territory (for example, Nunavut constitutes nearly 20 per cent of Canada's population but has only 22,000 people).

The salience of ethnicity is also affected by other considerations. The geographical concentration of a group is of course essential to territorial autonomy, although developing notions of corporate autonomy have opened up possibilities of limited self-government and participation in national institutions. Countries in which markers cut across groups are affected differently by ethnicity from where they are reinforcing; in the former, its salience is moderated by some commonality. India's extreme heterogeneity has been its strength, while the problems of Cyprus and Sri Lanka are bedevilled by bipolarity and the absence of cross-cutting cleavages. Ethiopia has numerous ethnic groups, but its politics have been determined essentially by the triangle of the Amhara, Tigray and Oromo peoples. If the markers converge with the dominant community in a neighbouring state, the central government is usually reluctant to grant autonomy to such groups (as evidenced by the policies of Sri Lanka, India and China). Autonomy in general is more likely to be conceded and to succeed when it is not explicitly based on ethnicity, yet it is precisely in these circumstances that there is the greatest agitation for autonomy.

AUTONOMY

Autonomy is a device to allow ethnic or other groups claiming a distinct identity to exercise direct control over affairs of special concern to them, while allowing the larger entity those powers which cover common interests. Autonomy can be granted under different legal forms. There is no uniform use of terms for the different kinds of arrangements for autonomy (for useful discussions, see Elazar 1987: ch. 2; Watts 1994a:7–10). I use 'autonomy' as a generic term, specialised terms being used to designate particular types of arrangements. The best known is federalism, where all regions enjoy equal powers and have an identical relationship to the central government. Traditionally, federalism has not been used as a way to solve problems of ethnic diversity, although two old federations, Switzerland and Canada, were adopted in part to accommodate ethnic diversity. Classical federalism, where all regions have equal powers, may not be sufficiently sensitive to the peculiar cultural and other needs of a particular community, which require a greater measure of self-government. Federal systems where one or more regions are vested with special powers not granted to other provinces are known as 'asymmetrical' (Agranoff 1994; Boase 1994; Brown-John 1994; Stevens 1977; Watts 1994a).

The federal model may be regarded as unnecessary if the need is to accommodate only one or two minority groups. In these situations, special powers may be devolved only to that part of the country where the minority constitutes a majority; these powers are exercised by regional institutions. Normally very significant powers are devolved and the region, unlike in a federation, plays relatively little role in national government and institutions. This kind of autonomy is referred to as 'regional autonomy' (Heintze 1998:10–11) or 'federacy' (Elazar 1987:7; Stevens 1977). By its nature, regional autonomy is asymmetrical, as in Hong Kong and in the 'historic communities' of Spain.

Both federalism and regional autonomy are characterised by constitutional entrenchment of autonomy. When territorial devolution of powers is not constitutionally protected, or not sufficiently protected, the arrangements are sometimes referred to as 'regionalism' (where central powers and institutions remain dominant, as in Italy) or 'decentralisation' (which is frequently a form of administrative transfer of powers, as in France). Local government can also be an effective way to give certain powers to a group, as the geographical scale is small and the prospects of its inhabitants being ethnically homogeneous are better. Some federations now constitutionally protect local government as a third tier of government for this very reason (Nigeria and Spain; but constitutional protection was rejected in India). When a federal-type state enters into economico-political regional arrangements like the European Union, a third constitutional tier appears (such as in Spain, Finland and Germany).

A major limitation of territorial devolution of power is that it is restricted to circumstances where there is a regional concentration of an ethnic group. Sometimes attempts are made to transcend this limitation by 'corporate autonomy', whereby an ethnic group is given forms of collective rights. Rights or entitlements protected under such autonomy can be personal, cultural or political. This book does not deal with corporate autonomy, except to the extent that it has played an important role in the political structure of a country, as in Cyprus at independence, or when it is part of territorial arrangements, as in the proposals for Sri Lanka which incorporate elements of consociationalism. Contemporary examples include the constitution of Bosnia–Herzegovina, which combines more traditional federalism with corporate shares in power and communal vetoes. A more limited version is the application to the members of a community of its personal or religious laws (covering marriage and family, and occasionally land, particularly for tribal communities) (see Ghai 1998:52–9). Sometimes group autonomy takes the shape of communal representation, whereby candidacy and voting are based on a communal electoral roll, as in Bosnia and Fiji and as proposed for Kosovo.

These different legal and political forms of autonomy are not always easily distinguishable. Spain is increasingly analysed in federal and not just regional terms. Papua New Guinea, although officially a 'decentralised state', has marked federal features. The choice of labels is not important for purposes of negotiation, and some deliberate fudging may indeed be beneficial, especially if the constitution seems to prohibit some options or where there is particular sensitivity about 'sovereignty' (as in China). Labels often refer to legal status – matters such as the degree of entrenchment and the method of division of subjects/powers – which may not always be a true guide to the scope of autonomy. Even when it is possible to be specific about the labels, a legal form may not exist to the exclusion of other forms. Thus, Canada has both symmetrical (for the most part) and asymmetrical (for Quebec) federalism, federacy or regional autonomy for Aboriginals, and a group council for Métis. Similar diversity is to be found in India. These devices are no longer regarded as alternatives or exclusive; contemporary variations in diversity, in terms of numbers, identity and resources, within a single state, requiring differential responses, may benefit from a combination of them.

These developments regarding federalism and autonomy have helped in the devising of arrangements for forms of self-government to suit varying circumstances and contingencies. In addition, there are variations in detailed arrangements within each category, such as in the division of powers between different layers of government, structures of government, the relationship between these structures at different levels, and the distribution of financial and other resources. While this flexibility is important in the negotiation process and facilitates compromises, there is the danger that it may lead to complex arrangements and systems, producing a lack of cohesion and the difficulties of governability. When negotiations enter a difficult phase, there is a temptation to devise some fancy scheme which may produce a temporary consensus which is hard to operationalise; thus, there is a conflict between immediate and long-term interests. Federal or autonomy arrangements are inherently hard to operate, requiring both high administrative capacity and political skills, and the embroidery on classical systems that tough negotiations may lead to can undermine the long-term prospects of settlement by their sheer weight or complexity, as in Papua New Guinea, Ethiopia and even Spain.

The definitions I have adopted concentrate on divisions of powers and corresponding institutions. It is frequently said that autonomy is also, perhaps more fundamentally, a process. It is also said that federalism connotes attitudes, a spirit of mutual respect and tolerance (Elazar 1987: ch. 3). These are undoubtedly important points, but I believe that, in a comparative study of this kind, the more 'neutral' definition in terms of powers and institutions serves our interests better. However, specific arrangements, and their experiences, cannot be understood without a consideration of process and values.

THE DISTINCTIVENESS OF ETHNICALLY BASED AUTONOMIES

Ethnically based federations or regional autonomies have different structures and orientations from federations like Australia or the United States. Naturally, ethnic federations emphasise diversity and multiplicity of values. Such federations are more likely to be the result of devolution or disaggregation, as in Canada, India, Spain, Papua New Guinea and Ethiopia. Because they start with a centralised structure and because there is unease about the political implications of devolution, national powers tend to be dominant and not infrequently to have the power to suspend regional governments. It is worth noting that Indian federation emerged at a time when state building through central management and homogenisation was the dominant paradigm; concessions to ethnicity were reluctant and grudging. Because, ideally, a region is supposed to provide ethnic or cultural homogeneity, the size of regions is likely to be uneven and agreement on boundaries hard. There is also likely to be more emphasis on self-rule than shared rule, particularly with regional autonomy. But, at the same time, there is likely to be greater regional representation at the federal level. Watts says that, 'in both Canada and Switzerland the "representational syndrome" whereby different linguistic, religious and geographical groups are carefully represented with each of the federal policy making bodies, including the federal executive, is very marked'. Klug's account of South Africa establishes the same point, indeed even more so since the principal form of 'autonomy' is not the exercise by regions of power in the regions but participation at the centre. In Ethiopia, a crucial role is ascribed to the House of Federation, composed of regional representation, where relations between regions and between regions and the federations are mediated and resolved.

The division of powers is likely to be more focused on cultural matters, like education, religion and arts, and the normal tensions of federalism, like fiscal redistribution or regional influence, take on an ethnic dimension and aggravate them. Distinctions between the private and public spheres may be less sharp than in other types of federations. Inter-regional mobility is likely to be contentious. The party structure may be different as there may be no great connection between national parties and regional parties. National parties often lack viable affiliates in particular localities; relations of centre and region depend significantly on this 'asymmetry'. As Smith (1995:9) notes, 'such enduring asymmetry can be symptomatic of inter-communal tensions and lead to pressures not only for greater autonomy but also for secession from federation'.

But, most of all, the major factor which distinguishes ethnic autonomy from classical federations is its asymmetrical features. Just as in liberal theory all individuals must be equally treated, so must regions in a federation. This approach is not very constructive when autonomy is used to acknowledge and manage ethnic differences. Asymmetry acknowledges the unevenness of diversities and opens up additional possibilities of awarding recognition to specific groups with special needs or capacities, such as indigenous peoples whose traditional culture is central to their way of life, or a minority linguistic group.

Asymmetry arises in various ways. Regional autonomy is by definition asymmetrical. Sometimes it is the result of a constitutional provision enabling regions to negotiate separately with the centre for autonomy and establishing a menu of which powers may be devolved (Spain, Papua New Guinea, Russia). Regions may make different use of concurrent powers. Regions may be endowed with the power to determine their own structures for the exercise of autonomy, leading to differences in constitutional arrangements. National laws may apply differentially for other reasons, the outstanding example being the 'notwithstanding' clause in Canada which enables a province to opt out of most provisions of the Charter of Rights under prescribed conditions, and another provision which limits the application of the charter in aboriginal areas by the supremacy of treaties between indigenous groups and the Crown. Asymmetry can also be used as a general technique for opting out of a scheme, or for a phased entry to full membership, as has happened frequently with the European Union. Other forms of asymmetry include special representation for a region at the centre (Quebec's entitlements to seats in the Senate and the Supreme Court), or special voting power given to the region at the centre (double voting or vetoes). Residents of a region may have special rights, at least in the region, that are not available to other citizens (as in the concept of permanent resident of the Hong Kong Special Administrative Region). The questions of the feasibility of negotiating and sustaining asymmetry are therefore fundamental to the design and operation of ethnic autonomy.

Perhaps it is not surprising that asymmetry has also become controversial; concerns about it have, for example, prevented a satisfactory resolution of Canada's constitutional problems. It is in Canada that the issue has been most extensively debated, in politics as well as in academe. Canadian scholars have argued that differences over asymmetry may be the undoing of ethnic or multinational federations, Milne (1994:159) noting an 'overwhelming' hostility towards proposals for asymmetry in

Canada (see also Kymlicka 1998a, 1998b). There is resentment in India at the privileged position of Kashmir (Kashyap 1990), although it has not emerged as a major political issue, perhaps because of Indo-Pakistani conflict over Kashmir. It is said that President Habibie offered independence to East Timor because he was afraid that the UN proposals of autonomy would set a precedent for other provinces of Indonesia, and that it would be politically difficult to restrict the high degree of substantive and institutional autonomy to East Timor.

One objection to asymmetry is that it is administratively and politically difficult to manage. The centre has to deal with regions with varying degrees of devolution and different institutional structures. This can pose problems in states as well developed as Spain; it can be a nightmare in states with less efficient bureaucracies or with politicians not given to compromise (as in Papua New Guinea and Ethiopia). A consultancy firm which advised Papua New Guinea on the implementation of decentralisation, expected to be asymmetrical under negotiated constitutional provisions, recommended the equal devolution of powers to all provinces, regardless of their capacity or willingness to assume these powers. If this proposal avoided one bureaucratic nightmare, it created another – poorly equipped provinces struggling to carry out new responsibilities which they neither understood nor wanted. The result was continuing domination by central bureaucrats and a not inconsiderable degree of inefficiency (Ghai and Regan 1992).

But the political problems with asymmetry are even more decisive. I have already referred to the difficulty of conceding autonomy on a purely ethnic basis. The difficulty is greater if only one or two groups are to enjoy autonomy. If the national government is inclined to support autonomy, it may have to generalise the conditions for granting it. In Papua New Guinea in 1976, negotiations for autonomy were conducted between the national government and the representatives of Bougainville. The assumption was that the arrangements under negotiation were for Bougainville only; and, in fact, Bougainville leaders insisted that only their province was to be entitled to them (to recognise their distinctiveness). However, the government realised that parliamentary support for these arrangements could not be guaranteed unless all provinces were given similar options. Similar developments took place in Spain, where all provinces or groupings of provinces were given roughly the same options as the 'historic territories'. Increasingly, Spain takes on the appearance of a federation, and a symmetrical federation at that. The devolution to provincial councils in Sri Lanka followed a similar trajectory, diluting the special claims of Tamils to autonomy.

Asymmetry is particularly controversial when the region benefiting from it wants equal or even superior representation in central institutions.

Logically, the region should not participate in decisions at the national level on areas which are within its autonomy, for then it would be making decisions for other regions, especially when the votes of its representatives hold the balance. When there is substantial asymmetrical autonomy, the moral or political right of the representatives of that region to count towards a parliamentary majority, thus determining the formation of the central government group, can be questioned. Claims might be made by the rest of the country that representatives from that region should be excluded from holding ministries whose portfolios cover areas within asymmetrical autonomy or, indeed, that the number of ministries given to them should be severely restricted. If there is equal representation for the autonomous region, other provinces will resent it; if the representation is less favourable, the region will tend to look inwards, political parties will tend to become regional and the region's integration with the state will weaken.

The conversion of asymmetry into symmetry would not necessarily be against the interests of the original claimants of autonomy. They would cease to be the object of envy and resentment. A greater number of beneficiaries would produce a more balanced state. It would also increase the capacity of regions to negotiate with the centre and extract higher benefits. But, for many groups, the exact amount of devolved power is less important than that they alone should enjoy some special powers, as a way to mark their status. If the powers they have are generalised, they increase their own demands for more, leading not only to a higher level of general devolution than is desirable or desired, but also pushing the special groups towards confederal solutions.

EXPERIENCES OF AUTONOMY

It is evident from the case studies in this volume that autonomy arrangements, appropriately arrived at and operated, can defuse and make more peaceful identity-based conflicts within states (as in India, Canada and Spain). Equally, autonomy has not been successful in other cases (Yugoslavia and Cyprus). It is resisted in Sri Lanka and agreement on federalism has eluded parties in Cyprus. I will try to draw some lessons from the case studies on why autonomy is resisted, when it is likely to be conceded and what factors explain its success or failure.

• The prospects of establishing autonomy arrangements are strongest when the state undergoes a regime change

Those who enjoy positions of power in the apparatus of the state are unlikely to give up their control of power willingly. A period of regime change provides opportunities for autonomy for a variety of reasons.

Those who are in charge of the transition may have been opposed to the previous centralised system. The framers of the 1994 Ethiopian constitution had fought against the centralisation of both Emperor Haile Selassie and his communist successors which had denied recognition to the ethnic diversity of the Ethiopian people, and thus stifled it (Nahum 1997:49–53). However, Paul explains the federalisation of Ethiopia on different grounds – as based on the strategy of the Tigray People's Liberation Front to conquer all of Ethiopia – and contrasts it with the more non-ethnic constitutionalism that pervades the Eritrean political ordering. The end of the old regime may usher in a new balance of forces that may necessitate or facilitate the restructuring of the state (as in Spain). The new or aspiring leaders may need to find allies, to be secured by the promise of autonomy (as with the rise of the communist regimes in the Soviet Union and Yugoslavia). The weakness of a new regime may be seized upon by groups wanting secession or autonomy by pushing their demands.

A common case of regime change has been the independence of a state, which provides an opportunity for a fresh look at the apparatus of the state and a structure to accommodate new social and political forces. Imperial rule produced many multi-ethnic colonies; centralised rule established during the colonial period was unacceptable to many communities when they gained independence. A large number of autonomy arrangements were established on independence (in India, Nigeria, Ghana, Kenya, Uganda, Papua New Guinea, Vanuatu and Indonesia). The end of British sovereignty over Hong Kong was facilitated by extensive autonomy under Chinese sovereignty. Sometimes, autonomy is established following a compromise among the local groups; sometimes, it is forced by the colonial power. The latter has been more common. It is less likely to ensure the successful implementation of autonomy because the majority resents the imposition (as in Cyprus). For that reason, few autonomy regimes in Africa have survived for any length of time after independence.

- Autonomy arrangements are likely to be established if the international community becomes involved in conflict resolution

At both the international and regional levels, there has been considerable support for autonomy, as reflected in emerging international norms. The increasing involvement of the international community in national conflicts has facilitated the application of these norms to the settlement of conflicts, as in Bosnia–Herzegovina, the Rambouillet proposals for Kosovo, Crimea, Palestine, and the continuing involvement of the United Nations in the search for a federal solution to Cyprus. Spanish aspirations of membership of European organisations was one factor in its conciliatory attitudes to the Basques and Catalonians. In Sri Lanka, the Indian government intervened to secure autonomy for the Tamils. It is not surprising that the international community, comprising states, is reluctant to see the dismemberment of states; autonomy seems a suitable compromise.

However, once autonomy is established, the international community is less willing to provide continuing support. It is reluctant to make long-term commitments, particularly as this involves continuing intervention in the affairs of a state, and is likely to require police or military manoeuvres and considerable sums of money (as evidenced by the failure of the United Kingdom, Turkey and Greece to honour their underwriting of the Cyprus constitution, and by the withdrawal of Indian troops from Sri Lanka).

- Autonomy arrangements are most likely to succeed in states with established traditions of democracy and the rule of law

Of autonomy arrangements in liberal societies, communist states and third-world states, most successful examples are in liberal societies (Ghai 1998). The record is worst in communist states, as in China where provisions for autonomy are negated through the overall control of the Communist Party. The reason that liberal societies have the best record is that they have established traditions of democracy and the rule of law. On the whole, pluralism is valued and there is respect for cultural and religious differences. Autonomy arrangements require give and take; they depend on frequent negotiations for the adjustment of relationships or in the implementation of the law. The law provides the framework for relations between the centre and regions and defines the powers of the respective governments. Disputes on the meaning of the law are resolved ultimately by the courts, whose decisions have to be respected by all parties concerned. Of the countries studied in this volume, Canada and, in recent times, Australia, come closest to this model, in relation to aboriginal peoples; and Spain is operating increasingly through a liberal order oriented to the rule of law.

- Autonomy is easier to concede and likely to succeed when there is no dispute about sovereignty

Autonomy has been a cause of great contention because it is associated with assertions of or qualifications on state sovereignty. Autonomy becomes less problematic if it can be disassociated from sovereignty. China's official position is that it would be prepared to discuss autonomy for Tibet if the Dalai Lama acknowledged that Tibet was an inalienable part of China. China was able to accept autonomy for Hong Kong in part because its leaders realised that it was inconceivable that the residents would ever try to secede. Franco's inheritors were prepared to discuss regional autonomy in Spain once agreement was reached on what is now article 2 of the 1978 constitution: 'The Constitution is based on the indissoluble unity of the Spanish Nation, the common and indivisible country of all Spaniards . . . ' The autonomy of linguistic provinces in India, which have no separatist ambitions, has been much less problematic than in Kashmir, whose status has been more controversial. Regional autonomy in Sri Lanka has become so difficult because of the secessionist claims of the Tamil Tigers. It reflects also a situation where autonomy is rejected by its potential beneficiaries precisely because acceptance would be seen to compromise their grander design of independence.

The success of autonomy negotiations may therefore depend on diffusing, fragmenting or fudging sovereignty. One method lies in the use of terminology; federation may imply splitting sovereignty and so the labels 'devolution', 'autonomy' or 'decentralisation' can be used to obscure the extent of autonomy (as in Spain or Papua New Guinea). The Ethiopian constitution finesses sovereignty by declaring that all sovereignty lies among its many diverse 'nations, nationalities and peoples'. This approach was foreshadowed in the 1974 Yugoslav constitution, which defined the units of the federation as 'states based on the sovereignty of the people' (a provision which also held the federation hostage to the 'people' of the different republics). Sometimes, it may be possible to fudge sovereignty by the use of competing international norms.

The reverse side of the coin is to make autonomy acceptable to the recipients by attaching the indicia of sovereignty to it – in the form, for example, of regional flags, distinct passports, regional stamps, or grand titles like republics and premiers.

- Autonomy is more likely to be negotiated and to succeed if there are several ethnic groups rather than two

Autonomy arrangements which bring together two communities have a poor record. They are, to start with, hard to negotiate. Negotiations between the Cypriot Greeks and Turks for a federation have led nowhere after more than twenty years. Autonomy discussions in Sri Lanka have been bedevilled by the Sinhala–Tamil polarity. The problem in Cyprus is that the Greeks want a strong centre and the Turks, strong regions; the former would enhance the role of the Greek community in the affairs of Cyprus, the latter would grant greater autonomy to the Turks. The collapse of the Ethiopia–Eritrea and Pakistan federations is attributed to the desire of the Ethiopian emperor and the West Pakistanis to use federal institutions to rule Eritrea and what is now Bangladesh, respectively. (If the need is to accommodate one or two small, geographically based minorities, regional autonomy rather than federalism may be a better solution.)

Even when agreement may be forthcoming, the federation may be hard to operate when there are basically two communities (or when, as in Canada now, the founding assumption of the federation of two communities has been outlived). Biracial federations with communities of about equal size have greater possibilities of conflict and limited scope for trade-offs. Tripolarity, while an improvement, is still fraught with problems, as in the original Nigerian federation (Watts 1994b:189–90). A larger number of groups allows for flexibility in arrangements and the establishment of a certain kind of balance and has the capacity to diffuse what are essentially bilateral disputes. A bigger constellation of interests has a stake in the success of federal arrangements and the clout to achieve this (well demonstrated by the Indian experience, where there are numerous linguistic, religious and regional groups, although the PNG–Bougainville experience shows that multipolarity cannot always diffuse bilateral problems).

Consequently, ways should be found to transform bipolarity into multipolarity. Nigeria achieved multipolarity (and some equality among the new regions) by dividing existing regions, particularly the dominant north, into several regions. Papua New Guinea based its regions not on the Papua–New Guinea divide or the highland–coastal–island divide but on the more numerous districts. Spain achieved multipolarity by extending the offer of autonomy to 'non-historic' communities, and Sri Lanka tried to make autonomy more palatable to the Sinhala by dividing the Sinhala-dominated area into districts and generalising autonomy.

Multipolarity is helpful if all territorial units are to be equal partners. Sometimes, multipolarity cannot be achieved in this way. Canada has become multipolar in recent years, with the claims of the aboriginals and recent immigrants, but this has served merely to complicate its problems. If multipolarity leads to differential or competing claims, implying asymmetry, negotiating agreement on autonomy can be very difficult.

- Autonomy arrangements which have been negotiated in a democratic and participatory way have a better chance of success than those which are imposed

Many systems of autonomy that were established in the dying days of colonialism were imposed rather than negotiated: the price that 'nationalist leaders' had to pay for independence. These leaders resented them and took early opportunities to dismantle them. In most instances, members of the groups for whose benefit autonomies were established had little understanding of the mechanisms. At best, the arrangements were inter-elite bargains. Some contemporary settlements may suffer from the same difficulties: agreements produced in the hothouses of hegemonic powers.

Participatory and negotiated settlements are more likely to have dealt with pressing problems, avoiding the superficiality of settlements produced under heavy external pressure. They are likely to represent a balance of interests. The parties have a stake in their success. The least successful of India's autonomies is Kashmir, which was not negotiated but provided for in response to a complex international situation, with Kashmiris not having been involved and other Indians resenting what they regard as unfair privileges for Kashmir.

It is important, as the Canadian Supreme Court has pointed out, that negotiations be conducted in good faith. If they are not, negotiations can be counterproductive. This point is well illustrated by the experience of Papua New Guinea. The relevant constitutional instruments provided for various mechanisms for consultation and mediation – particularly important as they also provided for the phased transfer of powers to provinces. Meetings were indeed regularly held, but the central government equally regularly disregarded agreements reached or recommendations made. This created great resentment in the provinces, particularly the eastern island provinces, including Bougainville (Ghai and Regan 1992).

The South African experience shows the importance of seriously negotiating claims of autonomy and in that process to change the perspectives of parties. In January 1994 the South African legislature adopted a new constitution which had been negotiated between various political groups, principally the African National Congress and the National Party. The Inkatha Freedom Party (largely Zulu) and some white groups stayed out of the settlement that produced the 1994 constitution until the principles of provincial autonomy and provision for a Volkstaat Council to pursue further proposals for self-government were accepted. This recognition by itself defused ethnic tensions and, as Klug shows, enabled subsequent agreement on a system of regionalism in which the provincial authorities participate in national law making.

The question of the role of referenda or plebiscites on autonomy – on which there seems to be no standard practice – is relevant here. First, there are technical problems to overcome: the form of the choice to be put to the people, and who can vote (everyone or only those in the proposed autonomy area). The Canadian experience of recent decades shows the 'destabilising' effect of referenda, although arrangements which do not enjoy popular support may also be hard to implement. A referendum under the influence of extremists may thwart an agreement which has been carefully negotiated to satisfy different, including minority, groups, when unpopular concessions might have been necessary. If there is substantial public support for autonomy, a referendum can consolidate the agreement and isolate politicians who may be opposed to it (as in Northern Ireland). Occasionally, a referendum can help to overcome the rigidities of the parliamentary process; President Kumaratunga of Sri Lanka has declared her intention to put autonomy proposals directly to the people if she cannot persuade parliament, and Bougainville leaders insist on a referendum on independence regardless of how favourable the autonomy proposals are. Sometimes, political leaders are ahead of the people; at other times, they are behind – this consideration affects the role of the referendum.

- An independent dispute settlement mechanism is essential to long-term success

Autonomy is based on constitutional and legal provisions. The enforcement of these provisions, what we might call the principle of legality, is essential to the maintenance of autonomy. The most common form for this is the judicial: courts are traditionally concerned with solving constitutional disputes. They are qualified for this task because of their well-established independence and competence and the rules of due process which ensure a fair hearing of all parties. Courts also enjoy considerable respect in the community and are thus well placed to provide authoritative and binding decisions.

Papua New Guinea provided a limited and residual role for the courts in intergovernmental relations. But the political processes it envisaged did not produce harmony or progress, because the centre had little interest in autonomy. When the existing autonomy was invaded by the centre, it was the judiciary which came to the assistance of the provinces, although courts had not previously supported provincial autonomy (Ghai and Regan 1992). In India, the recent more interventionist stand of the judiciary has helped to put some curbs on the arbitrary suspension of regional governments by the national government. Experience in Spain has been somewhat similar; a key decision of the Constitutional Court was necessary to overcome legislative and bureaucratic obstacles to constitutionally guaranteed autonomy. The experience in Sri Lanka is mixed; in the early days of decentralisation, the courts reinforced the centralising bias of the national government but have adopted a more pro-devolution approach recently. In South Africa, the Constitutional Court was given a key role in determining whether the final constitution conformed to the principle of decentralisation. It has played a valuable role in adjudicating disputes between the centre and the provinces and in maintaining a balance between them. In the former Yugoslavia, the only communist federation with a constitutional court, the court was unable to stem the disintegration, despite its rulings on the legislative and administrative competence of state institutions geared to the maintenance of the federation – political forces were firmly in control by then. In Hong Kong, the absence of secure guarantees of autonomy which can be enforced through independent courts is a major weakness. The final powers of interpretation vested in the Standing Committee of the National People's Congress, a political body under the control of the

Communist Party, have effectively negated the autonomy. Ethiopia, drawing from similar springs of Leninist jurisprudence, also provides for the role of interpretation and dispute settlement in a political body, the House of Federation. The weakness of its judicial system will in all probability mean that large parts of the federal arrangements will not be implemented and will become subject to political manipulation.

It is not necessary, and indeed it may not be desirable, that courts should be the first port of call when a dispute arises. A political settlement of disputes can strengthen autonomy (and the consensus on autonomy) more effectively than a court decision. Also, there are some kinds of disputes, such as the allocation of funds or forms of intergovernmental cooperation, which cannot be regulated through rules; a bargaining and negotiating process is more suitable. Unfortunately, experience shows that this process cannot always be relied upon, for the centre may disregard the representations of weak regions. The ultimate authority of courts should therefore be provided. Judicial decisions need not curb political bargaining; their function is to maintain constitutional parameters and, when necessary, to provide authoritative rulings to break political deadlocks (as the Canadian Supreme Court has tried to do, in contrast with the more 'authoritarian' style of its predecessor, the Privy Council). A balance between political and judicial processes is necessary to ensure the successful operation of autonomy. Indeed, courts in Canada and South Africa have attempted to prevent sharpening of conflict and to provide parameters for the political settlement of disputes.

- Careful design of institutional structures is essential for the success of autonomy

On the whole, international and regional norms say little about the content and structure of autonomy (although the Organisation for Security and Cooperation in Europe has produced some guidelines), and there is inadequate knowledge of various technical points in the drafting of autonomy arrangements. There is frequently such pressure for agreement on broad political principles that institutional details are paid insufficient attention. It is not possible here to expand on what would be useful structures; instead, I will draw attention to some key considerations:

(a) Autonomy arrangements should be properly guaranteed. Sometimes this can be done through treaties, but experience has shown that these are seldom effective. They should be entrenched in the domestic constitutional order. This is common for federalism but not always for regional autonomy. It is best to entrench autonomy in

21

such a way that the consent of the region is necessary for change (the reduction of autonomy in Papua New Guinea was facilitated by the absence of such entrenchment).

(b) In federations by disaggregation and in regional autonomy, provision is often made for the centre to issue directives to the regional government in specified areas. The central government has also the power to suspend regional government for prescribed reasons. These provisions can sour centre–regional relations and limit the exercise of regional autonomy (well illustrated in India and Papua New Guinea). Such provisions should be avoided, if possible; where they are considered necessary, adequate safeguards against the abuse of power should be inscribed in the law.

(c) Democratic structures are necessary for the exercise and protection of autonomy. Democratic politics in a region both compel regional leaders to protect autonomy as well as empower them to do so. Male-sevic explains the failure of autonomy in the former Yugoslavia by the absence of democratic politics. The weakening of autonomy in Hong Kong is the result of having a China-appointed executive and a non-democratic legislature.

(d) Agreement on autonomy is easier if guarantees of the rights of minorities which are created by autonomy arrangements can be secured. In Canada, provision was made from the very beginning of the federation for provincial minorities to appeal to the centre against discrimination, but this power was seldom used and is unlikely to be used now. Considerable attention has been paid to devices for the regional protection of minorities. Most constitutions now include bills of rights which preclude discrimination and other various forms of oppression. Local government structures and powers can be entrenched (as in Nigeria). There can be special representation for minorities in councils; this is often linked to forms of power sharing (as in Sri Lanka). There can be cultural councils for minorities, as in Estonia and Hungary. The most elaborate schemes have been established in Bosnia and Herzegovina and in the proposals for Kosovo, inspired by Lijphartian consociationalism. China has autonomy whenever there is a concentration of a minority, so that, within autonomous regions, there may also be autonomous townships, and so on.

(e) Of particular importance in ethnic autonomy is the method for the division of legislative and executive competence. There are different ways of division, depending on whether the relations between the centre and regions are seen as 'cooperative' or 'separate'. 'Cooperative' federalism, where governments at different levels coordinate policies, is more fashionable now, given the complexity of economic and social life, but, for ethnic autonomy, there may be considerable desire for 'separation' so that regional autonomy for cultural and other policies can be exercised without regard to central directions. It is important to avoid divisions and institutional arrangements which rely heavily on cooperation. It is easier to provide for 'separation' in regional than federal autonomy.

- Autonomy does not promote secession; on the contrary, true autonomy prevents secession

A principal reason for the refusal to grant autonomy is the fear that it will lead to secession. Strongly opposed views are held on this point: many people argue that autonomy brings secessionist claims to an end and strengthens the hand of the moderates of all parties. Others say that autonomy increases the resources and strengthens the identities of regional minorities, frequently justifying a claim of secession under the principles of self-determination.

The evidence is not conclusive but tends to discredit the claim that autonomy leads to secession. It may be important to make a distinction between federations by 'aggregation' and those by 'disaggregation'. In the first case, the federation is based on mutual consent and voluntariness, and it is on the whole forward looking. It is in the second case that there is a particular worry about secession, as federal arrangements are often a concession to overwhelming pressures or threats (it is interesting that of the examples of voluntary federalism, as in Canada and Switzerland, the attempted secession by a province or canton is unlikely to be resisted by the others).

The breakup of the Soviet Union and the federation of former Yugoslavia was the result of the failure to implement a genuine federation. This is less true of Yugoslavia; the federation there had tried to bring together people who had a long history of enmity but provided relatively few opportunities for the development of a real Yugoslavian identity. Both federations had relied heavily on the Communist Party to hold them together, preventing an organic unity. Also, the central authorities used ethnicities in opportunistic ways, not calculated to promote good inter-ethnic relations. In any case, the situations in the USSR and Yugoslavia are more correctly analysed less as secessions than as implosions of federations. Perhaps less so in Yugoslavia, the separation of constituent parts followed rather than caused the breakdown of the central authorities.

The settlement of 1976 in Papua New Guinea, when some parts of Bougainville wanted to secede, established a wide-ranging decentralisation and settled the Bougainville problem. An elected provincial government was established, responsible to an elected local assembly. With its human and physical resources, it quickly built an enviable reputation for efficiency and was assessed by various inquiries as the most effective and accountable of the provincial governments. Regular elections were held and its leaders played a full role in national politics. As Ghai and Regan show, the troubles of 1989 had a common source – the inequitable distribution of the income from the copper mine – but this time it was not a provincial-wide protest but had its origins in disputes among the community which owned the land on which the mine was located and concerned the internal distribution of royalties. The local, democratic forces to which autonomy gave rise were as much the victims of the anger and violence of the rebels as the central authorities. The grant of autonomy to Bougainville had helped to strengthen its links to the rest of the country, for it eliminated some genuine grievances and established a democratic order internally connected to the national system. There is little doubt that, without the 1976 autonomy, the rebellion of 1989 would have garnered more support in Bougainville – so autonomy has prevented rather than promoted secession.

These case studies point to the need to distinguish secession from the termination of a federation. There may be little to mourn in the second case – it suggests that ethnic communities have decided, mutually, to lead separate lives. Autonomy is important for ethnicity because it represents a compromise, a balance between those who want a tight, unitary system of government and those who may prefer separation. It loses that function if the wish to separate is mutual and the separation is achieved without strife or recrimination.

CONCLUSION

The question of autonomy is central to many conflicts today. Autonomy can play an important, constructive role in mediating relations between different communities in multi-ethnic states. It can defuse conflicts. It is a particularly appropriate mechanism for the protection and promotion of the culture and values of a community. But it is not an easy device to operate. Great political and technical skills are required to structure and make it work. Given the difficulties of managing multi-ethnic states, autonomy is a valuable option, notwithstanding its own difficulties.

But autonomy can also be fragmenting, pigeonholing and dividing communities. Sometimes, in an attempt to preserve the integuments of a state, autonomy is so structured that it is difficult to find the common ground on which the communities can find a moral or political basis for coexistence. Autonomy, particularly federal autonomy, is built around the notion that the people of a state are best served through a balance between the common and the particular. If the emphasis is so much on the particular, then separation may be the better option, notwithstanding the proliferation of states. The secret of autonomy is the recognition of the common; certainly it seems to be the condition for its success. Perhaps about thirty years ago, too much emphasis was placed on the 'common' and for this reason autonomy was narrow and contingent. Today we may be placing too much emphasis on the particular. It may be necessary to consider devices that stress the common bonds and construct the institutions that hold people together, as Nigeria did with the principles to 'federalise' the centre in the 1979 constitution – as in the election of president, the composition of the federal executive or the registration of parties – to promote broad interregional support, to counter the tendency towards disassociating that comes with disaggregating ethnic autonomy (Kirk-Greene 1983). Autonomy should be chosen not because of some notion of preserving 'sovereignty' but in order to enable different groups to live together, to define a common public space.

NOTE
I thank the Research Grants Committee of Hong Kong for assistance with my research on autonomy systems.

REFERENCES
Agnew, John 1995. 'Postscript: federalism in the post-cold war era', in Graham Smith (ed.) *Federalism: The Multiethnic Challenge*. London: Longman.

Agranoff, Robert 1994. 'Asymmetrical and symmetrical federalism in Spain: an examination of intergovernmental policy', in Bertus de Villiers (ed.) *Evaluating Federal Systems*. Cape Town: Juta.

Boase, Joan Price 1994. 'Faces of asymmetry: German and Canadian federalism', in Bertus de Villiers (ed.) *Evaluating Federal Systems*. Cape Town: Juta.

Brass, Paul 1991. *Ethnicity and Nationalism*. New Delhi: Sage Publications.

Brown-John, Lloyd 1994. 'Asymmetrical federalism: keeping Canada together?', in Bertus de Villiers (ed.) *Evaluating Federal Systems*. Cape Town: Juta.

Elazar, Daniel 1987. *Exploring Federalism*. Tuscaloosa: University of Alabama Press.

Eriksen, Thomas H. 1993. *Ethnicity and Nationalism: Anthropological Perspectives*. London: Pluto Press.

Ghai, Yash 1998. 'Decentralisation and the accommodation of ethnicity', in Crawford Young (ed.) *Ethnic Diversity and Public Policy: A Comparative Inquiry*. Basingstoke: Macmillan Press.

Ghai, Yash and Anthony Regan 1992. *The Law, Politics and Administration of Decentralisation in Papua New Guinea*. Waigani: National Research Institute.

Hannum, Hurst 1990. *Autonomy, Sovereignty, and Self-determination: The Accommodation of Conflicting Rights*. Philadelphia: University of Philadephia Press.

Heintze, Hans-Joachim 1998. 'On the legal understanding of autonomy', in Markku Suski (ed.) *Autonomy: Applications and Implications*. The Hague: Kluwer Law International.

Horowitz, Donald 1985. *Ethnic Groups in Conflict*. Berkeley: University of California Press.

Kashyap, Anirban 1990. *Disintegration and Constitution*. New Delhi: Lancer Books.

Kirk-Greene, A.H.M. 1983. 'Ethnic engineering and the "federal character" of Nigeria: boon of contentment or bone of contention?', *Ethnic and Racial Studies* 6(4):457–76.

Kothari, Rajni 1988. 'Ethnicity', in Rajni Kothari, *Rethinking Development in Search of Humane Alternatives*. Delhi: Ajantha Publications.

Kymlicka, Will 1998a. 'Is federalism a viable alternative to secession?', in Percy B. Lehning (ed.) *Theories of Secession*. London: Routledge.

—— 1998b. *Finding Our Way: Rethinking Ethnocultural Relations in Canada*. Toronto: Oxford University Press.

Lynn, Nicholas and Alexei Novikov 1997. 'Refederalizing Russia: debates on the idea of federalism in Russia', *Publius* 27(2):187–203.

Milne, David 1994. 'Exposed to the glare: constitutional camouflage and the fate of Canada's federation', in F. Leslie Seidle (ed.) *Seeking a New Canadian Partnership: Asymmetrical and Confedral Options*. Ottawa: Institute for Research on Public Policy.

Nahum, Fasil 1997. *Constitution for a Nation of Nations: The Ethiopian Prospect*. Lawrenceville, NJ: Red Sea Press.

Parekh, Bhiku 1993. 'The cultural particularity of liberal democracy', in David Held (ed.) *Prospects for Democracy: North, South, East and West*. Cambridge: Polity Press.

Rex, John and David Mason (eds) 1986. *Theories of Race and Ethnic Relations*. Cambridge: Cambridge University Press.

Smith, Graham 1995. 'Mapping the federal condition', in G. Smith (ed.) *Federalism: The Multiethnic Challenge*. London: Longman.

—— 1996. 'Russia, ethnoregionalism and the politics of federation,' *Ethnic and Racial Studies* 19(2).

Stevens, R. Michael 1977. 'Asymmetrical federalism: the federal principle and the survival of the small republic', *Publius: Journal of Federalism* 7(4):117–203 (special issue on Federalism and Identity, ed. Ivo D. Duchecek).

Thornberry, Patrick 1998. 'Images of autonomy and individual and collective rights in international instruments on the rights of minorities', in Markku Suski (ed.) *Autonomy: Applications and Implications*. The Hague: Kluwer Law International.

Tully, James 1995. *Strange Multiplicity: Constitutionalism in an Age of Diversity*. Cambridge: Cambridge University Press.

Walker, Graham 1997. 'The idea of nonliberal constitutionalism', in I. Shapiro and W. Kymlicka (eds) *Ethnicity and Group Rights*. New York: New York University Press.

Watts, Ronald 1994a. 'Contemporary views on federalism', in Bertus de Villiers (ed.) *Evaluating Federal Systems*. Cape Town: Juta.

—— 1994b. 'Discussants comments', in F. Leslie Seidle (ed.) *Seeking a New Canadian Partnership: Asymmetrical and Confederal Options*. Ottawa: Institute for Research on Public Policy.

PART 1

OPERATING AUTONOMIES

CHAPTER 2

FEDERALISM AND DIVERSITY IN CANADA

RONALD L. WATTS

THE RELEVANCE OF THE CANADIAN EXAMPLE

In a book aimed at exploring the role of federal political systems and autonomy arrangements in the management of ethnic differences and conflicts, this chapter focuses on the lessons, positive and negative, provided by the Canadian experience. While, in many respects, there are significant contrasts between Canada and other federations that must always be borne in mind, there are some features of the Canadian federation which make it particularly relevant to the examination of the interface between federalism and ethnic diversity. Unlike some other federations, such as the United States and Switzerland which were created by the aggregation of pre-existing states and cantons, the formation of Canada involved a substantial devolutionary process. A major part of its creation as a federation in 1867 was the splitting of the formerly unitary Province of Canada into two new provinces (Ontario, predominantly English-speaking and Protestant, and Quebec, predominantly French-speaking and Roman Catholic), each autonomous and responsible for its own affairs in those areas where the two communities were sharply divided. To these provinces were added two smaller provinces (New Brunswick and Nova Scotia).

The Canadian founders, concerned about maintaining effective unity, in 1867 adopted a predominantly federal structure that combined provincial autonomy with some constitutional quasi-unitary central controls over the provinces. Thus, the Canadian federal constitution, like those later established in India and Malaysia, and most recently in South Africa, was a hybrid combining a basically federal form with some unitary features. These unilateral central powers were frequently exercised in the early decades of Canada's history and they still remain in its constitution, but they have fallen into almost complete disuse in the second century of its existence.

Canada provides an example where statesmen have wisely been more interested in pragmatic political solutions having the character of hybrids than in theoretical purity. As a consequence, next to the United States and Switzerland, it is the oldest federation in the world. What is more, unlike the other two, Canada has not suffered a major civil war during the past two centuries, and it has achieved this by emphasising tolerance, negotiation and mutual adjustment. Furthermore, the continued vigour and vitality of the French Canadian community, concentrated in Quebec, shows that a federal system involving extensive provincial autonomy and a constitutionally asymmetrical recognition of the distinctive language, education and civil law of Quebec can accommodate a major federal minority, even though that may at times be a source of controversy.

A particularly relevant feature has been the Canadian innovation of combining federal and parliamentary institutions. The United States and Switzerland adopted federal institutions which emphasised the dispersion of power through the separation of the executive and the legislature. Canada was the first federation to incorporate a system of parliamentary responsible government in which, within each order of government, the executives are responsible to their legislatures. This combination of federal and parliamentary institutions has subsequently been adopted in Australia and in many other federations (often in a republican form, with a president), such as Austria, Belgium, Germany, India, Malaysia, Spain and South Africa. Canada provides the original example of the impact that parliamentary central institutions, with their majoritarian character and concentration of power in the executive, can have upon the dynamics of politics within a predominantly federal system.

One other feature giving Canada a particular relevance is that, during the past three decades, it has been going through the intense 'mega constitutional politics' engendered by public debate on possible reforms to its constitutional structure. The debates have focused on many issues similar to those in other multi-ethnic federations, especially issues relating to the appropriate degree of centralisation or provincial autonomy, the recognition and protection of major minority groups, and the role of a charter of rights.

CANADA'S CONSTITUTIONAL AND POLITICAL EVOLUTION

Canada was designed in 1867 as a centralised federation, with the key powers of the day vested in the federal government in Ottawa. Although, in recognition of the differences between English and French Canadians, most matters of cultural significance were assigned to the provinces, a strong federal government was established to be responsible for those matters where they shared common interests. Indeed, the federal government was also assigned a strong paternalistic oversight role with respect to the provinces. Despite that beginning, Canada over 132 years has become highly decentralised, for several reasons. Provincial areas of responsibility, such as health, welfare and education, which were considered of little governmental significance in the nineteenth century and which were therefore assigned to the provinces, have mushroomed in importance in the twentieth century, thus greatly enhancing the role of the provinces. In addition, judicial interpretation of the constitutional distribution of powers has broadly favoured the provincial governments over the federal government. Since 1960, a strong Quebec nationalism has helped to force the process of decentralisation, from which other provinces have also benefited.

The result is that Canada has powerful and sophisticated governments, both in Ottawa and in the provinces, engaged respectively in 'nation-building' and 'province-building'. This has created both interdependence and competition between governments, resulting in elaborate forms of intergovernmental coordination as well as, at times, intense intergovernmental conflict.

Federal unity has remained a recurrent political problem since the rise of a powerful separatist movement in Quebec in the 1970s. Repeated attempts to amend the constitution – one, in 1982, partially successful but the others unsuccessful – have failed to staunch the growth within Quebec of support for secession, and may even have encouraged it. In addition to the ongoing debate about the recognition and status of Quebec in the federation, there are decentralist pressures from a number of other provinces which are economically strong, and a continuing debate about the declining levels of financial support which the federal government has been offering to the provinces, particularly in the social policy field.

FACETS OF CANADIAN DIVERSITY

Impact of diversity on the operation of the federation
An important factor affecting the operation of the Canadian federal system is the political culture that is expressed in the attitudes, beliefs and values that affect the political behaviour of politicians and citizens in Canada. A marked feature of this political culture is that it is fragmented and plural in character. This diversity is illustrated by the strength of regionalism, by the fundamental duality between the French-speaking majority in Quebec and the English-speaking majorities in the other nine provinces, by the policies of bilingualism and multiculturalism, and by the tension between the supporters of North American continentalism and the supporters of Canadian self-sufficiency and nationalism.

31

Differences in regional attitudes and interests affect politics throughout Canada. A number of factors have contributed to this. Important have been differences in the economic base of the provinces, such as different products and differing degrees of industrialisation and urbanisation. Furthermore, extensive trade with the United States has contributed to strong north–south links cutting across the east–west ties among Canadians. Differences in ethnic and cultural composition of the population in each region as a result of earlier patterns of immigrant settlement have given the Atlantic provinces, Quebec, Ontario, the prairie provinces and British Columbia, each a distinctive cast. Different historical traditions have also contributed to regional consciousness, as provinces were settled in different periods and joined the federation at different times. Geography has also been a major factor. With most of the population spread along a narrow ribbon – 5000 kilometres long and 200 kilometres wide – on the border with the United States, those at the eastern and western extremities have felt remote from central Canada. Furthermore, Canadians living near the Atlantic have tended to look to Europe for trade and international contacts and those near the Pacific, especially British Columbia, have naturally looked in the opposite direction to Asia for trade opportunities.

The result has been considerable variation in attitudes and values, and a strong sense of regional consciousness and distinct provincial identity (Task Force on Canadian Unity 1979:21). This has had an important impact on the dynamics of Canadian politics. It has emphasised both the importance of provincial governments and the requirement within federal institutions, such as the cabinet, for the representation of members from all the provinces.

Given the variety of attitudes and beliefs, and the fragmented and plural nature of the political culture, Canadians have historically depended on 'elite accommodation' as a way of holding the country together. Agreements among the political leaders of different regions and language groups, arriving at negotiated compromises, have been a characteristic feature of Canadian political dynamics. These are reflected in the processes of both 'executive federalism' in intergovernmental relations, featuring interministerial negotiations as a predominant pattern, and the emphasis on a 'proportionality syndrome', that is, 'representativeness' of different regions and groups within the federal cabinet and, indeed, virtually all federal organisations.

Quebec and Quebec nationalism

One of the principal reasons for the adoption of a federal system was to accommodate the differences between the two linguistic and cultural groups. This duality has been both the motivating force to maintain a viable federal system and, at the same time, the root cause of the pressures that might lead to disintegration.

The province of Quebec, which includes just under 25 per cent of the Canadian population, is not a province like the others. In the 1867 constitution, two provisions in particular recognised this. One guarantees the use of the French and English languages in the Quebec legislature and in national institutions such as the parliament and courts (Constitution Act 1867, s. 133). The other preserves the civil law system in Quebec and a common law system in the rest of the country (Constitution Act 1867, s. 94). Thus, there are in Canada two completely different approaches to the law of property, contracts and family matters.

The evolution of Canadian federalism and federal institutions has been greatly influenced by this duality. For example, the Act establishing the Supreme Court of Canada provides that three of the nine judges on the court must come from Quebec in order to have judges trained in the civil law hear appeal cases originating from Quebec. There is also a convention to alternate the position of Chief Justice of Canada between a Supreme Court judge from Quebec and one from other parts of Canada.

To be sure, many francophones tracing their origins to Quebec live throughout Canada but they are, in most other provinces, a relatively small minority. Nevertheless, while francophones at 4.6 per cent of the population are a minority in Ontario, their numbers, at about half a million, are not insignificant. In the province of New Brunswick, a very substantial French-speaking minority constitutes about one-third of the population. The Acadians, as the French Canadians in New Brunswick are known, have a very different history in Canada from that of the francophones of Quebec. While the Acadians are also French-speaking, their culture is distinctive. It is these French minorities in other provinces and also the English-speaking minority in Quebec that led to the provisions in the 1867 constitution, and later the Charter of Rights and Freedoms of 1982, for special educational arrangements relating to religious and linguistic minorities within provinces (Constitution Act 1867, s. 93; Constitution Act 1982, s. 23), and also the special provisions recognising both English and French as official languages for the province of New Brunswick (Constitution Act 1982, ss. 16(2), 17(2), 18(2), 19(2), 20(2)).

In the province of Quebec, francophones constitute over 80 per cent of the population, a decided majority. Within and for the province, the government of Quebec has always seen itself as having a special role in protecting the French language and culture. One policy area pursued in recent decades by successive provincial governments to accomplish this objective has been through language legislation. Since the early 1970s, the provincial legislature has enacted various statutes safeguarding and enhancing the French language in the province. The most significant law is known colloquially as 'Bill 101'. Originally enacted by the Parti Québécois government in 1977, the formal title is the Charter of the French Language. Under this charter, fully supported by both Quebec federalists and separatists, priority is given to the French language within Quebec for all official and provincial purposes. This has contributed positively to the continued flourishing of the French language and to a vibrant sense of community in a territory that is surrounded by a continent of English-speaking jurisdictions.[1] That is not to say that minorities within Quebec have been submerged. While French is clearly the official and predominant language, provision for English-language schools and universities is maintained by the provincial government, and the services provided to the English-language minority are, if anything, clearly more extensive than those available to the French-language minorities in the nine English-speaking provinces.

Over the years, language policy at the federal level has also been a recurring source of friction between the two major linguistic communities. As a result of recommendations arising from an inquiry into bilingualism and biculturalism policy, the Parliament of Canada enacted the Official Languages Act in 1969. The Act established English and French as Canada's two official languages for all federal government activities. One purpose of the legislation was to ensure that the one million francophones living outside Quebec could receive federal government services in French. Another was to make all francophones feel comfortable anywhere in Canada, not just in Quebec. As a result, all federal government programs throughout the country are available in French and English. Manitoba, Ontario and New Brunswick – all with significant French-speaking minorities – have also developed comparable language policies for the delivery of provincial services.

In 1982, when Canada adopted its Charter of Rights and Freedoms as part of the Constitution Act 1982, English and French were entrenched as the two official languages and given constitutional protection (ss. 16–22). In addition, to protect official language minorities within provinces, the charter guarantees minority language (French or English) education rights, supported by public funds, wherever numbers warrant (s. 23). The guidelines for determining 'where numbers warrant' vary from province to province.

With respect to the actual functioning of Canadian federalism, over the years Quebec has been the most vocal and vigorous advocate of provincial autonomy and the leading proponent of a more decentralised form of federalism. Other provinces, such as Ontario and Alberta, have also strongly championed provincial rights and autonomy but not as persistently and consistently as Quebec.

Since 1960, the continuing search for greater autonomy and the strong sense of identification with the Quebec 'nation', as opposed to the Canadian 'nation', has given rise to nationalist movements and political parties within Quebec. Underlying this trend was the modernisation and industrialisation of Quebec during and immediately after World War II, which by the 1960s had brought to the fore a new middle class determined to be *maîtres chez nous* (masters in our own house). In the subsequent three decades, the previous strategy of *survivance* was replaced by *épanouissement*, the desire of Quebeckers to blossom and fulfil not only their traditional cultural identity but also their economic identity through greater provincial control of their economic affairs. This intensified Quebec nationalism has fed two distinct streams of political action: a greater emphasis upon the powers of the provincial government within a reformed federation (as espoused by the federalist Quebec Liberal Party), and a drive for sovereign independence from Canada (advocated by the sovereignist Parti Québécois). In the past twenty years, these parties have alternated in power provincially in Quebec, the Liberals governing in 1970–76 and 1985–94, and the Parti Québécois in 1976–85 and since 1994. The Parti Québécois has in its official platform the goal of Quebec sovereignty. The most recent manifestation of this drive was the 30 October 1995 referendum, sponsored by the Quebec government, which just narrowly failed to obtain majority support. Thus, an important feature of Quebec politics of the past thirty years has been the division within Quebec society between 'federalists' (supporting continued membership in the federation) and 'sovereignists' (supporting a sovereign Quebec, with some continued loose confederal links with Canada). To date, in two referenda (1980 and 1995) and in current opinion surveys, a majority (sometimes very narrow) has preferred the former.

At the same time, there is considerable pressure within Canada for reform to head off separation. One approach under consideration would involve the transfer of legislative authority to all the provinces for fields such as labour market training (which to a large extent has already occurred), communication and culture desired by the federalists within Quebec. This would involve decentralising further what is already one of the most decentralised federations in the world.[2] Another approach, already reflected in the 1867 constitution in the areas of civil law and language, is to increase the degree of 'asymmetry' among provinces. This alternative envisages that Quebec alone would receive additional legislative authority, reflecting its unique circumstances. In recent decades, proposals to develop an increased asymmetrical relationship for Quebec have been questioned in other provinces on the grounds that asymmetry would conflict with the principle of provincial equality and, in the eyes of some critics, would imply a privileged position for Quebec.

Multiculturalism

Multiculturalism as a policy has been an outgrowth of the great variety of lands from which immigrants have come to settle in Canada since the federation was formed. Because Canada has become 'a homeland of many peoples', federal policy has attempted to recognise this wider cultural variety. A constitutional expression of this was the recognition of Canada's multicultural heritage in the Charter of Rights and Freedoms adopted in 1982 (s. 27).

In the nineteenth century, most Canadians traced their ancestry to either the United Kingdom or France. Throughout the twentieth century, this pattern changed, with settlers coming from a variety of countries in Europe, the Caribbean and Asia. While these immigrants have integrated into mainstream society, the 'melting pot' approach encouraged by the United States has not been followed in Canada. Instead, governments have adopted policies of multiculturalism which encourage immigrants to preserve their cultures.

As such policies have taken root, there has been some conflict between multiculturalism and the fundamental linguistic and cultural dualism reflected in the original constitutional agreements. The Charter of Rights and Freedoms contains a recognition of multiculturalism and directs the courts to interpret it 'in a manner consistent with the preservation and enhancement of the multicultural heritage of Canadians' (Constitution Act 1982, s. 27). Federal policies on multiculturalism emerged in the 1970s and, in part, were a response to the growing perception in western Canada that the interests of other cultures were being ignored in the debate over Canadian duality. The conflict between multiculturalism and the basic dualism also surfaced during constitutional discussions in the 1980s over the Meech Lake Accord, and was reflected in a proposed clause shielding the multicultural provision of the charter from the proposed 'distinct society' clause applying to Quebec.

Aboriginal peoples

In addition to Quebec nationalism and policies of multiculturalism, Aboriginal policies have also required special attention. Prior to the arrival of European settlers, Aboriginal peoples lived throughout Canada. They completely reject, therefore, statements to the effect that the English and French are the two founding nations. They argue that they were in Canada long before the occurrence of European settlement, which helps to explain the phrase 'First Nations' used by Indian peoples to describe themselves.

Aboriginal peoples in Canada today number over one million, representing 3 per cent of the population. The term 'Aboriginal peoples' currently encompasses four groups: some 250–300 Indian bands living on their reserves, calling themselves 'First Nations' and loosely linked in an 'Assembly of First Nations'; Indians living off the reserves, having mostly migrated to the cities, and for whom the Native Council of Canada speaks; the Métis, descended from the intermarriage of early French fur-traders and Indians and who settled in the western wilderness before other settlers arrived there, now numbering about 200,000 and represented by the Métis National Council; and the Inuit (once referred to as

Eskimos), the majority of whom live in the Arctic in the Territory of Nunavut where they now number about 25,000 and for whom the national organisation is the Inuit Tapirisat.

The place of the Aboriginal peoples remains an issue of political importance in Canada because of their recent rising consciousness about maintaining their own way of life. They argue that they never gave their sovereignty to the settlers and that they therefore have an inherent right to self-government. In 1997 a Royal Commission on the Aboriginal Peoples issued a five-volume report dealing with their relation to the Canadian political system.

Under the 1867 constitution, 'Indians and lands reserved for Indians' is a head of legislative jurisdiction (s. 91(24)) assigned to the Parliament of Canada. This provision was intended to protect the Aboriginal peoples from settler majorities governing the provinces. As a result of a Supreme Court decision, the Inuit in the Arctic were included within the scope of this provision (*Re Eskimos* [1939] SCR 104). Over the years, the federal government employing this jurisdiction developed a series of policies to manage Indian and Inuit affairs. Provincial policies for Indians have been minimal, except in instances authorised by federal statute or in situations where the federal government has disavowed any responsibility, such as for the Métis people and many Indians in urban areas. The principal federal statute dealing with Indians, the Indian Act, has included a provision authorising provincial laws of general application to be enforced. Consequently, provincial laws on education, health and child welfare do apply on Indian lands. Aboriginal land claims have been a matter requiring federal–provincial cooperation because most of the land, and the accompanying natural resources, being claimed by Aboriginal peoples is provincially owned public land.

A federal structure provides both opportunities and problems for accommodating the aspirations of Canada's indigenous peoples. Where they are geographically concentrated and constitute a majority of people in a region, the provision of territorial autonomy may enable them to become self-governing. Furthermore, since the original relationship between many indigenous groups and the Canadian state was based on treaties, there has developed a theory of 'treaty federalism' in which treaties are seen as the fundamental political relationship between the Aboriginal peoples and Canada, existing alongside the 'provincial federalism' of the Constitution Act 1867 (Henderson 1993; Hueglin 1997; Tully 1995:118–39). Indeed, a part of the Charlottetown Agreement 1992 (ss. 41–56) proposed, within a comprehensive set of constitutional reforms, the establishment of self-government for indigenous peoples as a third order of government (since the units would be of a much smaller scale than the provinces) within the Canadian federation, but the agreement failed to achieve ratification as a constitutional amendment. Since then, progress has been on a piece-meal basis. In 1995 the federal government announced a new policy framework for Aboriginal self-government, based on a pilot project established in the province of Manitoba in late 1994. The emergence of autonomous Aboriginal governments will require their integration into and synchronisation with the existing federal system, which would then reflect three orders of government: federal, provincial and Aboriginal. Currently, these arrangements are the subject of negotiations among the federal government, the provincial governments and the various indigenous peoples.

Two further points of interest relate to the changing position of Aboriginal peoples in Canada. The three territories represent large, sparsely populated northern areas to which a large measure of autonomous self-government has been granted but which, because of their limited population and financial dependence on the federal government, are unable to sustain the full range of self-government normally exercised by the provinces. In 1999, following a referendum and negotiation of the arrangements, a third territory was carved out of the former Northwest Territory. Nunavut now provides the Inuit people with autonomous self-government in a territory where they form 80 per cent of the population. It occupies an area nearly 20 per cent of Canada's land mass but has a population of only 25,000. The creation of Nunavut is one illustration of how federalism has been able to accommodate indigenous aspirations for self-government.

Second, the Indian peoples of northern Quebec, an example of a minority within a federal minority, have steadfastly resisted being included in a separate, politically independent Quebec. In the 1995 Quebec referendum, over 95 per cent of these First Nations people voted against separation, insisting that if Quebec separates from Canada they should have the right to separate from Quebec to remain within Canada. Since the vast hydro resources of northern Quebec are vital to its economic future, this is a prospect fiercely repudiated by Quebec sovereignists, who have attempted to win over the support of the Aboriginal peoples but have so far failed to succeed.

Efforts to resolve these issues
As a result of these various pressures during the last three decades, Canada has gone through four phases of constitutional deliberations (Watts 1996). The first of these, directed particularly at Quebec's concerns, culminated in the Victoria Charter that resulted in tentative agreement. In the end, however, it failed to receive the endorsement of the Quebec government. The second round, during 1976–82, followed the election in 1976 of the first sovereignist Parti Québécois government. Issues relating to Quebec were central in this phase but a wider range of concerns was also

addressed. This round resulted in partial success with the passage of the Constitution Act 1982. This added new formal constitutional amendment procedures and the Charter of Rights and Freedoms to the constitution. Nevertheless, it left major issues relating to Quebec unresolved and Quebec therefore seriously dissatisfied. The third round, in 1987–90, involved the attempt to ratify the 1987 Meech Lake Accord, intended to reconcile Quebec by meeting five points sought by the then federalist Liberal government of Quebec.[3] Initially hailed as a major achievement towards accommodating Quebec, in the end when the time limit of three years for ratification expired, two of the ten provinces (Newfoundland and Manitoba, together representing only 6 per cent of the Canadian population) had failed to ratify. The fourth round, in 1991–92, embodied an extensive and inclusive range of constitutional reforms in the Charlottetown Agreement of 1992. These were directed not only at accommodating Quebec but also at the concerns of other parts of Canada, including the Aboriginal peoples. Although the complex set of compromises had the unanimous support of the federal prime minister, all the premiers of the ten provinces and two territories, and the leaders of all four of the national Aboriginal organisations, a subsequent Canada-wide referendum produced support from only 46 per cent of the electorate. Rejected both in Quebec and in the rest of Canada, it proceeded no further to ratification.

The failure to ratify the Charlottetown Agreement has meant that many of the issues that gave rise to the past thirty years of 'mega constitutional politics' in Canada have remained unresolved. Particularly serious is the issue of Quebec's place in the federation. In the 1994 Quebec elections, the sovereignist Parti Québécois returned to provincial power after a decade out of office. It immediately set about organising a referendum on sovereignty, which was rejected by a very narrow majority of 50.6 per cent. The resultant public mood in Canada has largely been one in which Quebeckers feel frustrated and cynical about the repeated promises of constitutional change which have failed to come to fruition, and Canadians outside Quebec have become weary and wary of the constant preoccupation with constitutional deliberations. Nevertheless, by 1998 the emphasis upon incremental rather than comprehensive constitutional adjustment and upon intergovernmental negotiation rather than unilateral government action and improved economic and political circumstances had improved the mood somewhat, and opinion surveys indicated some decline in the level of support within Quebec for the Parti Québécois and for independence.

THE FEDERAL ACCOMMODATION OF DIVERSITY

The Canadian experience has implications for the federal accommodation of ethnic diversity within federations more generally.

The general issue

The contemporary period has been marked not only by global pressures for larger economic and political units but also, in certain regions, by strong pressures for ethnic nationalism. As Forsyth (1989) and Wiessner (1993) have noted, the uniting of constituent units that are based on different ethnic nationalisms into some form of federal system appears to be one way of containing pressures for fragmentation. But multi-ethnic federations have been among the most difficult to sustain, as Nigeria, Pakistan, India, Malaysia, Canada, Belgium and Spain, as well as the effort to federalise Europe, have illustrated. This has led some commentators, such as Elazar (1993), to question whether federations composed of different ethnic units simply run the risk of eventual civil war. There is no doubt that fundamentally mono-ethnic federations, such as the United States, Australia and Germany, have faced fewer difficulties. Nevertheless, the persistence of federal systems in Switzerland and Canada for over a century, in India for half a century, and in Malaysia for over three decades suggests that under certain conditions multi-ethnic federations can be sustained. Given that the management of ethnic nationalism is a crucial issue in the contemporary world, we need to consider the structures and processes required to enable federal systems to accommodate ethnic nationalism.

In an analysis of conflict resolution within federations, Gagnon (1993) was right to remind us that such political systems should be assessed not by whether they can eliminate conflict but, rather, by their ability to manage it. Conflict is an inherent component of all societies. Federal systems that have persisted have done so not because they have eliminated conflict, but because they have managed it.

The relation of federal solutions to territoriality

Federal systems, by their very nature, represent a territorial form of accommodation. The applicability of a federal solution depends, therefore, on the degree to which ethnic diversity is geographically concentrated and so can be territorially demarcated.

Although some authors, such as Elkins (1995), have explored the possibility of non-territorial federal arrangements for power sharing, and there has been some consideration in Canada of non-territorial forms of self-government for Aboriginals not concentrated on reserves, there is no question that most federations, including Canada, have been based primarily on a territorial matrix. Their effectiveness in accommodating shared-rule with self-rule for constituent ethnic groups has depended, therefore, upon the degree to which these groups have been geographically concentrated. For instance, in Canada, the fact that over 80 per cent of French Canadians live within Quebec, and constitute over 80 per cent of the population there, has meant that the provincial government of Quebec has been in the position to provide francophone Quebeckers with an effective political unit for serving their distinct interests.

Intra-provincial minorities

The fundamentally territorial character of federal systems raises issues about the safeguards for intra-provincial minorities. Rarely do the elements of diversity within a federation fall neatly and precisely into geographical units. In the case of Canada, as noted earlier, although francophone Quebeckers form an overwhelming majority within that province, close to 20 per cent of the population are anglophones or allophones.[4] Furthermore, in a number of the English-speaking provinces (most notably, New Brunswick and Ontario), there are significant francophone minorities. Two constitutional devices are intended to protect those who are in a minority position within a province. One provides a right of appeal to the federal government. Such a provision was included in the Constitution Act 1867 in relation to religious minority education, although this federal power has in fact never been exercised (s. 93 (3), (4)). The other incorporates in the constitution a bill of rights protecting individual rights. The 1982 Charter of Rights and Freedoms includes an extensive list not only of individual rights but also of group rights in relation to minority language educational rights, multicultural groups and Aboriginal peoples, all judicially enforceable (ss. 1–34).

The existence of intra-provincial minorities raises a special problem where there is a significant secessionist movement within one of the constituent units of the federation and may, in fact, act as a brake upon such a movement. In the case of Quebec, both the anglophone and allophone population concentrated in the Montreal area, and the Aboriginal peoples in northern Quebec, voted overwhelmingly against separation in the 1995 referendum, tilting the balance.

The special problem of bicommunal federations

A particular problem arises in federal systems that are bicommunal in character and composed of only two constituent units. The literature on the particular difficulties of bipolar or dyadic federations is not encouraging (Duchacek 1988). Examples include the eventual splitting of Pakistan and Czechoslovakia. The problems of Cyprus and Sri Lanka also illustrate the special difficulties in bicommunal situations. The problem has generally been that the usual insistence upon parity in all matters between the two units has tended to produce deadlocks. This is because there is no opportunity for shifting alliances and coalitions, which is one of the ways in which multi-unit federations are able to resolve issues. In two-unit systems, the resulting cumulatively intensifying bipolarity has usually led to their terminal instability.

In the Canadian federation, there is a strong bicommunal element, given the fundamental English-speaking and French-speaking division. But, while in terms of linguistic communities Canada may be bipolar, as a federation it has been composed of more than two units and Quebec has from time to time allied itself in federal politics with various English-speaking provinces. Furthermore, the English-speaking provinces have often taken different positions from each other on many issues, thus moderating tendencies to polarisation between the two linguistic communities. From time to time there have been proposals for converting Canada into a confederation of two units: Quebec and a nine-province federation of the 'Rest of Canada'. Among such proposals have been those advanced by the Parti Québécois in 1979–80 and 1985 (Watts 1998). Such proposals have usually been met with strong resistance, however.

One feature that has been important to reducing polarisation between the two major communities has been the practice of emphasising representation of all major groups within federal institutions. By practice rather than by constitutional requirement, the position of governor-general has rotated between English-speaking, French-speaking, and non-English-or-French representatives, the federal cabinet has always contained a substantial number of francophone Quebec ministers, and three of the nine Supreme Court justices have been from Quebec. Also, the two major federal political parties have alternated their leadership between leaders from Quebec and those from the rest of Canada. During the last thirty years, this has resulted in the office of federal prime minister being held by three Quebeckers and three non-Quebeckers. Indeed, as a result of particular electoral circumstances, the three Quebeckers actually held office for twenty-eight of those thirty years. Furthermore, because Quebec represents a quarter of the federal population and because there are significant differences among the other provinces, any major federal party that hopes to gain office through an electoral majority in the House of Commons has found that, in practice, it must win substantial support in both Quebec and in English-speaking Canada, and this has induced a dynamic whereby major federal political parties attempt to bridge the bicommunal divide.

Asymmetry within federal systems

The issue of asymmetry among the constituent units within a federal system has attracted considerable attention in recent years. Fuelling this interest has been the debate in the European Union about the integration of Europe involving a 'variable geometry' and proceeding at 'variable speeds', and the debate within Canada about Quebec as a 'distinct society' differing from the other provinces. Attention has also been attracted by the asymmetrical constitutional arrangements or practices within Spain, Belgium, India, Malaysia, Russia and most recently the United Kingdom. These examples indicate that constitutional asymmetry among provinces or states in a federal system may, in some instances, be the only way to resolve situations where much greater impulses for autonomy exist in some constituent units than in others.

In the case of Canada, the distinctive character of Quebec led to the recognition of some constitutional asymmetry at the time of the establishment of the federation (Constitution Act 1867, ss. 22, 23, 93(2), 94, 97, 98, 133). Since then, further asymmetry has developed both constitutionally and in practice (Milne 1991). Much of the intensive constitutional debate in Canada has turned around the issue of the degree to which the current asymmetry might be increased to accommodate Quebec's concerns and the degree to which this might undermine equality among the provinces (Watts 1999:63–8). This Canadian experience suggests that constitutional asymmetry may be an essential element in accommodating distinct groups within a federation but also that there may be limits beyond which asymmetry itself may contribute to divisiveness.

Division of powers and interdependence within federal systems

Classical expositions of federalism emphasise the importance of ensuring that each level of government within a federation is independent from interference or domination by the other (Wheare 1963). Perhaps more than in any other federation, the original distribution of powers in Canada attempted to achieve this by assigning virtually all jurisdiction either exclusively to the federal government or to the provinces (Constitution Act 1867, ss. 91, 92). Only two matters were left to concurrent jurisdiction: immigration and agriculture (Constitution Act 1867, s. 93). This contrasts with virtually every other federation where, typically, substantial areas of concurrency were identified in the constitution.

But all federations, including even Canada with its emphasis upon exclusivities of jurisdiction, have found that it is impossible in practice to divide jurisdiction and policy making into watertight compartments. Over time, numerous areas of overlap and interpenetration in the functions of different levels of government have developed. This has made necessary in all federations extensive forms of intergovernmental consultation and collaboration, a pattern that has certainly been true of Canada, where these processes have involved a multiplicity of councils and committees of officials, ministers and first ministers (Watts 1989).

Where such extensive intergovernmental relations have proved necessary, ensuring that provincial self-rule is not undermined has been a constant concern.

A particularly important aspect has been the financial relationships between governments within the Canadian federation. Because over time the value of different tax sources and the cost of different expenditure responsibilities inevitably vary, it is difficult in any federation to maintain in balance the revenue capacity and expenditure requirements of each level of government. As in other federations, in Canada this has required intergovernmental agreement on frequent adjustments involving financial transfers from the federal government to the provinces. In addition to adjustments required by these vertical imbalances between levels of government, there have also been horizontal imbalances among provinces due to disparities in their fiscal capacities. As a result, Canada has developed an equalisation scheme under which the federal government makes unconditional financial transfers to the less wealthy provinces to reduce the disparities among them. Furthermore, in 1982, the commitment to the principle of equalisation payments and to promoting equal opportunities was embodied in the constitution (Constitution Act 1982, s. 36). This recognises that one of the most corrosive factors undermining federal harmony may be disparities in resources among the constituent units and that action to moderate such disparities is essential to federal solidarity. In Canada, the major recipients of financial equalisation assistance from the federal government have been Quebec and the Atlantic provinces.

Federal representative institutions

There are two fundamental aspects in the organisation of any federation: the institutions for autonomous 'self-rule' of the constituent units, and the processes for 'shared-rule' for dealing with shared objectives. The latter provide the glue to hold the federation together. The former alone, without effective arrangements for the latter, would merely lead to disintegration.

All federations have found it necessary, in establishing the institutions and processes for effective shared-rule, to take some account of regional diversity. Mere majority rule is bound to leave minorities concentrated in particular regions with the view that they have no say and therefore no stake in the processes of shared-rule. Even predominantly mono-ethnic federations, such as the United States, Australia and Germany, have therefore found it necessary to adopt bicameral federal legislatures, with representation by population in one chamber and equal or weighted representation of the constituent units in the second chamber. The need for such arrangements – and for employing, either by constitutional requirement or conventional practice, a representational balance of different internal groups within the various federal institutions – has been all the more essential in multi-ethnic federations. For instance, in both Canada and Switzerland, the 'representational syndrome' whereby different linguistic, religious and geographical groups are carefully represented within each of the federal policy-making bodies, including the federal executive, is very marked.

This draws attention to two particular points. First, where the federal institutions involve a parliamentary form of government with a cabinet responsible to the lower house, for example in Canada, Australia, India, Malaysia and Austria, inevitably the second chamber's relative power, and therefore ability to represent the diversity of regional interests, has been weaker than in federations such as the United States and Switzerland in which the principle of separation of executive and legislature has been adopted. Germany, by creating the Bundesrat with certain constitutionally guaranteed veto powers which in practice operate in relation to over 60 per cent of all federal legislation, has to some extent counteracted this usual trend within parliamentary federations. By contrast, in Canada, the federal appointment of senators has only further weakened its legitimacy and role as a body to represent regional and minority interests. That is why the call for Senate reform has been so persistent in Canada.

Second, in the processes for shared-rule, it is not just the institutional structures but the way in which political parties operate and the inter-relationships between federal and state (or provincial) branches of political parties that affect the extent to which a federation-wide consensus may be developed. This has been an important factor in Canada.

The role of the judiciary
Judicial review serves two primary functions within a federal system: resolving conflicts between federal and provincial governments, over the jurisdiction assigned to each, by interpreting the constitutional provisions governing the distribution of powers; and facilitating adaptation of the federal system without resort to constitutional amendment. The latter is achieved by interpreting how new policy areas, not envisaged at the time the federation was established (for example, in the Canadian case: air travel, nuclear energy, pollution policy and energy policy), may fall within the areas of jurisdiction identified in the constitutional distribution of powers.

During the nineteenth century and the first half of the twentieth century when Canada was a colonial federation, the Judicial Committee of the Privy Council (JCPC) in the United Kingdom served as the ultimate appeal court on the Canadian constitution. The Judicial Committee's judgments in a number of major cases, especially during the period

1890–1930, had a strong decentralising impact on the Canadian federation.[5] Because, unlike many other federations (such as the United States and Australia), the Canadian constitution specifically enumerated exclusive provincial powers, this enabled the JCPC to give a generous interpretation to these, especially the provincial authority over property and civil rights, and a narrow interpretation of the federal powers relating to trade and commerce, foreign treaties and 'peace, order and good government' (Cairns 1971). This contrasted with the pattern of judicial review in the United States. There, in the original constitution, to emphasise the initial decentralist thrust, the states were simply assigned the unenumerated residual jurisdiction. Ironically, the Supreme Court, relying on the doctrine of 'implied powers', was therefore able to expand the enumerated federal powers at the expense of the non-specific residual state powers. Thus, where judicial review in the United States contributed in the long term to increasing federal powers and to greater centralisation, the JCPC in interpreting the Canadian constitution maintained a strong protection of provincial powers against federal intrusion. In this way, the JCPC contributed to converting the Canadian federation, which was more centralised than the United States at its origin, into one that became more decentralised.

The Supreme Court of Canada was created in 1875 and since 1949 has been the final court of appeal on constitutional questions. Although its judges are appointed by the federal government, in practice the tradition of impartial judicial interpretation has been maintained. Studies analysing its decisions have generally concluded that, on matters relating to the jurisdictions of the federal and provincial governments, its judgments have been balanced without especially favouring one at the expense of the other (Russell et al. 1989:9, 131–288).

During the past twenty years of mega constitutional politics in Canada, the Supreme Court has been called upon to decide some very important constitutional issues. During the period 1980–82, there were three important cases in which the court ruled on the validity of the processes for constitutional amendment. In the *Senate Amendment* case and the *Patriation* case, it ruled that constitutional amendments affecting the fundamental federal character of Canada required the assent of a substantial number of provinces,[6] although, in the *Quebec Veto* case, the judgment was that Quebec did not by itself possess a veto on constitutional amendments.[7] More recently, the Supreme Court ruled in a historic case that Quebec did not have the right to secede from Canada unilaterally, but added the qualification that, if Quebeckers indicated in a referendum by a clear majority in response to a clear question that they wished to secede (the measures of clarity were left unspecified), the rest of Canada would have an obligation to negotiate the terms of secession taking into account the interests of all parties, including Quebec, the rest of Canada and minorities in Quebec, and also the fundamental organising principles of federalism, democracy, constitutionalism and the rule of law.[8] Thus, the court attempted a balanced judgment to avoid inflaming passions among either federalists or secessionists.

One notable development affecting the role of the courts was the addition to the constitution in 1982 of the Charter of Rights and Freedoms. Interpreting the charter has enormously expanded the number of cases before the Supreme Court and this now represents the largest portion of its work (Russell et al. 1989:10–13, 385–678). Because the charter relates not to the powers of federal and provincial governments in relation to each other, but to relations between governments and individual citizens, this area has attracted increased citizen interest in the Supreme Court and its procedures and the method of appointment to it. The inclusion of certain minority group rights in the charter has also meant that the court has come to play a major role in their protection.

Prime Minister Trudeau, in championing the adoption of the charter in 1982, had envisaged it as a document that would unite diverse groups by emphasising the common fundamental rights shared by all Canadian citizens. In large measure, it has been successful in this objective. Even within Quebec, surveys indicate significant support for it. Quebec nationalist politicians have been critical of it, however, as limiting Quebec's traditional jurisdiction over property and civil rights.

A number of provinces, including Quebec, have their own charters of rights. Wherever there are both federal and provincial charters, there is always the possibility of a charter duel, but in such cases the courts have normally judged that the federal charter, in so far as there is conflict, must prevail. What provincial charters have done, however, is to supplement or extend the rights available to their own citizens and minorities beyond those set out in the federal constitution. Indeed, when the Supreme Court in 1988 struck down a section of Quebec's controversial language law,[9] it did so on the grounds that it conflicted with the Quebec charter rather than with the federal charter (Russell 1993:146–7).

The impact of the Charter of Rights on Aboriginal autonomies and rights has been moderated by the inclusion of section 35, which recognises and affirms existing Aboriginal and treaty rights. Thus, since 1982, the courts have had the task of balancing these rights and the other rights set out in the charter.

Autonomy as a factor for divisiveness or unity
The question is sometimes raised, especially where a federation is created by devolution from a previously unitary political system, as to whether a federal system by encouraging and facilitating regional autonomy is merely a step on the way towards secession and disintegration. Indeed, this was a very real and expressed fear during the debates of the Constituent Assembly of

India and more recently in relation to devolution in South Africa and the United Kingdom. The rise of the secession movement within Quebec is often pointed to as such an example.

There is, however, also evidence to suggest that granting a substantial measure of autonomy and self-government to distinct groups within a polity may in fact contribute to enhanced unity. Indeed, the Canadian experience in 1867 was that much of the previous disharmony was reduced by replacing the previous unitary system under the Act of Union of 1840 with a federal system. The previous union had produced political conflict between the French and English populations and a series of impasses. By creating a distinct self-governing province of Quebec, with its French-speaking majority having control over matters of cultural and social significance, many of the previously contentious issues were siphoned off from the realm of federal politics, leaving the federal sphere to focus on shared objectives and policies. It is true that during the past thirty years there has been significant secession movement, but it has been the product of a desire for national self-determination rather than induced by the existence of autonomy. Certainly, all the evidence points to the fact that, if there had not already been provincial autonomy, the movement would have been much stronger, not weaker. It is not insignificant that referendum results and repeated recent public opinion surveys have persistently pointed to the fact that a large majority of Quebeckers want greater autonomy, but combined with continued association with the rest of Canada.

An important point to note is that unity as an objective should not be confused with homogeneity or uniformity. Where such a confusion has occurred, it has almost always fostered counter-pressures for separation and secession. Unity, to be effective in a multi-ethnic situation, should be understood as harmony in diversity. It involves the recognition of diversity within a harmonious whole. A noted French Canadian Prime Minister, Wilfrid Laurier, at the beginning of this century, once described federation as being like a majestic cathedral in which the various elements – the granite, the marble and the oak – were each clearly distinct but together were combined in an inspiring architectural harmony.

The adaptability of federal systems
Federal systems have sometimes been criticised as inflexible and rigid because of their emphasis upon constitutionally entrenched legal structures. Given the complexity and legalism inherent in federal constitutions, there is some validity to this contention. Nevertheless, an examination of the history of such federations as the United States (founded as a federation in 1789), Switzerland (converted to a federation in 1848), Canada (federalised in 1867) and Australia (federated in 1901) shows that they

have displayed considerable flexibility in adapting to changing conditions over a century or more. And this has included multi-ethnic federations like Canada and Switzerland. Canada, over more than 130 years, has undergone enormous changes in the process of its evolution. What has been significant is that much of this has occurred, not through formal constitutional changes but through incremental and pragmatic adjustments reached through political negotiation, intergovernmental agreements and consensus. During the past three decades, efforts at comprehensive and radical constitutional transformation have repeatedly failed, and it is now widely recognised that a pattern of piecemeal adjustment is likely to be more successful in the long run. That has certainly been the case in most federations elsewhere (Watts 1999:121–2).

A number of authors have attributed the prosperity, stability and longevity of many federations to the effectiveness of federation as a flexible form of political organisation. Martin Landau (1973), for instance, has argued that the multiple channels of decision making provide failsafe mechanisms that contribute to the reliability and adaptability of federations as political systems, compared with hierarchical or unitary systems, in responding to changing circumstances and needs.

Prerequisites for effective federal solutions
In the analysis of conflict resolution within federal systems, the importance of particular structures and processes is borne out by the Canadian experience. But perhaps most important of all in enabling a federal system to manage internal conflict is the existence of a supportive federal political culture emphasising constitutionalism, tolerance and the recognition of distinctive regional groups (Elazar 1993).

Past Canadian experience confirms the importance of such a political culture (Watts 1999:120–1). More important than its formal structures has been public acceptance of the basic values and processes required for the effective operation of the federal system. This includes an emphasis upon constitutionality, tolerance and compromise. It also involves the explicit recognition and accommodation of multiple identities and loyalties within an overarching sense of shared purpose and identity. Efforts to deny or suppress the multiple identities within its diverse society have, in Canadian experience, almost invariably led to contention, stress and strain. It would appear that, in any federation encompassing a diverse society, an essential requirement is acceptance of the value of diversity and of the possibility of multiple loyalties expressed through the establishment of constituent units of government with genuine autonomous self-rule over those matters most important to their distinct identity. At the same time, equally important has been the recognition of the benefits derived from shared purposes and objectives. The importance of these values is something that each generation of Canadians has had to relearn when faced with internal crises, such as those in relation to the place of Quebec within the federation.

The importance of tolerance as an essential element in the political culture necessary for an effective federation, especially a multi-ethnic one, points to the vital link between democratic institutions and processes and successful federations. Those who define democracy solely in terms of majority rule sometimes argue that federal structures and processes, by providing checks and balances against pure majority rule, limit democracy. The fault in such an argument lies, of course, in the definition of democracy in purely majoritarian terms rather than in terms of popular participation and consent to policy decisions. Indeed, federations, by providing for majority rule within different constituent units and by processes involving the participation and consent of the various distinct groups in federal decision making, maximise democracy in a broader sense.

CONCLUSION

Like all federations, Canada continues to undergo a constant evolution of its structure and practices. While still operating under the basic federal structure established by the Constitution Act 1867, much of that evolution has occurred not through constitutional amendment but through pragmatic development of intergovernmental practices and collaboration. These have responded to internal political, social and economic pressures and to changing conditions and circumstances. During its history, the federation has been faced with many challenges and crises to which, so far, its federal processes have managed to respond.

The current sovereignist movement within Quebec once again presents the federation with a severe challenge. Yet there are some signs that, as before, Canada will adapt. Popular support within Quebec for sovereignty, although still strong, has declined somewhat since 1995 and a substantial majority of Quebeckers are reluctant to break their links with the rest of Canada.

Much will depend on whether, in the immediate years ahead, the structure, practices and political culture of the Canadian federation will enable it to continue to respond adequately to the challenges facing it.

NOTES

1 Census reports indicate that the proportion of French speakers within Quebec has actually increased in recent decades.
2 For a comparison of Canada with other federations in terms of their degree of decentralisation, see Watts (1999:71–81).
3 The 1987 Meech Lake Accord proposed that the Canadian constitution be amended to recognise Quebec as a 'distinct society' within Canada, that

Quebec's veto over constitutional amendments be restored, that the Quebec government have an enhanced role over immigration into that province, that there be compensation for provinces opting out of federal–provincial shared-cost programs, and that Quebec representation on the Supreme Court of Canada be entrenched.

4 Allophones are largely immigrant groups whose mother tongue is neither French nor English.

5 See, for instance, *Hodge* v. *The Queen* (1883) 9 App. Cas. 117, and *Liquidators of the Maritime Bank* v. *Receiver General of NB* [1892] AC 437.

6 *Re Senate* [1980] 1 SCR 54; and *Re Amendment of Constitution of Canada* [1981] 1 SCR 753.

7 *Re Constitution of Canada* [1982] 2 SCR 793.

8 *Quebec Secession Reference* (1998) 161 DLR (4th) 385.

9 *Quebec* v. *Ford et al* [1988] 2 SCR 712.

REFERENCES

Cairns, A. 1971. 'The judicial committee and its critics', *Canadian Journal of Political Science* 4, 301–45.

Duchacek, I. 1988. 'Dyadic federations and confederations', *Publius: The Journal of Federalism* 18(2):5–31.

Elazar, D.J. 1993. 'International and comparative federalism', *PS: Political Science and Politics* 26(2):190–5.

Elkins, D.J. 1995. *Beyond Sovereignty: Territory and Political Economy in the Twenty-first Century.* Toronto: University of Toronto Press.

Forsyth, M. (ed.) 1989. *Federalism and Nationalism.* Leicester, UK: Leicester University Press.

Gagnon, A.-G. 1993. 'The political uses of federalism', in M. Burgess and A.-G. Gagnon (eds) *Comparative Federalism and Federation: Competing Traditions and Future Directions.* Hemel Hempstead, UK: Harvester Wheatsheaf, 15–44.

Henderson, J.Y. 1993. 'Affirming treaty federalism', submission to the Royal Commission on Aboriginal Peoples.

Hueglin, T.O. 1997. 'Exploring concepts of treaty federalism: a comparative perspective', paper prepared as part of the Research Program for the Royal Commission on Aboriginal Peoples, For Seven Generations, Libraxus CD-ROM.

Landau, M. 1973. 'Federalism, redundancy and system reliability', *Publius: The Journal of Federalism* 3(2):173–95.

Milne, D. 1991. 'Equality or asymmetry: why choose?', in R.L.Watts and D.M. Brown (eds) *Options for a New Canada.* Toronto: University of Toronto Press, 285–307.

Russell, P.H. 1993. *Constitutional Odyssey: Can Canadians Become a Sovereign People?* 2nd edn. Toronto: University of Toronto Press.

Russell, P.H., R. Knopff and T. Morton 1989. *Federalism and the Charter.* Ottawa: Carleton University Press.

Task Force on Canadian Unity 1979. *A Future Together: Observations and Recommendations.* Ottawa: Supply and Services Canada.

Tully, J. 1995. *Strange Multiplicity: Constitutionalism in an Age of Diversity*. Cambridge: Cambridge University Press.

Watts, R.L. 1989. *Executive Federalism: A Comparative Analysis*. Kingston: Institute of Intergovernmental Relations.

—— 1996. 'Canada: three decades of periodic federal crisis', *International Political Science Review* 17(4):353–71.

—— 1998. 'Examples of partnership', in R. Gibbins and G. Laforest (eds) *Beyond the Impasse: Toward Reconciliation*. Montreal and Kingston: McGill-Queen's University Press.

—— 1999. *Comparing Federal Systems*. 2nd edn. Kingston and Montreal: McGill-Queen's University Press.

Wiessner, S. 1993. 'Federalism and architecture for freedom', *European Law Review* 1(2):129–42.

Wheare, K.C. 1963. *Federal Government*. 4th edn. London: Oxford University Press.

CHAPTER 3

FEDERALISM AND DIVERSITY IN INDIA

VASUKI NESIAH

FROM DEMOCRACY AND PLURALISM TO CONFLICT MANAGEMENT

India is constituted by an extraordinary heterogeneity. Religion and language alone constitute a truly remarkable diversity. Hindi is the official language but only a little over a third of the population are Hindi speakers (Census of India 1988:x). Fifteen languages are recognised in the constitution, fourteen of them official languages of various states. In addition, there are hundreds of other linguistic communities spread throughout India. Similarly, Hindus, Muslims, Christians, Sikhs, Buddhists and adherents of a number of other smaller religions shape India's religious diversity. At one level, Hinduism may be seen as the religion of the majority; on the other, Hinduism is itself pluralised and fragmented by region, caste, and so on. In fact, the sheer proliferation of sects and local traditions are such that demographers find it impossible to track the internal diversity within different religious communities. Of course, religion and language are just two nodal points of ethnic identity and community; caste, tribe and region also constitute India's ethnic diversity.

Diversity is both India's most spectacular strength and its most formidable challenge. For the architects of the Indian constitution, federalism was a constitutional device that could engage this diversity in the project of nation building. It embodied and institutionalised those values that represented their own hopes and aspirations for independent India: democratic, pluralistic and politically stable. Federalist ideology can be situated in what Amartya Sen (1997:18–27) calls 'classical nationalism'. Classical nationalism forged in the context of empowering, first, an independence struggle and, then, an independent nation was invested in the idea of a united India.[1] In line with this, federalism was designed to give multiple, heterogeneous communities an institutional mechanism for engaging with the nation at large and, through that engagement, to give them a material and imaginative stake in India as a whole. In this vein, the Sakaria Commission (1988) has noted that the Indian system 'as it emerged from the Constituent Assembly in 1949' was a sui generis hybrid of a federal and unitary constitutional structure, 'in which the predominant strength of the Union is blended with the essence of cooperative federalism'. In fact, 'Unity in Diversity' was the celebrated slogan of Indian federalism and was reflected in its constitutional embodiment. Today India is a union of twenty-five states, ranging in size from Uttar Pradesh, which has a population of well over a hundred million, to Sikkim with approximately 400,000.[2] In addition, there are six union territories and Delhi, the national capital territory.

Yet today, fifty years after independence, as we evaluate the experience of federalism, any democratic and pluralistic values that informed its architecture have received scant institutional embodiment. There are many symptoms of the impoverishment of federalist principles and policies in India, but among the most notorious and telling records of this is the rigid control exerted by the centre over the chief ministers of state governments. Bhagwan Dua (1988:121–2) notes that 'only a few chief ministers, who are supposed to represent autonomous centres of power in their own right, have ever survived in office for any length of time if they were caught on the wrong side of the power structure in New Delhi. India seems to have lost the opportunity to develop a federal system based on partnership between the centre and the states.' Notwithstanding federalist principles in the constitutional structure, the Indian political system appears to have greater resonance as a unitary framework.[3] As enumerated in articles 155–6 of the constitution, state governors, appointed by and accountable to the centre, have a certain discretion to override elected state officials. The notorious article 356, enabling the suspension of state governments, is symptomatic of an 'anti-federalist' ethos. Thus, the constitutional rules of the game have either remained ineffective or, worse, enabled erosion of the autonomy of state governments.

Against this backdrop, this chapter seeks to analyse the relationship between federalism, diversity and democracy in India.

A CONTESTED TERRAIN

Ethnic diversity and the constitution
India has sometimes been described as a nation where everyone is a minority. Cross-cutting lines of identity and difference can be tracked along multiple axes: language, religion, caste, tribe, region, and so on. These are layered over factors such as class and gender that add further complexity to the country's demographic profile. As Bajpai (1997:38) has noted, while these differences may divide India, 'the absence of a

nationwide cleavage along ethnic lines' also provides a 'source of stability', since 'religious, caste, tribal, linguistic and regional differences do not converge on a single fault line'. We can contrast India with countries such as Cyprus and Sri Lanka where the national imagination has been held hostage by a polarised conception of ethnic difference, where all heterogeneity has been mapped onto a single fault line. India's federal structure would appear to have a greater chance of success in addressing ethnic difference, since centre–state relations will not be overdetermined by single high-stakes cleavage; a more diffused and multipronged dynamic could prevail.

If there are cross-cutting lines of diversity in the Indian polity, the constitution carries cross-cutting mechanisms to address that diversity. We can identify four approaches to diversity in the Indian constitution. First, the constitution attempts to tailor mechanisms that enable an inclusive and dialogical relationship between minority communities and the state; in this vein, federal institutions attempt to channel linguistic and regional diversity. Accompanying the federal schema is the language policy. While Hindi is the official language, English is to be used as an additional language for official matters and, most importantly, states can conduct affairs in their regional language. Similarly, the 'three language formula' recommended by the National Integration Council in 1961 required that 'all schools' have 'compulsory teaching in three languages: the regional language and English, with Hindi for the non-Hindi states and another Indian language for the Hindi-speaking states' (Hardgrave and Kochanek 1986:131).

Second, in other contexts, the constitution encourages the proactive intervention of the state in overcoming differences and their social and political consequences; affirmative action programs for scheduled castes and tribals are illustrative here. India continues to be fraught with deep caste hierarchy and discrimination. However, as Galanter (1989:185) says, 'If one reflects on the propensity of nations to neglect the claim of those at the bottom, I think it's fair to say that this policy of compensatory discrimination has been pursued with remarkable persistence and generosity (if not always with vigor and effectiveness) over the past thirty years'.

The constitution crafts a third approach to diversity by limiting state power and safeguarding a sphere of autonomy so that differences can be protected and enhanced without threat of assimilation and subjugation. This approach may be exemplified by the way in which the principle of secularism has been interpreted to offer religious minorities a protected sphere through the regime of personal laws. Secularism is sometimes understood in the classical liberal sense that religion is zoned out of the public sphere, or sometimes understood as being multi-religious, with parity in respect of all religious traditions (Sen 1997:22).[4] Concern with religious unity has been so overwhelming that there is a determined

55

refusal to allow federal boundaries to recognise religious divisions. Even when the federal map of India was reorganised, it was on linguistic grounds, and 'an important principle was reaffirmed: religious appeals were to be kept out of the official politics and language of the state' (Corbridge 1995:106).

Finally, a fourth approach to diversity lies in establishing a norm of equality for both individuals and groups, to guide the application of the specific guarantees and protections that run through other pieces of the constitutional framework; here we may cite those provisions entrenching the fundamental rights of all citizens against discrimination. Galanter (1989:155) situates this as part of the constitution's

> general program for the reconstruction of Indian society . . . it clearly sets out to secure to individuals equality of status and opportunity, to abolish invidious distinctions among groups, to protect the integrity of a variety of groups – religious, linguistic, and cultural, to give free play to voluntary associations, the widest freedom of association to the individual, and generally the widest possible freedom consonant with the public good.

Ultimately, these provisions protect not only minorities but also minorities within minorities.

If the different approaches to diversity have worked in complementary ways, historical change has also added to the complexity. As illustrated by the now famous *Shah Bano* case,[5] tensions between different approaches to diversity have gained increased urgency. New sources of diversity have been foregrounded; old approaches to diversity have begged for new strategies. Questions have been raised about whether particular constitutional strategies have helped or hindered the goals at which they aimed. For instance, if affirmative action programs have attempted to address the hierarchies of caste differences, critics have argued that foregrounding caste categories, in a redistributive effort, has only entrenched caste identity. Similarly, if secularism was to provide religion with a protected sphere within which it had autonomy, the boundaries of that sphere have been experienced as walls that limit religious expression as much as being boundaries that restrict state intrusion. Our received constitutional discourse of secularism alienates and excludes those (the vast majority of Indians?) who do not conceptualise their political identities and affiliations in a secular idiom. Does the mirage of neutrality subscribed to by the discourse of modernity and secularism nurture an exclusive and exclusionary mode of political participation? Does this in turn nurture the dominant agendas, the entrenched hierarchies and inequalities sustained by such an exclusionary discourse, privileging only a narrow political vocabulary as intelligible to the system, recognised and legitimated by state institutions?

All of these four approaches to diversity have one thing in common: the constitution envisions a public sphere where the state is constructed as an all-encompassing sieve through which we run claims of identity, community and difference. Claims of diversity are addressed to the state, mediated through the state and formulated in terms that speak to state power. As illustrated not only by *Shah Bano* but also by the tortured history of centre–state relations, even in those cases where the constitution sets limits on the sovereign to guarantee an arena of freedom, the sovereign has the power to set its own limits and rezone the line that limits its power.

Diversity and federalism

The British introduced a skeletal model of the current federal system through the Government of India Act in 1935 (Setalvad 1960:168–79). Using the boundaries drawn in this Act as a starting-point, the Constituent Assembly sought to breathe federal life into the administrative units in the constitution of independent India. The Constituent Assembly went about its project with considerable scepticism, suspicion and resentment of the 'divide and rule' motivations of the colonial legacy with which it had to work. We may infer that the stance towards federalism was itself informed by these initial sentiments. The 1956 States Reorganisation Act redrew the original borders along linguistic lines. Since then, some additional border changes have taken place, and some calls for border changes have been defeated. There have been calls for a second States Reorganisation Act. We have also witnessed calls for secession, citing 'cultural distinctiveness and economic and social disparities' (Hardgrave and Kochanek 1986:145). Hitherto, all calls for secession have been quelled by accommodation of some grievances and/or by force.

Indian federalism entails a basic division of powers, with a 'concurrent list' enumerating shared powers such as civil and criminal law, and planning; a 'state list' enumerating state powers such as education, agriculture and welfare; and a 'union list' enumerating the centre's powers, from defence and foreign affairs to income taxation, banking, and so on, and with all residual powers reverting to the centre as well. In addition to the wide range of powers allotted to the union list, 'the paramount position of the Centre is underscored by the power of Parliament to create new states, to alter boundaries of existing states, and even to abolish a state by ordinary legislative procedure without recourse to constitutional amendment' (Hardgrave and Kochanek 1986:116). Under emergency powers, the constitution allows the federal government to 'convert itself into a unitary one'. Moreover, even when not operating under emergency conditions, 'parliament can make laws with respect to any matter falling in the state list for a temporary period'. The constitutional structure is sometimes described as quasi-federal because of this centralising bias. 'The underlying emphasis is on the indestructibility of the Indian Union and not of the States' that make up that union (Mathur 1990:6).

Indian federalism is a contested terrain, characterised by shifts in the lines of diversity it engages with and the nature of that engagement. For instance, since the 1935 Act had drawn the borders of federalism for administrative convenience, these boundaries did not necessarily resonate with the relationships of identity and community that constituted people's lives. As Thakur (1995:71) notes, 'there was little opportunity for regional identities to coalesce around the existing political units'. The organisation of states along linguistic lines was a longstanding demand directed at the constitutional framers; however, the dynamics of Hindu–Muslim tensions, and then partition, overtook questions of linguistic diversity in that inaugural moment of Indian federalism. However, linguistic regionalism re-emerged as a force after independence, and particularly after the reorganisation of states along linguistic and cultural lines (Thakur 1995:71) and the establishment of Hindi as the official language in 1965. As Yash Ghai (1995:24) notes, with the States Reorganisation Act in 1956 the basis of Indian federalism was transformed from administration to ethnicity. Linguistic identity, as expressed by federal boundaries, has flowed into ethnic and regional identity, sometimes giving rise to 'sons of the soil' movements contesting internal migration from other states within India.[6] Some assertions of regional identity can be understood as responding to the evolution of federalism in centrifugal directions,[7] just as the centrifugal tendencies of the Indian nation-state can be located in its anxieties about an emerging regionalism.

Shifts in the relationship between federalism and diversity are also attested to by the waxing and waning of federalism as a take-off point for mobilising religious identity. While Indian federalism is said to have its basis in language and region, given that lines of diversity, and even the different components of the constitution's approach to diversity, intersect and overlap, federalism cannot but address questions that go beyond linguistic and regional identity. The shift in Punjab from linguistic nationalism to religious nationalism is but one marker of this complexity. In fact, when the constitutional framers began their project, federalism had significant purchase as part of the package of religious diversity, particularly as the Muslim League in their negotiations with the Congress Party had demanded federalism. Once partition was announced, this rationale for federalism declined considerably, although it was kept prominently alive with the crisis in Kashmir, Punjab, and so on. Today, with the Bharatiya Janata Party's electoral capture of national government, the relationship between federalism and Hindu–Muslim relations has arisen again.[8]

Religion is not the only cross-cutting cleavage impacted by federalism. The struggle of the left-wing government in West Bengal to resist centre directives regarding land reform, agricultural taxes, and so on conveys this dynamic along the axes of class differentiation within West Bengal. Thus, although Indian federalism is concerned principally with ethnicity, the dialectic between federalism and society, between institutional form and social relations, cuts diversity along a number of axes. These intersecting and overlapping cleavages both complicate and pluralise our conceptions of diversity, while also bringing into the federal equation various other sources of difference and hierarchy, such as class, that are not explicitly addressed by the constitutional form of federalism.

These are just a few cursory touchstones of the complex terrain charted by the relationship between federalism and diversity. Another layer of complexity is added by the provision for asymmetrical federalism in certain special cases. One of the most obvious instances of this is the constitutional provision (art. 370) for Kashmir's different status. Similarly, Indian federalism also entails constitutional demarcation of autonomous regions within states for tribal communities. Such internal differentiation is the norm, not the exception, of centre–state relations, as in Kashmir where explicit rules provide for institutional asymmetry, but also, as in the West Bengal example, in the more informal and everyday negotiation of federalism on substantive issues.

In sum, much of this discussion of change and continuity, intersection and overlap suggests that the defining alliances and tensions of diversity are not offered a priori for federalism to then address; rather, there is an ongoing dialectical process that is mutually constitutive.

INHERITED ARGUMENTS

This section seeks to synthesise arguments about federalism and diversity by drawing attention to three different paradigms that have informed classical nationalism: administrative, contractual and democratic. I define the administrative paradigm as seeing federalism as a mechanism to promote the stability, legitimacy and territorial integrity of the Indian state. I define the contractual paradigm as one aimed at multicultural power sharing; against the spectre of communalism, federalism was to enable constitutional negotiations between the diverse communities of India. It emphasises the pluralist ambitions of federalism. I define the democratic paradigm as interested in institutional arrangements that would encourage sub-national communities to have a measure of autonomy in shaping the realities of their lives. Its impulses are communitarian and participatory.

Each of these worked to shape, promote and legitimate particular visions of federalism. The social struggles that informed the conflicts, negotiations and compromises between different paradigms for federalism surface in the gulf between decentralisation as management and decentralisation as participatory democracy, the gulf between the aspirations of the centre and the aspirations of local communities, the claims of inter-ethnic justice and the realities of inter-ethnic fratricide. All three paradigms have persisted, with different arguments foregrounded at different times by different constituencies. Each of these mobilised a justificatory language, a discourse of legitimation, for conceptualising and justifying a federal framework. The specific agenda and political programs they prioritised sought (with different levels of effectiveness) to give substantive shape and content to the federalist project as it was concretised and institutionally elaborated. Classical nationalism's fashioning of federalism as a response to diversity strained to accommodate all three arguments, despite the different social visions they embodied.

The administrative paradigm
As noted earlier, the Government of India Act in 1935 introduced elements of a federal structure that was built upon and remodelled at independence. For the British, the creation of a sub-national state system was a way to deflect and diffuse calls for self-government (Setalvad 1960:170). Thus, the instrumental rationale for the legislative demarcation of centre and periphery was present even at that inaugural moment. In the post-1947 period, the administrative purposes of the centre gained prominence in the justificatory language of the federalist project in at least two contexts. First, in responding to the competing claims of the heterogeneous communities that made up India, federalism was seen to enable the centre's efforts in managing, accommodating and domesticating conflicts in the interest of maintaining the stability of the Indian state and its boundaries. Along these lines, Stuart Corbridge (1995:104) describes federalism as a 'myth' of governance directed towards the 'consensual management of India's many ethnic groups and subnationalities'. Second, in the discourse of modernisation and state economic planning, federalism was seen to promote efficiency and effectiveness in the dissemination and implementation of national development policy.[9]

Both these objectives are illustrated in the recommendations of the States Reorganisation Commission of 1953. Following political unrest in a number of states, particularly in the south, the commission was appointed to examine the question of linguistic federalism. It argued that reorganisation should be informed by four principles: 'First, any reorganisation plan must preserve and strengthen the unity and security of India; second, linguistic and cultural homogeneity would be taken into account in reorganisation plans; third, financial, economic and administrative efficiency should be considered in the effort; and fourth, reorganisation must be compatible with development plans' (Bajpai 1997:61–2). Only the second of these principles is responsive to the linguistic nationalism that prompted the appointment of the commission. The other three principles speak to the other administrative priorities that the centre wanted federal constitutional arrangements to support and facilitate. The constitutional drafting of federal boundaries for the expression of ethnic claims is also, simultaneously then, the project of regulating communities, of making them available for state power.

The federal device is often perceived as the constitutional mechanism that channels the state into a compatible fit with the nation; here, we also see the reverse process: the 'nation constituting' dynamic of a statist vision of self-determination. The constitutional project here not only subordinated sub-national identities to national identity but also reconfigured them as those that could find expression through the procedural avenues of federalism. The nation has to be constituted, therefore, as that which can be expressed through a unitary and centralised notion of the state.

Within the administrative paradigm, the relationship between state and nation repeatedly rides a number of polarities that give the state pre-eminence in constituting the nation. The state is situated in both the forward-looking movement of determining India's place in modernity and the retroactive fashioning of the kind of India that is fit for modernity. The state represents both an externalising process of engagement with the international order and an internally directed process of giving fixity and coherence to the Indian self. The state emerges as an objective placeholder for self-determination, embarrassed by, and seeking to overcome, the subjective constitution of self that is represented by the nation.

In fact, every time the federal compact has been revisited by the central government, it has done so only when its administrative project has been jeopardised, when the Indian self constituted by the discourse of sovereignty threatened to unravel into the heterogeneity that constituted the nation. A rising tide of regional linguistic nationalism that snowballed into violent protests in Andhra prompted the States Reorganisation Bill of 1956. The 1960 restructuring of the state of Bombay into Maharashtra, with Marathi as the official language, and Gujarat, with Gujarati as the official language, came in response to violent unrest and civil strife in that region. Similarly, the Punjabi-speaking population of Punjab had been agitating for a redrawing of state boundaries even at the time of the States Reorganisation Bill. However, the 1966 re-demarcation of Punjab into Punjab and Hariyana came only when, first, that agitation was perceived to have become a threat to the stability of the Indian state and, second, the patriotic role of the Sikhs in the Indo-Pakistani war of 1965 indicated that greater autonomy for the Sikhs would not be a threat to territorial integrity. Thus, a Sikh-dominated state appeared to be compelled by administrative interests in preserving stability, while there was also some assurance that such a state would not jeopardise administrative interests in the security of the border between India and Pakistan. As many commentators have observed, the demands of ethnic minorities have been ignored until 'prolonged agitation' thrusts those demands into the agenda of administrative imperatives, and then there has been 'a combined response of force and accommodation' (Hardgrave 1988). In one way or another, in all of the instances discussed above, federalism was revisited as a response to public pressure. However, for the most part, federalism did not develop as a democratic institutionalising of popular will, a pluralistic renegotiation of the constitutional compact. Rather, after an extended effort to simply maintain the status quo, the central government reluctantly accommodated regional demands by mobilising federalism to manage conflict and domesticate unrest.

The federal model shaped in the shadow of this paradigm emerges as conservative and statist, its mapping of the relationship between state and nation evocative of images of the state as Leviathan, all-encompassing and standing in for all.[10] In this paradigm, the centre is represented as concerned with national/general interests, while the local is tied to narrow and particularistic interests. The central government represents the unitary and all-encompassing community that is the Indian nation-state. It diffuses, resolves and rises above conflict, rather than being constituted by conflict. In its idealised model, the national government is informed by a unitary and homogeneous idea of the state, rather than one that is differentiated and internally contested. Local communities, in contrast, are tied to sectarian interests and partial perspectives. These particularistic interests are contained and deflected within the sphere of the domestic political structures of regional governments.

At its strongest, the administrative model is concerned with how federalism enables the centre to mobilise disparate regions towards centrally determined agendas, channelling, and thereby domesticating, participation through centrally defined mechanisms for political engagement. A pragmatic central administration may find that national policy is enhanced and conflict deterred if federalism can provide the periphery with an institutional mechanism for voice, for bottom–up feedback within centrally constituted boundaries. The local community itself stands to benefit from the trickle-down benefits of economies of scale, and other institutional and ideological benefits of an extra-local national political structure.[11]

At its weakest, the administrative paradigm has reduced federalism to central control. The arbitrary assertion of central government authority seems to have been only further entrenched with every political crisis, assimilating even those endeavours that had aimed at curbing the centre's authoritarian tendencies.[12] Indira Gandhi's rule may have been the worst offender in this regard; Dua (1988:129) notes that she 'destroyed many of the boundaries between federal and state politics and mutilated many of the institutionalised rules of the political game'.[13] We find federalism's particular historical manifestation was often that which promoted and sustained the Congress Party machinery.[14] There is a pronounced irony in how the centre's repeated success in tilting institutional arrangements in its favour is intricately coupled with heightened anxieties and insecurities about the reach and resilience of its authority. Yet this is an irony that is not quite a paradox. It has been noted before that a state's strong arm is often evidence of its weakness, not its strength. And this seems to be the case in the Indian experience, where the centre's most perverse excesses against state autonomy not only tilted the balance in the centre's favour but also led, invariably, to the progressive delegitimation and destabilisation of the central government itself. The Punjab crisis provides a striking illustration of this; Corbridge (1995) sees the processes that led the Khalistan issue to crisis proportions 'as a monstrous by-product of an extraordinary period of mismanagement of Centre–State relations by Mrs Gandhi', where the centre's refusal to negotiate a 'fair settlement of these grievances' at an early stage engendered a much more powerful challenge to the centre, proving 'suicidal, both for the region as a whole and for Mrs Gandhi herself'.

The contractual paradigm

The contractual paradigm lays emphasis on the pluralist commitments of federal structures in enabling voice for sub-state communities.[15] The centre is defined through its procedural promise rather than its substantive content. The idealised image here is one where distinct cultural groups plug into the federal contract as a fair and stable set of background rules that will allow them to bargain and negotiate an agenda of power sharing from positions of relative equality.

In this spirit, right from the outset, the contract model may allow for more flexibility in the constitutional framework. For instance, asymmetric federalism may get legitimation here as allowing diverse communities to negotiate the federal compact to best suit their particular interests and aspirations. Thus, Kashmir may quite rightly draw its own unique relationship to the centre to reflect its particular history and demographic make-up. The fraught history of Kashmiri federalism is accompanied by a constitutional contract that allows for far-reaching autonomy – in theory, even if not in practice (Bhatt 1976). Article 370 of the constitution recognises the special status of Jammu and Kashmir in the Indian union. This is the only former princely state that not only has its own constitution but is also where the residual powers fall to the state and not to the centre.

Taking Kashmir's constitutional status as a case in point, we see how the contract model's commitment to fashioning federalism to enhance ethnic pluralism may then enable a plurality of federal relationships.

I term this image of federalism 'contractual' because it is so fundamentally informed by the images of community and state in classical liberal discourse on the social contract. This paradigm can be seen as extending the classical liberal model of the state's relationship to the individual to the model of the state's relationship to sub-national communities. The hypothetical contract between these communities and the centre gains legitimacy by being situated against the backdrop of incessant conflict that characterises the state of nature or, in this case, the images of primordial communal conflict that shaped colonial administrators' constructions of India. Classical nationalist discourse posits community both as India's legacy and India's aspiration. Communal harmony is read back in narratives about India's past and projected forward in narratives about India's future. However, the spectre of communal conflict persists in the present. This polarity between communal harmony and communal conflict structures the nationalist imagery.[16] Federalism's institutional elaboration of the 'unity in diversity' formula is an attempt to ride this polarity in ways that enable and encourage communal harmony at a national level. In this context, cashing in their sovereignty and contracting into a federal constitutional framework institutionalises the political and legal arrangements to move from an India rent by communalism to an India encouraging multiculturalism.

In ways that echo liberal individualist conceptions of autonomy, federalism is seen as enabling sub-national communities to define their autonomy in terms of the space for self-determination outside of central control; that is, what Jerry Frug (1993) has sometimes termed 'a not in my back yard' idea of autonomy and state action. The centre's mandate is such that it can impinge on that space only when constitutional fundamentals are at stake. In contrast to the administrative paradigm, the centre plays a subordinate role in defining the substantive content of Indian nationhood.[17] It is better conceived as setting in motion the procedural mechanisms through which the substantive claims of sub-national communities are asserted and negotiated in line with constitutional commitments. The legitimacy of contractual arrangements is predicated on a sub-national community having a cohesive and unitary voice; moreover, with some implicit homology between voice, identity and interests that is then embodied in the representative functions of the regional governments. There is an assumed fixity to these associative affiliations that federal arrangements attempt to codify through boundary drawing. In its idealised vision, the cumulative voices of all these states get filtered through the institutional arrangements of federalism, to be harnessed together in imagining the community that constituted Indian nationhood, represented in these arrangements by the central government.

The neutrality of the state, as between multiple and diverse cultural claims, is crucial to the legitimacy of the contract paradigm. A modern nation-state committed to pluralism and religious equality is said to jealously guard the boundaries between religion and state. Historically, many minorities have found federalism attractive precisely because federal arrangements of state power were seen to aspire towards impartiality and posited the approximation of such impartiality as a measure of state legitimacy. Sub-national communities invested in the federalist promise that an impartial state would structure institutional arrangements to 'neutralise' (or make diffuse) the factional privileges of dominant ethnic groups. These communities have attempted to use the 'unrealised ideals' of the promise of impartiality against the ideological and institutional practices of exclusion experienced by Indian minorities.

Historically, the claim to impartiality has been tied principally to secularism and the refusal to allow federal boundaries to recognise religious divisions. As the case of Kashmir illustrates so sharply, however, this refusal quickly and problematically slips into the claim to neutrality, slips into the questionable claim that secular federal boundaries do not empower some religious communities at the expense of others. This slip equates secularism with fairness and substantive neutrality.[18] Commitment to the ideal of impartiality entailed in this vision promotes the idea of a neutral state concerned with reason not passion, statecraft not politics, federalism-constituted mechanisms of statehood encouraging nationalist rationalisation and normalisation of procedures for unity in diversity. This conception of the role and character of the state lends itself to a statism that overlaps with the administrative approach to federalism. This model of the state legitimates bureaucratic and hierarchical decision making and thereby removes some of the most critical arenas of collective decision making from the purview of social contestation and political challenge.[19] In this sense, the impact of a 'neutral' conception of the state reaches beyond the problems and possibilities of federalism, to questions of participation and community in the Indian public sphere at large.

As we noted at the beginning of this section and have elaborated on in the preceding paragraphs, the contract paradigm's modelling of federalism as a framework for diversity is predicated on a distinction between legal and political structures, on the one hand, and culture, on the other; or, in an alternative formulation, procedure and substance. Thus, the model is also committed to an idealised image of federal arrangements as fashioned by commitments and processes that are culturally neutral, because they are either culturally universal or culturally empty. This is accompanied by an image of culture and cultural identity as independent of, and always already prior to, the legal and political structures that enable expressions of collective identity and interests. Classical nationalism invoked something of a 'separation of spheres' argument, where one's political identity was understood with reference to the nation, rather than to the sectarian commitments of religion and other sources of individual or collective identity and allegiance (Sen 1997:23–7). As Sen (1997:18, 20) describes it, classical nationalism was characterised by 'a systematic attempt to focus on unity, rather than discord within India', with emphasis on 'the synthesising tendencies of Indian culture'.[20] Diversity was seen as a problem to be overcome by a political discourse and institutional structure aimed at unity and consensus. It is in this context then that federalism can be understood in terms of a mandate for producing unifying and unitary approaches to a single national community. Depoliticising and diffusing religious identity was in the forefront of classical nationalist claims to the political identity of 'Indianness'.

The democratic paradigm
The democratic paradigm argues for federalism because of the participatory and communitarian merits it associates with decentralisation. It is the paradigm that is most invested in the new third tier of federalism, namely the institutions of local government. It speaks to how 'Indianness' is to be forged through invocation, not only of shared values and traditions but also of participation and voice. Decentralised structures would encourage sub-national communities to have a measure of autonomy in shaping the realities of their lives, to take into account their particular cultural/linguistic/regional identities, interests and aspirations. In addition, the experience of close collective engagement in the political process encourages the forging of solidaristic ties, and the general deepening of cohesion and cooperation within the community. Giving people a voice also gives them an investment, a stake in the welfare of their community. The energy of political participation revitalises democracy and infuses citizens with civic virtue. It has been argued that the administrative imperatives that initially introduced the federal structure were taken over by more democratic impulses in the process of the anticolonial struggle. Reframing the federal question, 'the democratic urges of the people struck . . . and political articulations became interlined with social reform and cultural resurgence. The need to conduct administration in the language of the cultural regions was felt as part of this process of political participation and articulation' (Ashish Banarjee, in Ghai 1995:23). If the vastness that is India militates against principles of democratic accountability and participation, it is federalism, and particularly

the third tier of federalism, that translates that vastness into a vital, democratic political system.

The Gandhian voice of the democratic paradigm cites pre-colonial village political structures as the historical inspiration for decentralisation in the post-colonial era. This was one of the most powerful nationalist myths tracing the continuities and discontinuities of indigenous democratic aspirations. In the context of the third tier of federalism, the democratic paradigm's celebration of the local emerges against the shadow of the colonial empire coordinated from the halls of Westminster and against the spectre of the homogenising and centralising impulses of the new state. The romanticised conception of the local celebrates the third tier as carrying the potential for participatory, consensual government, in contrast to the centralised hierarchies of the colonial and post-colonial state.

Invocations of the indigenous origins of democratic traditions in India stand alongside colonial claims about the introduction of democratic and representative institutions into Indian political life. Sceptical of both these narratives, Khilnani (1997:17) argues that, 'contrary to India's nationalist myths, enamoured of immemorial "village republics", pre-colonial history little prepared it for modern democracy. Nor was democracy a gift of the departing British.' Instead, I think he is quite right in locating democracy in the tumultuous energies and strains of the post-colonial experience. In fact, Indian democracy, as is true of Indian federalism, is a hybrid system, carrying within it different conceptions of democracy. In this context, it has been suggested by Ashish Nandy and others that most Indians invest in a vision of participation and community that stands in some tension with the vision of citizenship that we situate in the representative institutions of the Indian state.[21]

In order to extend the reach of democracy to 'most Indians', there was an attempt to give constitutional status to the local government institutions of the Panchayat Raj in 1989. To an extent, the success of devolution from the state level to the local government level is tied to successful devolution from the centre to the state. The Panchayat Raj bill fell victim to centre–state tensions, and the third tier of federalism did not achieve constitutional standing. Granting constitutional recognition to the role and power of the Panchayat Raj would give the institution a political legitimacy and accord it a juridical respect that it now lacks. However, although constitutional status may be 'a necessary prerequisite', ultimately participatory democratisation can be enabled and sustained only through the development of a 'political culture' that internalises those norms (Rao 1995:78).

If our discussion up to now has given an account of Indian federalism as a narrative of disillusionment, this narrative does not even begin to tell the whole story of diversity and democratisation in Indian political life.

We need to move outside the narrow strictures of constitutional debate and traditional party politics to broader questions of culture and civil society, looking not only at those issues deemed 'national' but also to the level of the 'local' and 'transnational'. A number of contemporary theorists argue that there has been a 'growth of democratic politics in India' and point to 'the Chipko Movements . . . women campaigning for stronger liquor laws, or farmers movements . . . challenging the urban bias in the development process . . . the efforts of . . . battlers against corruption and injustice . . . movements and individuals . . . seeking to mobilise "authentically Gandhian" conceptions of politics as empowerment' (Corbridge 1995:111–12).[22] And to this list we may add many other efforts, 'a million little mutinies' (Naipaul, in Corbridge 1995:114) – a million little mutinies conveying discontent and disillusionment, while also seeking change, democratisation and justice that some have characterised, helpfully or unhelpfully, as new social movements (Wignaraja 1993). Across a range of issues, we see movements that are participatory and innovative, working within conventional channels and outside of them, internally diverse but also adding diversity to the agenda of local and national politics in challenging and transformative ways.[23] Rajni Kothari (1994:39, 53) has suggested that this multiplicity of political and social efforts, these 'fragments', exist 'without the totality being merely fragmentary'. His identification of 'a common thread' running through these discourses as 'the long term struggle for democratic values' is echoed in Corbridge's (1995:112) analysis that 'all of these movements affirm the vitality of the democracy that has taken root in India since Independence, even if they are employing political tactics and grammars that are sometimes at odds with the normalising and modernising ambitions of the Nehru years and India's major political parties'.[24]

While many of these movements may not be formulated in the discourse of federalism, the directions in which they point have relevance for how Indian federalism re-imagines democracy and diversity. In fact, the move beyond a single party, the coalition governments and shifting party alliances that characterised national electoral politics in the 1990s were themselves a promising sign of a more internally differentiated and fluid conception of what constitutes the centre in the shaping of centre–state relations over the next half a century. In this context, it is striking that, for the most part, legal analyses of federalism have not explored these alternative directions as presenting an opportunity for institutional innovation.[25] An understanding of the nature of Indian federalism that is limited to a scrutiny of constitutional provisions expresses a formalism all too common in legal scholarship. Just as reducing economic life to fiscal policy carries a peculiarly centralising dynamic, a focus only on 'official' politics constitutes an abandonment of politics in a deeper sense. We need to open up our understanding of federalism to an engagement with the everyday negotiation of citizenship. We need to attend to the issues raised by what many have called the 'unwritten constitution',[26] namely the broader civic dialogue that takes place in popular culture, the daily political and economic struggles of individuals and collectives. We need to interrogate some of the conceptual underpinnings of 'official' federalism and rezone our conversation around federalism in that gulf between the written and unwritten constitution. Our practical and theoretical understanding of federalism and diversity needs to explore these differentiated and heterogeneous public spheres – neither uncritically celebrating the unwritten constitution nor ceremoniously rejecting it, but foregrounding it in seeing federalism as an ongoing project, not a constitutional fait accompli.

ALTERNATIVE MAPPINGS .

In speaking of the ambivalence and contradictions that run through the 'imaginary homelands' of his community, Salman Rushdie (1991:15) describes their identity as 'at once plural and partial'.[27] This is an evocative and helpful starting-point as we reconsider questions of diversity in India and think through the institutional arrangements that resonate with that plural and partial landscape. With the simultaneous dynamic of sub-state nationalism and globalisation, changed historical contexts give new meanings to institutional arrangements mobilised in an earlier moment; the continuities and discontinuities of modernity and tradition have unsettled and reconfigured the role of the postcolonial state; distinctions of ethnicity, language, region and nation are rendered indeterminate, pluralised and resignified; new solidaristic networks and new conflicts have meant that questions of identity and representation are revisited and reworked.

This chapter has explored the contested terrain of what federalism has meant in India: arguments about who it was supposed to be serving, what visions informed its historical elaboration, what goals it promotes. I have tried to unpack the conceptual paradigms that have informed classical nationalist approaches to federalism and diversity. One is struck by the persistence of this framework, its far-reaching material and imaginative weight in structuring political struggle. However, enhancing federalism in India is not merely a project of reform – getting more powers on the state government list or more revenue for the regions, although, for the most part, all that is to be encouraged. Fundamentally transforming federalism in India calls for much more radical redirecting, institutional experimentation and imaginative exploration.

Lack of space precludes an extended investigation of alternative normative and programmatic foundations for federalism. However, let me conclude by briefly sketching a metaphoric picture of a federalism informed by alternative foundations. The 'unity in diversity' formula envisioned federalism as a pyramid-like structure, with the state at its pinnacle. Against this I would like to counterpose the *nacharam* as an alternative architectural metaphor for a federalism informed by the normative ideals alluded to above. The *nacharam*, literally 'four-sides', is a common style of house in the Jaffna Tamil community of Sri Lanka. Its defining characteristic is a common four-sided garden in the middle of the house: all rooms, from the kitchen to the living room, open out onto this garden. The garden itself opens up to the sky and lets in both rain and sun. The *nacharam* house may not have a fixed boundary between public and private, as the sights, sounds and smells from different rooms spill over and into each other. People criss-cross the garden and each other as they move about the house; the garden is used for a multitude of purposes throughout the day – from drying spices, to children playing.

This chapter has not researched the histories that narrate how the spatial dynamics of the *nacharam* house have been the site of, and given specific shape to, relations of gender, age, caste and class. We take as background fact that the *nacharam* is not only compatible with conflict but also with relationships coded with hierarchy and disempowerment. All that is suggested here is that, in contrast to the pyramid model, the spatial metaphor of the *nacharam* foregrounds such conflict, foregrounds the strains and interdependencies of intersecting paths in ways that suggest an alternative approach to federalism.

Rather than conceiving of claims and interests as mediated through the state, here they are mediated through the daily interaction of multiple localities. We may need to think creatively of decentralisation in ways that empower political participation without depending on the state as the central reference point, either as the forum to which we take our claims or, relatedly, as the critical mediating institution through which we conceptualise citizenship and political membership. We need to guard against federalism as simply the proceduralisation of democracy into a political management technique for the centre, or the domestication of politics within naturalised categories of nation and state. The *nacharam* is suggestive of the possibility of revisiting questions of public/private, inside/outside, to reshape the social terrain. For instance, this unsettling of boundaries reminds us that, acknowledging the internal diaspora that crosses federal boundaries, we need to structure a federalism that is responsive to mobility in opening up questions of citizenship in relationship to multiple sovereigns. With a spatial layout that foregrounds the inevitability of communication, the *nacharam* also foregrounds 'the gaps, ambivalence and conflicts' that characterise the communicative sphere. The *nacharam* points to how both independence and harmony invariably operate as ever-elusive goals, promising an illusory safe space. Instead, the unavoidable crossing of paths attests to how interdependence brings both collaboration and conflict, the promise and risk of a participatory politics. The use of the *nacharam* garden for a plurality of ends by shifting constituencies is suggestive of the need to rethink the fixity of membership and identity, the constant process of renegotiating and pluralising the vocabulary of the public sphere. If the *nacharam* garden provides a centre for the house, it is a centre characterised in Rushdie's terms, 'plural and partial'.

NOTES

I would like to acknowledge my gratitude to Neelan Tiruchelvam for his inspiration in my research for this chapter. I also thank Jerry Frug, Ashish Nandy, Imtiaz Ahmed, Yash Ghai, Tayyab Mahmoud, Ameena Hussein-Uvais and S. Nanthikesan for their comments and other assistance.

1 Classical nationalism's ways of framing the problem crucially shaped the terrain on which we negotiate claims of federalism and diversity. Most crucially, we may point to its founding myths – the dichotomy between universality and particularity, modernity and tradition, and communal harmony and communal conflict – which it mapped onto centre–state relations, myths captured in the 'unity in diversity' formula.

2 The 1989 figures ranged from 133,034,415 for Uttar Pradesh to 379,662 for Sikkim (see Annexure 1 in Mukarji 1990).

3 Tellingly, the constitution does not actually use the word 'federalism', opting instead for 'union'. It has been suggested that the retreat from federalism came after the announcement of partition, as the principal *raison d'être* for decentralisation had slid into secession (see Markanandan 1991; Sathyamurthy 1997; Thakur 1995:70).

4 For many, these two senses of 'secular' are evocative of the distinction between the Nehruvian and Gandhian visions of politics.

5 *Mohammed Ahmed Khan* v. *Shah Bano Begum* AIR 1985 SC 945 (in which a divorced Muslim woman successfully argued before the Supreme Court that her entitlement to maintenance on divorce was not limited to that provided by Muslim law).

6 Hardgrave and Kochanek (1986) remark that these 'nativist' movements have arisen in regions where culturally distinct migrants from outside the state are perceived to be blocking opportunities for 'locals' to advance (see also Thakur 1995:146; Weiner 1978).

7 'The very diversity of India, however, generated strong centrifugal pressures . . . Yet it may also be the case that consciousness of regional identities has in many cases been a reaction to over-centralisation of Indian politics' (Thakur 1995:70–1).

8 The 1991 elections may have been a turning-point here, with Bharatiya Janata Party victories in what has been referred to as the Hindu heartland of Udhya Pradesh, Madhya Pradesh, Himachal Pradesh and Rajasthan.

9 Increasingly, even institutions such as the World Bank are beginning to see questions of minority protection and inter-ethnic equality as critical to the development effort, and to incorporate these issues into good governance

criteria, and so on (see LST 1995). The identification of the central government with the image of the nation builder is not unconnected to the image
of the central government as rationalist planner (on this latter point, see
Chatterjee 1994).

10 The post–Indira Gandhi era of 'command' federalism is perhaps the most
perverse manifestation of this equation, where 'India became Indira' (Dua
1988:133).

11 It may be argued that, even today, a federalism predicated on state-centred
notions of unitary community have continued salience in facing the external
threat of globalisation, and that the forces of global economic integration
could actually exploit decentralisation. For instance, it may be argued that a
strong and cohesive sense of the Indian nation-state and its boundaries
stands as the last defender of the losers in the new world economy. Rather
than promoting democracy and pluralism, decentralisation could come to
mean the progressive dismemberment of local communities through the
invasive forces of the market.

12 Once again we turn to Dua (1988:133–4), who notes that 'the Janata government of Morarji Desai' which came into power protesting Indira Gandhi's
proclamation of emergency rule and 'promised to restore their lost power to
state leaders, in fact ended up creating greater insecurity among the chief
ministers'.

13 However, even Nehru's much-acclaimed style of consensus politics fell short
of a commitment to a truly decentralised system of power sharing. In fact, his
commitment to the Congress Party trumped any commitment to federalist
principles; 'the net result of this was that no non-Congress chief minister
lasted his full term of office in the Nehru era' (Dua 1988:128).

14 Rajiv Gandhi himself 'commented that centre–state relations in India had
been reduced to the connection between Congress Party headquarters in
New Delhi and its branch offices, with the former exacting obedience in
return for largesse' (Datta-Ray 1995:83).

15 Comparativists locate two alternative models of 'origin', as it were, for federalist systems. Countries such as the United States and Germany are cited as
aimed at uniting 'people in different political units, who nevertheless shared
a common language and culture'. In contrast, countries such as Canada, Nigeria and Yugoslavia sought 'the use of federalism to unite people who seek the
advantages of membership of a common political unit, but differ markedly in
descent, language and culture' (Forsyth 1989:4). It is in this latter model that
the contractual paradigm situates the Indian investment in federalism.

16 Against the shadow of orientalist constructions of India as Homo hierar-
chichus, nationalists strived to produce a harmonious model of community, as
reflective not only of the shared cultural traditions of the past but also of the
possibility of harmonious community in the independent India that marks the
future – ostensibly, replicating European models of national community. In
effect, it was framed as a choice between inter-ethnic fratricide, on the one
hand, and multi-ethnic unity, on the other. The fear that India would disinte-
grate into a multitude of sectarian conflicts was invoked in attracting and sustaining advocates for classical nationalism's unitary and centralised vision of

community. Ironically, it may turn out that, in fact, nationalism and communalism developed in tandem and have sustained each other precisely through invocation of their opposition (see Pandey 1990; and also Chatterjee 1986).

17 Simultaneous with the differences in their conceptual lenses, we also note that the aims of the contract paradigm also have resonances with the administrative paradigm. Thus, in the contract paradigm, federalism is simultaneously a tool for the recognition of cultural minorities and a tool for their integration. Here, too, there is a slippage between federalism enabling, and federalism managing, expressions of cultural identity. 'It provides a framework for inter-ethnic bargaining and so converts conflicts into disputes that are susceptible to formal processes' (Ghai 1995:2).

18 Unfortunately, the legacy of the debate about citizenship in the West has often been uncritically mapped onto other contexts and has too often shaped the lens through which we have constructed and fashioned the terms of political life in India. Some may argue, for instance, that the Gandhian view of secularism charts a conception of universalism in the public sphere in a way that has little resonance with that which has been more formative and influential in the European enlightenment tradition.

19 Partha Chatterjee (1994) explores this issue in the context of state planning.

20 These concerns become more acute in the context of the reach and power of contemporary communalism. In a moment in history when India is fighting the divisive and exclusionary forces of Hindu chauvinism, it may be argued that it is risky, and even irresponsible, to undermine an accommodationist national community that seeks to project a united sense of 'Indianness'. The classical nationalist legacy of a secular and impartial state may be our last defence against the unprecedented momentum that has attached to the Hindu fundamentalist drive for state power in recent years.

21 Corbridge (1995:112) quotes S. Kaviraj on this paradox of Indian politics: 'The paradox . . . is that if Indian politics becomes genuinely democratic in the sense of coming into line with what the majority of ordinary Indians would consider reasonable, it will become less democratic in the sense of conforming to the principle of a secular, democratic state acceptable to the early nationalist elite.'

22 Corbridge also cites the work of other theorists, such as Guha (1989), Kaviraj (1991), Kothari (1994), Kumar (1993), Nadkarni (1987), and Omvedt (1991). See also Sathyamurthy (1997).

23 This range and diversity is conveyed, for instance, by the heterogeneity of agendas and strategies that have characterised women's struggles in India over the past two decades, both under the banner of feminism and through conventional channels seeking law reform and so on, as well as the broader sphere of de-institutionalised political action. For a range of perspectives on feminist struggle in India, see Cossman and Kapur (1996), Desai (1988), Kishwar and Vanita (1987), and Krishna Raj (1990).

24 Kothari (1994:38), too, notes that these 'million little mutinies' also connote a shift and, in fact, a pluralising of the grammar of politics, saying that here engagement 'is conducted in a wide range of political (as distinct from linguistic) dialects'.

25 For a critical discussion of constitutional discourse, see Sudarshan (1994).
26 As Ashish Nandy and others point out, in many ways the 'unwritten constitution' has overtaken the written constitution in reshaping the character of federalism and democracy in India (ICES organised Conference on Federalism
   and Diversity, held in New Delhi, August 1997). The gulf between the written
   and unwritten constitutions tracks the democracy deficit that informs the
   dominant vision of federalism.
27 Rushdie is speaking specifically of the South Asian expatriate community in
   Britain.

REFERENCES

Bajpai, Kanti 1997. 'Diversity, democracy and devolution in India', in Michael E.
   Brown and Sumit Ganguly (eds) *Government Policies and Ethnic Relations in
   Asia and the Pacific.* Cambridge, MA: MIT Press.
Bhatt, Roop Kishen 1976. 'Kashmir: the politics of integration', in Iqbal Narain
   (ed.) *State Politics in India.* Meerut: Meenakshi Prakashan.
Census of India 1988. Series 1, Part IV B(I). New Delhi: Registrar General and
   Census Commission.
Chatterjee, Partha 1986. *Nationalist Thought and the Colonial World: A Derivative Dis-
   course.* London: Zed.
—— 1994. *The Nation and Its Fragments: Colonial and Postcolonial Histories.* Delhi:
   Oxford University Press.
Corbridge, Stuart 1995. 'Hindu nationalism and mythologies of governance in
   modern India', in Graham Smith (ed.) *Federalism: The Multiethnic Challenge.*
   London, New York: Longman.
Cossman, B. and Ratna Kapur 1996. *Subversive Sites.* New Delhi: Sage.
Datta-Ray, Sunanda K. 1991. 'Keeper of the law: scope for presidential action',
   Statesman Weekly, 22 June, cited in Thakur 1995:82–3.
Desai, N. (ed.) 1988. *A Decade of the Women's Movement in India.* Bombay: Himalaya
   Publishing House.
Dua, Bhagwan 1988. 'India: a study in the pathology of a federal system', in B.H.
   Sharuddin and Ifthikhar AMZ Fadzli (eds) *Between Centre and State: Federalism
   in Perspective.* Kuala Lumpur: Institute of Strategic and International Studies.
Forsyth, Murray (ed.) 1989. *Federalism and Nationalism.* Leicester: Leicester Uni-
   versity Press.
Frug, Jerry 1993. 'Decentering decentralization', *University of Chicago Law Review*
   60:253.
Galanter, Marc 1989. *Law and Society in Modern India.* New Delhi: Oxford Univer-
   sity Press.
Ghai, Yash 1995. *Decentralization and the Accommodation of Ethnic Diversity.*
   Colombo: ICES.
Guha, R. 1989. *The Unquiet Woods: Ecological Change and Peasant Resistance in the
   Himalaya.* New Delhi: Oxford University Press.
Hardgrave, Robert 1988. 'The Northeast, the Punjab, and the regionalisation of
   Indian politics', in B.H. Sharuddin and Ifthikhar AMZ Fadzli (eds) *Between
   Centre and State: Federalism in Perspective.* Kuala Lumpur: Institute of Strate-
   gic and International Studies.

Hardgrave, Robert and Stanley Kochanek 1986. *India: Government and Politics in a Developing Nation*. San Diego: Harcourt Brace Jovanovich.

Kaviraj, S. 1991. 'On state, society and discourse in India', in J. Manor (ed.) *Rethinking Third World Politics*. Harlow: Longman.

Khilnani, Sunil 1997. *The Idea of India*. London: Hamish Hamilton.

Kishwar, M. and R. Vanita (eds) 1987. *In Search of Answers: Indian Women's Voices from Manushi*. London: Zed Press.

Kothari, R. 1994. 'Fragments of a discourse: towards conceptualization', in Sathyamurthy (ed.) 1994.

Krishna Raj, M. (ed.) 1990. *Feminism: Indian Debates*. Bombay: Research Centre for Women's Studies, SNDT Women's University.

Kumar, R. 1993. *A History of Doing: An Illustrated Account of Movements for Women's Rights and Feminism in India, 1800–1990*. London: Verso.

LST (Law and Society Trust) 1995. *Minority Protection and Development Cooperation*. Colombo: LST.

Markanandan, K.C. 1991. *Sarkaria Commission and Constitutional Perspective*. Jalandhar: ABS Publications.

Mathur, Kultheep 1990. 'Centre–state relationship: political and general theme paper', in R.C. Dutt (ed.) *Centralism and Devolution of Power*. New Delhi: Lancer.

Mukarji, Nirmal 1990. 'Decentralization below the state level', in R.C. Dutt (ed.) *Centralism and Devolution of Power*. New Delhi: Lancer.

Nadkarni, M. 1987. *Farmers Movements in India*. Delhi: Allied.

Nandy, Ashish 1990. 'The politics of secularism and the recovery of religious tolerance', in Veena Das (ed.) *Mirrors of Violence: Communities, Riots and Survivors in South Asia*. New Delhi: Oxford University Press.

Omvedt, G. 1991. 'Shetkari Sanghatana's new direction', *Economic and Political Weekly Federalism:The Multiethnic Challenge*, 2287–90.

Pandey, Gyan 1990. 'The colonial construction of "communalism": British writing on Benares in the nineteenth century', in Veena Das (ed.) *Mirrors of Violence: Communities, Riots and Survivors in South Asia*. New Delhi: Oxford University Press.

Rao, G.R.S. 1995. 'Constitutional impact on federalism in India', in Justice Krishna Iyer et al. *Democracy and Federalism*. Secunderabad: Andhra Pradesh Judiciary Academy.

Rushdie, Salman 1991. *Imaginary Homelands*. London: Granta.

Sakaria Commission 1988. *Report of the Commission on Centre–State Relations*. Nasik: Government of India Press.

Sathyamurthy, T.V. (ed.) 1994. *State and Nation in the Context of Social Change*. New Delhi: Oxford University Press.

—— 1997. 'Impact of centre–state relations on Indian politics: an interpretative reckoning, 1947–1987', in Partha Chatterjee (ed.) *State and Politics in India*. New Delhi: Oxford University Press.

Sen, Amartya 1997. 'On interpreting India's past', in Sujata Bose and Ayesha Jalal (eds) *Nationalism, Democracy and Development: State and Politics in India*. New Delhi: Oxford University Press.

Setalvad, M.C. 1960. *The Common Law of India (The Hamlyn Lectures)*. London: Stevens and Sons Ltd.

Sudarshan, R. 1994. 'The political consequences of constitutional discourse', in Sathyamurthy 1994.

Thakur, Ramesh 1995. *Government and Politics of India*. Basingstoke: Macmillan.

Weiner, Myron 1978. *Sons of the Soil: Migration and Ethnic Conflict in India*. Princeton: Princeton University Press.

Wignaraja, Ponna (ed.) 1993. *New Social Movements in the South: Empowering the People*. London: Zed.

CHAPTER 4

AUTONOMY REGIMES IN CHINA: COPING WITH ETHNIC AND ECONOMIC DIVERSITY

YASH GHAI

The preamble of the constitution of the People's Republic of China proclaims it

> a unitary multinational state created jointly by the people of all its nationalities . . . Socialist relations of equality, unity and mutual assistance have been established among the nationalities and will continue to be strengthened. In the struggle to safeguard the unity of nationalities, it is necessary to combat big nation chauvinism, mainly Han chauvinism, and to combat local national chauvinism. The state will do its utmost to promote prosperity of all the nationalities.

It also says that 'Taiwan is part of the sacred territory of the People's Republic of China' and that it is the 'inviolable duty of all Chinese people, including compatriots in Taiwan, to accomplish the great task of reunifying the motherland'. The preamble acknowledges the leading role of the Communist Party and the guidance of Marxism–Leninism and Mao Zedong Thought.

These formulations provide a useful clue to understanding Chinese minority policies. China classifies its population into fifty-five ethnic or nationality groups, of which fifty-four are regarded as minorities. The fifty-fifth group is the Han, although they are less homogeneous than official policy recognises. 'Han chauvinism' refers to Han arrogance towards and contempt for minorities, rooted in Confucian perception of them as 'barbarians', and 'local chauvinism' refers to minorities' assertions of self-determination. China is governed by the Communist Party under the Leninist doctrine of 'democratic centralism', which effectively gives the monopoly of power to a small group of party leaders. This concentration of power is reinforced by administrative centralisation, with the emphasis on a 'unitary' state. The preference for a unitary state, despite China's huge size and diverse population, is closely connected to the leadership's obsession with state sovereignty. This obsession prevents a significant constitutional accommodation of ethnic and political diversity. 'Autonomy' is the centrepiece of China's policy, both to hold its minorities together and to expand its jurisdiction through the reunification of Greater China. Coupled with a weak legal system, the preoccupation with sovereignty and centralisation fails to provide an effective guarantee of the distribution or sharing of power, reducing 'autonomy' purely to an administrative device.

Such a political structure is unlikely to be able to cope with problems emerging from the shift to the market and the emphasis on economic development. These problems are connected with rapid social change which can be profoundly disturbing to the traditional lifestyles of most minorities, growing disparities between them and the Han majority, and the consequent consciousness of their identity, especially in the border areas. The situation about minorities is complicated by the fact of its expansive view of what territory belongs to China (Heberer 1989:120–2); any remote connection in the past seems enough to legitimate its claims, even though there may have been a substantial period of independence since that original connection. Pye (1975:488) says that, for 'reasons which spring deep from within the Chinese spirit and which have been reinforced during the era of Western encroachment and of the "Unequal Treaties", the Han Chinese have developed a powerful sense of their territorial identity, which, some might say, overrides their sense of cultural identity'. For that reason and the fact that most minorities are located on its western and southern borders, China's minority policies are connected with its foreign and diplomatic policies. National security is deeply implicated in its minority policies, especially since the emergence of independent Muslim states on its western flanks and an evangelising Taliban in Afghanistan, and continuing foreign criticism of its Tibetan policies. All of these factors combine to compel a rather active state role in ethnic classifications and policies.

MINORITIES AND BASIC POLICIES

Minorities constitute only 8 per cent of the population, which in absolute figures is a significant size (60 million). They occupy 60 per cent of the land area, which contrasts with the densely populated areas inhabited by the Han. They are therefore natural areas for the resettlement of the Han. These lands contain some of the most valuable mineral and other resources in China, which are vital to its plans for economic development and modernisation. Since minority people are less technically skilled than the Han, Han technicians and entrepreneurs have been moving into these areas. Minorities also live in border areas; over 90 per cent of border populations are minorities. For security reasons, large sections of the army have been stationed there – another cause of the Han influx. Many areas which are predominantly populated by minorities now have substantial numbers of Han people and, in places, they constitute a majority. There is considerable resentment of this influx, which is aggravated by increasing economic disparities between them and the local people.

Minorities show great diversity in social structure, languages, cultural and religious traditions, and economic development. A large proportion of minorities belongs to Islam or Buddhism. Ten minorities adhere to Islam, just over 17.5 million in total. The largest of these are the Hui, who are dispersed throughout the country and who speak the local Chinese dialects. The next largest, and politically the most active, minority are the Uygur (7.2 million), who live in Xinjiang which is also the home of other Islamic minorities: Kazakh, Kirghiz, Tadjik, Uzbek and Tartar (Gladney 1996:20). Buddhists as a minority are principally to be found in Tibet. Although the Chinese criteria for identifying a minority does not include religion, and the ruling party forbids its members to profess a religion, it is clear that there is a close connection between religion and ethnicity, and some of the best-known challenges to Chinese rule have had a religious base. Minorities vary greatly in size, from the nearly 9 million Hui to a mere 5000 Tartar. They also vary in the degree of concentration, with the Hui the most dispersed and the Uygur the most concentrated. Because of these variations, minorities impact differently upon the larger national system. The smaller ones, and those away from the border areas, are more prone to assimilation. The larger, concentrated minorities tend to be more resistant and have secessionist tendencies.

During the imperial period, China was content that smaller entities around it accepted its suzerainty, and it let the people rule themselves. After the 1911 revolution, the Kuomintang took a more active interest in them and assumed that, under the influence of modernisation as well as Han superiority, minorities – even Tibetans, Uygurs and Mongols – would be assimilated. They pursued the policy of sinicising minorities, something akin to internal colonialism, relying on indirect rule but also finding that local leaders built their own power base and were reluctant to implement national policies. Tibetans refused, successfully, to have anything to do with them and even succeeded in expelling their armed forces. The subsequent military engagement of the nationalists with the communists left little time for minority matters. After their own victory, the communists tried to bring minorities and neighbouring entities within the national fold. But, until recently, this did not result in any great contact between minorities and the Han people, and, for the most part, there has been little serious ethnic conflict. But, for reasons outlined earlier, the situation is changing, and there are already two strong secessionist movements: among the Uygur in Xinjiang, and the Tibetan. China has had to give more attention to its minority policies in recent years. But, even earlier, it had elaborated policies for incorporating minorities into the national political system, through a combination of Marxist analysis of 'nationalities' and Han nationalism (Pye 1975:511).

Lenin's principles for dealing with minorities during the course of the revolution which overthrew the tsarist regime in Russia were developed in order to secure support for the Bolsheviks among the numerous non-Russian peoples in the former empire (for a classic study of the Leninist approach to the question, see Connor 1984; see also Roeder 1990–91). They were promised self-determination, including the right to secede if they wished, but if they stayed they would be granted significant autonomy to pursue cultural, linguistic and other policies. By according such prominence to ethnic considerations at the expense of the identity of and through economic interests, the theory was in basic conflict with the underlying premises of Marxism. Meant as a temporary concession to what was regarded as a passing force of nationalism, its implementation and practice were fraught with contradictions. Institutional and other policies (including the dominance of the Communist Party) were employed to attenuate self-determination and federalism, but ultimately they were the undoing of the federation (Ghai 1998b:37–41).

Under the influence of the Soviet Union, the Chinese Communist Party adopted Leninist policies in 1931, promising minorities self-determination, and even secession, to enlist their support against the nationalists. As Connor (1984:91) notes, this approach served the communists extremely well. However, such policies were soon abandoned, self-determination being downgraded to 'autonomy' within a unitary framework, promoting political integration with cultural diversity. Using labels to decide on the degree of rights to be conferred à la soviet system, China downgraded ethnic groups from 'nations', which would have justified autonomous republics, to 'nationalities', entitling them at best to an autonomous region. There is now ample evidence that Mao never intended to honour the earlier commitment, once the party was secure in its hold over power (Gladney 1996:88–92; Schram 1985:86–7). Connor (1984:91–2) remarks that Mao's decision to cloak his party in the ethno-national garb of the country's dominant element appears out of tune with Lenin's cosmopolitan viewpoints, but it was probably instrumental in its rise to power. The change of policy was probably also due to the impact of foreign powers on China's border regions, where most minorities lived (Mackerras 1994:72, ch. 4; Pye 1975:511). Even this reduced concept of self-government has not been followed consistently. The most serious repudiation of autonomy and the cultural rights of minorities occurred during the Great Leap Forward and the Cultural Revolution – the issue was no longer seen as a 'nationality' issue but as a class struggle; earlier policies were condemned as a 'bourgeois reactionary line' and regional autonomy as 'obliterating the essence of the dictatorship of the proletariat' (Heberer 1989:24). It was not until the 1982 constitution that autonomy provisions were restored.

Imposed identity
Central to the Chinese communists' strategy of managing ethnic relations has been the state's monopoly on imposing identity. This is done through categorising groups as 'nationalities'. China used Stalin's four criteria (common language, territory, economic life, and culture) for determining whether a group qualified for this status. Stalin denied the relevance of 'national consciousness' not entirely based on objective criteria. The Chinese soon discovered the limits of these criteria but did not formally abandon them, although they were applied with considerable flexibility to reflect China's reality, as is obvious in designating the Hui – who share neither language nor territory, economic life or culture – a nationality (Gladney 1996:68–9). The Chinese were more alert to subjective criteria but officially drew the line at religion, despite contrary practice.

In 1953, groups were invited to submit claims to being a minority – 400 did so; this was whittled down to fifty-five by the State Council 'after scientific investigations', carried out by a large number of anthropologists and linguists. Many claims have still to be processed and there are a number of persons and communities who do not yet fall into any category. There is no doubt that, despite the engagement of scientists, there was a large measure of arbitrariness, to suit the political convenience of the time (as with the improbable recognition of the Hui). Cynics might say that the whole exercise was part of statecraft to manage and control ethnic politics.

Those who are not registered by the state are unable to organise communal activities or institutions. Those who are recognised have to channel their political and economic activities along predetermined channels, under party supervision and control. The intrusion of wider concerns into categorisation is also evident from the classification of minorities into 'backward', 'feudal', and even 'more backward', using the Han civilisation as the yardstick. Gladney (1996) observes that 'nationality status marks one group from another, and is stamped on one's identity card. Like class, nationality in China objectifies social relations and modes of production, in that some minorities are given certain privileges and encouraged to maintain cultural and economic niches'. He emphasises the importance of state categorisation for, even if people consider their group to be a 'nationality', this has no practical significance in terms of its corporate existence or benefits without official recognition of its status. Conversely, 'even if one does not regard oneself as ethnic, but is a member of a nationality designated by the state, such as the Manchu, one may be stigmatised by an identity stamped on one's work card one might not want'. He concludes that, 'in the multi-ethnic world of China, the state's panoptic power is improved if those under supervision and control are divided into certain cells or accepted categories of ethnicity and tradition' (Gladney 1996:78, 312). The fragmentation of minority groups contrasts with the obscuring of linguistic and cultural distinctions among the Han.

Arbitrary and bureaucratic though the categorisation and recognition may be, the consequences are complex. The eagerness of groups to seek recognition has fluctuated, depending on whether the current fashion is the suppression of minorities or their conciliation. In the latter context, recognition carries with it particular advantages: autonomy, preferential policies (Sautman 1998), special political representation, and protection of their language. The practice allows possibilities of shifting and crossing categories, which permits manipulation and mobility by those subject to it. Moreover, however arbitrary the grouping, it tends to create a new consciousness of common identity and provides prospects, and even legitimacy, of joint action (as Gladney 1996 has shown with respect to the Hui, and White 1998 for the Naxi) – and as is evidenced by experience elsewhere (Anderson 1983). White (1998:10) also observes another contradiction that, while the prevailing discourse is premised on hierarchical distinctions, encompassing narratives of socialist modernity, unilinear social evolutionism and the Chinese 'civilizing project', 'there is also a discourse premised on notions of authenticity, in which certain "traditional" cultural practices (both minority and Han) are valorised by the state and written into official policies'. Perhaps White overstates the case, for, as I argue below, the emphasis on 'authenticity' seems to extend little beyond exotic folklore. There are clear limits to independent politics or autonomous policies outside the framework of party decisions. But there is no denying that some minorities have a developed sense of identity and others are likely to acquire it, which will not fit into the scheme of things envisaged by the party. The central authorities will be driven to further interventions to manage the problems, which may provide additional stimulus to the sense of separate identity. Whether the principal instrument for managing ethnicity – autonomy – is up to the task is what I turn to next.

AUTONOMY: SCOPE AND INSTITUTIONS

Ethnic autonomy

Just as the state has played the central role in defining and recognising minorities, so it has in defining autonomy. The terms of autonomy have not been negotiated with the leaders of minorities any more than they were for Hong Kong or Macau, the colonial powers being presented with a fait accompli (Ghai 1999). Although Mao had promised secession or federalism to the minorities in the 1930s and 1940s (Schram 1985:81–3), what was eventually devised was an exceedingly weak form of autonomy. Autonomy has also been used for two other purposes: to promote special economic zones and the reunification of Hong Kong, Macau and potentially Taiwan. Economic zones fall outside the scope of this study, as in a strict sense does reunification autonomy. However, some comments are made on the latter, since it has been argued, particularly by Tibetan leaders, that Hong Kong's type of autonomy would be more suitable for them than the present ethnic autonomy. An analysis of reunification autonomy also helps to put ethnic autonomy in perspective.

State as well as party constitutions establish a hierarchy of institutions and, through the concept and practice of democratic centralism, seek to centralise power and authority. Autonomy for minorities is part of a broader package which is elaborated in article 4 of the 1982 constitution: the equality of all nationalities, preferential treatment of minorities to accelerate their economic and cultural development, a minority's freedom to the use and development of its language and the preservation or reform of its 'folkways and customs', and regional autonomy where minorities live in 'concentrated communities'.

An examination of the 1982 constitution and the 1984 Law on Regional National Autonomy does not disclose a clear concept of autonomy. In principle, there are three types of arrangements: an autonomous area for a minority may be established if all the inhabitants belong to it; if there is another minority which is concentrated in a district, that district might form the basis of autonomy for it; and, if there are several minorities, a multinational autonomous area might be set up. There are three principal types of autonomous areas: region, prefecture, and county (art. 30 of the constitution); and where within an autonomous area there is a town with the concentration of another minority, a nationality township may be designated for its benefit (art. 12 of the Law). Such areas may only be declared where a minority is 'concentrated' – but there is no specification of its proportion of the total population of the area. There are 5 autonomous regions at the provincial level (Inner Mongolia, Xinjiang, Guangxi, Tibet, and Ningxia), 31 autonomous prefectures, 105 autonomous counties, and about 3000 nationality townships. The decision to so declare an autonomous area depends on 'local conditions such as the relationship among the various nationalities and the level of economic development, and with due consideration for historical background' (art. 12 of the Law). The decision to establish an autonomous area is made by the State Council (art. 89(15)) on the recommendation of lower-level state organs after relevant consultations, including with the minority concerned (art. 14 of the Law). It would therefore follow that there are no hard criteria and that no minority can claim autonomy.

The governing bodies of autonomous areas are called 'organs of self-government' (art. 95 of the const.); they have all the powers of organs of government at local level – that is, people's congresses with their standing committees and people's governments – but have some additional powers which constitute the primary element of their autonomy (art. 115 of the const.), including the enactment of 'autonomy regulations' (art. 116), although this term is nowhere defined. One of their primary tasks is to adapt state laws and policies to local circumstances (art. 115), and if a resolution, decision or instruction of a higher state organ is unsuitable for the autonomous area, the organs of self-government may modify it or cease to implement it (art. 20 of the Law). Within the general terms of state laws and plans, they may undertake a number of measures, such as the allocation of resources, international trade, and the exploitation of natural resources. They have some fiscal autonomy, being free to determine the expenditure of money allocated to the area by the state (art. 117 of the const. and art. 33 of the Law) and to allow larger exemptions from taxation than under the state law (art. 35 of the Law). They may maintain local security forces for the maintenance of public order (art. 120 of the const. and art. 24 of the Law). They have a particular responsibility for the development of the culture, languages and customs of the minority (art. 119 of the const. and art. 38 of the Law), as well as for the economic and social development of the area (arts. 25–28 of the Law). Organs of state power at higher level are required to help to accelerate the development of autonomous areas by various preferential policies and special grants (art. 122 of the const. and chap. VI of the Law).

Both the constitution and the Law attempt to ensure that the organs of self-government as well as other state bodies in the autonomous area are effectively under the influence of persons from the minority nationality (through the chairs of organs of self-government as well as membership of administrative services – arts. 113 and 114 of the const. and arts. 16, 17, 23 and 46 of the Law). In principle, the language of administration, courts and procuracy should be that of the minority (art. 134 of the const. and arts. 21 and 47 of the Law). Cadres of Han nationality posted to the area 'should learn' the spoken and written language of the areas, and cadres from the minority nationality should learn Mandarin (art. 49).

These provisions do not add up to a system of autonomy as generally understood. 'Autonomy' is of course not a term of art, but it does imply very significant powers of independent decision making, at the legislative and executive levels, and independent resources, particularly finance and public service, to exercise them. In China, the discretion of the organs of self-government in the discharge of these responsibilities is limited (Heberer 1989). Their policies and activities must be conducted within the general framework of national laws (and there is no indication that 'autonomy regulations' may contravene state laws). Fundamentally, the broad framework within which the system operates denies true autonomy of choice of policy, for the organs of self-government are bound by the key principles of the Chinese state system: socialism, democratic dictatorship and centralism, subordination to institutions at the next higher level, within the overarching domination of the Chinese Communist Party (CCP). Most regulations or policies require the consent of higher state organs and, in some cases, of the State Council itself (as for establishing local security forces or engaging in international trade). They have to work ultimately under the unified leadership of the State Council (art. 15 of the Law). Their financial and other resources depend on grants from the centre. There is no mechanism to resist the encroachments on their powers by the centre. Any 'autonomy' given by the law can be negated through the directives or influence of the CCP – for example, key positions in autonomous areas are covered by the nomenklatura (and there is no requirement in the CCP constitution that party secretaries in these areas be members of their nationalities: in fact, most of them are Han).

Special economic zones
This concept of autonomy is clearly different from ethnic autonomy, described above, and from the economic autonomy of the special administrative regions ('reunification autonomy'), described below. Special economic zones provide, at first sight, a middle ground; their rationale is experimentation with new economic forms, providing a substantial role for foreign investment in the private economy, but within the framework of 'socialist modernisation'. To take the Special Economic Zone of Shenzhen (one of three such zones in Guangdong Province) as an example, it has been set up 'in order to develop external economic relations and technical exchanges and support the socialist modernisation programme' (art. 1 of the Regulations on Special Economic Zones in Guangdong Province, 1980). It facilitates direct investments or joint ventures by 'foreign citizens, overseas Chinese, compatriots in Hong Kong and Macao' – primarily for export purposes, because domestic sales require special permission and attract customs duties (art. 9). Special facilities and fiscal and other concessions are offered to investors which are available only to investors in these zones (see, for example, arts. 4, 5, 10 and chap. III)). An investment can only be made after it has been approved and licensed. Special laws may be enacted, establishing a different regime of laws, particularly commercial laws. However, neither policy nor administrative decisions are made by Shenzhen authorities. The management of the zones comes under the authority of the Guangdong

Provincial Administration of Special Economic Zones, which is to exercise 'unified management of special zones on behalf of the Guangdong Provincial People's Government' (art. 3). Key functions in relation to the management are vested in this authority (arts. 7, 9, 11 and chap. V). Important policy decisions are made by the provincial authorities, who have to negotiate with and seek the approval of the State Council and in some instances, where regulations are concerned, of the National People's Congress (NPC) or its standing committee. Although the social and economic impact of special zones has been infinitely greater than that of autonomous regions, the former have little autonomy; they are merely instruments to carry out policy decided by the normal institutions of the state. In that sense, they provide no precedents for the tensions that may arise from the exercise of autonomy and how the central authorities may handle them – this is not to say that policies pursued through special zones have not been the subject of acute controversies within the party and the government.

Tibet

For these precedents, we have to turn to the experiences of national autonomous regions. On the whole, these areas have not been problematic from the CCP's point of view, and since 1979 they have enabled minorities to enjoy their culture and customs without giving them a significant measure of self-rule. Two problematic areas have been Tibet and Xinjiang – and, in both instances, strong indigenous religious traditions (Buddhism and Islam, respectively) have been critical factors, aggravated by intolerance of them during the Cultural Revolution. The Tibetan situation is also complicated by disputes over the legal basis of Chinese sovereignty, with sharp differences between those applying modern international law, which proclaims Tibet's right to independence, and the Chinese authorities, who invoke traditional notions of its hegemony (Heberer 1989:122–4). China's relationship with Tibet, in some form of suzerainty, is ancient, but over the years the links had weakened, partly under European machinations, and British influence over Tibet increased in the early part of the twentieth century – and Tibet operated largely as an independent state. During the 1911 Chinese revolution, Tibet fought with and drove out the Chinese. It was only after the communist victory over the Kuomintang that China started to assert its claims, deciding in 1950 to 'liberate' Tibet, motivated in part by considerations of defence as well as communist dislike of Tibetan theocracy. After preliminary talks between the Chinese and Tibetan authorities, Chinese troops invaded Tibet and captured the eastern part, Chamdo. Under threats of further violence, the Tibetan authorities negotiated a seventeen-point agreement with the Chinese on 23 May 1951 ('Agreement on Measures for the Peaceful Liberation of Tibet').

The Agreement provided for the return of Tibet to the 'big family of the Motherland – the People's Republic of China' and the presence of the People's Liberation Army in Tibet to consolidate 'national defences'. The People's Republic of China was to be responsible for all external affairs. In return, various guarantees were given to Tibetans: the right to exercise national regional autonomy 'under the unified leadership' of the Central People's Government; no change to the existing political system in Tibet, including the status, functions and powers of the Dalai Lama; respect for the religious beliefs, customs and habits of the Tibetan people and the protection of lama monasteries; and development of the spoken and written language and the school education of Tibetans. It was also agreed, as regards reforms, that there would be no compulsion by the central authorities and that the 'local government of Tibet should carry out reforms of its own accord, and, when the people raise demands for reform, they shall be settled by means of consultation with the leading personnel of Tibet' (art. 11). The question of reform (and the associated question of the status of monasteries) was fundamental, since 'reform' was regarded by many Tibetans as implying the introduction of elements of communism and threatening their separate way of life – as late as 1956, Zhou En Lai assured the Indian government that China did not intend to force communism on Tibet (ICJ 1959:8).

A committee was to be set up to ensure the implementation of the Agreement, consisting of personnel from the central government and 'patriotic elements' from various sectors in Tibet, although the Preparatory Committee for the Tibetan Autonomous Region was not established until October 1955. The Agreement failed to resolve differences between the Chinese and the Tibetans. For a while, attempts were made to govern Tibet in accordance with it, but there were conflicts of aims and interpretation. There was increasing resentment among large sections of Tibetans at what they perceived to be direct Chinese rule and an assault on their way of life. The Agreement was formally repudiated on 11 March 1959 by a declaration of independence by the Dalai Lama and his government. The Chinese began a siege of the Potala Palace where the Dalai Lama lived and bombarded it and other monasteries. The Dalai Lama escaped to India, which weakened the forces of secession and resistance to China. Tibet was further integrated into the regular administrative system of China and 'reforms' pushed through. In 1965, the Tibet Autonomous Region, under the general scheme for minorities, was established.

The Tibetan and Chinese versions of why the Agreement failed are diametrically opposed (see ICJ 1959). The Tibetans accused the Chinese of total disregard of the Agreement, saying that China ignored provisions for the internal autonomy of the Tibetan government and refused to support its proposals for reform while, at the same time, pressing Chinese reforms in the face of local opposition; that the preparatory committee, despite significant Tibetan membership, acted to rubber-stamp Chinese decisions; and that the local public service was taken over, the dominance of the Chinese army established and communist ideology propagated. A study of laws passed by various organs of 'self-government' provides no evidence of any meaningful exercise of autonomy; indeed, it shows that Tibet, and autonomous areas generally, enjoy less autonomy than ordinary provinces (Keller 1994).

There was transmigration of Han people to Tibet, while Tibetans were moved to other parts of China, thus diluting their numbers in Tibet (and autonomous prefectures were established for them elsewhere). Monasteries were raided, their income taken away and religious texts destroyed, as part of a general onslaught on their religion and social system. The Dalai Lama's position was constantly undermined (and 'puppets' co-opted), and with it the general structure of Tibetan society. In all of these ways, the political system was transformed, contrary to the guarantee in the Agreement. Tibetans questioned Chinese interpretation of the territorial extent of Tibet, for parts of what they regarded as traditional lands, particularly eastern Tibet (Chamdo), were excluded from the scope of the operation of the Agreement. There were allegations of widespread violation of the rights of Tibetans, including the large-scale killing of monks, the suppression of freedom of expression and association, and the use of forced labour. China was also accused of genocide because of its suppression of Tibetan religion and culture and because of its migration policies.

The Chinese riposte was that the Dalai Lama and his government had refused to cooperate with the Chinese authorities in accordance with the Agreement; that 'people' wanted reforms, requiring the central government, in accordance with the Agreement, to consult them in order to effect them (the Tibetan interpretation being that it was the Tibetan government which had to undertake the consultation); and that various 'reactionaries' under the influence of 'imperialists' had attempted to undermine Chinese authority. The Chinese attempted to impose their control through violence and the force of arms, which provoked open revolt among the Tibetans. Severe Chinese retaliation followed, with the Dalai Lama leading many Tibetans into exile in India. The onset of the Cultural Revolution (1966–76) was a further blow to the Agreement. Under the reversal of Chinese policy towards minorities, most monasteries were destroyed as part of a systematic attempt to destroy Tibetan religion and culture, and there was a terrible repression which has left deep and bitter scars.

With the end of the Cultural Revolution and the recognition of its ravages, particularly towards minorities, previous conciliatory policies were reinstated (as in the 1982 constitution). Attempts were made by Deng Xiaoping to start a dialogue with the Dalai Lama to return to China; he

declared his willingness to discuss any arrangements short of independence. The Dalai Lama has renounced claims of independence and suggested arrangements which are similar to the earlier relationship, under
which China would be responsible for foreign affairs, with a phasing out
of its defence responsibilities and with other matters under Tibetan
autonomy. But no agreement could be reached on the terms for his
return, particularly on the scope of autonomy to be enjoyed by Tibet.
Tibetan resentment at Chinese rule has continued, and various protests
against it have been staged – and have received wide international pub-
licity. The most serious were in March 1989 – a combination of ethnic
and economic dissatisfaction – to which China reacted with great feroc-
ity and imposed martial law, thus ending another, more attenuated, stage
of autonomy. Although both sides have expressed willingness to talk, the
terms of a meeting have eluded them (Smith 1996).

Xinjiang

Xinjiang has a largely Muslim population with kin across the boundary
into what was the Soviet Union but are now Kazakhstan and Tadjikistan.
The main group is Uygur, who until recently constituted over 80 per cent
of the population. Various groups of people tried to secede from China
throughout the twentieth century, either as independent republics or to
join with Turkey (with which some have linguistic connections). For a
short while, an Eastern Turkestan Republic was established, centring
largely around three districts in the far north-west of Xinjiang. China has
dealt with secessionist tendencies through armed suppression as well as
negotiation – and through its diplomacy with the Soviet Union or the
Russian Federation (for example, the Turkestan republic was attacked by
Soviet troops in 1934 – both China and Russia had a common interest in
suppressing Islamic irredentism).

   In 1946 the Kuomindang government made a peace agreement with
the Eastern Turkestan Republic, promising self-government. Under it,
the people of Xinjiang would have the right to elect officials, with one of
the provincial vice-chairmen to come from one of the three troubled districts. Discrimination on the basis of religion would be punished, and primary and secondary schools would teach in the language of the local
nationality (in addition to courses in Chinese). The culture and arts of
the nationalities would expand freely, and there would be freedom of
publication, assembly and speech (see Benson 1990:185–7 for full text).
China did not honour the agreement:

> The central government continued to push to extend its control in Xin-
> jiang, while the Chinese military interfered continually in the region's civil
> affairs. They aimed to prevent the reforms required by the agreement. Nat-
> urally enough, local Han bureaucrats were fearful of their own power if

autonomy took root, and they were quite happy to co-operate with the military. A coalition government led by Zhang Zhizhong [Han chairman of Xinjiang] was supposed to have a 70:30 ratio of minority nationalities to Han Chinese but it was never put into effect. Chinese-appointed bureaucrats remained firmly in control of Xinjiang, and as they were in other provinces in China. (Mackerras 1994:66–7)

When the Communist Party came to power, it also tried to negotiate (by which time, relations had worsened due to disregard of the earlier agreement). Xinjiang was made a province in 1955, and some leaders of the Turkestan republic were persuaded to join the new administration. It was subsequently brought under the regime of national autonomy, but sporadic protests against Chinese rule have continued, especially during the period of Sino-Soviet tensions. The breakup of the Soviet Union has led to a resurgence of Islamic consciousness and identity (as in other parts of the world), and this has clearly worried China. Large numbers of troops (and other Han civilians) have been stationed in Xinjiang, for domestic and external reasons, also aggravating the situation. Due to restrictions on the entry of journalists and foreigners, it is hard to form a clear impression of the present situation, but there are occasional reports of unrest and its armed suppression. In recent years, resistance to Chinese rule has grown and China has responded with increased repression, including numerous executions. It has also worked on the diplomatic front to stave off support to secessionists from neighbouring Islamic states and Russia, by entering into joint ventures and other forms of economic cooperation with them. The rulers of these states feel themselves threatened by 'fundamentalists', as the secessionists are labelled. That label has also obstructed the efforts of radical Uygurs in mobilising support in the West – in sharp contrast to the success of Tibetan exiles.

Autonomy tensions
From this brief discussion of two experiences of 'autonomy', the following tentative conclusions may be drawn. The first is that there is no consistent theory of autonomy, because Marxist-Leninist formulations (never significant in their place of origin) have never really been adopted, despite the rhetoric. The meaning ascribed to autonomy is somewhat different from its normal significance. It generally means arrangements for governance in which a particular community or locality has substantial powers of decision making regarding policy and administration, and control over fiscal resources. Specific institutional structures are necessary to exercise this autonomy, including an impartial machinery for adjudica-

tion which maintains the boundaries that define autonomy. It would seem that the Chinese authorities understand autonomy to refer to arrangements which recognise the distinctiveness of culture of particular communities, promote their economic and social development, and allow for a measure of community participation in the affairs of the locality. These arrangements have to operate within a regime of national laws, policies and institutions which serve to place severe limitations on the discretion of the local community. There is no independent mechanism for boundary keeping, so there are no safeguards against inroads into autonomy. The Communist Party maintains its overall control; and here there is no requirement of local participation or discretion.

Second, autonomy is conceived of in ethnic terms: it is to combat Han chauvinism and to recognise the cultural distinctiveness of minorities. The emphasis, somewhat superficially, is on language and folklore rather than on the deeper springs of ethnic identity, like religious or historical traditions. Both Tibetan Buddhism and Xinjiang Islam provide an alternative world view to that of Chinese communism and, therefore, cannot be easily accommodated within the wider PRC system. This immediately alerts us to the limitations of autonomy: not only has there to be an ethnic claim to autonomy but autonomy must also stand constantly subordinate to the interests of the state, as defined by the central government. The current emphasis on economic development has eroded autonomy and threatens the way of life of these communities, as the natural resources of their regions are exploited, frequently with the introduction of Han workers, and the environment degraded. Each time the implications of autonomy for restrictions on central policies and initiatives become obvious, autonomy is suppressed, allegedly against the wishes of the local communities. The legal terms of autonomy agreements are disregarded when it suits the centre. The PRC legal system is still relatively underdeveloped and there is, apart from the political imperatives, considerable confusion as to who has what power and what regulations are in force. Autonomy seems to be tolerated only in so far as it does not affect the project of the Communist Party – even though, in the first place, autonomy is granted only to the weak and the peripheral. Autonomy is tangential to the national system – hence, its impact in terms of theory and doctrine is little. China has been more concerned to elaborate theories of sovereignty and national unity (and external nonintervention) than local autonomy or self-government.

Consequently, China has not developed any sophisticated mechanism to deal with assertions of autonomy that it finds distasteful – and thus denies the very premise of autonomy. There are no institutions for dialogue, mechanisms for defining issues between parties, or procedures for negotiation or adjudication (compare the protracted negotiations in Canada or India to settle ethnic claims). There is a tendency to use extreme measures, such as the use of armed force, which does little to solve the underlying issues but serves only to aggravate them and escalate the conflict. This approach is remarkable, considering that China is in such a dominant position vis-à-vis communities which are promised autonomy. On the other hand, it has to be acknowledged that, in general, China has had considerable success in dealing with its minorities, and unrest or challenges to its authority have been limited. The overwhelming dominance of the Han of course helps in this regard – but, all over the world, ethnic protests and demands for self-government have achieved a very high degree of salience (tearing countries apart), and it is not unrealistic to assume that China's border communities may bestir themselves in the near future. There is also the growing 'regionalisation' of Han China, which might limit the capacity of the centre to deal with ethnic disputes unless better procedures – and a higher degree of tolerance – are developed.

ONE COUNTRY, TWO SYSTEMS: 'A HIGH DEGREE OF AUTONOMY'

As a result of the weakness of ethnic autonomy, attention has turned to the potential of the system first offered to Taiwan in 1981 but applied so far to Hong Kong (in 1997) and Macau (in 1999). Welcoming the establishment of the Hong Kong Special Administrative Region, the Dalai Lama urged the adoption of 'one country, two systems' ('octs') for Tibet. He considers that the 1951 agreement with China was made in the same spirit as 'octs' but had an unfortunate history. He has suggested that foreign affairs and defence should be handled by China, 'then the rest of the business such as education and economy and preservation of spirituality or cultural heritage, these Tibetans should handle fully'.[1] Deng Xiaoping (1993:14) had predicted wide use of this formula in helping to 'eliminate flash points and stabilise the world situation'. The Muslims in Mindanao (the Philippines) have expressed a preference for the Hong Kong formula, and it is significant that the autonomy proposals for East Timor, developed by Portugal and Indonesia under United Nations auspices, bore a remarkable similarity to 'octs'.

Despite its origins, there is no reason why 'octs' cannot be applied in different circumstances, but it is important to recognise that the autonomy it provides was not conceived of for the purpose which is the focus of this book, namely the accommodation of ethnic claims. Its origins lie in the need to accommodate, as part of the reunification strategy of the PRC, the economic, social and political systems in Hong Kong, Macau and Taiwan (all perceived as inhabited by Han Chinese) with the Leninist principles of political and economic organisation on the mainland. The juridical basis for this formula was incorporated in the 1982 constitution, which authorised the NPC to establish special administrative regions and to institute 'systems' therein in 'the light of specific conditions' (art. 31). This broad formulation was adopted to accommodate precise arrangements that would be agreed with the Taiwanese, as well as somewhat different systems for Hong Kong and Macau. Under this article, China has enacted Basic Laws for Hong Kong and Macau which confer very substantial 'autonomy' on them. Whether the 'octs' formula has the potential for Greater China or the rest of the world ascribed to it by Deng is doubtful, for, while the substantive powers of Hong Kong are now well understood, the institutional arrangements for their exercise are not. In order to understand the real nature of 'octs', it is helpful to examine these aspects: the powers transferred to Hong Kong, the institutional arrangements within Hong Kong and their articulation with mainland institutions, the essential purpose of the system, and the constitutional guarantees.

Hong Kong has been delegated powers over all areas except defence and foreign affairs.[2] Even in the case of foreign affairs, there is a considerable delegation so that Hong Kong can maintain its international trading and other economic relations, enabling it, for example, to keep its membership of international and regional economic and financial institutions and to conclude commercial treaties with other states. The transfer of powers is reinforced by the maintenance of separate systems in Hong Kong: its market economy; its currency, fiscal, tax and budgetary system; its legal and judicial system based on common law; its regime of rights and freedoms; and its immigration controls. Since most of these were in place before the transfer of sovereignty, 'octs' sprang to life instantaneously on 1 July 1997, requiring none of the bureaucratic approvals and delegations that so often delay the implementation of autonomy.

The weakness of 'octs' lies in the institutional arrangements. A close analysis makes it abundantly clear that China wanted to retain effective control over Hong Kong affairs, notwithstanding its slogan of 'Hong Kong people ruling Hong Kong'. The internal political system is heavily weighted in favour of the chief executive, the head of the government, who has firm control over the legislative process through vetoes, not only over bills but also over the introduction of legislative proposals. The chief executive is appointed by the Chinese government and cannot be dismissed by the Legislative Council, even on impeachment, except with the approval of the Chinese. On the other hand, the chief executive has limited powers of dismissal of the legislature in the event that they are in conflict. The weakness of the legislature is compounded by its partially non-democratic character. A majority of its members are elected through narrow functional constituencies, or a special committee, which privilege business and conservative interests who are, in turn, committed to support China. Consequently, the executive is both unable and unwilling to stand up to the Chinese government, and the more autonomy-minded members of the legislature are unable to hold the government accountable or to secure Hong Kong's autonomy. Although other chapters in this volume argue that autonomy is not possible without democracy, China was able to devise 'octs' only because of the lack of democracy in Hong Kong. A democratic Hong Kong would not fit into 'one country' – as China is finding in relation to Taiwan. But this very fact imposes and defines the restrictive scope of 'octs' autonomy.

The Chinese authorities articulate not only with the Hong Kong executive but also with its legislature and judiciary. The NPC reviews Hong Kong legislation and has the power of veto over laws which its standing committee deems to violate Basic Law provisions regarding responsibilities vested in the Chinese authorities. It has also the power to interpret the Basic Law, overriding decisions made by Hong Kong's highest court. These powers are very wide and can also be used to change the Law.[3] It has become clear now that the Hong Kong judiciary is incapable of protecting autonomy. For other reasons, too, the autonomy is without any reliable safeguards. The prevailing orthodoxy is that the relationship of the Chinese authorities to Hong Kong is determined not only by the Basic Law, despite art. 159 governing its amendment which aims at restricting the powers of the Chinese authorities (which would have provided some safeguard), but also by the PRC constitution, which places no limits on the powers of the NPC or, effectively, the State Council.

It will be clear from the above account that the real purpose of 'octs' is not to confer autonomy on the people of Hong Kong but to devise a framework for managing an alternative type of economy – the market economy – which stood in such sharp contrast to the Chinese planned economy at the time the negotiations for the transfer of sovereignty were conducted. The separation of Hong Kong's systems owes less to respect for its distinct lifestyle than to the perception that they are a necessary adjunct to its economy. It is because the Chinese authorities have invented 'octs' for this specific purpose that the Communist Party was quick to dismiss the Dalai Lama's request for it, claiming that Tibet had already been integrated into China's socialist economy and political system.

These considerations make 'octs' an unlikely candidate for the reunification of Taiwan, whose status cannot be negotiated away by a colonial power. Taiwan is larger, with a population of nearly 20 million, has a robust economy and a developed democratic system, and is well armed. China recognises these factors and has offered Taiwan, in additional to what is in Hong Kong's Basic Law, the right to 'run its own party, political, military, economic and financial affairs'. Moreover, Taiwan 'may keep its military forces and the mainland will not dispatch troops or administrative personnel to the island. On the other hand, representatives of the government of the special administrative region and those from different circles of Taiwan may be appointed to senior posts in the central government and participate in the running of the national government' (PRC State Council 1993:III:3). Implicit in 'octs' is that the mainland system represents 'one country' and thus subordinates other parts to its dominant ideology and power. Such an outcome is unacceptable to Taiwan which has, for over fifty years, run itself as an independent state; it sees 'octs' as a method for annexation (Republic of China 1994:285). It is more comfortable with the notion of 'one country, two political entities' as an interim solution, while negotiations on unification proceed between two equal and independent entities (a procedure currently unacceptable to Beijing). Taiwan believes that the present time is not propitious for unification, for unification can take place only on the basis of common ideology and values (a view which represents a total rejection of the ideology or feasibility of 'octs'). In its view, the ideology of unification must be democracy and human rights, as outlined in the 'Three Principles of the People' enunciated by Sun Yatsen. Once the two entities practise these values, 'the unification of China will come naturally' (Republic of China 1994:286). There is considerable merit in Taipei's analysis, for such different moral and economic systems cannot be held together unless there is a basic symmetry of power, otherwise they would splinter off. But, if there is asymmetry, one part would seek to dominate the other. Beijing, on the other hand, has stated that, unless Taiwan consents to 'octs', it may have to use force to bring about reunification.

CONCLUSION

With at least three types of autonomy, China seems comfortable with asymmetry. The range of arrangements is further multiplied when we consider the variations within each type of autonomy. Were Taiwan to join the 'motherland' on the basis of some form of autonomy, it would inevitably be on yet another set of arrangements. It is possible that Chinese ease with asymmetry is due to the fact that it is considered not to matter, since all forms of autonomy are subordinated to the supremacy of the Communist Party, manifested in the NPC and the State Council. The constitutional distinction, if not the precise legal differences, between 'octs' and ethnic autonomy has more or less been obliterated by the December 1999 decision of Hong Kong's Court of Final Appeal,[4] following upon the standing committee's interpretation of the Basic Law, that acknowledges the unlimited and unchallengeable power of the NPC to impose any meaning on the Basic Law.[5]

Ethnic autonomy bears little relation to the concept of autonomy as it is understood in the countries that form the subject of other chapters in this book. In China, there is no negotiation on autonomy; what passes for an offer is in fact an imposition. International underpinnings, as there are for 'octs' through joint declarations with the UK and Portugal, are of little moment. There are no reserved lists of autonomous powers, there are no constitutional guarantees that are policed by any independent umpire, there is no regional democracy that is not subverted by democratic centralism. There are no credible spokespersons for autonomy. There are no prospects that regional politics or preferences would influence national policies or institutions.

A major difficulty in establishing genuine autonomy, assuming that Beijing really wanted to do so, lies in the weakness of China's constitutional and legal systems. Until 'octs', China did not have to confront the issue of constitutional entrenchment. However, the autonomy promised Hong Kong could not be delivered unless it was constitutionally entrenched. It was entrenched in the Basic Law but not in the PRC constitution. Not that it would have mattered, for the notion of the supremacy of the constitution is alien to both China's imperial and communist traditions. At one stage, it looked as if Hong Kong's judiciary, steeped in the common law, might be able to provide some protection for autonomy. It did make a valiant effort in a famous judgment in January 1999,[6] but retribution was quick, both from Hong Kong's mainland-appointed government and from Chinese authorities. Nor is the notion of hierarchy of norms and fields of competence, so essential to autonomy, easily feasible in China's chaotic legal order (Ghai 1999:128–33).

There is nothing surprising in China's experience of autonomy. Maleševič demonstrates, in this volume, the near impossibility of securing genuine autonomy in a communist system. The Communist Party is too avaricious and powerful to allow it. Autonomy is a useful tool for obfuscation and manipulation. In China's case, autonomy is problematic also because of the huge size and clout of the national government; autonomous areas are pygmy-like in comparison and, except for areas covered by 'octs', are inhabited by 'barbarians'.

China's singular lack of capacity or desire to establish and manage autonomy bodes ill for its future. With the shift to a market economy, and the decentralisation of power which that brings about, the increasing irrelevance of the communist ideology and the legitimacy of the Communist Party, regional disparities, and growing ethnic consciousness and resentment of discrimination suggest that the new economic and social order cannot be managed through the frame of a Leninist state. Regional autonomy, or even federation, may be necessary to provide a framework for negotiating competing regional and ethnic claims. But, for the time being, federation is taboo and autonomy is tolerated only so long as it is subordinated to Beijing.

NOTES

I thank the Research Grants Committee of Hong Kong for the assistance provided for my research on Hong Kong's constitutional system.
1 Interview with Phillipe Noubel on the European Internet Network, <http://www.insidechina.com/tibet/kanaubt1.html>.
2 For a detailed account, see Ghai (1999); for a summary, see Ghai (1998b). For differences in Macau, which largely follows the Hong Kong model, see Ghai (2000a).
3 This view of its powers has been endorsed by Hong Kong's Court of Final Appeal (see Ghai 2000b).
4 *Lau Kong Yung v. Director of Immigration* [1999] 4 HKC 731.
5 *The Interpretation by the Standing Committee of the National Peoples Congress of Articles 22 (4) and 24 (2) (3) of the Basic Law of the Hong Kong SAR of the PRC.*
6 *Ng Ka Ling v. Director of Immigration* [1991] 1 HKLRD 315.

REFERENCES

Anderson, Benedict 1983. *Imagined Communities: Reflections on the Origin and Spread of Nationalism.* London: Verson Press.
Benson, Linda 1990. *The Ili Rebellion: The Moslem Challenge to Chinese Authority in Xinjiang 1944–49.* Armonk, NY: M.E. Sharpe.
Connor, Walker 1984. *The National Question in Marxist-Leninist Theory and Strategy.* Princeton: Princeton University Press.
Deng Xiaoping 1993. *On the Question of Hong Kong.* Hong Kong: New Horizon Press.
Ghai, Yash 1998a. 'Decentralisation and the accommodation of ethnicity', in Crawford Young (ed.) *Ethnic Diversity and Public Policy: A Comparative Inquiry.* Basingstoke: Macmillan Press.
—— 1998b. 'Autonomy with Chinese characteristics: the case of Hong Kong', *Pacifica Review* 10(1):7–22.
—— 1999. *Hong Kong's New Constitutional Order: The Resumption of Chinese Sovereignty and the Basic Law.* Hong Kong: Hong Kong University Press, 2nd edn.
—— 2000a. 'The Basic Law of the Special Administrative Region of Macau: some reflections', *International and Comparative Law Quarterly* 49:183–98.
—— 2000b. 'The NPC and its consequences', in J. Chan, H.L. Fu and Y. Ghai (eds) *Hong Kong's Constitutional Debate: Conflict of Interpretation.* Hong Kong: Hong Kong University Press.

Gladney, Dru C. 1996. *Muslim Chinese: Ethnic Nationalism in the People's Republic.* Cambridge, MA: Harvard University Press.

Heberer, Thomas 1989. *China and Its National Minorities: Autonomy or Assimilation.* Armonk, NY: M.E. Sharpe.

ICJ (International Commission of Jurists) 1959. *The Question of Tibet and the Rule of Law.* Geneva: ICJ.

Keller, Perry 1994. 'Human rights under Chinese municipal law', in Robert McCorquodale and Nicholas Orosz (eds) *Tibet: The Position in International Law.* Stuttgart: Hans-Jorg Mayer.

Mackerras, Colin 1994. *China's Minorities: Integration and Modernisation in the Twentieth Century.* Hong Kong: Oxford University Press.

PRC State Council 1993. *The Taiwan Question and Reunification of China.* Beijing: Taiwan Affairs Office and Information Office, State Council.

Pye, Lucian 1975. 'China: ethnic minorities and national security', in Nathan Glazer and Daniel P. Moynihan (eds) *Ethnicity: Theory and Experience.* Cambridge, MA: Harvard University Press.

Republic of China 1994. *Relations across the Taiwan Straits* (Taipei: Mainland Affairs Council, Executive Yuan), as reproduced in Jean-Marie Henchaerts (ed.) 1996 *The International Status of Taiwan in the New World Order: Legal and Political Considerations.* London: Kluwer Law.

Roeder, Philip 1990–91. 'Soviet federalism and ethnic mobilisation', *World Politics* 43:196–232.

Sautman, Barry 1998. 'Preferential policies for ethnic minorities in China: the case of Xingjiang', in William Safran (ed.) *Nationalism and Ethnoregional Identities in China.* London: Frank Cass.

Schram, Stuart R. 1985. 'Decentralisation in a unitary state: theory and practice, 1940–84', in Stuart R. Schram (ed.) *The Scope of State Power in China.* Hong Kong: Chinese University Press.

Smith, Warren W. Jr 1996. *Tibetan Nation: A History of Tibetan Nationalism and Sino-Tibetan Relations.* Boulder, CO: Westview Press.

White, Sydney D. 1998. 'State discourses, minority policies, and the politics of identity in the Lijiang Naxi people's autonomous county', in William Safran (ed.) *Nationalism and Ethnoregional Identities in China.* London: Frank Cass.

CHAPTER 5

HOW THE CENTRE HOLDS: MANAGING CLAIMS FOR REGIONAL AND ETHNIC AUTONOMY IN A DEMOCRATIC SOUTH AFRICA

HEINZ KLUG

Ethnic interests have shaped the quest for federalism in South Africa (Friedman 1993a; Horowitz 1991; Welsh 1993). However, federal arrangements have also been advocated by those seeking to protect non-ethnic interests.[1] While the dominant ethnic-driven claim for federalism has provoked serious resistance, concerns about democratic accountability and effective local administration as well as regional political interests help to explain the vibrancy of the federal elements in South Africa's new 1996 constitution. I will argue that the particular constitutional outcome, which rejects particular forms of federalism while embracing a strong regionalism, is a direct consequence of both the political majority's reaction to particular ethnic claims as well as an attempt to incorporate a broader demand for the recognition of regional and ethnic diversity.

To explain this outcome, in which provincial governments wield limited powers yet provincial legislatures play a direct and constitutionally important role in the formulation and passage of national legislation in accordance with enshrined principles of cooperative government, it is necessary to understand both the history of federalist claims in South Africa and their particular role in the democratic transition and constitution-making process. In this context, it is also necessary to outline the ways in which ethnic demands have been recognised in the constitution and the alternative constitutional mechanisms which have been established to address these issues.

FEDERALISM'S SOUTH AFRICAN HISTORY

South Africa is a land of fairly pronounced regionalisms, including some historically distinctive regions – such as Namaqualand, the Western

Province, the Eastern Province, the Highveld, the Eastern Transvaal, and the Northern Transvaal – which, despite their geographic, economic and even social distinctiveness, have never coincided with the historic provincial boundaries (Welsh 1994:243–4). However, it is important to recognise that the apartheid project was based quite fundamentally on the spatial division of the country into racial and ethnic blocs. By the beginning of the democratic transition in 1990, apartheid policy and practice had defined and created six self-governing territories and four independent states within the internationally recognised boundaries of South Africa.

Starting with the all-white National Convention in 1909, which negotiated the formation of the Union of South Africa (Davenport 1977:147–69), fears and designs of domination have marked the history of federalist claims in South Africa. Although the convention agreed on the basic issues – the forging of white political unity in the face of African anti-colonial resistance (Roux 1964:87–100), and economic advantage (Thompson 1975:347)[2] – the Natal delegation's demand for a federal structure for the new state reflected a fear by English speakers in Natal that they would be dominated by the nationally more numerous Afrikaans speakers (Davenport 1977:120–46). While Natal lost its demand for a federal constitution, a few remnants remained in the creation of an upper house of parliament, based on equal representation from the four provinces, and elected provincial councils with powers to make ordinances on a number of issues, the most significant being non-tertiary education. These provisions were, however, mere sops to Natal opinion as provincial governments could be unilaterally changed by parliament,[3] and provincial ordinances required central government endorsement before they became law. Even the Senate's limited ability to reject bills could be overcome by a simple majority of the two houses sitting jointly.

Significantly, while the Union constitution paid lip-service to the fears of English-speaking colonials in Natal, the non-ethnic demand for federal arrangements designed to protect the non-racial franchise in the Cape colony was explicitly rejected. Instead, both the parity of English and Afrikaans as well as the Cape franchise were constitutionally entrenched, even if ineffectively in the case of the franchise. The political legacy of this early non-ethnic claim for federalism was kept alive by the small white parliamentary opposition but was completely overshadowed by the apartheid balkanisation of the country. This process reached its apogee in the apartheid regime's proposal for the formation of a Constellation of Southern African States, in which the territory of South Africa would be forever divided into separate ethnically defined entities.

Responding to the process of decolonisation which was sweeping through Africa in the late 1950s, the apartheid regime sought to extend franchise rights to the African majority, but only within geographically bound and fragmented entities. Referred to by the apartheid regime as the policy of 'separate development' (Basson and Viljoen 1991:307–18; Richardson 1978), this policy led to the creation of four 'independent' bantustans and aimed to engineer a permanent balkanisation of the country.[4] Rejected by the majority of South Africans and the international community as a violation of black South Africans' right to self-determination (Klug 1990), 'separate development' became a process of denationalisation in which black South Africans became foreigners, regardless of an individual's place of birth or preference.

In the face of increasing internal resistance and international isolation, the apartheid regime looked in the late 1970s to the political reincorporation of the Indian and Coloured communities as a means of broadening its social base. This led to the adoption of the 1983 constitution which purported to adopt a consociationalist model by extending the franchise to 'Indians' and 'Coloureds' in a tricameral legislature with its jurisdiction distributed according to a vague distinction between 'own' and 'general' affairs. However, two mechanisms ensured that power remained safely in the hands of the dominant white party (the National Party). First, government was effectively centralised under an executive state president with extraordinary powers. Second, all significant decisions within the legislature – such as the election of president – could be resolved by the 4:2:1 ratio of representatives, which ensured that even if the 'non-white' houses of parliament voted in unison, the will of the 'white' house would prevail. The exclusion of the African majority from this scheme and resistance from within the two target communities (Indian and Coloured) meant that the 1983 constitution was practically still-born. The escalation of resistance and rebellion, which began in late 1984 and led to the imposition of repeated states of emergency from mid-1985, sealed its fate.

This legacy holds important implications for the debate over federalism and ethnicity in South Africa. While it is possible to argue that the apartheid regime's designs for ethnic homelands and even a constellation of states envisioned at best a confederal arrangement in which colonial domination would remain intact, and that its adoption of proportional consociationalism among the white, Coloured and Indian minorities lacked the essential parity required by a consociational model, this manipulation of ethnicity discredited the demands for ethnic federalism which emerged in the democratic transition. Furthermore, it is important to recognise that, despite this history of ethnic fear and manipulation, ethnic divisions, whether by language, religion, race or tribal affiliation, have never completely coincided with geographic or political boundaries. Even where, such as in KwaZulu-Natal, there is a single dominant Zulu-speaking group, national patterns of economic development have resulted in a significant dispersion of members of that group into other regions of the country. Nevertheless, it was this same region that mounted the strongest claim for regional autonomy in the transition to democracy, driven by the claims of Zulu nationalism and fears of ethnic domination within the African majority, as well as by the political interests of the former KwaZulu government's ruling Inkatha Freedom Party (Mare 1992; Mzala 1988).

NATION BUILDING, ETHNICITY AND CULTURAL DIVERSITY

Claims for the recognition of ethnicity posed the greatest threat to South Africa's democratic transition. While all the parties said they wished to respect cultural diversity, contestation over the nature of that diversity forced negotiators to confront claims, made by the apartheid regime and its allies since the early 1970s, that the policy of separate development was based on the protection of different cultures. Although this justification ignored the reality of ethnic and racial hierarchies and of racist domination of the black majority, it remained a significant source of many separatist claims during the negotiations.

While African National Congress (ANC) negotiators remained committed to building a non-racial South Africa, the power and fear generated by a history of ethnic identification could not be ignored. Through the forty years of apartheid, at least, South African ethnic diversity was reinforced and re-created through government sponsorship of separate ethnic administrations, and separate language radio and television stations. Although controlled by apartheid propagandists, these purported to serve the needs of cultural diversity. The reproduction of this 'diversity' in the creation of bantustan elites and the promotion of ethnic 'tribalism' created an apartheid legacy which will continue to affect debates and political struggles over issues of national development and democracy. In contrast, the ANC was premised at its founding in 1912 on the desire among African leaders to create a single nation, unifying Africans against colonial domination, regardless of ethnic affiliation. Over the century, the quest for national liberation witnessed numerous reformulations aimed at extending the category of oppressed in ethnic and class terms, while simultaneously presenting an alternative vision of a single, non-racial South African nation free of ethnic domination.

Despite the non-racial project's success in creating a united front against apartheid – most visibly in the Congress Alliance and later the United Democratic Front – questions of cultural diversity in language and education policies continued to plague the democratic movement. This tension between a commitment to non-racialism and the recognition of cultural and other group-based differences has mediated the ANC's communitarian traditions and led to an embracing, in part, of individualism, constitutionalism and preferential policies. These proposals have not, however, placated those whose political standing remains tied to distinct group or ethnic identities and difference.

Although opinion polls prior to the 1994 elections revealed limited popular support for any ethnic-based party, ethnic assertions began to resonate across the political spectrum both during negotiations and in the election campaign. Addressing a 20,000-strong Inkatha rally on 5 April 1994, an Inkatha regional secretary threatened that, 'if our demands cannot be addressed, then there is no election on the 27th of April . . . We will do everything in our power to destroy any attempt by any state organ used by the ANC to divide the Zulu nation' (Lorch 1994:A13). Like Buthelezi's Inkatha, hard-line white separatists continued to insist on ethnic diversity. Faced with the conclusion of negotiations for the transition to a democratic order in October 1993, an odd assortment of parties, including Inkatha and right-wing white segregationists, formed the 'Freedom Alliance', demanding that the new constitution enshrine ethnic identities. This trend led to the appearance of new and as yet unsupported claims, the most flamboyant being made by a 'coloured separatist movement' demanding an independent state stretching across the Southern and Western Cape, with Cape Town as its capital.[5] Even the ANC was drawn into this debate, challenging Buthelezi's claim to speak for South Africa's eight million Zulu speakers. Speaking at a rally in Durban, Nelson Mandela celebrated Zulu history as part of the struggle to build a nation and told 60,000 ANC supporters that 'it is impossible to separate the threads that make the weave of our South African nation'.[6] Although not overtly addressed in the transitional 1993 constitution, the impact of mobilised ethnic claims on this first round of constitution making was reflected in a range of constitutional provisions – including the structuring of a government of national unity – designed to ensure minority participation in governance (Ellmann 1994).

Despite the obvious salience of ethnic and racial identities in the South African context, it is important to recognise how the apartheid legacy in effect precluded a focus on ethnic divisions in the construction of the post-apartheid state. First, the very existence of the 'independent' bantustans, which had been denied recognition by the international community, gave the ANC's demand for a unitary South Africa important international support. Second, the continued resistance of these entities to reincorporation – particularly Bophuthatswana, whose political leadership refused to sign the declaration of intent at the first formal negotiations (Codesa I) because it implied reincorporation – and the Inkatha Freedom Party's repeated withdrawal from the negotiations, threats of secession and finally alliance with white right-wing parties completely opposed to democracy only strengthened this rejection of any federal arrangement based on the existing geographic and political divisions. Finally, the ANC's own antipathy to any recognition of ethnic claims was explicitly stated in its 1988 constitutional guidelines which went so far as to suggest the future prohibition of political parties which advocate or incite ethnic or regional exclusiveness or hatred (ANC 1988).

NEGOTIATIONS AND THE F-WORD

Entering negotiations, the three major political parties held distinct if developing views on federalism, regional government and diversity. For the ANC, a future South Africa would have to be based on a common citizenship and identity which could only be achieved through a collective effort to overcome apartheid's legacy (ANC 1994:1–3). The National Party (NP), on the other hand, conceived of a future in which local communities would be able to voluntarily choose to pursue their own living arrangements without interference from the state (NP 1991a, 1991b:12). To this end, the NP advocated a government of limited powers and proposed that different communities should be able to veto legislative action – if not directly at the national level, then indirectly at the local level through self-government based on local property rights and through the creation of a firewall between public and private activity (NP 1991a:15–18). Finally, the Inkatha Freedom Party (IFP) advocated complete regional autonomy which it described as 'federalism', as a means to ensure the self-determination of particular communities. The IFP's federalism would require not only that national government be a government of limited, enumerated powers but also that the national constitution would remain subject to the constitutions of the individual states of the federation.[7] Although labelled federalism, the essence of the IFP proposal was a system of confederation.

In specific terms, the ANC proposed a combination of elements which, on the one hand, would ensure the participation in the legislature of any group that could achieve 5 per cent of the national vote through a system of proportional representation and, on the other, would address the legacy of apartheid. Constitutional provisions to address that legacy were contained in the ANC's proposed bill of rights (ANC 1993) and comprised five different prongs which together would work to produce a system of both formal and substantive equality. The most significant of these for the debate on regionalism was a provision for regional equalisation designed to address the dualistic structure of South Africa's regional development.

The NP government entered negotiations promising its constituency that the government's bottom-line would be a system of power sharing that would secure the interests of different communities – characterised at first racially, then as different ethnic nations and ultimately as distinct minorities. Attempting at first to provide an acceptable version of the failed 'consociationalism' of the 1983 constitution, the NP proposed a revolving presidency and a bicameral legislature, with the upper house – consisting of 'minority representatives' – having veto powers over all legislation. After being criticised for relying on a thinly disguised framework of racial vetoes, the NP modified its approach, demanding an extended period of transition and advocating what it described as 'constitutional rule in a participatory democracy' (NP 1991a). This proposal promoted a combination of individual rights, communal vetoes and consociationalism. Together, these elements were structured to produce a framework designed to insulate private interests and action from public power, with the net effect of allowing those with the resources and desire to pursue a system of privatised apartheid.

At the national level, the protection of individual rights was to be restricted to positively enforceable political and civil rights,[8] while legislative power was to be dominated by a regionally constituted upper house of a bicameral legislature. Significantly, regional representation, while analogised to the system of equal state representation in the US Senate, would in fact involve a second level of equivalence which would ensure 'minority' veto power. While regions would have equal representation, each region's delegates would be made up of an equal number of representatives from every political party achieving more than 5 per cent of electoral support in the region (NP 1991a:12). The effect of this scheme would be to ensure that parties representing significant racial or ethnic minorities would receive enough seats in the Senate to effectively veto any legislation threatening their interests accumulated under apartheid.

Relying on this particular construction of a bill of rights and federalism to protect individual and community interests at the national level, the focus of the NP proposal shifted to the local level, conceiving local government as a form of consociationalism based on property rights and presenting it as securing 'participatory democracy'. According to this proposal, votes for local government would be apportioned equally between a general voters roll and one restricted to property ownership within each voting district (NP 1991a:16–17). Local government would thus enable different racial groups consigned by apartheid to different geographic areas to retain control over their local arrangements.

While the NP focused its concern on local control, the IFP early on committed itself to the consolidation of its interests in one region of the country: KwaZulu-Natal. Although, at the beginning, the IFP demanded parity in the negotiations with the ANC and the NP government, it retreated to the advocacy of regional autonomy in an attempt to perpetuate its existing advantage as a homeland government into the post-apartheid era

(Ottaway 1993:64–72). Described as federalism, the form of regional autonomy advocated by the IFP and its allies in the Freedom Alliance[9] was closer in substance to the form of state autonomy contained in the US Articles of Confederation.[10] In terms of the IFP notion of federalism, the different regions would constitute autonomous states whose constitutions would dictate interpretation of the 'federal' constitution (IFP draft constitution 1993). In other words, any application of the federal constitution to issues within a region or to conflicts between regions would have to be consistent with the constitutions of the relevant regions (art. 92).

This conception of 'autonomous federalism' is further revealed in the IFP's proposed Constitution of the State of KwaZulu-Natal the draft of which was adopted by the KwaZulu Legislative Assembly in late 1992. Declaring the sovereignty of KwaZulu-Natal to be 'indivisible, inalienable and untransferable' (art. 3), this constitution would have required South African armed forces to obtain permission before entering KwaZulu-Natal (art. 67(b)), required South Africa to obtain consent before levying tax (art. 67(d)), created an 'autonomous' central bank (art. 81), and granted a KwaZulu-Natal Constitutional Court exclusive jurisdiction to decide whether South African laws were valid within the region (arts. 67(c) and 77).

At the federal level, the IFP proposed a government of limited powers in specific areas, including a common monetary system, national defence, nationality and immigration, foreign affairs, federal judicial organisation, intellectual property rights, and external commercial relations (IFP draft constitution 1993: art. 65(a)). The national legislature would also be empowered to pass general principles of legislation in the areas of environmental regulation, banking, interstate commerce and economic development as well as framework legislation to facilitate interstate negotiation over policies in these areas (art. 65(a)). Finally, any federal legislation would have to be passed by both houses of parliament, effectively giving the Senate – made up of four representatives elected from each state – a veto over national legislation (art. 70(a)).

The federal government would be further disempowered under the IFP's proposals by the creation of a series of independent commissions to control and regulate federal government activity. Apart from a number of internationally cognisable bodies, such as a judicial service commission (art. 75), a civil service commission (art. 83) and an electoral commission (art. 84), the proposal introduced the notion of independent policy-making institutions into the heart of traditionally government-controlled activities and called for the establishment of a series of such commissions, including a privatisation commission (art. 81), a regulatory relief commission (art. 85) – to repeal or amend burdensome, unnecessary or inadequate regulations – an environmental commission (art. 87), a consumer affairs commission (art. 88), and an economic development commission (art. 86). A significant feature of these commissions was that their membership was to be appointed from a variety of sources, including the president, federal parliament, and private bodies including the national chamber of commerce, consumer groups and representatives of industry (arts. 81(a), 85(a), 87(a) and 88(a)). This introduction of different factions into the heart of government was a unique aspect of the IFP proposal, which in the South African context would have worked to promote established interests whose racial character would, for some time, remain largely the product of apartheid's allocation of economic and social resources.

THE CHALLENGE OF REGIONALISM

In the process of negotiating the 1993 constitution, there were significant changes in the positions of the three major players as well as important continuities which became cobbled together in the interim constitution. Most fundamentally, the ANC's demand for a unitary state came to be interpreted to mean national sovereignty over the 1910 boundaries of South Africa, rather than meaning a central government with pre-emptive power over regional authorities. With this new emphasis, the issue of federalism/regionalism, rejected initially by the ANC because of its historic association in South Africa with the emasculation of governmental powers, became a central feature of the constitutional debate.

The adoption of the language of 'strong regionalism' by both the ANC and the NP government also reflected NP acceptance that the veto powers of the upper house of the legislature would be limited to regional matters and that its notion of political party-based consociationalism would be formally restricted to local government structures. Although the NP government accepted the demise of its specific proposals, many of the provisions of the 1993 constitution, and in particular its guarantee of a five-year 'government of national unity', satisfied many of the goals implicit in the apartheid government's earlier proposals.

Unlike the ANC and the NP, however, the IFP refused to concede its central claim to regional autonomy and, in its alliance with white pro-apartheid parties, threatened to disrupt the transition. Although factions of the IFP seemed ready to contest the elections for the KwaZulu-Natal regional government, party leader Chief Gatsha Buthelezi interpreted his party's poor showing in pre-election polls as cause to promote an even more autonomous position, encouraging and supporting King Goodwill Zwelethini in his demand for the restoration of the nineteenth century Zulu monarchy, with territorial claims beyond even the borders of present-day KwaZulu-Natal.

Although the protagonists of a federal solution advocated a national government of limited powers, the 1993 constitution reversed the traditional federal division of legislative powers by allocating enumerated powers to the provinces. This allocation of regional powers – according to a set of criteria incorporated into the Constitutional Principles and in those sections of the constitution dealing with the legislative powers of the provinces – was, however, rejected by the IFP on the grounds that the constitution failed to guarantee the autonomy of the provinces. Despite ANC protestations that the provincial powers guaranteed by the constitution could not be withdrawn, the IFP objected that these were only concurrent powers and that the national legislature could supersede local legislation through the establishment of a national legislative framework covering any subject matter. This tension led to an amendment to the 1993 constitution before it even came into force. The amendment granted provinces prevailing powers in enumerated areas of legislative authority: agriculture; gambling; cultural affairs; education at all levels except tertiary; environment; health; housing; language policy; local government; nature conservation; police; state media; public transport; regional planning and development; road traffic regulation; roads; tourism; trade and industrial promotion; traditional authorities; urban and rural development; and welfare services.

Although the provinces had the power to assign executive control over these matters to the national government if they lacked administrative resources to implement particular laws, the constitution provided that the provinces had executive authority over all matters over which they had legislative authority as well as matters assigned to the provinces in terms of the transitional clauses of the constitution or delegated to them by national legislation. The net effect of these provisions was continued tension between non-ANC provincial governments and the national government over the extent of regional autonomy and the exact definition of their relative powers.

THE ROLE OF THE NEW CONSTITUTIONAL COURT

It is in this context that three particular cases were litigated before the Constitutional Court in 1996, cases in which we may trace the role of the new court in addressing the challenge of regionalism in a post-apartheid South Africa. All three cases involved, among other issues, claims of autonomy or accusations of national infringement of autonomy by the province of KwaZulu-Natal where the IFP was declared the marginal winner of the regional vote in 1994. As such, they represent three moments in which the court was called upon to help shape the boundary between contending claims of constitutional authority to govern, unresolved by the negotiated settlement. While two of the cases directly implicated actions of the KwaZulu-Natal legislature and its attempts to assert authority within the province – in one case, over traditional leaders and, in the other, the constitution-making powers of the province – the first case involved a dispute over the National Education Policy Bill which was then before the National Assembly.[11]

Objections to the bill focused on the claim that it 'imposed national education policy on the provinces' and thereby 'encroached upon the autonomy of the provinces and their executive authority'. The IFP argued that the 'bill could have no application in KwaZulu-Natal because it [the province] was in a position to formulate and regulate its own policies' (*NEB* case, 1996: para. 8). While all parties accepted that education was defined as a concurrent legislative function under the interim constitution, the contending parties imagined that different consequences should flow from the determination that a subject matter is concurrently assigned to both provincial and national government.

KwaZulu-Natal and the IFP in particular assumed a form of pre-emption doctrine in which the National Assembly and national government would be precluded from acting in an area of concurrent jurisdiction so long as the province was capable of formulating and regulating its own policies. Rejecting this argument, the Constitutional Court avoided the notion of pre-emption altogether and, instead, argued that the 'legislative competences of the provinces and Parliament to make laws in respect of schedule 6 [concurrent] matters do not depend upon section 126(3)', which the court argued only comes into operation if it is necessary to resolve a conflict between inconsistent national and provincial laws (para. 16). The court's rejection of pre-emption is an interpretation of the constitution which enabled both national and provincial legislators to continue to promote and even legislate their own imagined solutions to issues within their concurrent jurisdiction without foreclosing on their particular options until there is an irreconcilable conflict.

Having avoided siding categorically with either national or provincial authority, the court argued that, even if a 'conflict is resolved in favour of either the provincial or national law the other is not invalidated', it is merely 'subordinated and to the extent of the conflict rendered inoperative' (para. 16). Supported by the comparative jurisprudence of Canada (para. 17) and Australia (para. 18), the court was able to make a distinction between 'laws that are inconsistent with each other and laws that are inconsistent with the Constitution' (para. 16), and thereby to argue that, 'even if the National Education Policy Bill deals with matters in respect of which provincial laws would have paramountcy, it could not for that reason alone be declared unconstitutional' (para. 20).

While the Constitutional Court's approach clearly aimed to reduce tensions inherent in the conflict between provincial and national governments, particularly in relation to the continuing violent tensions in

KwaZulu-Natal, it also took the opportunity to explicitly preclude an alternative interpretation. Focusing on argument before it which relied upon the US Supreme Court's decision in *New York* v. *United States*,[12] the court made the point that 'unlike their counterparts in the United States of America, the provinces in South Africa are not sovereign states' (para. 23). Furthermore, the court warned that 'decisions of the courts of the United States dealing with state rights are not a safe guide as to how our courts should address problems that may arise in relation to the rights of provinces under our Constitution' (para. 23). In effect, the court's approach was to begin to draw a boundary around the outer limits of provincial autonomy, while simultaneously allowing concurrent jurisdiction to provide a space in which different legislatures could continue to imagine and assert their own, at times contradictory, solutions to legislative problems within their jurisdiction.

The scope of such a definition of concurrent jurisdiction was immediately tested in a case challenging two bills before the KwaZulu-Natal provincial legislature, which purported in part to preclude national action affecting the payment of salaries to traditional authorities in KwaZulu-Natal.[13] In this case, brought by ANC members of the KwaZulu-Natal legislature, the objectors argued that the bills were unconstitutional, as they attempted to 'frustrate the implementation of the [national] Remuneration of Traditional Leaders Act', by preventing the Ingonyama (Zulu King) and traditional leaders 'from accepting remuneration and allowances which might become payable to them in terms of the national legislation'. Furthermore, the object of this provincial legislation 'was to create a relationship of subservience between them [traditional leaders] and the provincial government', an object outside the scope of the provinces' concurrent powers with respect to traditional authorities (*Amakhosi* case, 1996: para. 16).

Faced with intractable political conflict between the IFP and the ANC in KwaZulu-Natal, the court reasserted its duty to interpret legislation narrowly, so as to avoid constitutional conflicts, and upheld the legislative competence of the KwaZulu-Natal legislature and the constitutionality of the two bills. In effect, the court allowed the KwaZulu-Natal legislature to continue to imagine its own authority in this area, merely postponing clear questions of conflict between the national and provincial legislation to a later date. The outer limits of the court's tolerance for alternative constitutional visions was, however, reached in the third case, in which the court was asked to certify the Constitution of the Province of KwaZulu-Natal.[14]

Although the KwaZulu-Natal draft constitution had been unanimously adopted by the provincial legislature, the Constitutional Court held that there are 'fundamental respects in which the provincial Constitution is fatally flawed' (*KZN Constitution* case, 1996: para. 13) and therefore declined to certify it. The court considered these flaws under three headings. Two sets of problems were essentially procedural in nature and involved attempts by the KwaZulu-Natal legislature: (1) to avoid the court's determination of the text's inconsistency with the interim constitution (paras 36–38); or (2) to suspend the certification process itself until particular sections could be tested against the final constitution (paras 39–46). While the court rejected these devices as being in conflict with the certification process and attempting to circumvent the process, respectively, the most significant problem with the text was the KwaZulu-Natal legislature's usurpation of national powers.

Referring to the court's decision on the education bill (*NEB* case), in which it made a 'distinction between the history, structure and language of the United States Constitution which brought together several sovereign states . . . and that of our interim Constitution' (para. 14), the court held that parts of the proposed KwaZulu-Natal constitution appeared to have 'been passed by the KZN Legislature under a misapprehension that it enjoyed a relationship of co-supremacy with the national Legislature and even the Constitutional Assembly' (para. 15). Drawing a clear boundary around the permissible constitutional aspirations of the IFP in KwaZulu-Natal, the court rejected the draft text's attempt to both 'confer' legislative and executive authority upon the province (para. 32) and to 'recognize' the authority of the government and 'competence' of the national parliament in other respects (para. 34). While recognising the right of the IFP-dominated KwaZulu-Natal legislature to exercise its powers to draft a provincial constitution, even possibly including its own bill of rights, the court clearly rejected the attempt by the IFP to assert its vision of regional autonomy beyond the core meaning of the negotiated compromise represented by the 1993 constitution. Furthermore, the court clearly silenced the extreme option of provincial sovereignty, stating that the assertions of recognition were 'inconsistent with the interim constitution because KZN is not a sovereign state and it simply has no power or authority to grant constitutional "recognition" to what the national Government may or may not do' (para. 34). Even as its vision of regional autonomy became increasingly isolated, the IFP still imagined that it could be achieved within the parameters of the 1993 constitution. Its rejection by the Constitutional Court silenced this particular attempt but did not foreclose on the IFP's vision of greater regional autonomy.

Instead of suffering defeat, the IFP was able to take solace from the court's refusal, on the same day, to certify the draft of the final constitution, and in particular its decision that the draft final constitution had failed to grant provinces the degree of autonomy they were guaranteed in the constitutional principles.[15] However, when the 1996 constitution was finally certified by the Constitutional Court,[16] the IFP remained dissatisfied over the limited degree of provincial autonomy recognised. But, by then, as the governing party in KwaZulu-Natal, it was not about to exit the system. Instead, it joined the other opposition parties in saying that they would take the opportunity in the following year's legislative session to review the constitution, thus keeping their claims alive.[17]

CONSTITUTION MAKING AND THE RECOGNITION OF DIVERSITY

South Africa's democratic transition was premised on a two-stage process of constitution making. The first round, while buffeted by popular participation, was ultimately under the negotiating parties' control. In contrast, although the second round was formally constrained by a complex set of constitutional principles contained in the interim constitution (South Africa Constitution 1993, Fourth Schedule), it was driven by an elected Constitutional Assembly made up by a joint sitting of the National Assembly and the Senate of South Africa's first democratic parliament (s. 68).

The sections of the interim constitution providing for the creation of a final constitution clearly influenced the distribution of power in the Constitutional Assembly. While requiring that a new constitution be passed within two years from the first sitting of the National Assembly (s. 73(1)), chapter 5 of the interim constitution required that at least two-thirds of all members of the Constitutional Assembly vote for the new constitution (s. 73(2)).[18] In addition, sections of the final constitution dealing with the boundaries, powers and functions of the provinces had to be adopted by two-thirds of all members of the regionally constituted Senate, giving the provinces established under the interim constitution an important lever of influence in the Constitutional Assembly (s. 73(2)). However, once the negotiating parties reached a compromise requiring the Constitutional Court to certify that the final constitution was consistent with the constitutional principles (s. 71(2)), the different parties focused their attention on the content of the principles as a way of continuing their struggles for particular outcomes with respect to regional powers and racially or ethnically defined governance.

The constitutional principles contained an amalgam of broad democratic principles consistent with the new international post–cold war consensus on constitutionalism and a host of details specific to the needs of the negotiating parties. The most dramatic of these specific provisions were those requiring the recognition of the Zulu King and the provision of a Volkstaat Council, which were added by amendment shortly before the April 1994 elections as a way to include parts of the Freedom Alliance, particularly the IFP and the Afrikaaner right-wing led by former South Africa Defence Force head General Constant Viljoen. The inclusion of this plethora of constitutional principles not only enabled the elections to go forward and the democratic transition to proceed, but they also served to defer a range of substantive issues into the next phase of constitution making. Although individual principles were open to varying interpretations, the interaction of the different principles revived many of the conflicts their inclusion had been designed to lay to rest. A significant difference, however, was that these conflicts would henceforth be played out in a completely different arena.

Faith in the constitutional principles was at first vindicated when the Constitutional Court declared the text of the final constitution 'unconstitutional', despite its adoption after last-minute political compromises by 86 per cent of the democratically elected Constitutional Assembly. While the court's denial of certification was based to a large extent on the failure to, on balance, grant sufficient powers to the regions, the court was also careful to point out in its unanimous, unattributed opinion that, 'in general and in respect of the overwhelming majority of its provisions', the Constitutional Assembly had met the predetermined requirements of the constitutional principles. In effect, however, this was a very limited and circumscribed ruling, as the major political parties rejected any attempt to use the denial of certification as a tool to reopen debates. Instead, the Constitutional Assembly focused solely on the issues raised by the Constitutional Court.

While, in the second certification judgment, it recognised that the powers and functions of the provinces – the most contentious issue in the whole constitution-making process – remained in dispute between the parties, the court held in essence that the removal of the presumption of constitutional validity of bills passed by the National Council of Provinces (NCOP) had tipped the balance.[19] Thus, despite the recognition that provincial powers and functions in the Amended Text remained less than or inferior to those accorded to the provinces in terms of the interim constitution, this was not substantially so (SCJ: para. 204(e)), and therefore no longer a basis for denying certification.

THE FINAL CONSTITUTION'S REGIONALISM PROVISIONS

Although traditional notions of federalism assume the coming together of formerly sovereign entities and their retention of certain specified powers, South Africa's 1996 final constitution represents an increasingly common means of constitutionalising the relationship between different spatial jurisdictions within the nation-state. South Africa's constitutional regionalism is one in which the constituting act created a structure in which powers are allocated to different levels of government and includes a complex procedure for the resolution of conflicts over governance – between the respective legislative competencies, executive powers, and relations with other branches and levels of government. Unlike its German, Indian and Canadian forebears however, South Africa's constitution places less emphasis on geographic autonomy and more on the integration of geographic jurisdictions into separate functionally determined roles in the continuum of governance over specifically defined issues. While provision is made for some exclusive regional powers, these are by and large of minor significance, all important and contested issues being included in the category of concurrent competence.

Unlike prior South African constitutions, the 1996 constitution entrenches three distinct levels of government – national, provincial and local – and makes detailed provision for both their constitutional autonomy and their interaction. Unique in this regard is the inclusion of one specific chapter detailing the governmental structure of the country and laying down general principles of interaction between these different spheres of governance.[20] Most significant among these principles is the provision requiring organs of state involved in an intergovernmental dispute to make every reasonable effort to settle the dispute and to exhaust all other remedies before it approaches a court to resolve the dispute (s. 41(3)). Cooperative governance, in this sense, integrates the different geographic regions and discourages them from seeking early intervention from the courts; rather, they are forced into an ongoing interaction designed to produce interregional compromises.

While the basic structure of South Africa's constitutional regionalism is reflected in the division of functional areas of legislative power into areas of concurrent and exclusive legislative competence, specified in schedules 4 and 5 of the constitution, the substance of this constitutional design is contained in provisions: (1) requiring joint or collaborative decision making; (2) regulating inter-jurisdictional conflict; and (3) securing limited fiscal autonomy. First, the constitution provides for a second house of the national parliament – the NCOP – directly representing the provinces in the national legislative process through their provincial delegations, appointed by the legislatures and executives of each province (ss. 60–72). It then provides that most bills must go before the NCOP, although the nature of the latter's role in each bill's passage will depend on the subject matter involved (ss. 73–77). Constitutional amendment of the founding provisions (chap. 1), the bill of rights (chap. 2) or those sections dealing specifically with the provinces, the NCOP or provincial boundaries, powers, functions or institutions, all require the support of at least six of the nine provinces. Ordinary bills must also go before the NCOP but procedure for their passage within the NCOP will depend on whether the bill involves a matter assigned by the constitution to a particular procedure, is a matter of concurrent jurisdiction or is an ordinary bill not affecting the provinces.

Unless it is an ordinary bill not affecting the provinces and therefore may be passed by a mere majority of the individual delegates to the NCOP, the decision will be made on the basis of single votes cast on behalf of each of the provincial delegations. Furthermore, the constitution requires an Act of Parliament to provide a uniform procedure through which provincial legislatures confer authority on their delegations to cast votes on their behalf (s. 65(2)). Conflicts between the National Assembly and the NCOP over bills affecting the provinces are negotiated through a mediation committee consisting of nine members of the National Assembly and one from each of the nine provincial delegations in the NCOP. It is this elaborate system of structures and processes that creates a system of enforced engagement integrating provincial and national interests at the national level. The requirement that provincial legislatures mandate their NCOP delegations serves in this context to further integrate the legislative process, thus projecting provincial interests onto the national agenda while simultaneously requiring the regional bodies to debate nationally defined issues, both processes designed to limit provincial alienation.

Second, provision is made for the constitutional regulation of inter-jurisdictional conflict that may occur in the exercise of both legislative (ss. 146–150) and executive (ss. 100 and 139) powers. It is these provisions that effectively denote the limits of this new regionalism. In the case of executive authority, mirror provisions allow either the national or the provincial executives to directly intervene at the provincial and local level, respectively, if a province or local government cannot or does not fulfil an executive obligation in terms of legislation or the constitution (ss. 100 and 139). Although these provisions establish numerous safeguards against their potential abuse, they nonetheless pose an important limit to provincial and local autonomy. In the case of legislative authority, a whole section of the constitution deals specifically with the circumstances under which national legislation will prevail over provincial legislation in areas where the two levels of government enjoy concurrent authority. Significantly, however, the default position is that, unless the conflicting national legislation meets the criteria laid down in the constitution, it is the provincial legislation that will prevail (subsection 146(5)). While this seems to grant more authority to the provinces, in fact, the broad criteria establishing national authority over provincial competence, including where the national legislation provides for uniform national norms and standards, frameworks or policies (subsections 146(2) and (3)), means that provincial competence will provide a very thin shield against national legislative intrusion. It must be remembered, however, that the provinces will be significant participants in the production of such national legislation through the NCOP. Central authority is, however, further privileged by the inclusion of a provision establishing particular circumstances, including the need to maintain national security, economic unity or essential national standards, as the basis upon which national legislation may be passed, overriding even the exclusive subject matter competence secured for the provinces with respect to those areas defined in schedule 5 of the constitution (s. 44(2)).

The third important feature of South Africa's 'strong regionalism' is the constitutional protection of fiscal distributions to the provinces so that they might, to some extent, fulfil their constitutional mandates and provincial policies independent of the national government. Again, however, this mechanism is characterised by an emphasis on integration through the Financial and Fiscal Commission, an independent constitutionally created body which advises parliament and the provincial legislatures on, among other things, the constitutional mandate that parliament must provide for the equitable division of revenue among the national, provincial and local spheres of government (s. 214). But the national government is again privileged in that the taxing power of the regional and local governments is constitutionally constrained (ss. 228 and 229) and made dependent upon national legislation (s. 228(2)(b)), and, as in the case of executive authority, it has a carefully constrained power through the national treasury to directly cut off transfers of revenues to the provinces – at least for 120 days at a time (s. 216). The outcome is a system of mediating sources of authority which neither guarantee regional and local autonomy nor allow the national government to simply impose its will on these other spheres of government.

COOPERATIVE GOVERNMENT AND 'WEAK' REGIONALISM

In the end it is not surprising, given the anti-apartheid context, that South Africa's new constitution does not satisfy the federal aspirations of those parties whose demands were based on ethnic claims and aspirations. Yet it is notable that the new structure has a number of profoundly federal characteristics, particularly evident in the creation of the NCOP and the direct role given to provincial legislatures in the formulation of national legislation.

Despite the rhetoric of 'strong' regionalism, the new system of cooperative government precludes any significant regional autonomy and grants even less exclusive control to the provinces than did the interim constitution. The notion of 'cooperative government' is based, according to Professor Nicholas Haysom, legal adviser to former President Mandela and a member of the ANC Constitutional Committee, on a break with the nineteenth century approach to federalism which allocated 'areas of responsibility to one particular area of government only'. What the new South African approach does, argues Haysom, is to 'give the different areas of government the right to legislate on the same topic or area but only in respect of their appropriate responsibilities. Responsibility, in turn, is decided relative to appropriate interest, capacity and effective delivery but the apportionment of it is more complex than merely isolating an area of social life and parceling it out to a single sphere of government' (quoted in Bell 1997:72).

While the exact scope of regional power in this formulation remains unclear, it is evident that the Constitutional Court will have a very important role in mediating the continuing struggle over the exercise of power between the different levels of government. Although this has already begun, as indicated in my discussion of the 1996 cases involving KwaZulu-Natal, the effects of these conflicts and the general lack of administrative capacity in many of the newly formed provinces have already been brought to the attention of the central government, which is increasingly concerned about the inability of the provinces to perform their functions.[21]

CONCLUSION

Dharam and Yash Ghai, in an analysis of constitutional frameworks designed to tackle problems of ethnicity in South and South-East Asia, identified three distinct constitutional approaches (Ghai and Ghai 1992:79; Ghai 1994:1–16). The first approach assumes that ethnic problems are transitional and that the constitution should not inhibit the necessary process of national integration. The second approach assumes that ethnic minorities need more than individual or even group protection against arbitrary discrimination. This approach requires ethnic minorities to have a share in power that will enable each group to participate significantly in decision making. The third option is an intermediate position in which specific but limited provision is made to address the concerns of particular communities.

South Africa's democratic transition represents a context in which these different alternatives often represented the preferences of different political claimants and have to different degrees been incorporated into either the transitional constitutional arrangements,[22] or are reflected in the final 1996 constitution. While the adoption of proportional representation and strong language and cultural rights in the constitution is consistent with both the nation-building project of the ANC and the aspirations of different ethnic minorities, it is the incorporation of specific mechanisms – such as the Commission for the Promotion and Protection of the Rights of Cultural, Religious and Linguistic Communities, as well as the special role guaranteed to 'traditional leaders' – which offer particular ethnic claims some recognition in the final constitution.

This recognition has not, however, been carried over into the struggle over regional autonomy and federalism.

Although the constitutional mandate of cooperative government may indeed represent an innovative response to the issues of decentralisation and the devolution of power, it neither recognises claims for regional autonomy nor does it give any space for the promotion of ethnic claims to self-governance. Indeed, the 1996 constitution responds to ethnic claims through a combination of individual rights and indirect political recognition through the functioning of proportional representation. Most explicitly, there was the adoption of a limited number of group mechanisms to deal with those ethnic claims which continued to threaten the political order. However, given the history of ethnic claims and the rejection of ethnic balkanisation imposed by the apartheid regime, the rejection of ethnic demands for more explicit spatial autonomy and the exclusion of the f-word, or federalism, is not surprising.

More interesting, however, is the impact that the discourse on federalism and regional autonomy had on the reconstruction of the South African polity. Although there is no way of knowing now just how centralist an unmodified version of the ANC's original vision would have been in practice, it is safe to assume, given the attempts by the national leadership to intervene in regional and local ANC party politics since 1994, that there would have been much less space for regional autonomy. For the IFP and the NP, on the other hand, the legitimisation of a discourse of autonomy, if not federalism, has allowed them to continue to assert their own visions for the two provinces they control: KwaZulu-Natal and Western Cape, respectively. What is striking is how the failure of complete autonomy or federalism has in fact forced these parties to reshape their own visions of regional autonomy. While any analysis of these changes will have to take into consideration the post-apartheid transformation of both these parties, including the impact that the findings of the Truth and Reconciliation Commission is having on their support and internal politics, there is already evidence of a significant dissipation of the demands for autonomy that marked the democratic transition. Briefly, the IFP in KwaZulu-Natal has moved from a position of near-total antagonism to the ANC to one in which portions of the party have even been prepared to discuss merger with the ANC. The NP, on the other hand, is engulfed by its own internal ethnic divisions as it attempts to integrate the Coloured support it relied upon to win control of the Western Cape.

The fate of regional autonomy and federalism in South Africa may also be considered from the perspective of governance since 1994. While both the Western Cape and Gauteng seem to have established fairly effective regional polities, the other seven regional governments have been plagued by different degrees of conflict and lack of competence stemming from the severe lack of capacity at the local and regional level.

This brief history indicates that the adoption of a pure federal system with the degrees of autonomy initially demanded by the IFP and the NP would have most likely floundered. While governance continues to be reworked and even strengthened in South Africa, this process has been very dependent upon a very close interaction between the national ministries and the regional and local governments. The federal elements contained in the 1996 constitution, and especially the important role given to provincial legislatures in the national legislative process through the NCOP, thus represent the beginning of a new South African regionalism rather than the embrace of federalism as a means to deal with a long history of colonial and ethnic conflict.

NOTES

1 An important early example of this was Olive Schreiner and W.P. Schreiner's advocacy of federalism at the time of Union, in which they were attempting to protect the non-racial franchise in the Cape colony (First and Scott 1980:256–64).

2 See also A Review of the Present Mutual Relations of the British South Africa Colonies, 1907, Cd. 3564.

3 The elected provincial councils were in fact abolished with very little protest in the 1980s.

4 For an early critique of the policy of separate development and the idea of bantustan development, see Mbeki (1984:73–94).

5 *Weekly Mail & Guardian*, 1–7 October 1993, p. 9, col. 4.

6 *New York Times*, 25 October 1993, p. 1, col. 3.

7 Inkatha Freedom Party, The Constitution of the Federal Republic of South Africa (draft, 18 June 1993), reprinted in Blaustein (1971).

8 Government's Proposals on a Charter of Fundamental Rights (2 February 1993).

9 The Conservative Party (a member of the Freedom Alliance) submitted its 'Constitutional Proposals of the Conservative Party for a Peaceful South Africa' to the Technical Committee on Constitutional Issues of the Multi-Party Negotiating Process, arguing for a confederation, with relations between the states negotiated by treaty and not by an overarching constitution (Amato 1994:62–3, 84–98).

10 Act of Confederation of the United States of America, 15 November 1777 (see Jensen 1976:86–94).

11 *Ex Parte Speaker of the National Assembly: In Re Dispute Concerning the Constitutionality of Certain Provisions of the National Education Policy Bill 83 of 1995*, 1996 (3) SA 289 (CC) [hereinafter *NEB* case].

12 505 US144 (1992).

13 *Ex Parte Speaker of the KwaZulu-Natal Provincial Legislature: In Re KwaZulu-Natal Amakhosi and Iziphakanyiswa Amendment Bill of 1995; Ex Parte Speaker of the KwaZulu-Natal Provincial Legislature: In Re Payment of Salaries, Allowances and Other Privileges to the Ingonyama Bill of 1995*, 1996 (4) SA 653 (CC) [hereinafter *Amakhosi* case].

14 *Ex Parte Speaker of the KwaZulu-Natal Provincial Legislature: In Re Certification of the Constitution of the Province of KwaZulu-Natal, 1996,* 1996 (4) SA 1098 (CC) [hereinafter *KZN Constitution* case].
15 See *Ex Parte Chairperson of the Constitutional Assembly: In Re Certification of the Constitution of the Republic of South Africa, 1996,* 1996 (4) SA 744 (CC).
16 See *Ex Parte Chairperson of the Constitutional Assembly: In Re Certification of the Amended Text of the Constitution of the Republic of South Africa, 1996,* 1997 (2) SA 97 (CC).
17 *Mail and Guardian,* 11 November 1996.
18 The acceptance of a two-thirds threshold involved an important shift in position for the National Party which had attempted to require a seventy-five percent majority to pass a new constitution within the constitution-making body. This demand led to the collapse of negotiations within the Codesa framework (Friedman 1993b: 31).
19 *Ex Parte Chairperson of the Constitutional Assembly: In Re Certification of the Amended Text of the Constitution of the Republic of South Africa, 1996,* 1997 (2) SA 97 (CC) at paras 153–157 [hereinafter Second Certification Judgment (SCJ)].
20 See Chapter 3: Cooperative Governance, Constitution of the Republic of South Africa, Act 108 of 1996 [hereinafter all references to constitutional sections are to the 1996 constitution].
21 See Ministry for the Public Service and Administration (1997).
22 Such as the provisions for 'consociational' local government until 1999.

REFERENCES

Amato, Rob 1994. *Understanding the New Constitution.* Cape Town: Struik.
ANC (African National Congress) 1988. 'Constitutional guidelines for a democratic South Africa', reprinted in *Hastings International and Comparative Law Review* 12:322.
—— 1993. *A Bill of Rights for a New South Africa.* February.
—— 1994. *The Reconstruction and Development Programme.* Johannesburg: ANC.
Basson, D. and H. Viljoen 1991 [1988]. *South African Constitutional Law.* Cape Town: Juta.
Bell, Paul 1997. *The Making of the Constitution: The Story of South Africa's Constitutional Assembly, March 1994 to December 1996.* Cape Town: Churchill Murray, for the Constitutional Assembly.
Blaustein, A.P. and G.H. Flanz (eds) 1971. *Constitutions of the Countries of the World.* Dobbs Ferry, NY: Oceania Publications.
Constitution of the Republic of South Africa, 1993.
Constitution of the Republic of South Africa, 1996.
Constitution of the State of KwaZulu-Natal, 1 December 1992.
Davenport, T.R.H. 1977. *South Africa: A Modern History.* London: Macmillan.
Ellmann, S. 1994. 'The new South African constitution and ethnic division', *Columbia Human Rights Law Review* 26:5.
First, Ruth and Ann Scott 1980. *Olive Schreiner: A Biography.* New York: Schocken.
Friedman, S. 1993a. 'The nature of the divide', in S. Friedman and R. Humphries (eds) *Federalism and Its Foes.* Johannesburg: Centre for Policy Studies, 9–26.

—— (ed.) 1993b. *The Long Journey: South Africa's Quest for a Negotiated Settlement.* Braamfontein: Ravan Press.

Ghai, D. and Y. Ghai 1992. 'Ethnicity, development and democracy', *Peace and Conflict Issues after the Cold War.* UNESCO.

Ghai, Y. 1994. 'Ethnicity and governance in Asia: a report to the Ford Foundation' (draft). Also available as 'Ethnicity and governance in Asia' in *The Thatched Patio* 7(1):1–16.

Government's Proposals on a Charter of Fundamental Rights, 2 February 1993.

Horowitz, Donald L. 1991. *A Democratic South Africa?* Berkeley: University of California Press.

Inkatha Freedom Party (IFP) 1993. 'The Constitution of the Federal Republic of South Africa (draft), 18 June 1993'; reprinted in A.P. Blaustein, South African Supplement 93–6 (October 1993) to Blaustein and Flanz (eds) 1971.

Jensen, Merrill (ed.) 1976. *The Documentary History of the Ratification of the Constitution: Volume I: Constitutional Documents and Records, 1776–1787.* Madison: State Historical Society of Wisconsin.

Klug, H. 1990. 'Self-determination and the struggle against apartheid', *Wisconsin International Law Journal* 8(251):294–5.

Lorch, Donatella 1994. 'Arms ban is defied at rally by Zulu Party', *New York Times*, 6 April.

Mare, Gerhard 1992. *Brothers Born of Warrior Blood: Politics and Ethnicity in South Africa.* Johannesburg: Ravan Press.

Mbeki, G. 1984. *South Africa: The Peasants' Revolt.* 2nd edn. London: International Defence and Aid Fund for South Africa.

Ministry for the Public Service and Administration 1997. *The Provincial Review Report.* August.

Mzala 1988. *Gatsha Buthelezi: Chief with a Double Agenda.* London: Zed Books.

National Party 1991a. *Constitutional Rule in a Participatory Democracy: The National Party's Framework for a New Democratic South Africa.* Pretoria: National Party.

—— 1991b. 'Constitutional plan', *Nationalist* 11(9), November.

Ottaway, M. 1993. *South Africa: The Struggle for a New Order.* Washington DC: Brookings Institution.

Richardson, Henry J. 1978. 'Self-determination, international law and the South African Bantustan Policy', *Columbia Journal of Transnational Law* 17:185.

Roux, Edward 1964. *Time Longer than Rope: A History of the Black Man's Struggle for Freedom in South Africa.* Madison: University of Wisconsin Press.

Thompson, L. 1975. 'The compromise of union', in M. Wilson and L. Thompson (eds) *The Oxford History of South Africa. Vol. II: South Africa to 1870.* Oxford: Clarendon Press.

Welsh, David 1993. 'Regional institutions: a South African perspective', in Bertus de Villiers and Jabu Sindane (eds) *Regionalism: Problems and Prospects.* Pretoria: Human Sciences Research Council, 140–53.

—— 1994. 'Federalism and the divided society: a South African perspective', in Bertus de Villiers (ed.) *Evaluating Federal Systems.* Cape Town: Juta.

CHAPTER 6

AUTONOMOUS COMMUNITIES AND THE ETHNIC SETTLEMENT IN SPAIN

DANIELE CONVERSI

Of many recent experiments in ethnic conflict management, Spain's has been one of the most successful. This success is due in part to the specific pattern of democratisation experienced by Spain since the late 1970s, finally enshrined in the new democratic constitution (December 1978).

Spanish nationalism can be understood as a response to peripheral nationalisms, at least as much as peripheral nationalism is a response to Spanish nationalism. Throughout this century, the bogey of 'separatism' has been used by Madrid elites to buttress centralism against any concessions to regionalism. In turn, intolerance of regional aspirations bred peripheral nationalism. However, the tension has slowly given shape to an interesting synthesis which attempts to bridge the gap between the two.

Since the nineteenth century, two forms of Spanish nationalism have competed: one espoused by Madrid's elites, the other by elites in Barcelona. One is rigidly centralist, the other concerned with carving out a space of autonomy for other regions. Basque nationalism, on the other hand, with its separatist program, simply opted out of the project of reconstructing Spain. I have argued elsewhere that the state played a major role in shaping both types of nationalism, although the internal dynamics of political elites were also important (Conversi 1997).

THE HISTORICAL BACKGROUND

The objective of a homogeneous Spain has competed with a pluralist vision of Spanishness since the beginning of the nineteenth century and both are part of a centuries-long political practice in which centralising attempts clashed with regional resistance. They engendered contrasting

122

conceptions of the term 'nation', which in turn changed its meaning between the time of the first Spanish constitutions (1812 and 1837, when the nation was already defined as sovereign) and the present day (Arbos 1986).

In the second part of that century, two visions of nationhood crystallised: the unitarian organicism of most Spanish elites, and the republican federalist tradition which found its greatest support in Catalonia. The main ideologue of the second group, Francisco Pi y Margall (1824–1901), used the term *nacionalidades* ('nationalities') to distinguish the historical regions with a sense of nationhood and common descent from the politically dominant Spanish 'nation' (Pi 1979). Pi translated *Du principe fédératif* (Proudhon 1921) and other works of Pierre Joseph Proudhon (1809–65), becoming moreover one of the inspirations for Barcelona's anarchism. He became the president (February 1873) of the First Spanish Republic, when federalism merged with local particularism degenerating into cantonalism, as ever smaller towns chaotically declared their 'independence' (Hennessy 1962). He defined the federation as

> a system by which different human groups join and submit [power] to the entirety of the members of their own species for their common goals, without losing their autonomy in what is unique to them . . . It establishes unity without destroying variety and it might succeed in reuniting the whole of mankind without altering the character of nations, provinces and peoples, or threatening their independence. (Pi 1979:93–4)

Despite the decline of republican federalism, a strong federalist element persisted in Catalonia. Catalan nationalism was first formulated by a disciple of Pi y Margall, Valenti' Almirall (1841–1904), and later fully articulated by Enric Prat de la Riba (1870–1917) who subsequently became president of a newly created inter-provincial government, the *Mancomunitat* (1914–17) (Conversi 1997:30–2). The dominant trend, particularly under the moderate bourgeois leadership of the millionaire Francesc Cambó (1876–1947), remained a Spain-wide project to reconstruct the country from the vantage point of its historical regions. Catalonia's first autonomy statute was approved during the Second Spanish Republic (1931–39) (Roig 1978), an interlude abruptly ended by the Francoist victory in the civil war (1936–39).

A radically different movement emerged in the Basque Country (Euskadi), where Sabino de Arana y Goiri (1865–1903) created a more exclusivist form of nationalism, blending neo-traditionalism, clericalism, racialism, and linguistic nationalism (Conversi 1993:189–200; Conversi 1997). Arana was not influenced by the federal tradition; rather, his political platform can be seen as a direct response to, and in dialectic antagonism with, the policies of the Spanish state. Basque nationalism was born largely as a reaction against the abolition of traditional provincial privileges (*fueros*) and the process of increasing centralisation following the Basque defeat in the Second Carlist War (1872–76). This anti-centralist reaction merged with an anti-modernist and anti-urban trend which was in turn an answer to the misery and uprooting caused by rapid industrialisation (de la Granja 1994).

In both cases, nationalist formulations responded to the behaviour of state elites. Whenever the state reacted tolerantly towards nationalist aspirations, peripheral demands were softened. In contrast, whenever the state increased its repression against the most salient aspects of regional specificity, the movements grew more radical.

The idea of a strong homogenised state was a recurring fetish for Madrid's conservative elites and was drastically implemented with the imposition of a single language, Castilian (Spanish), through a centralised education system. A Jacobin prerequisite for rule and order was that the language of the empire (*idioma del imperio*) be totally congruent with culture, state and territory.

In 1959, a group of Catholic technocrats inaugurated a stabilisation plan, involving the introduction of a market economy. In 1963, the *milagro económico* (economic miracle) began and Spain's growth rate outpaced all developed economies, except Japan. A minimum of free expression was needed to encourage the influx of capital required for Franco's grandiose development plans. But all possible interstices were exploited by the Catalan resistance, and at least since 1945 a linguistic renaissance began in cloistered, reclusive circles, gaining momentum and gradually expanding its sphere of action. Its unexpected vigour supplied common ground for an ideologically variegated democratic opposition in the region.

In contrast, in the Basque Country (Euskadi), a group of radical youth formally founded ETA (*Euskadi 'ta Askatasuna*) in 1959, the very year in which Franco decided to put an end to Spain's 'splendid isolation'. Because of the lack of freedom of expression, ETA slowly evolved from an intellectual cultural elite into an organisation fully dedicated to armed struggle.

By the early 1970s, Spain had become a crucible for ethnic mobilisation unparalleled in Europe. When General Francisco Franco died on 20 November 1975, nationalist mobilisations were increasing so rapidly that the country's territorial integrity seemed to be seriously at risk. On 11 September 1977, over one million people marched in the streets of Barcelona and other Catalan towns demanding 'freedom, amnesty and a statute of autonomy'. On 4 December, similar demonstrations occurred throughout Andalusia when nearly a million marched demanding Andalusian autonomy. New regional challenges surfaced in Galicia, Asturias and Aragon. In the Basque Country, ETA stepped up its attacks on Spanish military and paramilitary targets to unprecedented levels and, in the final part of the decade, almost 100 people were killed annually in ETA-related violence (Clark 1990). At the same time, the army and the old Francoist cadres confined to their 'bunkers' were ready to strike at the earliest opportunity to re-establish their authority; the term 'bunker' was often used in Spain to cover 'the extreme right committed to fighting democracy from the rubble of Francoism' (Preston 1986:232).

THE 1978 CONSTITUTION

As with the demise of most dictatorial regimes, the democratisation process in Spain was tightly bound up with the accommodation of minority aspirations (Heywood 1995). At the same time, the prospect of democracy provided the first real possibility for free expression of nationalist feelings submerged for decades.[1]

The constitutional process began on 15 June 1977, the date of the first democratic elections in post-Franco Spain, and ended with the approval of the constitution, which was passed by the *Cortes Generales* in a plenary meeting of the Congress of Deputies and the Senate (31 October 1978). It was ratified by referendum (7 December) and finally sanctioned by the King before the *Cortes* on 27 December (Esteban 1989). Although the elections were not specifically designed to generate a constitutional agenda, most elected MPs (*diputados*) promptly adopted this objective (Peces-Barba 1988). On 26 July a 36-member Constitutional Affairs Commission was set up which, in turn, appointed a seven-member working party with the specific task of drafting the constitution (Tamames 1985). This was only thirteen days after the establishment of the *Cámara Baja* (Congress of Deputies or lower house) and the *Cámara Alta* (Senate or upper house) – from 1939 to 1977, the *Cortes* had comprised a one-chamber legislature. The main reason for this speed was pressure from the press, academia and most political parties after Franco's death (Gunther et al. 1986:34–6). Indeed, the process really began a few hours after the installation of the *Cortes Generales*; at the opening ceremony, King Juan Carlos announced: 'The Crown – interpreting the Cortes' aspirations – desires a Constitution which grants space to the individualities of our people and guarantees their historical and current rights' (see Attard 1983).

Without propounding a rigid normative approach to the national question, the 1978 constitution embodies a difficult balance between two historical elements of Spanish history: the federalist and the centralist. It took bits and pieces from the peripheral pluralist vision (as particularly developed in Catalonia), while maintaining elements of the older pattern of a strongly united sense of Spanishness. While some forms of organic essentialism are maintained, the ideal of homogeneity is altogether discarded. Its place is filled by a new appreciation for regional differences, together with a supra-ethnic unitary symbol, the monarchy. Regional differences are seen as enriching the national texture – rather than threatening it, as feared by the older Francoist cadres. This malleable Janus-faced approach is particularly evident in article 2 of the *Titulo Preliminar* (Introductory Section), which reads: 'The Constitution is based on the indivisible unity of the Spanish Nation, common and indivisible fatherland (*patria*) of all Spaniards. It acknowledges and guarantees the right to autonomy of the nationalities and regions which form it and the solidarity among them.'

Any possible fully federalist reading of the constitution is pre-empted at the outset by the stress on 'unity' in this article. The most important point is its acknowledgement of the existence of other 'nationalities' (*nacionalidades*) within a united and indivisible Spanish 'nation' (*nacion*). But, given the centralist legacy discussed above, how easy was it to reach an agreement over such a crucial issue? Was not there a strong opposition from both poles of the political spectrum? Indeed, recognition of the term 'nationalities' was not achieved easily (Solé 1985:95ff). The Right, dragging with it a great part of other political forces, tried vigorously to sabotage any mention of the word '*nacionalidades*'. However, both the Catalan nationalists and the communists firmly objected to its being dropped. The constitution's gestation lasted for sixteen months, during which the draft passed through several committees and was subject to over a thousand amendment proposals. Whereas compromise was more easily achieved over most of the 169 articles, 'a large part of the amendments presented to the draft (*anteproyecto*) were directed against Article 2'. The concept of 'nationalities' became the greatest stumbling-block. After lengthy discussion, the term was retained, but not before the article was thoroughly modified in order to stress the unitarian and indivisible character of Spain. Jordi Solé i Tura, one of the seven 'framers' of the constitution, recalls that art. 2 'is a veritable synthesis of all the contradictions looming during the constitution-making process . . . It is an authentic point of encounter between different conceptions of the Spanish nation . . . In it, two great notions of Spain merge' (Solé 1985:100–1).

Aside from heartland 'Castile' (often identified by peripheral nationalists as Spain *tout court*), three culturally and nationally based historical regions are usually identified within Spain: Catalonia, Euskadi (Basque Country) and Galicia (with the arguable addition of Andalusia). These are never explicitly mentioned in the constitution, leaving scope for subsequent interpretations as to the criteria to determine whether a particular region qualifies for autonomy. The obvious device was to extend decentralisation to most other regions, thereby diminishing, in a relative sense, the potential impact of Basque and Catalan autonomy.

Article 145 provides that 'no federation between Autonomous Communities will be permitted under any circumstances', an attempt to curb unifying trends among the regions, which were a real possibility in some potentially 'irredentist' areas. Pan-Catalanism spoke in the name of Valencia and the Balearic Islands, while in Euskadi the question of an '*irredenta*' Navarre contributed to the fuelling of nationalist fire (Blinkhorn 1974). Present-day peripheral nationalists still complain that the creation of many regions was an attempt to break down 'national unity' by gerrymandering. Yet the process has succeeded in softening the overall impact of radical nationalism. Once the constitutional process was accomplished, seventeen 'autonomous communities' (*Comunidades Autonomas*) emerged on the official map, some of which were entirely new creations.[2]

Among the fundamental rights solemnly proclaimed by the Spanish nation, there is the need to 'protect all the Spaniards and peoples of Spain in the exercise of their human rights, their cultures, traditions, languages and institutions' (preamble). The nation is openly multilingual and the protection of regional languages is explicit. Conferring official legitimacy on the regionalisation process, art. 3 runs:

> Castilian is the official language of the State. All Spaniards have the duty to know it and the right to use it. The other Spanish languages will also be official in their respective Autonomous Communities according to their own Statutes. The richness of the distinct linguistic modalities of Spain represents a patrimony which will be the object of special respect and protection.

Linguistic pluralism is also emphasised in art. 20 (para. 3), related to parliamentary control of the media: 'The law shall regulate the organisation and parliamentary control of the means of social communication owned by the State or any public entity and shall guarantee access to those means by significant social and political groups, respecting the pluralism of society and the various languages of Spain.' Thus is eliminated an important parameter of traditional Spanish centralism: the idea that there should be a congruence between nation, state and language – in other words, that a state should have only one language – lest its unity be threatened.

The term 'nation' (*nacion*) and its adjective 'national' (*nacional*) are applied exclusively to Spain as a whole.[3] But there is obviously some confusion with the term 'Spanish nationality' (*nacionalidad espanola*) which means, in the singular, 'citizenship', while in the plural it is supposed to refer to regions and nationalities (see art. 2 quoted above – *nacionalidades y regiones*). Article 11 provides:

> (1) Spanish nationality [*nacionalidad*] is acquired, preserved, and lost in accordance with provisions established by law.
> (2) No one of Spanish birth may be deprived of his nationality.

Through the concept of popular sovereignty, the Spanish nation is seen as the inherent subject of the constitutional process. The very first words of the preamble read: 'The Spanish Nation, desiring to establish justice, liberty, and security, and to promote the well-being of all its members, in the exercise of its sovereignty proclaims its will . . .' In art. 1 of the *Titulo Preliminar*, Spain is again seen as the subject and protagonist of the popular will:

> (1) Spain constitutes itself into a social and democratic state of law which advocates liberty, justice, equality, and political pluralism as the superior values of its legal order.
>
> (2) National sovereignty resides with the Spanish people, from whom all the powers of the state derive.

As generally established in the *Titulo Preliminar*, Spain is not a federal but a unitary state. However, its open character allows for a wide range of possible developments in the direction of regional autonomy, which may ultimately result in the emergence of a federal system. This openness is assured by the fact that the constitution can be interpreted in different ways, at least in matters related to the division of power between the central state and the regions. Openness also means that the functioning of the present system depends almost entirely on the political will of the party in office. In particular, the Senate does not function as a house of equal regional representation, as is usual with federations (Guibernau 1995:239–56). Salvador Giner and Luís Moreno (1990) identify another unfederal feature of the Spanish constitution: the reconfirmed, even heightened, role of the provinces (*provincias*) as intermediate institutions between the autonomous communities and the city councils. Solé i Tura (1985:103) argues that 'the main political defeat for the supporters of the autonomies[4] was the constitutional recognition of the continuity of the provinces'.

There are at least three problems associated with this survival of nineteenth century provincial institutions (*Diputacions*).[5] First, they add to Spain's already heavy bureaucratic burden by often unnecessarily replicating functions carried out by the regional governments or municipal institutions.[6] Secondly, some of the autonomous communities have only one province (Asturias, Balearic Islands, Cantabria, La Rioja, Madrid, Murcia, and Navarre) and these communities would be advantaged in comparison to multi-provincial communities, for instance in political representation and in the distribution of public funds. Moreover, some of the latter are new creations.[7] Hence, they have often been viewed as the product of centralist gerrymandering. Finally, the majority of senators are elected from the provinces (which have remained the usual electoral constituency also for the deputies). This is despite the fact that art.

69 defines the Senate as 'the chamber of territorial representation' which was originally meant to represent the interests of the autonomous communities.

These limitations aside, the constitution starts as a defence of Spain's unity, even to the point of reproducing some older centralist tenets, but it de facto grants self-government to the autonomous communities and, in particular, pays full respect to regional cultures. In this way, it opens the door to the possibility of federal arrangements, even though it remains *au fond* unitarist.

Without this compromise, the conflict between opposite nationalist visions would inevitably have escalated. Such escalation or even deadlock might have led to one of two alternative outcomes: the revocation of basic democratic freedoms, or the outright disintegration of the Spanish state. The timing of the constitutional change, the favourable international conditions and, finally, the will and ability of national elites to negotiate a wide gamut of settlements rendered this nightmare scenario unlikely.

THE POST-CONSTITUTIONAL DEVOLUTION PROCESS

The Spanish constitution can hardly be understood without considering the decisive role played by Catalan and Basque nationalism in the debates preceding its approval (Conversi 1997). The experience of regional autonomy enjoyed by Catalonia under the Republic (1931–38) was often taken as a point of departure for elaborating contemporary concepts of regional autonomy. 'The Catalan example proved to be the only one of negotiation over the transfer of powers. Since the Catalan regime was the first to be developed, its powers were subject to more bargaining. Subsequent regional entities, such as the Basque General Council, would have to follow the pattern established by the Catalan Generalitat' (Clark 1979:349). But, for the Basque nationalists, the prewar model lacked many guarantees and thus needed to be deepened and expanded (Gonzalez 1974).

In the referendum of December 1978, 87.8 per cent of those who voted throughout Spain endorsed the constitution – with the notable exception of Euskadi. Nearly all Basque nationalist forces opposed it, while the moderate PNV (Basque Nationalist Party, which had also refrained from taking a stand in the parliamentary vote) invited its supporters to abstain (see Hills 1980; Tamayo 1988). The reasons for the boycott related mostly to perceived ambiguities about Basque local rights. The abstention rate reached 56 per cent in the two most nationalist provinces: Guipuzcoa and Bizkaia (Vizcaya). This shows how little legitimacy the Spanish state had in Euskadi, a situation which provided fertile ground for the continuation and spread of violence.[8]

129

The next important step was to transform the constitution's regionalist ideal into practice by creating the instruments of regional self-government. With its robust tradition of autonomy preceding the civil war, Catalonia was obviously an ideal candidate to be granted this honour first. The Statute of Autonomy of Catalonia (*Estatut*) was approved in 1979 after a popular referendum in which 61 per cent of those eligible voted, of whom 88 per cent supported the statute. Catalonia achieved an autonomous government (the *Generalitat*) and its own parliament. The statute's charter declared Catalan as Catalonia's own language (*llengua propria*), although it had to share the status of 'official language' (*llengua official*) with Castilian (Generalitat 1979).

A popular referendum also ratified the approval of the Basque Autonomy Statute in 1979, with 61 per cent voting and 89 per cent in favour (Ayestarán 1979). Jesús María de Leizaola (1896–1980), president of the Basque parliament in exile, returned from France, ending the 43-year-old 'government in exile'. In April 1980, Carlos Garaikoetxea, leader of the PNV, became the first post-war *lehendakari* (head of the Basque government).[9]

In short, Spain was transformed from a highly centralised bureaucracy into a quasi-federal system, which includes the possibility of evolving towards a fully-fledged federal structure. Political commentators as well as nationalists avoid calling the present system a 'federation', since there is much ambiguity in regard to the powers attributed to the regions – which, however, have the possibility to negotiate them with Madrid. Also, the constitution's heavy emphasis on the idea of Spain's indivisibility and quasi-organic unity are not typical federalist features.

Irrespective of their relative artificiality or historical depth, all of the autonomous communities embarked on a process of boundary building, which included the invention of symbols as well as the rediscovery and rewriting of regional cultures, through the establishment of major projects of cultural compilation. Since 1978, the autonomous communities system has inspired the formation of new regional parties, often compelling state-level parties to adapt locally by at least regionalising their names. It has also generated a proliferation of local research in history, anthropology, economy, social science and culture in general. Once regions such as Cantabria and La Rioja had been created, their institutions activated a plethora of endeavours in many aspects of regional culture. The quintessence of these efforts was collected in vast compendia of local knowledge, comprehensive reference works, and book series.

Municipal and regional historians have been most active in this enterprise. In some regions, grassroots philologists have immersed themselves in a quest for archaic lexicons, revitalising lost languages as well as inventing new ones. Among the latter, the creation of a 'Cantabrian language', supposedly spoken in the region before Castilianisation, has not gained popular acclaim. Attempts to revive the *fabla aragonesa*, still spoken in a few Aragonese Pyrenean valleys, have met with mixed success. More successful has been the case of Asturian (nicknamed *bable*), spoken by fewer than 300,000 people and made co-official in the 'Principate' of Asturias (*Principau d'Asturies*).

Where language is not the distinctive regional element, other aspects of local culture have gained various degrees of institutional support. Yet the revival has often been spontaneous and local artists have had to endure dire economic conditions in order to survive. For instance, while the Andalusian government has promoted theatre, literature and the now international art of flamenco, most of the *nuevo flamenco* (new flamenco) scene has emerged spontaneously in Gypsy communities beyond the reach of institutional support.

In short, all regions have engaged in a process of cultural revival and community building, encouraged by the very existence of regional governments. Yet regions, as opposed to nationalities, still have difficulties in imagining themselves as cohesive and distinguishable communities – while Basque, Catalan and Galician senses of separate identity remain incontrovertible.[10]

For some people, however, the process of devolution went too far. Provoked by the rapid spread of democratisation and regional autonomy, as well as by ETA assassinations, the most conservative elements in the military tried to block the entire process. On 23 February 1981, a plenary session of the Spanish parliament was interrupted by a group of Civil Guards, led by Colonel Antonio Tejero, who seized the assembly and held the MPs prisoners for more than a day. A providential intervention by the king prevented the attempted coup from becoming an open military revolt.

The shock of this adventure had long-lasting implications for the young democracy and halted further progress, especially in matters of regional devolution. In a move conceived to pacify the 'bunker' and to quieten rumours of another, more serious, *golpe* (coup d'état), Madrid tried to pass a basic law (LOAPA, *Ley Orgánica de Armonizacion del Proceso Autonomico*). The law was officially designed to 'harmonise' the devolution process, but its covert aim was to curtail the powers of the two main autonomous communities – Catalonia and Euskadi – by standardising the political power and representation of each community. Its attempted introduction in 1982 stirred vigorous popular protest from most of the opposition.[11] Finally, in August 1983, the law was held to be *ultra vires* by the Constitutional Court and was dropped after its enormous unpopularity became clear.[12] In the 1982 general elections, the PSOE (Spanish Socialist Workers Party) won an absolute majority in the *Cortes*, crowning the transition process. For the first time, Spain was ruled by a socialist government.

However, Spain's impending accession to the European Community (1986) had a crucial importance. It has been argued that the European Union has exerted a vigorous influence in restraining the nationalism of its constituent nation-states, while it simultaneously worked as an accommodating framework for resolving region–state conflicts. Moreover, its powerful role in promoting respect for human rights, including cultural rights and the rights of minorities, cannot be denied. As is known, many of the EC founding fathers, such as Jean Monnet, identified regionalism as a means of defusing nationalist tensions (see Brinkley and Hackett 1991; Fontaine 1983). But an in-depth analysis of the EU's role should clearly distinguish between the pressures exerted on the Spanish political system prior to joining the European Community, and the ensuing developments.

Moreover, specific attention should be paid to the proliferation of European-level institutions representing the regions, analysing how these have influenced or countenanced regional nationalism. The most important of them is undoubtedly the Committee of Regions (Jáuregui 1997:152ff). The latter has worked as a structure for conveying and channelling regional interests. Catalan President Jordi Pujol has been one of its most active supporters, vigorously campaigning for its transformation into two separate chambers: one representing the municipalities and the other, the regions.

The economic dimension of European unity should also be discussed. Despite Spain's (as well as Portugal's and Greece's) unbroken authoritarian rule from the late 1930s until the 1970s, a decisive element has been the direct political assistance of Western European countries to the democratisation process through 'massive financial assistance and large-scale capital investment' (Agh 1993:234). Particularly important in this sense has been the European Investment Bank, based in Luxembourg and recently enhanced by the Treaty of Maastricht (Steinherr 1994).

ASYMMETRIC VERSUS SYMMETRIC FEDERALISM

In Spain, demands for autonomy have uncovered a growing gap between two models of 'federalism': the symmetrical model, dominant in the Castilian-speaking heartland, and the asymmetrical model, aspired to by the three historical nationalities. The latter can be defined as a 'combined system', with some federal units having greater self-governing powers than others (Kymlicka 1998a:14). A demand for some form of asymmetrical arrangement is likely to arise in federations that contain both regionally and nationally based units. In general, there cannot be ideal asymmetrical arrangements, and this is particularly the case of states riven by ethno-national conflicts, where regional demands, by nature changing and unpredictable, are not easily restrained or managed.

There are two forms of asymmetrical federalism: one dictated by the different size and demography of the units, the other determined by the different privileges and rights enjoyed by each unit – whether they are territorially or ethnically based (see Chapter 1).

In Spain, Catalonia, the Basque Country and Galicia have to compete with the other fourteen regionally based entities, some of which were arbitrarily created during the transition process to break up the dominance of Spain's majority nation, Castile. This territorial division could have avoided excessive asymmetry in size by introducing some level of non-ethnic symmetric federalism. However, the largest autonomous community, Castile-Léon (94,222 square kilometres), hardly compares with the smallest, La Rioja (5045). Demographically, the differences are also eye-catching: the Census of 1991 indicates a population of 6,940,522 in Andalusia, compared with La Rioja's 263,434 inhabitants. None of these communities belongs to any of the three historical nationalities; thus, the greatest level of asymmetry in both demography and size occurs between units belonging to the 'dominant nation' (if we include Andalusia in the wider Castilian area).

In practice, the Spanish 'federal' model offers a combination of both asymmetric and symmetric federalism. After an initial attempt to decree integral symmetry by means of a centrally imposed law (the LOAPA), Spain has not moved further towards such a goal. Instead, asymmetry has become the inevitable outcome of the increasing leverage acquired by both the Catalan and Basque autonomous governments at the negotiating table. More recently, their bargaining capacity has been enhanced by their electoral weight in both the lower and upper houses, when incomplete majorities (under both the socialist and, after March 1996, the conservative governments) needed nationalist support to obtain full majorities. Asymmetry may be costly, but in the end it is seen as increasingly unavoidable.

Asymmetry is hence an inevitable consequence of having to deal with regions characterised by different levels of intensity of ethno-national mobilisation. Yet a core question remains unanswered: Is asymmetric federalism intrinsically unstable? As Will Kymlicka (1998b:141) has observed for the Canadian case, the controversy arises from the widespread notion that granting special rights to a single autonomous community (on the grounds, for example, that it is a 'historical nationality') implies somehow a debasement of the other communities and the creation of 'classes of citizens'. In a previous article, Kymlicka (1998a:14) maintained that the asymmetrical model 'has proven extraordinarily difficult to negotiate', adding that in the long term asymmetry can lead to the erosion of 'social unity'. However, more recently, he has asserted that an asymmetrical status for 'nationality-based units' can also promote moral equality, since it ensures that the identity of distinctive or 'historical' nationalities receives the same consideration and support as the majority nation. But this defence of asymmetry presupposes the acceptance and self-definition of a state as a multinational federation. In our case, the acceptance of Spain as a genuinely pluri-national country is a prerequisite for asymmetry to work. Kymlicka's statement about the future of Canada can be applied, with minor nuances, to the case of Spain:

> I see no way to paper over these differences between the multination conception of Canada endorsed by most Quebecois and Aboriginal people and the single-nation conception endorsed by most English-speaking Canadians. Prior to 1982, it might have been possible to formulate a constitutional settlement that avoided the issue of national identities and loyalties. After all, the 1867 [British North American Act] did not discuss the values and identities of Canadians; nor was it expected to. But now the Constitution must be a framework that reflects our values, our aspirations and the best of what Canadians really are. (Kymlicka 1998b:148)

In other words, Canada's predicament lies in the insistence on provincial equality on the part of English speakers, rather than in Quebec's demand for asymmetry. A *modus vivendi* can only be reached with a division of powers along asymmetric lines. The fact that Quebec has already rejected secession twice proves in part that federalism is more stable than critics have so far argued. In the end, both English and French speakers are attempting to find a reasonable way of reconciling their demands, while building on mutual advantages by means of some asymmetric formula.

As for Spain, if asymmetry were fully accepted by most citizens, then regional demands for special autonomy would not be seen as obstacles to strengthening the role of the federal government, while nationalities would still be able to express their national aspirations without fear that the system was unreceptive to their needs (Arbos 1992; Requejo 1998a, 1998b).

ETHNICITY AND CULTURE: COMPLEMENTARY OR CONTRASTING FACTORS?

In pondering how to accommodate ethno-national differences, one should differentiate between 'ethnic' and 'cultural' diversity. In the social sciences, especially in the literature on nationalism, the terms 'ethnicity' and 'culture' are often confused – perhaps, sometimes, deliberately so. By ethnicity, we normally refer to a belief in putative descent (that is, a belief in something which may or may not be real). Ethnicity is thus similar to race, in that they both refer to descent. While ethnic descent is conjectural, racial descent requires a biological determinant. Both are obviously based on speculation and unfathomable myth.

Culture is, instead, an open project. You can become a member of a culture by learning its norms, traditions and codes, then sharing what you have learned by participating in cultural events. Even though the contractual element is not conspicuous (one often needs to be raised in a particular culture in order to be fully familiar with it), some give-and-take is implicit: 'I belong to this culture in so far as I can share its benefits while contributing to its maintenance and development.' Since culture is necessarily based on tradition and continuity, and it is hence passed through generations, it is often confused with ethnicity. But its exclusivist association with a single ethnic group is relatively modern.

The confusion between ethnicity and culture is helped by the fact that the former usage is quite new: in fact, in English, the term 'ethnicity' appeared only in the 1950s.[13] Yet a more important reason for this confusion may be that cultural continuity is stressed rather than cultural innovation. The conservatism of the concept of culture is emphasised by sacrificing its outstretching and creative power, as well as its capacity of expansion beyond rigid ethnic parameters. All cultures must have an assimilative core to survive. Assimilation means precisely that a member from another cultural group is allowed to become an in-member by simply adopting and sharing its basic elements. Assimilation is not an exclusive prerequisite of dominant cultures. Small cultures need to assimilate newcomers as well if they wish to survive.[14]

Although it is possible to conceive it in universalist terms, human culture can be broken down into multiple overlapping levels: civilisational, continental, religious, national, regional, provincial, local, tribal, sectional, individual – to the point of pure solipsism. It is important to stress that there is no single homogeneous or homogenisable universal culture (see Conversi 2000). A uniform 'world culture' would be an oxymoron, and the moment of its birth would also be the instant of its death. Like all forms of life, culture needs difference to survive. Culture is indeed based on diversity itself, and on the contact, encounter, competition, escape, isolation and conflict between different cultural systems.

This difference is important in order to understand Spanish federalism, in so far as culture and ethnicity have performed differently in each of the three 'historical nationalities'. In Catalonia, the cultural dimension has played a catalytic role in the entire devolution process. The Catalan language has operated as a key symbol and core value around which the entire democratic opposition converged during the transition period (Conversi 1990:50–70). This stress on culture has been vital in leading to peaceful language-centred forms of mobilisation, as well as to

135

intergenerational understanding (Conversi 1997). Moreover, it has worked as a powerful tool for integrating immigrants, given the mutual intelligibility between Castilian (Spanish) and Catalan (Conversi 1988).

On the other hand, ethnicity has played a much more central role in the Basque Country, partly because the regional language (Euskara) was, and is, spoken by a minority of the population and hence could not be used by nationalist leaders as a vehicle for national identity. On these grounds, the term 'ethno-nationalism' is often accepted by Basque politicians and scholars, whereas – if applied to Catalonia – it is flatly rejected by their Catalan counterparts. In Euskadi, the stress on ethnicity and descent has considerably complicated matters, given that, since the early 1960s, the region has experienced a massive influx of immigrants from other Spanish regions (Conversi 1989). I have argued elsewhere that the radical nationalists' strategy of anti-state antagonism has often attracted immigrants directly into Basque socio-political networks by challenging the state's monopoly of legitimate violence. Integration has thus been achieved by means of the immigrants' active participation in various levels of political activity, notably popular street demonstrations. This has not required, on their part, a native-like proficiency in the regional language nor a proof of their ethnic pedigree. It was the mere fact of participating in nationalist activities which led to their full acceptance into influential segments of the host society, the so-called *galaxia abertzale* ('patriotic galaxy', made up of hundreds of local civic groups of all sorts) (Conversi 1997:ch. 8). Indeed, the attempt to integrate the immigrants into the Basque nationalist struggle has been a key source of the oppositional logic which eventually led to the propagation of political violence (Conversi 1997).

Finally, unlike the previous two cases, in Galicia the majority of the population never abandoned the regional language (Galician), while immigration into the region has been minimal – rather, emigration towards the Americas and northern-central Europe has characterised modern Galician history.

CAN THE SPANISH EXPERIENCE PROVIDE A UNIVERSAL MODEL?

Spain has often been defined as a 'success story' along several evaluative dimensions: in terms of successful transition to democracy, democratic consolidation, elite bargaining, elite settlement, conflict resolution and, more recently, de-escalation and pacification – at least since ETA's 'total and indefinite' cease-fire (18 September 1998).[15] Although the truce came as a surprise, the entire Basque society had been mobilised for years in order to attain an end to terrorism. The main rationale of these mobilisations was that Euskadi had already achieved self-government and all efforts to expand its powers should be legally pursued within the framework provided by the Statute of Autonomy. Hence, violence had no longer any reason to exist; it was indeed counter-productive and against the interests of the Basque nation.

Whether Spain is a 'success' must take into account the perceptions not only of all major political parties involved but also of the various segments of society and of external or international actors. From the viewpoint of state elites, the maintenance of the state's territorial integrity within its existing borders is an indicator of success. On the other hand, from a peripheral nationalist perspective, it is the level of self-government so far achieved that becomes the measure of success. Obviously, there are points of incompatibility between the two conflicting poles of state centralism and peripheral separatism. The success of federalism can ultimately be measured by the extent to which it has effectively devised a long-lasting mechanism of accommodation, while avoiding the temptation to revert to one of the two extremes. In all of these respects, the Spanish transition has triumphed against all odds.

What is successful today may not necessarily remain successful tomorrow. Federalism works as an ongoing negotiating process, as well as a comprehensive political project. For this reason, it is liable to enter crisis as soon as one of the contracting parts unilaterally changes the game's basic rules. Hence, an indication of its success would include the difficulty or impossibility of both re-centralisation and separatism.

A major corollary is that federalism is a one-way route. Once one is embarked on its course, there is no turning back. An accepted federal arrangement cannot suddenly be unilaterally reversed without risking the violent break-up of the country (as in Ethiopia–Eritrea, Nigeria–Biafra, Abkhazia–Georgia, and the former Yugoslavia). In Spain, on the other hand, the quasi-federal framework proceeding from the 1978 constitution created an ideal structure for the slow eradication of political violence. (Despite its limited duration, ETA's 1998 cease-fire had seemed clearly to crown the success of the Spanish transition as a whole.) The granting of regional autonomy slowly but effectively cut the ground from under the feet of the supporters of political violence (the origins of which can be traced back to the abolition of local rights). The achievement of civil peace is certainly one of the most satisfactory indicators of a specific strategy's long-term success.

Finally, given the success of this 'model', one may be tempted to regard it as universally applicable. A few scholars have claimed that Spain's lesson can be transferred and applied to other countries, including Britain.[16] Parallels between Canada and Spain have also flourished, in both directions.

Canada has worked as an inspiration for many Spaniards, and Quebec's experience is considered by Catalan nationalists as the most suitable for emulation (see Keating 1996; Pares and Tremblay 1988). Moreover, during the early phases of post-communist transitions, East European leaders, commentators and scholars have looked to Spain as a possible paradigm.

The model can certainly have validity for polities experiencing rapid democratic transition, wherever a territorially concentrated nationalist movement poses a real challenge to the state. However, it is largely inappropriate in areas characterised by deep ethnic cleavages or simultaneous ethnic dispersion and intermingling. For instance, in ethnically mixed areas, such as in Transylvania and a few Asian countries, the model may not be applicable. As a matter of fact, federal units dominated by a single nationalist movement are likely to become ethnicised, rather than remaining purely territorial entities. This may result in the further ethnicisation of political life, with particularly regrettable consequences in mixed areas.

CONCLUSION

Assimilation and congruence between state and nation have been the traditional goals of Madrid's elites since at least the first failed centralisation attempts by the Conde-Duque de Olivares (1587–1645), whose policies resembled closely those of his French counterpart Armand Jean du Plessis, duc de Richelieu (1585–1642) (Elliott 1984, 1986). However, the most methodical attempt in this respect was carried out under the dictatorship of General Francisco Franco (1939–75), as before 1939 the Spanish state had failed to initiate a decisive process of 'nation-building' (Arbos and Puigsec 1980; Giner 1986:447). Spanish nationalism conceived the nation monolithically, in terms of *unidad de destino* (unity of fate). *Unidad* referred to an indivisible quality whereas the nation was metaphorically imagined as a human body, while *destino* meant that this unity was unquestionable and forever given: 'We are into it and we cannot escape it.'[17]

The transition to democracy brought a radically different vision of Spanishness, stressing a plural, inclusive identity for the country. The process of gaining full admission to the European Community was a further boost in this direction, providing a supplementary and overarching identity that diminished the importance of state boundaries. Finally, the monarchy became the ideal vehicle for the aspirations of a changing society, while embracing the different identities of Spain's diverse peoples. As some have argued, the king could be described as the true pilot of change (Powell 1991).

Post-Franco Spain has often been pointed to as one of the most successful cases of internal restructuring by a state in post-war Europe.

Under the pressure of powerful nationalist movements, the country was transformed from a centralist into a largely decentralised polity. A key ingredient of this restructuring was the need to deal with ethnic conflict, which in the Basque case has had a highly organised violent component.

The landmark event in this profound change was the approval of the constitution in 1978, a masterwork of political negotiation and balance between opposing trends, as it fully recognises the 'right to difference'. Perhaps alone among contemporary constitutions, the Spanish one blends unitarism and pluralism, allowing quasi-federal principles to be put into practice.[18] Unlike standard federalist constitutions, it stresses the unity of the state, but like most federalist constitutions the operative premise is that social peace can only be achieved by accommodating minority aspirations, and this cannot be achieved through majority rule.

Following Charles Taylor's (1992) notion of multiculturalism, nationalism can be regarded as a form of politics of 'recognition' (see also Kymlicka 1995; Shapiro and Kymlicka 1997). By recognising the right to ethnic and cultural difference, and by endeavouring to actively protect it, even encourage it, the universal need for recognition of most modern societies is addressed, albeit belatedly. As we have seen, the political debate immediately preceding the constitution's approval was centred on recognition. Such debate shows how the original antagonism between Spanish and peripheral nationalisms could be overcome via the creation of a new inclusive notion of Spanishness. It may be premature to judge whether this idea has already percolated into the consciousness of most Spaniards. Even though the new Spain has sought to accommodate ethnic aspirations, deeply ingrained memories of oppression linger on, and the legacy of the latter was a process of cultural assimilation which only recently has been halted – and even begun to be reversed. Yet we can stress that this pluralist vision has at least permeated political elites – which are the crucial actors and protagonists of nationalist mobilisation.

As ethno-national conflicts must be submitted to a process of continuous negotiation, this chapter does not claim that national conflicts in Spain are permanently settled. It is possible that, with another change of regime or new forms of socio-economic upheaval, ethnic strife may resurface. We have also seen that through a lengthy process of negotiation, a potentially explosive conflict has partially quietened down. Most importantly, the Spanish state acquired a new legitimacy among wider and wider sectors of the population, a legitimacy which it did not enjoy at the beginning of the transition period.

Perhaps nowhere in the world has pure coercion proved to be effective in nation building. Nearly everywhere, state repression has succeeded only temporarily and superficially in halting ethnic dissent. Most typically, it has generated powerful separatist trends which, once unleashed, have been hardly kept in check. The recent breakup of multi-national states, held together by decades of one-party rule, has confirmed the improbability that coercion will work in the long run as a tool for conflict management. In its most intolerant moments, Spanish nationalism has elicited opposing responses, as local elites countered centralising and assimilationist efforts (Linz 1973). Basque, Catalan and, to a lesser extent, Galician nationalism are all reactions to Madrid's past failure to accommodate regional aspirations. Due to the historical fiasco of the Jacobin centralised model, a more pluralistic vision of Spanishness has emerged, inspired by a previous federalist tradition.

NOTES

1 For a political science approach, see Gunther et al. (1986), and Linz (1970, 1975). For a general overview, see Conversi (1997) and Heywood (1995).

2 Recently, local historians have been mobilised in order to confer on these new administrative units a new regional dignity. Not everybody is satisfied with the present status: some regions claim a separate autonomy based on alleged historical roots. Thus, some organisations in Léon wish their region to 'secede' from the Autonomous Community of Castile.

3 On the constitution's use of *nacional* and related terms, see Solé i Tura (1985: 97–102), for the use of the term *nacionalidades* in art. 2.

4 There seems to be no better English equivalent for the Spanish usage; see Brassloff (1989:24).

5 Most contemporary Spanish provinces are the result of the administrative division by Javier de Burgos in 1833.

6 However, in the Basque case, the provinces (Alava, Guipuzcoa, Navarre, Vizcaya) have a much deeper historical legitimacy and functional role.

7 For instance, autonomy statutes were granted to Cantabria (province of Santander), an area whose ancient name was La Montaña, and La Rioja (province of Logroño), both regions culturally and historically part of Castile. Madrid has been detached from its hinterland, Castile, and established as a separate *Comunidad Autonoma*, a sort of 'federal district' on the pattern of Canberra, Washington and Mexico City.

8 On the crucial relationship between nationalism and legitimacy, see the seminal essay by Connor (1980).

9 On constitutional law and constitutional history in the Basque Country, see Escudero and Villanueva (1976); on Navarre's constitutional history, see Valentin (1986).

10 Constitutionally, all Autonomous Communities have the right to achieve the same privileges as the Basque Country and Catalonia. But it will be hard to create, in a few years, a distinctive culture such as the nationalities have developed over a much longer time.

11 Apart from all Basque and the Catalan nationalists, the anti-LOAPA front also included the communists (PCE) and the Andalusian regionalists (PSA). The law had been agreed on by the PSOE and the UCD (Democratic Centre Coalition) (Trujillo 1982).

12 For a legislative assessment of the LOAPA and the Spanish decentralisation process in comparative perspective, see Hannum (1990:263–79).

13 Hutchinson and Smith (1996:4) argue that 'the meaning of the term is equally uncertain. It can mean "the essence of an ethnic group" or "the quality of belonging to an ethnic community or group".'

14 Scattered pre-industrial communities were not totally isolated and normally allowed a limited numbers of 'outsiders' to join in and share their fruits on the implicit (or explicit) basic covenant that cardinal traditions, core values, and key symbols had to be treasured and enhanced.

15 On 28 November 1999, ETA announced the calling-off of its cease-fire, apparently to push the Spanish government into resuming talks, which had stalled.

16 Gallagher (1991) points out that such an experiment can function as a workable model in the relations between England and the Celtic fringe.

17 This holistic vision was indeed much more similar to the early Basque nationalist idea of Euskadi, even though the envisioned country was conceived as a free confederation of seven provinces. In the earliest stages, the province of Vizcaya may have played a central, but never a centralist, role.

18 Graham Smith (1995:7) recognises that it is often difficult to distinguish unitary states from states officially defined as federations.

REFERENCES

Agh, Attila 1993. 'The "comparative revolution" and the transition in central and southern Europe', *Journal of Theoretical Politics* 5(2):231–52.

Arbos, Xavier 1986. *La Idea de Nació en el Primer Constitucionalisme Espanyol* [The Idea of Nation in the First Spanish Constitutionalism]. Barcelona: Curial.

——— (ed.) 1992. *Federalisme* [Federalism]. Barcelona: Fundació Rafael Campalans.

Arbos, Xavier and Antoni Puigsec 1980. *Franco i l'Espanyolisme* [Franco and Spanish Nationalism]. Barcelona: Curial.

Attard, Emilio 1983. *La Constitución por Dentro. Evocaciones del Proceso Constituyente: Valores, Derechos y Libertades* [The Constitution from Within. Evocations of the Constitutional Process: Values, Rights and Liberties]. Barcelona: Argos Vergara.

Ayestarán, José Antonio (ed.) 1979. *Euskadi y el Estatuto de Autonomía* [The Basque Country and the Autonomy Statute]. San Sebastián: Erein, D.L.

Blinkhorn, Martin 1974. 'The Basque "Ulster": Navarre and the Basque autonomy question under the Spanish Second Republic', *Historical Journal* XVII(3):595–613.

Brassloff, Audrey 1989. 'Spain: the state of the autonomies', in Murray Forsyth (ed.) *Federalism and Nationalism.* New York: St Martin's Press.

Brinkley, Douglas and Clifford Hackett (eds) 1991. *Jean Monnet: The Path to European Unity.* New York: St Martin's Press.

Clark, Robert P. 1979. *The Basques: The Franco Years and Beyond.* Reno: University of Nevada Press.

——— 1990. *Negotiating with ETA: Obstacles to Peace in the Basque Country, 1975–1988.* Reno: Nevada University Press.

Connor, Walker 1980. 'Nationalism and political illegitimacy', *Canadian Review of Studies in Nationalism* VII (Fall):201–28.

Conversi, Daniele 1988. 'L'integrazione degli immigrati a Barcelona [The integration of immigrants in Barcelona]', *Studi Emigrazione/Etudes Migrations* 89:67–82.

―― 1989. 'Ethnic nationalism, immigration and political violence: notes from the Basque case', *Ethnic and Racial Studies* 12(3), July, 401–7.

―― 1990. 'Language or race?: the choice of core values in the development of Catalan and Basque nationalisms', *Ethnic and Racial Studies* 13(1), January, 50–70.

―― 1993. 'The influence of culture on political choices: language maintenance and its implications for the Basque and Catalan nationalist movements', *History of European Ideas* 16(1–3):189–200.

―― 1997. *The Basques, the Catalans and Spain: Alternative Routes to National Mobilization*. London: Hurst/Reno: Nevada University Press.

―― 2000. 'Nationalism and cosmopolitanism', in Athena Leoussi and Anthony D. Smith (eds) *Encyclopaedia of Nationalism*. Oxford: Transaction.

de la Granja Sainz, José Luis 1994. 'La invención de la historia: nación, mitos e historia en el pensamiento del fundador del nacionalismo vasco [The invention of history: nation, myths and history in the thought of the founder of Basque nationalism]'. Unpublished manuscript.

Elliott, J.H. 1984. *Richelieu and Olivares*. Cambridge: Cambridge University Press.

―― 1986. *The Count-Duke of Olivares: The Statesman in an Age of Decline*. New Haven: Yale University Press.

Escudero, Manu and Javier Villanueva 1976. *La Autonomía del País Vasco desde el Pasado al Futuro* [Autonomy in the Basque Country from the Past to the Future]. San Sebastián: Txertoa.

Esteban, Jorge de 1989. 'El proceso constituyente español 1977–1978', in José Felix Tezanos, Ramon Cotarelo and Andres de Blas (eds) *La Transición Democrática Española* [The Spanish Democratic Transition]. Madrid: Editorial Sistema.

Fontaine, François 1983. *Plus loin avec Jean Monnet*. Lausanne: Fondation Jean Monnet pour l'Europe/Centre de Recherches Européennes.

Gallagher, Tom 1991. 'Autonomy in Spain: lessons for Britain?', in Bernard Crick (ed.) *National Identities: The Constitution of the United Kingdom*. Oxford: Basil Blackwell/ *The Political Quarterly*.

Generalitat 1979. *Estatut d'Autonomia de Catalunya* [Catalonia Autonomy Statute]. Leaflet published by Generalitat de Catalunya.

Giner, Salvador 1986. 'Nacionalismo étnico: centro y periferia en España [Ethnic nationalism: centre and periphery in Spain]', in Francesc Hernández and Francesc Mercadé (eds) *Estructuras Sociales y Cuestión Nacional en España* [Social Structures and the National Question in Spain]. Barcelona: Ariel.

Giner, Salvador and Luís Moreno 1990. 'Centro y periferia: la dimension étnica de la sociedad española [Centre and periphery: the ethnic dimension of Spanish society]', in Salvador Giner (ed.) *Espana*. Madrid: Espasa-Calpe, vol. 1.

Gonzalez Casanova, José Antonio 1974. *Federalisme i Autonomía a Catalunya, 1868–1938* [Federalism and Autonomy in Catalonia]. Barcelona: Curial.

Guibernau, Montserrat 1995. 'Spain: a federation in the making?', in Graham Smith (ed.) *Federalism: The Multiethnic Challenge.* London/New York: Longman.

Gunther, Richard, Giacomo Sani and Goldie Shabad 1986. *Spain after Franco: The Making of a Competitive Party System.* Berkeley: University of California Press.

Hannum, Hurst 1990. *Autonomy, Sovereignty, and Self-determination: The Accommodation of Conflicting Rights.* Philadelphia: University of Pennsylvania Press.

Hennessy, Charles A.M. 1962. *The Federal Republic in Spain.* Oxford: Clarendon Press.

Heywood, Paul 1995. *The Government and Politics of Spain.* New York: St Martin's Press.

Hills, George 1980. 'Basque autonomy: will it be enough?', *World Today* 36(9):356–60.

Hutchinson, John and Anthony D. Smith (eds) 1996. *Ethnicity.* New York: Oxford University Press.

Jáuregui, Gurutz 1997. *Los Nacionalismos Minoritarios y la Unión Europea: Utopía o Ucronía?* [Minority Nationalisms and the European Union: Utopia or 'Ucronia'?] Barcelona: Editorial Ariel.

Keating, Michael 1996. *Nations against the State: The New Politics of Nationalism in Quebec, Catalonia and Scotland.* New York: St Martin's Press.

Kymlicka, Will 1995. *Multicultural Citizenship: A Liberal Theory of Minority Rights.* Oxford: Clarendon Press/New York: Oxford University Press.

—— 1998a. 'Is federalism a viable alternative to secession?', in Percy B. Lehning (ed.) *Theories of Secession.* New York: Routledge.

—— 1998b. *Finding Our Way: Rethinking Ethnocultural Relations in Canada.* Toronto: Oxford University Press.

Linz, Juan J. 1970. 'An authoritarian regime: Spain', in Erik Allardt and Stein Rokkan (eds) *Mass Politics: Studies in Political Sociology.* New York: Free Press.

—— 1973. 'Early state-building and late peripheral nationalism against the state: the case of Spain', in S.N. Eisenstadt and Stein Rokkan (eds) *Building States and Nations.* Beverly Hills: Sage Publications, vol. 2:32–116.

—— 1975. 'Totalitarian and authoritarian regimes', in Fred I. Greenstein and Nelson W. Polsby (eds) *Macropolitical Theory.* Vol. 3 of *Handbook of Political Science.* Menlo Park, CA: Addison Wesley, 175–411.

Pares, M. and G. Tremblay (eds) 1988. *Catalunya, Quebec: Dues Nacions, Dos Models Culturals* [Catalonia, Quebec: Two Nations, Two Cultural Models]. Ponencies del Primer Simposi, Barcelona, maig 1985. Barcelona: Generalitat de Catalunya.

Peces-Barba Martinez, Gregorio 1988. *La Elaboración de la Constitución de 1978* [The Elaboration of the Constitution of 1978]. Madrid: Centro de Estudios Constitucionales.

Pi y Margall, Francisco 1979. *Las Nacionalidades* [*The Nationalities*]. Barcelona: Producciones Editoriales (1st edn 1877, Madrid: Imprenta y Libreria de E. Martínez).

Powell, Charles T. 1991. *El Piloto del Cambio: El Rey, la Monarquia y la Transición a la Democrácia* [The Pilot of Change: The King, the Monarchy and the Transition to Democracy]. Barcelona: Planeta.

Preston, Paul 1986. *The Triumph of Democracy in Spain*. London/New York: Methuen.

Proudhon, Pierre Joseph 1921. *Du Principe Fédératif et de la Nécessité de Reconstituer le Parti de la Révolution*. Paris: Editions Bossard [Engl. trs. *The Principle of Federation*. Toronto/Buffalo: University of Toronto Press, 1979].

Requejo, Ferran 1998a. *Federalisme, per a què? L'Acomodació de la Diversitat en Democràcies Plurinacionals* [Federalism for What? The Accommodation of Diversity in Multinational Democracies]. València: 3 i 4 Edicions.

——— 1998b. *Zoom Polític: Democràcia, Federalisme i Nacionalisme des d'una Catalunya Europea* [Political Zoom: Democracy, Federalism and Nationalism from a European Catalonia]. Barcelona: Proa.

Roig i Rosich, Josep 1978. *L'Estatut de Catalunya a les Cortes Constituents (1932)* [The Statute of Catalonia and the Constituent Courts]. Barcelona: Curial.

Shapiro, Ian and Will Kymlicka (eds) 1997. *Ethnicity and Group Rights*. New York: New York University Press.

Smith, Graham 1995. 'Mapping the federal condition: ideology, political practice and social justice', in Graham Smith (ed.) *Federalism: The Multiethnic Challenge*. London/New York: Longman.

Solé i Tura, Jordi 1985. *Nacionalidades y Nacionalismos en España: Autonomías, Federalismo, Autodeterminación* [Nationalities and Nationalism in Spain: Autonomy, Federalism, Self-determination]. Madrid: Alianza.

Steinherr, Alfred (ed.) 1994. *30 Years of European Monetary Integration from the Werner Plan to EMU*. London/New York: Longman.

Tamames, Ramon 1985. *Introducción a la Constitución Española: Texto y Comentarios* [Introduction to the Spanish Constitution: Text and Commentaries]. 3rd edn. Madrid: Alianza Editorial.

Tamayo, Virginia 1988. *Genesis del Estatuto de Gernika* [Genesis of the Basque Autonomy Statute]. Gasteiz: Herri-Arduralaritzaren Euskal Erakundea.

Taylor, Charles 1992. *Multiculturalism and 'The Politics of Recognition': An Essay*. Princeton, NJ: Princeton University Press.

Trujillo, Gumersindo 1982. *LOAPA eta Konstituzioa/ LOAPA y Constitución: El Proyecto de LOAPA, desde la Perspectiva de Su Constitucionalidad* [LOAPA and the Constitution: The Project of LOAPA, from a Constitutional Perspective]. Vitora/Gasteiz: Servicio Central de Publicaciones del Gobierno Vasco, Secretaria de la Presidencia.

Valentin, Vazquez de Prada (ed.) 1986. *Cuestiones de Historia Moderna y Contemporanea de Navarra* [Questions of Modern and Contemporary History in Navarre]. Pamplona: Ediciones Universidad de Navarra.

PART II

FAILED AUTONOMIES

CHAPTER 7

ETHNICITY AND FEDERALISM IN COMMUNIST YUGOSLAVIA AND ITS SUCCESSOR STATES

Siniša Malešević

With the collapse of communist federations in the early 1990s, many scholars have questioned the value of federal arrangements for the maintenance of multi-ethnic societies. Some argue that federations give too much power to regions, which eventually leads to secession. For others, a federal arrangement is an insufficient form for the expression of regional and cultural differences and, consequently, it perpetuates internal conflicts and leads to disintegration of the federal state. However, federal arrangements per se are not necessarily good or bad. A great deal depends on the historical, political and social conditions of the particular society. What is crucial is the way in which the agreement between the constitutive units is reached. If the particular type of federal structure is imposed on the member states, it is more likely that the relationships between them will be a constant source of tension and conflict. If there are significant cultural and ethnic differences between the constitutive units, cultural questions will almost certainly become political questions which, in specific historical circumstances, can lead to collapse of the federal state.

Democratic constitutional arrangements do not define relationships between federal units once and for all, but provide for constant renegotiation and compromise. In the same vein, the 'national question' can never be resolved, as many communist governments claimed. Ethnic groups are prone to permanent re-evaluation of their position vis-à-vis other groups within the larger society. However, there is no clear answer to the questions: Why do some ethnic groups coexist peacefully in a particular state, while others develop hostile attitudes and engage in ethnic conflicts, wars or secession? Under which conditions does political recognition of ethnicity become threatening to federalism?

The changing nature of relationships between ethnic groups is a subject of dispute among social scientists. Some interpret the shifts in ethnic cohesion and ethnic animosities in terms of the behaviour of rationally motivated actors who manipulate cultural similarities for individual benefit. Thus, wide support for secession on an ethnic basis is explained as a rational outcome for utility-driven individuals. Socio-biologists, on the other hand, view ethnocentrism in terms of in-group–out-group relationships, as universal and biologically determined. For them, ethnicity is nothing but a form of extended kinship where individuals as the carriers of genes tend to maximise their inclusive fitness through kin selection; therefore, all plural societies whether organised in a unitary or federal way are, in the long term, predestined for collapse. Neo-Marxist theories of ethnicity explain ethnic relations as a special case of class relations which are largely determined by the economy and, in particular, by the capitalist mode of production. Symbolic interactionist perspectives stress the collective interpretation of group membership, where emphasis on ethnic distinctiveness is a strategy to improve the collective status of the group. In this perspective, what is crucial for the stability of inter-ethnic relations are not economic or political conditions but rather mutual symbolic interpretations and forms of understanding between the groups.[1] Finally, ethnic relations are also studied as power relations, where ethnicity is analysed as a means of making political claims as strategies of manipulation and mobilisation employed by power elites for political ends (Brass 1991; Cohen 1981).

In this chapter, relationships between ethnic groups in general, and between ethnicity and federalism in particular, will be analysed from the perspective of power-elite mobilisation. In other words, the emphasis will be placed on political factors as being the most important for the explanation of the changing relationship between ethnic groups in a federal state. The aim is to look at the dominant political actors and their motives, as well as at the structural and institutional constraints in reference to the ethnicity and territorial arrangements of the state. Political theories of ethnicity stress the competition of elites for resources and their manipulation of cultural, religious or linguistic symbols for political ends. As Cohen (1969:200) puts it precisely, 'ethnicity is essentially a political phenomenon, as traditional customs are used only as idioms, and as mechanisms for political alignment'. With the help of ethnic, cultural or religious symbols, masses are mobilised on an ethnic basis and confronted with other groups who are now perceived solely as culturally distinct and thus potentially threatening. Through ethnic mobilisation, a particular elite manages to articulate cultural and ethnic differences as political ones – to give a political meaning and significance to culture by reifying, and then politicising, its content. As Brass (1991:26) explains, the political instrumentalisation of ethnicity is more likely to occur in societies that undergo dramatic and uneven social change. Under such conditions, 'ethnic self-consciousness, ethnically-based demands, and ethnic conflict can occur only if there is some conflict, between indigenous and external elites and authorities or between indigenous elites'.

Political interpretations of ethnic relations are particularly convincing when state socialist societies and their offspring are analysed. Since these societies were characterised by the dominance of politics over all other spheres of social life where economy did not exist as an autonomous sphere, and since the decisions of major political actors (such as the Communist Party, charismatic leaders, political bureaucracy, the Politbureau) were crucial for the direction of development of the society, it is obvious that an analysis of these actors can yield a better understanding of the phenomenon under study. Brubaker (1996) has, for example, convincingly argued that, although nominally internationalist and anti-nationalist, communist states were very much nation-centred and, as such, responsible for the institutionalisation of 'nationness' as a category of everyday experience.

Working within the power-elite approach, this chapter aims to show, from the example of former Yugoslavia and its successor states, under which conditions federal and other decentralised arrangements can fail. It is often argued that Yugoslavia has disintegrated simply because it was a multi-ethnic federation with a long history of mutual animosities that were kept under control by the iron fist of a communist government. The argument in this chapter is exactly the opposite – Yugoslavia did not collapse because it was a multi-ethnic society of mutually antagonistic groups or because it was organised in a federal way, but because it was not a genuinely democratic federal state. The power elite of socialist Yugoslavia used decentralisation as a means of avoiding democratisation and liberalisation. Under pressure from below for further democratisation of society, the government shifted the question of popular political participation to the level of inter-republic relations. By giving more power to the party elites of individual republics instead of to its citizens, the Communist Party preserved its monopoly within the political system. Thus, what took place was not genuine decentralisation but, rather, quasi-decentralisation, which produced a set of loosely linked but internally highly centralised units – republics. To avoid democratisation, power was not devolved to the citizens of the individual republics but to the party elites of each constitutive unit.

The situation is in many ways similar for the successor states. Regardless of whether they are shaped as unitary states (Croatia, Macedonia), federations (FR Yugoslavia) or confederations (Bosnia and Herzegovina), they are basically unstable states whose political elites rely on decentralisation only as a last available resource in the internal power struggle. For that reason, they all face the same problems with ethnicity that drove socialist Yugoslavia to its end.

ACCOMMODATED ETHNICITY IN COMMUNIST YUGOSLAVIA

The relationship between ethnicity and federalism in communist Yugoslavia was a complex one. It shared some similarities with other state socialist countries, such as the USSR and Czechoslovakia, but the direction of its development shows more differences than similarities with these countries.[2] Being driven away from the rest of the communist world at a very early stage (1948) in the development of post–World War II Europe,[3] Yugoslavia had to somehow develop a different model of state socialism, including its distinct federal arrangements. Claiming to be a more genuine expression of socialist society, the Yugoslav government had to demonstrate abroad and at home that its political system was more just, free and equal to all its citizens as well as its constitutive units. For that reason, it engaged early on in periodical changes of its economic and political system as well as of its constitutional structures. Starting as a very centralised state in 1945, Yugoslavia was gradually transformed into an extremely loosely formulated federation that, by the time of its bloody collapse in 1991, had many actual features of a confederal state. In terms of the relationship between ethnicity and federalism, one can distinguish three phases in the development of the Yugoslav state: the period of gradual but constant decentralisation on the macro level, from 1945 to 1974; the period of radical macro-decentralisation and simultaneous micro-centralisation, from 1974 to 1987; and the gradual disintegration of the state from 1987 onwards that ended in the wars of 1991–95.

From party centralism to macro-decentralisation, 1945–1974

Unlike the Kingdom of Serbs, Croats and Slovenes that was established in 1918 and was from the beginning a Great Serbian project, the new Yugoslav state set up by Tito and the Communist Party recognised the existence and rights of all other major ethnic groups, in particular Montenegrins and Macedonians who were, because of their Orthodox religion, previously seen as Serbs, but also Bosnian Muslims who were in 1971 given the right to express themselves as a separate ethnic collective.

The aim of the central government was to legitimise itself, on the one hand, by providing each constitutive ethnic group with its own state largely along the lines of their historical territories, and, on the other hand, by unifying different ethnic groups in a single state that would be much more sensitive to ethnic issues than monarchist Yugoslavia. Hence, the country became officially a federation of six republics: Slovenia, Croatia, Bosnia and Herzegovina, Serbia (including its two autonomous provinces: Kosovo and Vojvodina), Montenegro, and Macedonia.

Although recognising the specificities of each ethnic group, the new regime aimed also at emphasising the similarities. This was not an easy task because of traditional and historic differences, among which the most important are the following: Slovenes and Croats were mostly Roman Catholic, had been under the control of the Habsburg Empire for several centuries, were more exposed to Western and Central European cultural influences, had more developed industrial infrastructure and were more urbanised, whereas Serbs, Montenegrins, Macedonians and Bosnian Muslims had been in the same period subjects of the Ottoman Empire, had less developed industry, were less modernised and urbanised and had traditionally belonged to Eastern Orthodox Christianity (Serbs, Montenegrins and Macedonians) or Sunni Islam (Bosnian Muslims). However, what was common for all of these groups were the same Slavic origins and the culture and language related to these common Slavic roots. With the exception of Slovenes and Macedonians, whose languages are different although not completely incomprehensible for other south Slavs, the other four ethnic groups speak the same language.[4] The only significant difference is that Serbs and Montenegrins predominantly use the Cyrillic script, whereas Croats and Bosnian Muslims use the Latin alphabet. These cultural similarities were further successfully connected by the new government to the ideal of a common struggle against the various imperial powers of the past. Another important point was the fact that, apart from the more recent past culminating in the World War II atrocities, the groups inhabiting the new Yugoslav state had little history of mutual animosity. Since, through most of their history, they had been subjects of different imperial powers, their collective memory of animosity and anger was aimed mostly at those powers and their representatives. Through the influence of nineteenth century pan-Slavism, and the Illyrian movement that preached that all south Slavs are branches of the same Illyrian tribe, the Yugoslav idea had a strong foundation and wide support, at least among intellectuals and various groups on the Left.

The new regime had to take all of these elements into account. As a result, in 1945 federalism was for the first time offered as a solution that would not only recognise these differences between ethnic groups but would also ensure that the common state remained intact. However, the new constitution secured that all central powers were in the domain of the federal government, which in fact meant in the hands of the Communist Party. Until 1948–49 Yugoslav federalism was largely a copy of the 1936 Soviet model. The Constitution of the Federal People's

Republic of Yugoslavia (1946) included in its first article the Leninist idea of the right to self-determination of individual republics and hence de jure right to secession from the federal state. Every constitutive republic in the federation had its own constitution, which, although designed and approved by the parliament of that individual republic, had to be in agreement with the federal constitution. Just as in the Soviet constitution, the republics had a large degree of autonomy on paper, while in reality power was highly centralised at the federal level.

The political and ideological clash with the Soviet Union meant that the Yugoslav government needed stronger popular support at home. In order to secure this support, the party was forced to liberalise its policies as well as to accommodate republican party leaderships by decentralising some of its powers.

Thus, the new 1953 constitutional law was much more decentralised and some crucial areas, such as the economy, media and education policy, were now to be decided at the level of the republics and not solely at the federal level. The political, economic and constitutional changes were accompanied by intensive industrialisation and political liberalisation, producing the most dynamic development in Yugoslav history, with GDP growing at 8.1 per cent annually in the period 1953–60.

However, the republics did not develop at an equal pace. The historically more advanced regions of the north (Slovenia, Croatia and the Serbian province of Vojvodina) developed faster and more intensively than the rest of the country. To accelerate development in the poorer regions, the federal government introduced a joint fund for such regions to which the wealthier republics had to contribute more than others. This fact, together with the simultaneous and gradual decentralisation of the state, had an impact on popular perceptions in Slovenia and Croatia that they had to carry an enormous burden. At the same time, the southern republics felt that they had been exploited by the richer republics of the north. This issue was to become a central point of disagreement in the 1960s.

The new constitution of 1963 did not solve this problem, merely reflecting the ambiguities and existing conflicts that had accumulated in the post-war period. Although the constitution maintained and even extended most of the rights given to individual republics in the constitutional law of 1953, it redefined and neutralised their status of being sovereign states as formulated previously. Instead, they were defined as 'state socialist democratic communities' (Caca 1988:164). Party leaderships in Slovenia and Croatia viewed this as a step backward, one which, together with the economic stagnation of the late 1960s,[5] contributed to the conflict between the republics' leaderships. The richer republics were opposed to making contributions to the fund for the underdeveloped republics. In the 1960s, first the Slovenian and, later on, the Croatian leadership started opposing the policy of redistribution of economic resources and demanded further decentralisation. The Croatian party leadership was particularly opposed to the existing currency system and pressed the federal leadership for a new system that would give each republic greater control over its foreign currency assets (Stokes 1993:227). For Croatia, this was a very important issue because of its disproportionate revenue from tourism.

The federal state responded by accepting a number of constitutional amendments that gave more authority to the republics and provinces. In addition, important changes had taken place within the main power holder: the League of Communists of Yugoslavia (LCY). Thus, for example, in 1968 the congresses of the republican branches of the LCY were held before the federal congress. As Hodson et al. (1994:1539–40) emphasise, 'this step was important in reversing the tendency of the republican congresses to simply ratify and adopt the policies decided by the federal congress'. However, by the end of the 1960s, resistance to centralisation had developed in Croatia into a national movement led by the leadership of the Croatian branch of the LCY.[6] In the early stages of the 'rebellion', Tito and the federal leadership attempted to accommodate the demands made by the protesters. So, for example, in 1971 each republic was given de facto veto power on the decisions made on the federal level. However, this and other moves did not satisfy the protesters, and Tito changed his position and crushed the movement, removing its leading members from power. Despite this draconian attitude towards the leaders of the Croatian national movement, Tito and the federal party leadership basically accepted most of the demands made by the leadership of the 'Croatian Spring' and initiated the radical change in the constitution in 1974 which practically gave all important powers to the republics and provinces.

The new and last constitution of socialist Yugoslavia defined the units of federation as 'states based on the sovereignty of the people' (Caca 1988:164).[7] For the first time, sovereignty was deduced from the individual republics rather than the federation, as previously. In addition to powers they already had, such as education, media policy and the economy, the republics acquired most of the powers that were in the domain of the federal government, such as the political system, finances and distribution of public funds, social services, policing, civil protection and defence, and jurisprudence. Apart from foreign policy and defence, all major decisions from then on were to be taken by the republics themselves. Effectively, from 1974 Yugoslavia had many more elements that would define it as a confederate state than its official name – federation – implied.

From macro-decentralisation to micro-centralisation, 1974–1987

Instead of solving existing problems, the reform of the federation and the implementation of the new 1974 constitution only accelerated the proliferation of conflicts between the republics and the federation. First, to avoid any more rebellions like the Croatian Spring, the party radically decentralised the federal state, but at the same time it strengthened its own role and further micro-centralised its branches all over the country. As Golubović (1988:256) rightly points out, 'the IX congress of LCY (1969) has reaffirmed the directive role of the party apparatus and legalized the route to re-etatization'. With these changes the Yugoslav state became what some commentators termed 'policentric etatism'.

Second, the constitution change opened up the problem of the party–state relationship. Whereas the state was now radically decentralised, the party was still organised according to the Leninist principle of democratic centralism. As Bilandžić (1985:411) had rightly predicted, since both of these institutions were engaged in the decision-making process and were supposed to act as a single unit, changing the principle of organisation and function for one (the state) and not for the other (the party) would lead to the situation where one would break up the other.

Third, while the new constitution completely decentralised the federal state, it preserved the existing centralised modes of decision making within the federal units. In other words, the outcome of the reform of federation was not genuine decentralisation but, rather, micro-centralisation at the level of the republics. However, since the party itself was still a highly centralised organisation, as long as it was in control it could prevent disintegrative tendencies. The charismatic authority of Tito and other veteran party leaders, and the strength of another centralised institution – the army – helped to maintain the federation for another few years.

The 1974 constitution institutionalised the principle of ethnically defined nationality as a central element of the political system. However, the monopoly on its articulation was still firmly with the party, which decided all important issues regarding national policies. Since the state was completely decentralised and since the party itself was gradually losing its legitimacy among the Yugoslav population, the party leaderships of the individual republics attempted, and were in a position, to gain legitimacy by shifting their problems elsewhere. Hence, economic stagnation or a shortage of political liberty was now interpreted as a result of the 'unequal position of our republic within the federation'. The message was simple: 'It is the neighbouring republic (Croatia, Serbia, Slovenia, and so on) that hinders our development.' Decentralisation of the state soon produced a quasi-multiparty system, with eight communist parties having a virtual monopoly over their territories. This situation was soon to lead to further and more intensive conflicts between the party leaderships of individual republics.

Tito's death in 1980 marked a new phase in the development of the Yugoslav state. This was the period of economic stagnation, huge inflation, an enormous unemployment rate, and political unrest in Serbia's Kosovo province. GDP fell from 8.8 per cent in the period 1956–64 to 0.4 in the period 1980–84 (Cohen 1993). The country also had huge international debts and the gap between the developed north-west and the undeveloped south-east continued to widen. The effects of the new constitutional arrangements were most apparent in the area of economic policy. The republics conducted their own economic policies and the fact that 65 per cent of all borrowings abroad were made by the republics and provinces themselves indicates how decentralised the state had become (Dyker 1990). The death of Tito meant that the last source of authority, and the last element binding the party leaderships together and keeping them from serious conflict, was gone. From now on, the struggle for political control would intensify.

It is important to emphasise here that, despite large-scale unrest in Croatia in the late 1960s and early 1970s, relations between ethnic groups in Yugoslavia, unlike those between the individual party leaderships, were reasonably good. As surveys in this period show, the levels of social distance between the main ethnic groups were very low, if not non-existent, and the rate of intermarriage was relatively high. Thus, in a 1964 survey, 73 per cent of the sample described relationships between Yugoslav ethnic groups as good. Similarly, in a 1966 survey, 85.3 per cent of Croats and 81.7 per cent of Serbs showed very slight or negligible ethnic distance towards other ethnic groups living in Yugoslavia (Dyker 1979). The results of surveys conducted in the 1980s showed a similar pattern (Katunarić 1986, 1987). In addition, the rate of inter-ethnic marriage for the period 1962–89 was regularly high. The average percentage of exogamous marriages was 12.63, ranging from as low as 6.98 per cent in Kosovo to 25.95 per cent in Vojvodina (Botev 1994). The real conflicts were on the top, rather than on the bottom, of the social pyramid.

The mid-1980s brought the first significant criticism of Tito's policies and of the state's highly decentralised structure. In 1985 a group of academics from the Serbian Academy of Arts and Sciences drafted a document, 'Memorandum', which set up the basis of Serbian ethno-nationalism. The document attempted to show that post-war Yugoslavia had been developed as an anti-Serb project and that 'Yugoslavia in its present form was no longer an adequate solution to the Serbian question' (Silber and Little 1995:30). The document was especially critical of the 1974 constitution, seeing it as designed to weaken Serbia by giving its two provinces semi-state status. It also insisted that Serbia's political weakness was reflected in its 'economic subjugation' by Slovenia and Croatia. The publishing of the Memorandum provoked outrage in the other republics, but it largely gained backing from Serbian intellectuals and silent support from some members of the Serbian LC Central Committee.

Promoting indirectly the ideas presented in the Memorandum and relying on growing dissatisfaction with the political system, widening economic crises and political crises in Kosovo, Slobodan Milošević managed in 1987 to gain power within the Central Committee of the Serbian branch of the LC. Unlike his predecessors, Milošević built his support base not among the party members and through usually institutional channels, but principally among the masses by organising 'spontaneous' street demonstrations, first in Kosovo and Belgrade and then in Vojvodina, Montenegro and the Serbian-populated areas of Croatia and Bosnia. He was the first communist leader since 1971 and the Croatian Spring to break the taboo of speaking to an audience consisting solely of one ethnic group (Serbs) and using ethno-national rhetoric. The involvement of the new leadership of the Serbian LC in the organisation of large-scale demonstrations on an ethnic basis meant that, from now on, politics would not be confined to party meetings and declarations. Pandora's box was definitely opened.

The results of micro-centralisation, 1987–1991

The intensive decentralisation of the federal state and the simultaneous micro-centralisation at the level of the individual republics in a one-party state situation inevitably led to fragmentation of the central party structure. After Tito's death, it was just a matter of time before individual party elites started fighting for political control over the federal centre.

Since Croatian political space was largely silenced after the political purges of 1971, and new cadres were elected and promoted only if firmly anti-nationalist, politics oriented towards ethnic mobilisation could develop only in the other two major centres – Belgrade (Serbia) and Ljubljana (Slovenia). Between 1987 and 1989, Serbian LC leadership supporters organised a number of street demonstrations in Kosovo, Vojvodina and Montenegro and managed to replace their party leaderships with those that were loyal to Milošević. In this way, Serbia controlled over four out of eight votes in the federal collective presidency and could block any decision on the federal level. This 'anti-bureaucratic revolution' provoked outrage in the other republics and especially in the most developed and most Westernised, Slovenia. Hence, this period was characterised by constant political struggle between the rising Serbian nationalism promoted by Milošević and the Serbian party leadership and a liberal and pro-Western, but also nationalist-oriented, Slovenian leadership led by M. Kučan. Under the influence of civil society groups and a change of general political climate, the Slovenian party leadership was more ready than any other LC leadership for democratisation and radical political change.

The changes that the new Serbian leadership undertook were finalised in March 1989 when a number of crucial constitutional amendments were adopted in the Serbian parliament. In doing so, Serbia took virtual control of Kosovo and Vojvodina, reducing their autonomy to a minimum, and thus became more powerful than the other republics in the federation. In addition, the Serbian government took over a number of functions that were in the domain of the federal state, such as appointing its own foreign minister. This was a precedent that other republics were to follow. Slovenian and, later on, Croatian reaction was swift. The Slovenian party leadership proposed a set of constitutional changes that were aimed at weakening the federal centre even further, by establishing an 'asymmetrical federation' in which Slovenia would take over from the federal government the right, among other things, to decide how to allocate the republic's wealth. By adopting these amendments, Slovenia strengthened even further the definition of its sovereignty in the 1974 constitution.

Slovenia and Croatia were also the first to organise genuine democratic elections in early 1990. The elections brought the opposition nationalist parties into power whose programs were clearly secessionist. By the end of that year, elections had been held in each republic. In Bosnia and Herzegovina and in Macedonia, nationalist parties also gained majorities and formed new governments, whereas in Serbia and Montenegro the LC changed its name to Socialist Party and Democratic Socialist Party, respectively, and won elections.

Slovenia and Croatia were now even less ready to accept the concept of Serbian leadership for the reorganisation of the federal state. On the Serbian leadership's demand for a more centralised state, they responded with the idea of confederation. The new Bosnian and Macedonian governments attempted to mediate by proposing compromises that were always rejected by the Serbian or the Slovenian side.

In this situation, the institutions of the federal government were gradually losing any significance and power. The collective presidency was largely paralysed and no group had a majority,[8] and the federal parliament was basically illegitimate since no federal elections had taken place. The only relatively functional institutions were the office of Prime Minister A. Marković and the army. However, neither of these two could succeed in preserving the federal state. The prime minister was losing the backing of the republics, while the army was internally divided not only between various ethnic groups but also between reformists (clearly a minority) and hardliners.[9]

Since the federal institutions were largely non-functional, negotiations on the status of the new organisation of the common state were held directly between the presidents of the republics. When, after many such meetings, agreement had not been reached, Slovenia and later Croatia, following successful referendums, decided in 1991 to proclaim their independence.

THE BREAKUP OF THE FEDERAL STATE

The results of the first democratic elections of 1990 have further polarised the political and constitutional crisis in the federation. The newly elected governments in Slovenia and Croatia not only differed ethno-nationally from those in Serbia and Montenegro but had also been ideological adversaries. While the north-west was now governed by right-wing nationalists whose primary aim was to secure an independent ethno-national state, to change the economic and political system and to try to join the European Union and other Western associations, the south-east was ruled by the same old left-wing nationalists whose principal goal was largely to preserve the existing economic and political system and to establish its hegemony within the federation and who showed little interest in joining Western alliances.

However, what was common to both sides was their firm determination to use all means available in realising their immediate interests. For this reason, both Serbian and Croatian ruling elites, which had become the main representatives of the two sides, had taken control of the mass media and engaged in delegitimisation of each other by means of an intensive media war. But the targets of delegitimisation were not so much opponent governments as entire populations – the Croats and the Serbs. For the first time since WWII, traditional and historical differences, such as religious denomination (Roman Catholicism v. Serbian Orthodox Church), script (Latin v. Cyrillic), and dialect (predominantly Serbian *ekavian* v. Croatian *ijekavian*), were extensively used to underline the distinctiveness of these two ethnic nations.[10] Hence, at the level of the masses, the political struggle was articulated as a cultural struggle. The message disseminated in the media was not that 'we cannot live with them because they do not share our ideas about the political and economic organisation of our society' but, rather, that 'we cannot live with them because they are culturally, religiously and historically different or inferior to us'.

The new elites were successful in mobilising ethnic differences for two main reasons. First, since the old communist regime was opposed to the use of historic, religious and cultural symbols of an ethnic nature but these were preserved strongly in the collective memory of people, the new elite was in a position to manipulate these symbols. Communist symbolism was quickly replaced with the old ethno-national symbolism (flags, coats of arms, religious motifs, old national heroes and myths). Because of their emotional appeal and ambiguity, these symbols were then relatively easily connected to some imaginary golden ethnic past. In the case of Serbs and Croats, this past could be symbolically traced to 'vast' medieval kingdoms of Serbia under Tsar Dušan and Croatia under King Tomislav. 'It is this ambiguity in their meanings that forges symbols into such powerful instruments in the hands of leaders and groups in mystifying people for particularistic or universalistic or both purposes' (Cohen 1979:103). Symbols become mighty weapons in a power struggle because of their 'irrationality' and their connection to the real or imaginary objects and acts that affect human feelings.

Second, because the communist regime had not allowed subtle discussion of the WWII massacres and genocide committed by the Ustashi regime against the Serbian population in the Nazi-sponsored Independent State of Croatia, nor of the crimes committed by Serbian Chetnik paramilitaries against Muslim and Croatian civilians, this space was open for new elites. Since these topics were official taboos but at the same time were alive and well in the collective memory, the new elites in power were now in a position to crudely manipulate these images and provoke fear. With the help of ethno-symbolism, new enemies replaced old ones. Instead of the 'capitalists', 'fascists' and 'Western imperialists', the new sources of fear became Ustashis/Croats, Chetniks/Serbs and Islamic fundamentalists/Bosnian Muslims.

In a situation of political uncertainty, economic hardship and state collapse, intensive attachment to ethnic group and consequently animosity and hatred towards other 'threatening' ethnic groups became the only source of security and certainty. The instrumentalisation of these emotions and interests by political elites was particularly evident in the mass media. The dissemination of propagandistic messages had a direct influence on entire populations, provoking old fears – for example, that the new Croatian state is just another version of the Nazi-sponsored and Ustashi-run Independent State of Croatia, or that all Serbs are Chetniks who only want to subjugate, exploit and oppress Croats as happened during monarchist Yugoslavia times.

Some of the actual policies of the new governments contributed further to these fears. The new Croatian constitution of 1990 defined the Republic of Croatia solely as a state of ethnic Croats and not as a state of all its citizens or, as it had been in the Constitution of Socialist Republic of Croatia, as 'the state of Croats and Serbs living in Croatia'. The new ruling party, the Croatian Democratic Community, removed Serbs from important state institutions, introduced the Latin alphabet as the only officially recognised script, and immediately changed political symbols and the names of the streets, provoking Belgrade to manipulate and 'awaken' nationalism among Serbs in Croatia. All these actions led to a widespread perception among Serbs in Croatia that, if Croatia became independent, they would become second-rate citizens. So, when in 1991 Slovenia and Croatia declared their independence, the territories where Serbs had a majority did not recognise the new Croatian government and started establishing their own institutions. With the backing of the Yugoslav army, now clearly pro-Serbian, they proclaimed their independent state of 'Serbian Krajina'.

The last moves of the federal government were to try to stop Slovenia's secession. Since Slovenia had no significant minorities, it could quickly and easily negotiate its secession with the Serbian side. This, however, was not the case with the Croatian secession. Having a large Serbian minority that had already established its own institutions in the rural areas of the state, Croatia could not follow Slovenia without conflict with the Serbs, a conflict which developed into full-fledged war in the second half of 1991. After six months, the war was partially stopped by UN intervention that confirmed the status quo. The period 1992–94 was one of non-war, non-peace in Croatia, and in 1995 the Croatian army conducted two military offensives, crushed the 'Serbian Krajina' state and established the authority of the Croatian state in these territories.

Much more horrific war soon followed in Bosnia and Herzegovina. The open conflict between the Serbian and Croatian governments could not but affect this multi-ethnic republic. As events started to unfold, the Serbian side in the new Bosnian government followed the position of the Serbian government in opposing the joint institutions, whereas the Bosnian Muslim/Bosniak[11] and Croatian ruling parties largely followed the views and policies promoted by the Slovenian and Croatian governments. In 1992 when the Bosnian government, following a successful referendum, decided to proclaim independence, war spread to the territories of Bosnia and Herzegovina where, again, the Yugoslav army openly sided with the Serbian paramilitaries. The Bosnian Serb side proclaimed its independent state, Republika Srpska, and was supported by the Serbian government, both militarily and financially. The war in Bosnia ended with the Dayton Accord, enforced by NATO and signed by all sides in 1995, dividing the country into two largely self-sufficient entities.

In 1992 Serbia and Montenegro proclaimed their common independent state – the Federal Republic of Yugoslavia. The new state was conceived as a continuation of the old federal republic. However, the international community did not recognise the new federation as the lawful successor of socialist Yugoslavia. On the contrary, the United Nations imposed economic and political sanctions on Serbia and Montenegro for their involvement in the Bosnian war.

ACCOMMODATED ETHNICITY IN THE SUCCESSOR STATES

The breakup of communist Yugoslavia resulted in the establishment of five new independent states: Slovenia, Croatia, Bosnia and Herzegovina, Macedonia, and the new federal Yugoslavia. Of these, only Slovenia was almost mono-ethnic; the other four still had large ethnic minorities. Despite the claims made by the nationalist governments that independence would solve the 'national question', the new states inherited many of the same problems that communist Yugoslavia had. The conflicts that were fought between the republics in the former state were now mirrored on a micro-scale in the republics themselves. Ethnic problems did not vanish with independence; on the contrary, for most of the new states, they increased and accelerated.

The initial response of the new governments was tighter centralisation, which only provoked even stronger demands for decentralisation and, in some cases, secession. To accommodate these demands, often after armed struggle, some of the new governments were forced to accept federal, confederal and other types of decentralised arrangements. Being largely mono-ethnic, Slovenia escaped these difficulties, which is why it will be omitted from further analysis. The remaining states had to respond to the decentralisation demands made by their minorities or regions. One (Bosnia and Herzegovina) was forced to reorganise itself as an extremely loosely formulated confederation, one (FR Yugoslavia) responded by nominally preserving the existing federal structure, while the other two (Croatia and Macedonia) aimed at accommodating minority demands by cultural rather than political decentralisation.

Bosnia and Herzegovina

The 1995 Dayton agreement defines Bosnia and Herzegovina as a sovereign state made up of two entities: the Federation of Bosnia–Herzegovina and the Serb Republic (Republika Srpska). The structure and constitutional arrangements of the new state are very unusual. Although the state is not officially defined either as a federation or as a confederation since one of its entities is a federation in itself, it is obvious that the relationship between the two entities is at least confederal. Some think that the most appropriate definition is 'asymmetric confederation' (Kasapović 1996). The powers of the central government are limited to foreign policy and trade, customs, monetary policy and banking, international and inter-entity law enforcement, and a few other less substantial issues. All

161

significant powers, such as defence, policing and the judiciary, are in the hands of the entity governments. Each entity has its own constitution, parliament, army and government. There are a few joint institutions, such as the Parliamentary Assembly, the Council of Ministers, the Constitutional Court and the collective presidency. The constitution provides that the representatives of the three main ethnic groups – Bosniaks, Serbs and Croats – have a veto over all important decisions. To enforce the functioning of these joint institutions, the Dayton agreement stipulates that foreign nationals be appointed to them. Thus, out of nine members of the Constitutional Court, the president of the European Court of Human Rights appoints three, who cannot be citizens of Bosnia–Herzegovina. In addition, the governor of the central bank is appointed by the International Monetary Fund. In this way, Bosnia and Herzegovina has both de facto and de jure elements of an international protectorate.

The NATO/UN soldiers and other UN personnel on its soil are there to guarantee that the provisions of the constitution agreed in Dayton are implemented. The powers of the international representatives in the country have increased several times since Dayton in order to accelerate their realisation. All these changes and safeguards provided by the international community have helped to stop the war and to move towards post-war development.

However, the society itself remains deeply divided. The war has not only homogenised ethnic groups living in Bosnia and sharpened their mutual animosities, but it has also institutionalised cultural differences. With the Dayton constitution, ethnicity has become territorialised and ethnic membership remains the key issue in any political discourse. As the results of the first post-war elections show, there is even greater support for the same ethno-nationalist parties that were in power during the war. Despite the proportional electoral system, 95 per cent of all seats were taken by three ethno-nationalist parties or party blocks (Kasapović 1996:19). Equally, strong international pressure on ethno-nationalists and energetic support for the opposition did not pay off in the elections of 1998. Hence, politics is reduced to a single dimension – ethnicity. The refugees are still not allowed to return to areas that are under the control of other ethnic groups. In the rare cases when they have been allowed to return, they find themselves objects of hostility and hatred by the ethnically different residents. The war has produced an exceptionally high degree of social distance and animosity between Serbs, Bosniaks and Croats. When asked whether they could live in peace in a single state with the other two groups, only Bosniaks thought so (80 per cent), while Serbs (89 per cent) and Croats (88 per cent) thought that 'war has permanently damaged inter-ethnic relations' and hence 'it is not possible for the three communities to live together' (Žunec 1998:203). When these results are compared with those of the 1989 surveys, in which 90 per cent of respondents had described inter-ethnic relations in the place they lived as good or very good and 62.75 per cent had agreed that 'one's nationality/ethnicity should be of no importance in choosing a life partner' (Pešić 1995), it is obvious that war has had a very deep impact on ethnic relations in Bosnia and Herzegovina.

Because of its very late intervention in the conflict with the Dayton Accord, the international community has only endorsed the status quo in Bosnia. The agreement was largely an ad hoc arrangement whose main aim was just to stop the war as soon as possible. So that all three warring parties would agree on its content, the document was vague and imprecise. As a result, it is interpreted differently by the three sides and the main joint institutions are still not functioning. The paralysis of the joint government was again solved in an ad hoc manner, by strengthening the powers of the Office of the High Representative of the International Community.

Despite the fact that the international community has provided the new Bosnian state with a superior legislative system that includes safeguards and guarantees for all three ethnic communities, there has been little progress on reaching consensual decisions. Almost all significant decisions for the new state – from the selection of the new flag and state symbols, joint currency and joint passports to the selection of joint car licence plates – were decided solely by the Office of the High Representative of the International Community. The elected representatives of the three communities could not agree on any of these issues. The new power elites benefit from such a situation because they can push ethnonationalist agendas as far as they want and hence legitimise themselves 'at home', knowing at the same time that the High Representative will have the last word.

All this suggests that Bosnia and Herzegovina is still far from being a genuine, democratic and independent state where issues of decentralisation can be discussed and decided from below with strong popular support. As long as the population of the state sees decisions by the international community as imposed, there is very little hope for the preservation of existing constitutional arrangements.

FR Yugoslavia

In 1992 the two remaining units of the socialist federation, Serbia and Montenegro, decided to preserve their federal arrangement and established the Federal Republic of Yugoslavia. The new state has been defined as a sovereign federation, but the individual republics have gained more powers than they had in the 1974 constitution. Thus, the 1992 constitution defines an individual republic as a 'state where the power belongs to its citizens' (Article 6). The republics have their own constitutions and can conduct their own foreign policy, individually join international organisations and enter into agreements with other states. Although the federation is, on paper, defined very loosely, its actual organisation is more complex and conflictual.

First, there is an obvious and huge difference in population and territory size between the two units. Serbia is ten times larger in terms of territory and twenty times in terms of population. Despite safeguards built into the constitution, such as vetoes and equal numbers of parliamentary representatives in the second chamber of the federal parliament (the Council of Republics), there is clear dominance by Serbia over federal policy.

Second, while both republics have large minority populations, Serbia also has two autonomous regions, Kosovo and Vojvodina, whose autonomy was greatly reduced with the amendments to the Serbian constitution in 1989 and with the new Serbian constitution of 1990. Since the majority Albanian population of Kosovo (90 per cent) do not accept the new position of their province within Serbia, they have boycotted all republican and federal elections since the collapse of communism. The response of the Serbian state has been fierce. The government not only appointed Serbian officials to the Kosovar state apparatus but it also closed down Albanian informational, educational and other vital institutions. Since then, existing mutual animosities between Serbs and Albanians have been on the increase. A survey conducted long before the war of 1999 showed that 77.9 per cent of the Serbian population thought that Albanians were dangerous for Serbia.[12]

The process towards a more centralised state that started in 1987 in Serbia is also reflected in the new federation. Since the establishment of the new state, the Serbian leadership has gradually attempted to integrate the federation and to strengthen the powers of the federal state.

Third, and most importantly, the charismatic authority of Milošević has, since 1989, been a decisive factor in the functioning of both Serbia and Montenegro. The new leadership of the Montenegrin LC was installed with his help and, until the election of 1997, was totally loyal to the Serbian leadership.

This unequal position of federal units could remain unchallenged only in extraordinary circumstances such as the war of 1991–95. While there was an external threat, Serbia and Montenegro presented a united front, but since the war ended the differences between the two have become more apparent. Apart from small variations in dialect, there are no significant ethnic differences between Serbs and Montenegrins (they share the same religion, 'culture', history, language). The conflict was to become exclusively political. First, the sanctions imposed on FR Yugoslavia in 1992 had a devastating effect on both economies. However, since one of the central sources of income in Montenegro was tourism, it suffered much more than Serbia. Even when the sanctions were removed, the continuation of anti-Western policies by the Serbian, and thus federal, leadership further deprived Montenegro of its tourism income.

Second, the Montenegrin political leadership had engaged more intensively in transformation of the economy by privatising many state-owned companies, while the Serbian leadership had maintained the status quo by avoiding privatisation. The parallel existence of two different economic systems appeared to be an important source of conflict. Third, the increasing threat of Serbian majoritarians at the federal level, which would potentially result in an unequal position for Montenegro in the federation and, in the long run, annihilation of Montenegrin statehood, culminated in the election of Milošević to the post of federal president in 1997.

Despite the fact that the 1992 constitution limits the powers of the federal president, Milošević has preserved his individual power and influence in his new post. This has provoked resistance in Montenegro, and the elections in 1997 and 1998 were victories for anti-Milošević candidates. The escalation of the conflict in Kosovo in 1998 and the war with NATO in 1999 have estranged the Montenegrin leadership even further. While there were elements of consociationalism (Lijphart 1968) built into the 1992 federal constitution and applied in reality by relying on a grand coalition of Serbia's and Montenegro's ruling parties, they completely disappeared with the split within the Montenegrin leadership in 1997.

All of these elements indicate that the new Yugoslav federation which has, simultaneously and paradoxically, features of both a confederal and a unitary state is very far from being a genuine and democratic federal state. It has not only been unable to 'solve' the ethnic conflicts inherited from its communist predecessor but it has also produced new ones, such as the issue of Sandjak's Muslims, Vojvodina's Hungarians and Croats. The animosity between the federal centre, Belgrade, and the rest of the country has been accelerating since the establishment of the new state in 1992.

Croatia and Macedonia

Although before the war Croatia was a multi-ethnic state, with more than 12 per cent of its population being Serbian, the two offensives by the Croatian army in 1995 resulted in the mass expulsion of its Serbian minority, and present-day Croatia is almost mono-ethnic. After its independence and under pressure from the international community, Croatia laid down in its constitution the basis for the two autonomous regions with a Serbian majority (Knin and Glina). During the war, the government was ready to negotiate an even greater degree of autonomy that culminated in the 'Z-4 plan' (see Žunec 1998), which, although never accepted by the leadership of the Serbian Krajina para-state, offered semi-federal status to Krajina Serbs. With Croatian victories on the battlefield, the offers were withdrawn. At present, only cultural autonomy is guaranteed to the Serbian and Italian minorities (the use of their native language and script), as well as their rather symbolic representation in the parliament (three seats are guaranteed for the Serbian minority). However, expulsion of the Serbian population certainly did not 'solve' the problem, because the international community expects Croatia to allow their return. In view of the fact that the war has caused deep mistrust and animosity, Serbs are reluctant to return individually, whereas Croats are opposed to their collective return. As many surveys conducted during the war and in the post-war period show, ethnic distance between the two communities is still exceptionally strong. For example, 15.3 per cent (in 1992) and 14.1 per cent (in 1993) of Croatian university students displayed an attitude of extreme aggressiveness towards Serbs (agreeing with such statements as 'I would like someone to kill them all' or 'I would personally exterminate them all') (Malešević and Uzelac 1997).

In addition to the Serbian problem, the new Croatian state, consisting of several regions that have distinctive identities and histories, also faces increasing opposition from regional autonomist movements. Since the new Croatian government largely centralised the Croatian state with the 1990 constitution, calls for decentralisation have been heard from various regions – Dalmatia, Slavonia and, especially, Istria. The region of Istria, which has its own cultural and historical identity and a large Italian minority, is the strongest opponent of central government. In all successive elections held in the post-communist period, it voted overwhelmingly for the regional autonomist movement (Istrian Democratic Alliance). The government response to Istrian demands for decentralisation was further centralisation that included reorganisation of state internal borders so that they cut across traditional and historic regional divisions, and changes to the electoral system to decrease the voice of the IDA and other such movements in the national parliament. All of these moves have provoked only animosity towards the centre – Zagreb.

Despite the fact that Macedonia is the only former Yugoslav republic to have escaped the horrors of war, it has also had to confront ethnic cleavages and the politicisation of ethnicity. Macedonia shares many of the same problems. The fact that one-third of its population is of Albanian origin and that ethnic Albanians constitute a majority in most of western Macedonia (Tetovo and Kumanovo regions) is in itself enough to signal that the ethnic factor cannot but play an important role in the political life of the new state. Even though the new Macedonian government has some elements of consociation, as formulated in Lijphart's early work (1968), it still cannot overcome deep ethnic divisions and the dominance of ethnicity in politics. Since its establishment, the new state has been ruled by a grand coalition of politically moderate Macedonian and Albanian parties, while at the same time excluding more extreme parties. However, power sharing between the two communities has not been equal and has been more the result of necessity than a genuine determination to develop a pluralist democracy. The use of a majoritarian electoral system, the resistance to any form of territorial autonomy and local self-government and the non-existence of a mutual veto system in relation to the vital interests of the two communities indicate that the Macedonian case is still very far from being a true consociation in the Lijphartian sense. Regardless of the political maturity of its government and the steps undertaken to accommodate ethnicity, the Republic of Macedonia is defined in its 1991 constitution, similar to the Croatian case, as 'the national state of Macedonians' instead of as 'the state of its citizens', the more moderate definition proposed by Albanian and civic-oriented parties.

In addition to its internal problems, Macedonia's external position has further contributed to radicalisation of the 'national question'. Being stretched between four largely hostile neighbours who do not recognise its full statehood (Greece), clearly show territorial aspirations (FR Yugoslavia, Albania) or do not recognise the existence of a separate Macedonian language and nationality (Bulgaria), Macedonia has had to balance its foreign policy to maintain its independence and at the same time to preserve internal peace. All of these unresolved problems have had an impact on the predominance of ethnic discourse in politics.

An inflexible politics of centralisation, the lack of democratic solutions in the accommodation of ethnicity and ad hoc responses to demands made by its ethnic minorities and regions have led both Croatia and Macedonia to a situation of permanent conflict between the centre and the 'periphery'. The change of political system alone did not solve the 'ethnic problem', and the similarities between the present-day governments and those of communist Yugoslavia in their approach to ethnic communities are clearly evident.

CONCLUSION

Communist Yugoslavia broke up because it produced in itself animosities and conflicts that it could not resolve. To maintain its political monopoly, the party attempted to deal with the accumulated differences and existing antagonisms by shifting the emphasis from the crucial issue of popular participation towards the question of territorial organisation of the federal state. The party-state evaded the central problems of democratisation and liberalisation by articulating them as questions of decentralisation. In other words, decentralisation was used as an ad hoc mechanism for decreasing the pressure from 'below'. In this way, the federal party gradually devolved power to the party leaderships of the individual republics instead of devolving it to its citizens. This policy resulted in the establishment of a quasi-multiparty situation, with eight communist parties competing for control of the centre. In this situation, all political issues were soon to become exclusively ethno-national issues. This was a prelude to war and the collapse of the joint federal state. Yugoslavia did not collapse because it was a multi-ethnic society or because of the political recognition of ethnicity via federalism. Yugoslavia collapsed because it was not democratic.

The relationship between ethnicity and decentralisation in the Yugoslav successor states shows that secession and the establishment of independent states does not automatically solve the problem. On the contrary, the new independent states share many of the same problems of communist Yugoslavia. With the possible exception of Slovenia, all successor states are in one way or another multi-ethnic societies that face the problems of territorial or corporate decentralisation. Regardless of the fact that they all define themselves as democratic states, their approach to the recognition of ethnicity is in many ways similar to that of communist Yugoslavia. The calls for decentralisation are answered only if the pressure from ethnic groups or the international community is so intense that there is no alternative. The adopted arrangements are viewed, once again, as an imposed necessity rather than a genuine will to build a democratically decentralised society. The issues of decentralisation are, as before, used as a potential weapon in the power struggle.

The case of Yugoslavia and its successor states indicates that the central question is not whether federalism is good or bad for multicultural societies but, rather, whether the arrangements between the federal units are negotiated in a democratic and voluntary way. In a truly democratic society, collective demands for cultural and ethnic recognition have to be recognised and accommodated. However, it is not recognition of ethnicity per se that is crucial but the process of its articulation. Ethnic differences and rights in a democratic society are part of the individual and collective rights of its citizens. If they are suppressed in any way, they will quickly become dominant forms of political identity. If they are recognised and accommodated, they will remain just one among the many segments of individual and group identity. As the Yugoslav case shows, in a situation where no other political space is open, in a multicultural society ethnicity will always dominate politics.

NOTES

1 For a more extensive discussion of all of these theories, see Malešević (1998a:105–21).

2 For example, Yugoslavia did not have the concept of 'titular nation' and the system of internal passports which were crucial in the institutionalisation of ethno-national federal units in the Soviet Union (see Brubaker 1996).

3 In 1948, after the Tito–Stalin split, the Yugoslav Communist Party was expelled from the Cominform, and Eastern European communist states broke off relations with Yugoslavia.

4 With the breakup of the common state in 1991, the common language, Serbo-Croat, has also officially disintegrated into Serbian, Croatian and Bosnian, although the differences between these three languages are no greater than those between American and British English. It is also important to note that there are differences in dialects among Serbo-Croat speakers but they cross-cut ethnic borders.

5 In the period 1966–70, GDP fell from 8.1 per cent to 5.8 per cent (Federal Bureau for Statistics 1986:10).

6 The Croatian national movement (also known as 'Maspok' or 'Croatian Spring') was launched in 1967 with a declaration about the position and name of the Croatian language which spread to other groups: separatist economists who wanted to see an independent Croatian state, liberals who demanded change of the political system, and students and cultural workers who stood for cultural nationalism and the separation of the Croatian language and culture from its amalgamation with the Serbian language and culture.

7 The status of Serbia's two provinces, Vojvodina and Kosovo, was also upgraded and they too had their constitutions as well as their representatives in the collective presidency of Yugoslavia.

8 Since the Serbian leadership had control over four votes (Serbia, Vojvodina, Kosovo and Montenegro), the voting usually ended up in a deadlock – 4:4.

9 It is important to emphasise here that Serbs were significantly overrepresented in the army.

10 For more about the delegitimisation strategies used during the war in former Yugoslavia, see Malešević and Uzelac (1997:291–8) and Malešević (1998b).

11 From 1990 onwards, the term 'Bosniak' (not Bosnian, which refers to all citizens of Bosnia–Herzegovina) was used more often by Bosnian Muslims to describe their nationality.

12 *Naša Borba*, 17 February 1997.

REFERENCES

Bilandžić, D. 1985. *Historija SFRJ: Glavni Procesi 1918–1985* [History of the Socialist Federal Republic of Yugoslavia: Main Trends 1918–1985]. Zagreb: Školska Knjiga.

Botev, N. 1994. 'Where east meets west: ethnic intermarriage in the former Yugoslavia 1962 to 1989', *American Sociological Review* 59:461–80.

Brass, P. 1991. *Ethnicity and Nationalism*. New Delhi: Sage.

Brubaker, R. 1996. *Nationalism Reframed*. Cambridge: Cambridge University Press.

Caca, Dj. 1988. 'Ustavni koncept socijalističkih republika i socijalističkih autonomnih pokrajina [The constitutional frame for the socialist republics and socialist autonomous provinces]', in *Ustavni Razvoj Socialističke Jugoslavije* [The Constitutional Development of Socialist Yugoslavia]. Belgrade: Eksportpres.

Cohen, A. 1969. *Custom and Politics in Urban Africa*. Berkeley: University of California Press.

—— 1979. 'Political symbolism', *Annual Review of Anthropology* 8:87–113.
—— 1981. *The Politics of Elite Culture: Explorations in the Dramaturgy of Power in a Modern African Society*. Berkeley: University of California Press.
Cohen, L. 1993. *Broken Bonds: The Disintegration of Yugoslavia*. Boulder: Westview.
Dyker, D. 1979. 'Yugoslavia: unity out of diversity?', in A. Brown and J. Gray (eds) *Political Culture and Political Change in Communist States*. London: Macmillan.
—— 1990. *Yugoslavia: Socialism, Development and Debt*. London: Routledge.
Federal Bureau for Statistics 1986. *Jugoslavija 1945–1985: Statistički Prikaz* [A Statistical Overview]. Belgrade.
Golubović, Z. 1988. *Kriza Identiteta Savremenog Jugoslovenskog Društva* [The Identity Crisis of Contemporary Yugoslav Society]. Belgrade: Filip Višnjič.
Hodson, R., D. Sekulić and G. Massey 1994. 'National tolerance in the former Yugoslavia', *American Journal of Sociology* 99(6):1534–58.
Kasapović, M. 1996. 'Izbori: kontekst i rezultati [Elections: a context and results]', *Erasmus* 18, October.
Katunarić, V. 1986. 'Sistem moći, socijalna struktura i nacionalno pitanje [The system of power, social structure and national question]', *Revija za Sociologiju* [Sociological Review] XXVIII:75–90.
—— 1987. 'Autoritarnost, etnocentrizam, seksizam i društvene grupe [Authoritarianism, ethnocentrism, sexism and social groups]', *Revija za Sociologiju* [Sociological Review] XXXIX:603–10.
Lijphart, A. 1968. *The Politics of Accommodation: Pluralism and Democracy in the Netherlands*. Berkeley: University of California Press.
Malešević, S. 1998a. 'Ethnic relations in contemporary sociological theory: one taxonomy', *Europa Ethnica* 3–4(55):105–21.
—— 1998b. 'Ustashas and Chetniks: delegitimization of an ethnic enemy in Serbian and Croatian war time cartoons', in C. Lowney (ed.) *Identities: Theoretical Considerations and Case Studies*. Vienna: IWM.
Malešević, S. and G. Uzelac 1997. 'Ethnic distance, power and war: the case of Croatian students', *Nations and Nationalism* 3(2):291–8.
Pešić, V. 1995. 'Društveni i državni aspekt multikulturalnosti u Bosni i Hercegovini [The social and state aspects of multiculturality in Bosnia and Herzegovina]', in *Interkulturalnost* [Interculturality]. Belgrade: IFDT.
Silber, L. and A. Little 1995. *The Death of Yugoslavia*. London: Penguin & BBC.
Stokes, G. 1993. *The Walls Came Tumbling Down: The Collapse of Communism in Eastern Europe*. Oxford: Oxford University Press.
Žunec, O. 1998. *Rat i Društvo: Ogledi iz Sociologije Vojske i Rata* [War and Society: Essays in the Sociology of the Military and War]. Zagreb: Jesenski i Turk & HSD.

PART III

SEEKING AUTONOMIES

ETHNICITY AND THE NEW CONSTITUTIONAL ORDERS OF ETHIOPIA AND ERITREA

JAMES C.N. PAUL

The 1994 Ethiopian constitution creates a unique federal state. Its preamble declares:

> We, the Nations, Nationalities and Peoples of Ethiopia . . . in the full exercise of our right to self-determination . . . [and] fully cognizant that our common destiny can best be served by rectifying historically unjust relationships . . . have adopted this Constitution through our [duly elected] representatives . . . [emphasis added]

The constitution goes on to reconstruct Ethiopia as a federation wherein 'all sovereign power resides', not in the people of Ethiopia but among its many, diverse 'nations, nationalities and peoples'. No distinction is made between a nation and a people. Both are defined as a group sharing a common language, culture, customs, history and identity. All such groups are endowed with a corporate right to constitute themselves into a self-governing state or local government within a state. Each enjoys an unconditional right to self-determination, including the right to secession (articles 8 and 39).[1]

In contrast, the preamble to the 1997 constitution of Eritrea – once a territory of the Ethiopian empire, but now (through force of arms and unilateral invocation of self-determination) Africa's newest independent state – declares:

> We the people of Eritrea, united by a common struggle for our rights and common destiny . . . [and] desirous that the Constitution be a covenant . . . founded in national unity . . . do ratify . . . [emphasis added]

The constitution recognises Eritrea's notable ethnic, regional and religious pluralism, but it tells us that these peoples, as a result of their collective exercise of self-determination, are now a single nation 'guided by the principle of unity in diversity' (preamble and art. 6).

Eritrea's past assertion of self-determination (as the collective right of all the peoples inhabiting a distinct historical territory to throw off an oppressive, alien regime) was never accepted by the Organization of African Unity (OAU). Ethiopia's present assertion (that the right inheres in all distinct ethnic groups) is certainly unacceptable. In Ethiopia, as elsewhere in Africa, the processes of state formation entailed the forcible aggregation of very different indigenous polities within borders arbitrarily drawn by imperial powers. In the early 1960s, the universal right to self-determination was invoked to justify the immediate conversion of Africa's colonial states into independent states. Since most of these juridical states were not yet empirical social formations, the OAU charter in effect sought to put the troublesome genie of self-determination back in the bottle once sovereignty was transferred (OAU 1963:preamble, arts. II(1)(c) and III(3)). But the cases of Ethiopia and Eritrea show the continued attraction of this problematic universal right in states afflicted with political turbulence reflecting their historical origins.

The two constitutions portray these difficulties. Many Eritreans and Ethiopians share common historical, cultural, religious and kinship ties. The boundary now separating them is an arbitrary line – the product of Italy's participation in the European scramble for colonial territories. The present leaders of both countries are Tigrinya speakers whose immediate ancestors lived on both sides of the Mareb River, which now constitutes an international border determining who is an Ethiopian of Tigrayan nationality and who is a Tigrayan of Eritrean nationality. Yet once, long ago, the Mareb flowed through the heartland of the ancient kingdom of Axum which is celebrated today by many people in both countries as the cradle of their civilisation.

As the border moves south and eastward of the Mareb, it passes through the lands of the Afar, a proud but isolated nomadic people occupying the inhospitable Danakil desert in Ethiopia and the arid coastal plains of southern Eritrea, where the strategic (for Ethiopia, but not Eritrea) Red Sea port of Assab is located. Historically, the Afar have hardly identified themselves as Eritreans or Ethiopians. Today those who live in Ethiopia are now declared to be a self-governing nation of the federation, enjoying an unconditional right to secession. Across the invisible, desolate border which they regularly traverse, a wandering Afar becomes, *mutatis mutandis,* an Eritrean national, governed from distant Asmara by a newly created, quite centralised government.

This chapter examines the constitutional evolution of the new Ethiopian and Eritrean states. It is useful to view the two countries as a single geopolitical area, because the history of each can hardly be taught without reference to the history of the other, and they are still interdependent in many ways. The avoidance of future civil war is crucial to both, and the security of each from their traditionally hostile Muslim neighbours depends on close relations.

However, Eritrea and Ethiopia now seem bent on fratricidal war – an event which confounds all neutral observers because it appears senseless and tragic. Ostensibly, the quarrel is over which state has sovereignty over a scrap of desolate highland territory along the northern border; apparently absurd errors in the maps used to mark the border in a set of nineteenth century Ethio-Italian treaties created this long-ignored problem. Neither government seems interested in arbitrating the dispute or in allowing the few people who live in this contested area to self-determine their citizenship; both seem to be using the crisis to stimulate patriotism and popular support. But a protracted war could bleed and bankrupt both countries and generate civil warfare within them. It is to be hoped that what follows in this chapter will not be mooted by such a calamity.

What are the prospects for success of these two radically different constitutional approaches to the problems of pluralism? The answer, to the extent that one is possible, must first depend on the criteria used to define success. It is now widely assumed that the essential tasks of reconstructing conflict-ridden states in Africa must centre on the interrelated and indivisible goals of promoting human security, human development and human rights. Thus, the creation of an integrated legal, administrative and political environment which fosters these objectives is probably a prerequisite to the promotion of social harmony by other means. Have the present regimes in Ethiopia and Eritrea created such environments?

HISTORICAL PERSPECTIVES

Arguably, there are several genres of Ethiopian history. One portrays the long history, political culture and expansion of the core Ethiopian polity from its Axumite origins through Haile Selassie's reign (Zewde 1991). A second portrays the impact of the creation of the 'Empire' of Ethiopia on the diverse peoples and polities incorporated into it (Tareke 1991). A third focuses on the causes, consequences and implications of the implosion of this relatively new imperial state (Harbeson 1998a). Obviously, all are controversial, and a synthesis of all three even more so.

The making of the empire
The first genre is important because, without it, the present Ethiopian state would not exist and because it depicts important elements of the political culture and identity of the Amharan, Tigrayan and other

175

assimilated groups who constituted the Habesha, a core pan-cultural group of peoples within Greater Ethiopia.

Themes of this history begin with a popular (and sophisticated) epic, a national legend which recounts the biblical and divinely blessed founding of Ethiopia by Menelik I, son of the Queen of Sheba and King Solomon of Israel. Further themes include the extraordinary durability of this polity over many centuries; the development, early on, of its own written languages and its distinctive Christian church, an institution which integrated the polity by transmitting a common culture providing a centre of community life, and a focus and source of Ethiopia's historic art, literature and monuments. Important, too, was the concept of the Solomonic dynasty, a line of monarchs descended from Solomon – who rule absolutely as 'king of kings', symbol of Ethiopian unity, defender of the church and of the independence of the Habesha from ever-threatening foreign enemies.

The political system was built on feudal-type, pyramidal social structures. At the top was the king of kings, later styled as emperor. Below him (and, at times, more powerful) were the higher nobility: the lesser kings, chiefs or warlords who controlled different territories by virtue of their power (rooted in forms of customary law) to collect rents and services from the peasants and to allocate a share of these spoils to their predatory soldiers, who constituted a third element of society. The church establishment, loosely governed by the archbishop, constituted a fourth element. At the broad base was the landholding, individualistic, but often exploited, peasantry who owed obligations to their overlords, the church and, nominally at least, the king of kings. Notions of social hierarchy, deference to authority and duties based on status even permeated peasant society: the head of the household was the master (*geteuch*) of his realm, and the ascribed status of others within it depended on factors such as age, sex and family relationships (Levine 1974).

Late in the nineteenth century, the historic Ethiopian polity emerged from anarchical feudal federalism to a new zenith. Warlords were brought to heel; foreign invaders, bent on imposing Islam (Egyptians and Mahdists from the north) or European colonisation (Turks and Italians advancing from Red Sea bases), were repulsed. The stunning, decisive defeats of Italian armies at Dogali in 1887, and especially at Adwa in 1896, preserved independence, revitalised the monarchy and inspired an Ethiopian imperialism.

Emperor Menelik II (1889–1913) subjugated a vast range of outlying kingdoms and decentralised polities in regions to the south, east and west of his newly established capital at Addis Ababa. He created much of Greater Ethiopia and thereafter settled its international borders by playing off the colonial powers which suddenly threatened to surround him.

Addis Ababa, situated at the very centre of the new empire, became linked to the sea by a rail line to Djibouti. These developments, and control of the fertile southern agricultural lands and coffee-producing Kaffa region, helped to assure a dominant position for the Shoan Amhara nobility in the new imperial state (Marcus 1975).

Menelik's 1896 (post-Adwa) treaty with Italy guaranteed Ethiopia's independence within settled borders in exchange for its recognition of Rome's sovereignty over the territory still occupied (after Adwa) by reinforced Italian armies based in Asmara. Thus was created (in a legal sense) a new, typically artificial colonial territory which Rome, celebrating its ancient empire, called 'Eritrea'. Menelik was praised for his *realpolitik*; but, in appeasing Italy's colonial appetite, he had sanctioned the partitioning of the Tigrayan peoples: those north of the Mareb River became subjects of an alien colonial regime; and those to the south remained independent Ethiopians, but they were now governed by a new Amharan monarchy in distant Shoa.[2]

Fifty years later, at the end of World War II, Haile Selassie, then at the apogee of his prestige, began a vigorous and ultimately successful international campaign to reunite Eritrea with Ethiopia. By 1952 the task of establishing the new empire seemed complete.

The peoples of the empire

Greater Ethiopia has been described as a multicultural museum, unique even in the African context of pluralistic states. Scholars have estimated that over seventy different dialects (belonging to the Semitic, Hamitic or Nilotic families) are spoken within its borders (Levine 1974:10).

The constitution converts most of these groups into nations or peoples endowed with the mystical qualities of juridical sovereignty. Yet there are striking differences between them in terms of size and resources, habitats and modes of subsistence, histories and homogeneity, political organisation and unity. Some are Habesha, part of the core polity; some were incorporated into the imperial state by force and thereafter exploited. Others were more peacefully annexed. Some assimilated the hegemonic, traditional culture; others were far less affected by it.

The empire spurred new social evolutions, affecting identities by creating new relationships between ethnic and religious communities. Addis Ababa became a multi-ethnic metropolis which generated new systems of expanded trade between regions. The creation of Haile Selassie's large, inclusive army, police and civil service produced new political opportunities and outlooks. The creation of a unified, national legal system and a modicum of new services generated new dependencies on the state.

Most of Ethiopia's many nations and peoples are too small, too lacking in resources and often too divided to wield much political clout. All really depend on a stable state for security, and maintenance of that stability depends on the development of politics within and between the Amhara, Tigray and Oromo nations which, together, constitute about 90 per cent of the population.

Amhara

The Amhara epitomise the problems of the concept of ethnicity now enshrined in the constitution. Arguably, they see themselves more as Ethiopians than as members of a unified ethnic group. Indeed, disunity has often characterised Amharan political culture. Intense patriotism is modified by loyalties to one's region and ancestral place. The emergence of Addis Ababa as the epicentre of politics, culture and development generated resentments in the northern Amharan regions, manifested by rebellious peasant protests against the regime's tax measures and disaffection among elites (Zewde 1991:217–18).

The winds of change blowing over Africa in the 1960s created new cultural and political fissures. A new elite, composed of educated, younger civil servants, teachers and army officers, became increasingly embarrassed by Ethiopia's backward condition. An ill-fated coup in 1961, led by young Amharan officers and civil servants who promised democratisation and structural reforms, had a profound impact, notably the politicisation of new generations of students. Enjoying some relatively free space in an otherwise closed political society, they became radicalised. Marxist dogmas were simplistically used to diagnose Ethiopia's plight and provide the remedy. Increasingly violent student demonstrations, disunity among political elites and the emperor's now advanced age presaged an increasingly uncertain future and the growing possibility of military intervention (Levine 1965; Zewde 1991). Thus, the upheavals which began in 1973 and ultimately led to a marginalisation of Amharan political power were, to a great extent, the result of the unravelling of the supposedly hegemonic Amharan nation.

Tigray

The Tigrayans (who constitute about 10 per cent of the total population) shared a long, common history, church and culture with their Amharan neighbours, and they, too, came to see themselves as victims, rather than beneficiaries, of Shoan rule. The late nineteenth century was, for Tigray, a time of tragedy. The heroic Tigrayan Emperor Yohannes IV perished in northern Eritrea during one of his endless battles against the Mahdi's invading armies. Thereupon, Menelik, king of distant Shoa, seized the Solomonic title and turned the course of empire to the south. His agreement with Italy to partition Tigray created a bitter legacy, and thereafter the region was marginalised in political and economic terms, experiencing steady population growth, environmental degradation, periodic famines and increasing impoverishment of the peasantry (Young 1997).

Thus, there developed a peculiar kind of nationalism in Tigray. The peoples of the region proudly identified with the historic Abyssinian polity (Axum is located in Tigray). At the same time, however, there was resentment against the Shoan regime, exacerbated by the Amharisation of education, culture and the language of public discourse.

In 1943, some Tigrayan nobles organised a rebellion against the emperor's efforts to centralise and control local governance. This insurgency was repressed, but those who had rebelled – known as the Woyene – became celebrated as popular heroes. In the 1970s, when civil warfare erupted in Ethiopia, radicalised Tigrayan university students were able to exploit and use this nationalism to develop a most effective army of young peasants, dedicated to the liberation of Ethiopia from Shoan domination and to the restoration of Tigray's proper place in the state (Young 1997).

Oromo

The Oromo (who probably constitute around 40 per cent of Ethiopia's population) moved from Kenya into many areas of the south during the sixteenth century. Thereafter, some groups advanced further north into Shoan highlands, eastward into the Harare region and westward into the regions of Wellega and Kaffa.

Oromo scholars and protagonists have recently portrayed their nation as a historic, homogeneous polity united by language, history and a system of decentralised governance which (it is said) was egalitarian and participatory, rooted in the celebrated Gada (age-group) system (Hassen 1990). But other scholars have long noted the diversity of the histories of different groups of the Oromo in the centuries following their extensive migrations into Greater Ethiopia. Clearly, they manifested an extraordinary capacity to adapt their way of life to different environments and host populations. Thus, many Oromo communities became Christian, adopting the ways of the Amhara and intermarrying with them. Others melded into the Islamic kingdoms of the south-west or the decentralised Muslim societies in the east; still others remained pastoral and rather independent (Levine 1974).

The Oromo experience of incorporation into Menelik's empire also varied. In some regions, the process was less violent and Oromo leaders were co-opted, by the award of titles and marriage, into the Shoan nobility. But, in the fertile regions south of Addis Ababa, subjugation was often brutal. The Shoan Amhara had long considered these territories as their own, and the Oromo living there were seen as uncivilised aggressors. Menelik conquered and expropriated these lands, keeping some, and

awarding fiefdom rights over others to Shoan nobles and permanent possessory rights to Shoan soldiers of merit – who became landholding
colonist settlers (*Neftagnya*). As commercial agriculture spread, Oromo
peasants on these lands became, in effect, 'tenants at will' or 'sharecrop-
pers' of *Neftagnya* or absentee landlords in Addis Ababa.

Islam
In times long past, the historic Christian kingdom was beleaguered by
jihad-motivated Muslim armies, attacking from the east. These invaders
penetrated the highlands, forced conversions and created pockets of
Islam which still exist today. Menelik's subjugation of neighbouring and
more distant Muslim regions was, in part, an attempt to make Christian
Ethiopia more secure. His annexation of Afar and Somali territories
brought into the empire warlike peoples whose ancestors, long ago but
in remembered history, had nearly destroyed historic Ethiopia. Haile
Selassie's annexation of Eritrea added a significant, historically hostile
Arabic-speaking population.

The effect of this long history was to criss-cross (Greater) Ethiopia
with lines of sub-tribal alliance and to create potential arenas of competition between the religions (Levine 1974:42). Haile Selassie, who had
married the daughter of a Muslim Oromo noble, recognised the need
for accommodation. The 1955 constitution guaranteed freedom to practise any religion. The emperor sanctioned *sub silentio* the continuation of
Sharia courts, even though his national codes purported to expropriate
all systems of religious and customary law; and he made a point of
bestowing gifts on Muslim charities. Today, after federalisation of the
erstwhile empire, Islam may become a more visible and potentially divisive political force.

Afar and Somali
The Afar and Somali Hamitic-speaking peoples have been converted by
the constitution into new nation-states. Actually, each of these nations is
part of a larger linguistic group, extending far beyond Ethiopia's borders. Thus, the politics of these new states in Ethiopia may be affected by
politics in Somaliland, Somalia, Djibouti and Eritrea – and even Arabia.
However, most Afar and Somalis live in nomadic communities. Their primary loyalties lie with their clan and locale (Lewis 1955; Markakis 1974).

Proud, independent and hostile to intruders, these communities were
never effectively governed from Addis Ababa; rather, methods of indirect
rule were used to maintain a semblance of peace. Yet the strategic importance of these vast regions suggests that the new federal government may
be challenged to find ways to keep their inhabitants loyal to the federation.

Peoples of the south and west
The many peoples of the southern and western regions are marked by cultural and political diversity and, in some cases, by historic inter-group feuds. Some are Nilotic Sudanic peoples; some have uniquely distinct cultures. Since all are too small and lacking in resources to enjoy (or perhaps want) political autonomy, they have been federated into several multi-ethnic states which are highly dependent on the central government. Much of this area is fertile and less densely populated. It constitutes a resource for future federal projects to resettle peoples from increasingly overcrowded and degraded lands in the highland north (Levine 1974).

Eritrea
Eritrea, when annexed in 1952, was said (by Haile Selassie) to constitute part of historic Ethiopia. That claim may have been true in respect to the Tigrinya-speaking highland areas, but other regions and groups had experienced quite different histories. The Sudanic pastoral peoples in the arid north had never been integrated into Ethiopia. Arabic-speaking peoples occupying coastal regions had become Muslims early on and, at different times, had been subjects of Egypt or of the Ottoman Empire. The Afar, occupying the inhospitable plains of the south, were separated from Asmara by a formidable geography and history.

Italian rule (1896–1942) was despotic and racist and it probably created an appreciation of freedom when, during World War II, British forces captured the territory and instituted a rather benign rule as temporary trustee for the United Nations. Eritrea, noted one scholarly British official, was an especially capricious creation of colonialism; the inhabitants were not, in any sense, a single people but, rather, a conglomerate of peoples linked to kindred groups in Ethiopia, Sudan or French Somaliland (now independent Djibouti) (Trevaskis 1960:129–30). The British occupiers instituted indirect rule and pursued policies envisioning an eventual exercise of self-determination which (they thought) would lead to a partitioning that would join the peoples of the erstwhile territory with their respective kindred groups.

In 1950, when the UN Assembly took up the future of Eritrea, an independence movement was organised by Arabic-speaking leaders. But a more visible and largely Tigrinya-speaking Unionist Party (supported by Ethiopia) favoured reunion, an outcome backed by the United States which was anxious to establish (with the emperor's consent) a military communications centre near Asmara.

A UN commission purported to consult with all interested parties, though there was no popular referendum to measure sentiment. In

December 1950, the General Assembly, 'taking into account the wishes and welfare of the inhabitants as well as the claims of Ethiopia based on historic, ethnic and geographical factors', approved the commission's proposal for federation which would provide for the *widest possible measure of self-government* in Eritrea – autonomy in all spheres except foreign affairs, defence, immigration and customs. This resolution was reluctantly accepted by Ethiopia (Paul and Clapham 1969:366–76).

A constitution for Eritrea, drafted by UN experts, was adopted by a specially elected Constituent Assembly. Unique in the context of its time, this was the first independence constitution in post-war sub-Saharan Africa. Eritreans were now citizens of their own quite autonomous state (with its own flag), as well as citizens of Ethiopia (under its flag). Adult males enjoyed clearly stated rights to form political parties and elect a unicameral legislature; and all Eritreans also enjoyed other liberally defined political and civil rights, including the right to retain their systems of personal law and land tenure, and their languages. An independent judiciary was empowered to enforce the constitution. A chief executive exercised powers which, in Ethiopia, were prerogatives of the emperor who, in Eritrea, was relegated to the ceremonial role of a constitutional monarch.

The federation was an exogenous creation of the United Nations, not an endogenous arrangement grounded in cooperation and compromise. Nor did it really reflect a federal system. Rather, a hastily constructed, quite autonomous, multi-ethnic, but ostensibly democratic, Eritrea was attached to a monarchial autocracy. The Ethiopian government, marginalised from the UN-dominated process which created a quasi-independent Eritrea, objected strenuously to this outcome, fearing that an Eritrea too autonomous and too democratic might undermine the stability of the federation and, indeed, Ethiopia.[3]

From the beginning, the Ethiopian government worked to undo the federation. The ensuing history is controversial, but the Eritrean version – important because it is now official Eritrean history – holds that, in 1962, the emperor's agents (using a combination of force and bribery) engineered a coup by inducing a fear-stricken rump of the Eritrean parliament to vote for abolition of the federation and for reunification. An imperial decree established that result: Eritrea's separate government, constitution and system of law were completely abolished and the territory became another province in the empire, ruled by an Amharan governor, backed up by Ethiopian security forces. The effects of this move became increasingly resented as people realised that they had been stripped of valuable rights, notably self-government, while experiencing Amharisation of their language, governance and schools (Iyob 1995).

The outcome was also tragic for the emperor. By 1973, Eritrea's provincial administration was becoming a garrison government, beleaguered by guerrilla nationalists. Embarrassing challenges to the legality of Ethiopia's abolition of the federation were pressed in the United Nations and in the OAU, while in Addis Ababa discussions among intellectuals about the territory's future status underscored the need for political change and uncorked the genie of self-determination.

The governance of the empire

Menelik's death brought dangerous political disarray until a junta enthroned Haile Selassie, who worked skilfully to consolidate monarchial power by displacing feudal-style local governance with a highly centralised and institutionalised system controlled by the monarch. Following Ethiopia's liberation in 1941, he began to use Western models to establish an ever-increasing number of specialised government departments, a civil service, a financial structure, a codified and integrated legal system, a professional army and police, schools and a national university (Paul and Clapham 1969; Zewde 1991).

Modernisation – an ambiguous term – is frequently used to describe his achievements. But, perforce, it was modernisation within an Ethiopian context: the traditional, hierarchical social structure and the feudal-type land tenures remained in place; the emperor established a unique kind of personal rule which blended old and new forms of veneration.

The contradictions of modernisation are revealed by analysis of the Janus-like constitution of 1955. De jure, it was the supreme law of the empire, governing even the emperor. It contemplated the establishment of an independent ministerial government responsible to both the monarch and parliament, notably an elected Chamber of Deputies endowed with legislative, fiscal and investigative powers. It called for a professional civil service and an independent judiciary apparently endowed with power to enforce the constitution, including its bill of rights.

These liberal provisions were overshadowed by the extensive prerogative powers reserved to the emperor, who exercised them expansively, periodically shuffling ministers and transferring, promoting or demoting officials and judges according to his pleasure. Adherence to hierarchical patterns of administration and pervasive secrecy weakened the initiative and morale of the new elites. Notions of hierarchy and status also maintained the vast social distance that separated both new and old elites from the peasantry and urban poor.[4]

Few ordinary Ethiopians were familiar with the content of their constitution, which had been laboriously drawn up in secret and adopted quickly by parliament, with no public debate. Elections were generally viewed with cynicism by the urban middle classes, and with apathy in the countryside where they were apolitical affairs dominated by landholding elites. Political parties, associational activities, an independent press and other structures enabling civil society participation in governance were effectively discouraged (Markakis 1974).

183

Local government was far more important to the vast majority of peoples. The constitution made no provision for either the modernisation or democratisation of this sector. Rather, the organisation and staffing of local administration was a prerogative of the emperor, who divided Ethiopia into provinces, districts and sub-districts, and, in theory, appointed governors for all of these units. Usually, at upper levels, they were Amhara, and Amharic was everywhere the language of local administration. The essential tasks were limited: security, tax collection and the maintenance of local roads; and they were administered through authoritarian processes, closely monitored by the Ministry of Interior (Markakis 1974).

Amharic was the prescribed language of governance and the legal system at all levels, and of education, the media and other public activities. This policy and the attempt to Amharise the history of Ethiopia and its culture were justified by arguments which resonated with modernisation theory: the need to establish a national identity. But Amharisation also inhibited the access of many to schooling and opportunities to develop social capital; it underscored social gaps which further marginalised peoples in peripheral areas; and, of course, it was often resented.

These conditions affected the character of development in Ethiopia which consisted, primarily, of separate state-managed, bureaucratised sectoral activities. In the latter 1960s, prodded by the World Bank and other donors, the government initiated several expensive, integrated rural development projects designed to bring packages of infrastructure, credit, technologies and improved services to agrarian households in the south. The projects were successfully co-opted by local and absentee landlords. They profited from a small-scale green revolution. But their Oromo tenants were converted into landless rural workers, and many were displaced and impoverished. Nor did the legal and administrative systems provide a means to redress their grievances (Cohen 1987).

By the early 1970s, most scholars of Ethiopia foresaw an imminent, serious crisis. Radicals anticipated a class-based revolution, leading to some kind of rule by – or for – 'the toiling masses'. Others hoped, albeit with pessimism, for a more peaceful transition to democracy, coupled with structural reforms. Despite the country's extraordinary pluralism, few scholars seemed to anticipate that the problematic concept of ethnicity might replace the problematic concept of class as the basis for political reconstruction of a state about to implode.

Revolution and dictatorship
In 1973, the government's attempt to conceal a terrible famine in the Wollo highlands (only a day's journey from Addis Ababa), and then its seeming inability to respond to this and other serious crises, confirmed

a growing view that the aged emperor was too feeble to manage his government.

There were strikes in Addis Ababa and an uncertain revolutionary situation emerged. The press suddenly exploded with letters on politics. For a brief period, it was as if a thousand flowers had bloomed. Then the Derg,[5] a clandestine, well-organised conspiracy within the military, gradually assumed control of the government, initially promising a benign transition to democracy, land reform and socialism. But, as its power was consolidated, more doctrinaire communist elements seized control, eliminating their moderate colleagues, deposing the emperor and then slaughtering him and leading members of his government and family in cold blood (Clapham 1988; Thomson 1975).

Student radicals organised the Ethiopian People's Revolutionary Party (EPRP) and demanded a civilian government. In the brutal Red Terror which followed, thousands of these young people and others suspected of sympathy with them were massacred. Lieutenant Colonel Mengistu Haile Meriam personally executed his immediate rivals and assumed dictatorial powers. Fond of mouthing Marxist slogans, burning with hatred, Mengistu was, in reality, Ethiopia's last and most brutal emperor and his Leninist regime was probably the most repressive in Africa during an era of military despotisms. It left legacies which have profoundly changed Ethiopia (Clapham 1988; Thomson 1975).

One was the shattering of Amharan political society. The Derg's regime was dominated by Amhara. Some were ideologically committed; most were its passive servants. But many Amharan elites opposed it and many of them were killed or imprisoned indefinitely. The economic base of many traditional elites was destroyed as a result of land reform, while thousands of the professional and other urban classes fled to escape the Derg's brutality. The student radicals who had organised the EPRP fled to the northern highlands to mobilise armed resistance. Military officers and others loyal to the emperor fled to Sudan to create another resistance force. Neither group was able to form a strong base of peasant support; both were ultimately suppressed by Derg forces. These and other events produced both a diaspora and brain drain of enormous proportions and considerable disunity and disarray among educated Amharan elites at home and in exile.

A second legacy was the escalation of the Eritrean conflict into full-scale war. When it first seized control, the Derg co-opted the popular, politically moderate General Aman Andom and installed him as its chairman. Aman was respected as an Ethiopian patriot, but he was also an Eritrean who openly sought a peaceful resolution of his homeland's grievances. Mengistu, a believer in the use of massive retaliation and terror to suppress opposition, soon arranged for the murder of Aman and the intensification of the Eritrean war. The effect was to galvanise popular opposition to the hated Derg.

A third legacy was the politicisation of much of Ethiopia's peasantry. The Derg brought about sudden, sweeping and welcome reform by nationalising all land and abolishing all forms of tenancy and feudal obligations. Local peasant associations were created to redistribute land-lord holdings to those who worked them. The result was to create a new breed of independent farmers in the south and, more broadly, a peas-antry endowed with a new sense of status and empowerment. But the Derg's claim of ownership and ultimate control of all lands was unac-ceptable to them, and its subsequent efforts to use the peasant associa-tions (and force) to collectivise production and to impose resettlement in new villages, price controls and other socialist measures were deeply resented (Clay 1988; Giorgis 1989).

A fourth result was civil warfare and the genesis of ethnic nationalism. In the early stages of the revolution, the nationalities question and the demands for self-determination were pressed by Oromo and Tigrayan radicals – and compounded by the Eritrean crisis. The Derg promised to create autonomous regions modelled after the Soviet constitution. But that policy was abandoned and talk of devolution was thereafter treated as sedition. Disaffected Tigrayan and Oromo radicals formed nationalist resistances and the Derg found itself waging many wars against its own peoples, with a brutality that only incited more rebellion.

Civil wars

In 1975, the rogue military government of Somalia, facing its own inter-nal crisis, sent an invading army into the Ogaden, ostensibly in response to calls for help from liberation fronts organised by clans in Ethiopia. The invasion was repelled, but many Ethiopian Somalis, now armed, were never pacified. Similarly, a small Afar Liberation Front, organised to resist the Derg's resettlement programs, threatened the vital desert highway linking Addis Ababa to the port of Assab.

In theory, the Oromo Liberation Front (OLF) presented the most serious challenge since it purported to speak for a plurality of Ethiopia's peoples. Its leaders, emphasising past genocidal crimes, called for estab-lishment of an independent Oromia – a vast territory which would include Addis Ababa and eviscerate Ethiopia. Most OLF leaders were urban elites and apparently failed to develop many strong grassroots, political bases and participatory party structures; rather, they attempted to create a military force. But they found it difficult to unite all of the dis-parate Oromo communities behind demands for an independent state.[6]

In contrast, the Tigrayan People's Liberation Front (TPLF) was organ-ised as a peasant-based political movement in the rugged northern highlands. The creation of party structures and participatory local governance took precedence over military mobilisation. Socialist indoctrination was displaced by Tigrayan nationalism and appeals were made to remembered ideological history: the heroism of the martyr-emperor Yohannes, the treachery of Menelik, the patriotism of the Woyene. The TPLF somehow mobilised resources to provide schooling and literacy training, basic health care and food supplies in the regions it controlled. In this context, a volunteer army was recruited with a mission to liberate all peoples of Ethiopia from the Derg's despotism (Young 1997).

There were two civil wars in Eritrea. The original independence movement had its origins in the post-colonial era and it turned to force after abolition of the federation. This Eritrean Liberation Front (ELF) has been described as a loose coalition of Arabic-speaking local factions, orchestrated by exiled leaders in Cairo. Despite protestations of secularism, it failed to gain wide support among Christians. A rival and more radical and disciplined Eritrean People's Liberation Front (EPLF) emerged, led by Tigrinya speakers, and it proceeded to destroy the ELF. It then pursued strategies similar to those of the TPLF, putting politics first, encouraging the building of participatory local governments and stressing the need for pan-ethnic nationalism. The Derg played into this strategy by creating a particularly brutal regime of military retaliation (Iyob 1995).

The TPLF established an uneasy military alliance with the EPLF in Eritrea, cooperating to sap the strength of the Derg armies. But their political relationship was difficult: the former's insistence on ethnic self-determination as the means of reconstructing Ethiopia was irreconcilable with the latter's ideology of multicultural nationalism and independence. Reluctantly, the TPLF accepted the EPLF's de facto control of Eritrea's future and abandoned its hope of reuniting the divided Tigrayan peoples. As its army swept southward, TPLF political cadres began organising ethnic-based political parties as allies in liberated regions. Success led to the formation of an umbrella party: the Ethiopian People's Democratic Revolutionary Front (EPDRF), a country-wide coalition of ethnic-based parties controlled by the TPLF leadership, overtly designed to govern Ethiopia in the future (Young 1997).

THE RECONSTITUTION OF ETHIOPIA AND ERITREA

The transition in Ethiopia

In May 1991, the Derg collapsed. As communism withered away, the TPLF moved quickly to reconstitute the state – by legitimating itself as a government, establishing an essential foundation for a federal constitution, creating de facto one-party rule, marginalising Amhara and Oromo opposition, and liquidating the Eritrean problem.

Legitimation was established by quickly shedding the peculiar Marxist ideology and embracing the rhetoric (if not all of the substance) of liberal democracy, and by convening a national conference to adopt an interim constitution, a charter for a Transitional Government of Ethiopia (TGE). Composed primarily of leaders of ethnic parties spawned by the civil war, the conferees reflected a dramatic shift of political power from Shoan urban elites to new politicians from hitherto marginalised regions. The EPDRF dominated the proceedings and secured cooperation from the OLF by promising it a role in the TGE's Council of Ministers.

The charter established the framework for the provisional government and promised self-determination and self-government for all nations and peoples. Thereafter, legislation was drawn up which carved the country into new ethnic regions which would be governed locally by elected councils. A manifesto explaining this unprecedented legislation suggested that ethnicity had replaced class as the official basis of politics in Ethiopia. It seemed likely that the new regions would be transformed into quasi-sovereign states by the future constitution.[7]

The 1992 elections to choose the regional councils became a talismanic event. The EPDRF parties worked to consolidate their local power while the TGE's Tigrayan army forcibly demobilised OLF forces in the countryside. The OLF was still unprepared to compete for votes in many parts of Oromia, as was AAPO – the Addis Ababa-based All Amhara People's Organisation – in the Amhara Region. All opposition parties demanded the postponement of elections. The TGE refused. Charges of bad faith and evil designs were exchanged. The TGE then charged its OLF ministers with sedition and forced them (and others) into exile; the AAPO's leaders were harassed, and senior Amhara in the civil service and the university suspected of some kind of disloyalty were summarily dismissed. The election was badly managed and, wherever a local (notably OLF) opposition party appeared, gross abuses were practised against it. The EPDRF won a sweeping, but decidedly flawed, victory which established a de facto one-party state (Joireman 1997).

The TGE's acceptance of a referendum in Eritrea calling for independence further convinced its many Amharan opponents that the historic Ethiopian nation was to be balkanised and destroyed.

The federal constitution of Ethiopia
In 1993, the TGE established a Constitutional Commission to prepare a draft instrument for submission to a specially elected Constitutional Assembly, vested with plenary powers to promulgate a final organic law. Democracy and rule of law were promised; the issue of federalism was left open.[8]

President Meles Zenawi urged the broadest possible public participation in this project in order to promote civic education, experience democracy and exercise self-determination. That hope was never realised;

there was little meaningful public participatory debate, especially debate which focused on devolution versus ethnic federalism, let alone ethnic sovereignty or self-determination. Again, opposition parties withdrew. Instead of debating the content of the constitution, they denounced the legitimacy of the whole project. Just as the EPDRF controlled the Constitutional Commission's work, so it controlled the election, and then the deliberations, of the Constitutional Assembly.

In view of the constitution's content, it seems regrettable that the processes for making it were so flawed. It is an unusual document in terms of its historical, empirical and theoretical premises and its articulation of the right of self-determination; its bill of rights; its construction of a federal system; its blending of parliamentary and presidential models; and its contradictions. It has been characterised as a tour de force to resolve potential conflict, as a treaty between the nations and the peoples of Ethiopia, who are portrayed as its authors. Alternatively, it might also be seen as part of an ingenious divide-and-rule political strategy which enabled the TPLF (constituting 10 per cent of the population) to legitimate its power. Perhaps, too, it reflects a residue of the TPLF's Marxism.[9]

The bill of rights is unusual. One of its thirty-five articles sets out the *corporate* rights of nations and peoples. All the rest elaborate, in quite liberal terms, the *individual* rights of Ethiopians. All of these rights must be interpreted in a manner conforming to the International Bill of Rights and international instruments adopted by Ethiopia, including the conventions on the rights of women, children and others. Thus, the constitution appears to incorporate a very large body of international human rights law.[10]

The right to development is also guaranteed and defined as a right of all people of Ethiopia to enjoy rights to participate in the processes of development; and the basic aim of development activities should be to enhance the capacities of citizens and to meet their basic needs. Presumably, claims of self-determination cannot be used to derogate any of these rights, and the federal government is enjoined to enact federal laws to promote and protect their exercise. To that end, it must create a federal human rights commission.[11]

A House of People's Representatives, elected for five-year terms to represent the people, has the power to select the prime minister, who is given presidential prerogatives to command the armed forces, to control the cabinet and to appoint all high civilian officials and federal judges. Tenured also for a five-year term, the prime minister would seem to enjoy considerable independence from the legislature (chap. 8, arts. 72–74).

The enumeration of federal powers includes authority to enact laws governing: all foreign and interstate commerce; enforcement of all rights guaranteed by the constitution; the conduct of elections; labour relations; a national system of money and banking; development policies

189

(including the setting of standards in education); environmental protection and exploitation of natural resources; public security and a national police force; and states of emergency and threats to public order in any state. The federal government must also enact national codes of penal, commercial and employment law, and a family law code to protect the constitutional rights of spouses and children (art. 55).

Ownership of all land is also vested in the federal government, which must enact legislation to establish the possessory rights of peasants and pastoralists, to provide for long-term leases for private investors and for the private exploitation of resources. (Owners of immovables – houses – retain rights to possess, lease and sell this property.) Finally, and critically, the federal government enjoys the lion's share of revenue sources (notably customs) and the power to allocate its funds to the states for specified development purposes (art. 96; Cohen 1995).

All residual powers, such as they may be, are vested in the states (art. 52; Cohen 1995).

A House of Federation is established to mediate conflicts among the states, and between them and the central regime. It is portrayed as a council composed of representatives of the nations and peoples (each group is represented by at least one member, and an additional one for each million persons). Its functions also include the power to seek resolution of misunderstandings between states; to mediate all demands for self-determination; and to ensure the fair allocation of federal subsidies to the states. Very significantly, it enjoys an apparently exclusive power to interpret the constitution. Any constitutional issue arising in the courts must be taken up to the House of Federation, via a rather cumbersome (and probably costly) interlocutory process for decision by this hybrid political–arbitral body (arts. 61, 62, 64, 82, 83 and 84). Vesting constitutional review in a non-judicial body may make sense as a means to resolve politically sensitive issues of state versus federal power, but it plainly undercuts the power of the courts to enforce the expansive rights guaranteed to all Ethiopians by the constitution.

Thus, the constitution contains glaring contradictions. The powers allocated to the federal government reflect a mistrust of the kind of federal system elsewhere proclaimed. The powers denied the courts to enforce the bill of rights reflect a mistrust of the rule of human rights law. A right to secede, as an integral element of self-determination, is granted; but the long, complex procedure which must be followed to exercise this right suggests that it exists more in theory than in fact.

The constitutional construction of Eritrea
In 1991, the victorious EPLF moved quickly to consolidate its control over Eritrea's political future, but slowly to create that future. Finally, in 1993,

a provisional government was legally established, structured along the lines of the TGE. Then, through a national conference, the EPLF converted itself into the People's Front for Democracy and Justice (PFDJ). Describing itself as a national civic movement, it looked more like a vanguard political party. All other political organisations (and, indeed, most non-government organisations) were quietly suppressed, usually by appeals to elites to maintain unity by avoiding political discourse.

A broad-based Constitutional Commission was created in 1994. Its chairman (an eminent scholar) has portrayed its initial period (1994–96) as an effort to construct a dialectic between process and substance by encouraging the widest possible participation in its work. The commission based this approach on both a theory of self-determination and lessons drawn from African history. Exclusion of the public from the process of making constitutions marginalised their political significance and led to their breakdown, and this explains the many 'false start[s] that [have] dogged . . . post colonial Africa'. The commission hammered on this theme so that Eritreans would fully appreciate the importance of their active participation in the work of creating a democratic state (Sellassie 1998).

Faced with an initially diffident, diverse, 80 per cent illiterate and largely rural population, the commission mobilised popular radio talkers, singers, theatrical performers, poets and hastily trained school teachers to help it organise hundreds of local assemblies where public discussion of constitutional issues was integrated with entertainment and tradition. A first round of meetings focused on basics: the need for a new national identity; the nature and value of democracy and universal rights; and the role of a constitution in establishing these. A second round turned to institutions and methods to realise accepted goals. Some questions discussed were touchy: should there be a system of federalism to reflect the country's regional and cultural diversity? Or some other system of ethnic representation? What place should religion have in government? How can fair elections be ensured? Presidential versus parliamentary systems? A massive number of reports (now in the official archives) record the local discussions of these and other issues. We are told that the public decisively rejected federalism and ethnic representation and left it to the legislature to create a system of local government (Constitutional Commission of Eritrea 1995; Sellassie 1998).

A preliminary draft constitution was then submitted to the National Assembly for publicised debate, and thereafter a revised draft was taken back for a third round of popular discussions. At last, in 1997, a final draft was adopted by an elected Constituent Assembly, with minimal revision. This short-form constitution establishes Eritrea as a unitary state, governed (like Ethiopia) by a National Assembly which chooses a president endowed with independent executive powers and tenure during his term in office. The bill of rights guarantees (with little equivocation) all basic civil and political rights. Powers of judicial review are vested in a Supreme Court, while the structure of lower, independent courts is left to the National Assembly (Constitutional Commission of Eritrea 1995; Eritrean constitution, art. 2, chaps. 3 and 6; Sellassie 1998).

It was left to the provisional government to determine exactly when and how the constitution was to be implemented through enactment of legislation establishing the machinery for the election of the National Assembly. By failing to act, the provisional government has postponed those elections indefinitely. The interim president has deplored the dangers of the very system of competitive party politics which the constitution envisions. As of October 1999, the legal status of the constitution remained problematic. Eritreans have repeatedly been urged to abstain from politics.

A promised devolution and democratisation of local government also seems delayed because of fears of encouraging pluralism. Rather, local government and the administration of a new land law which displaces the traditional system of community control are administered top–down by the central government. Despite years of popular struggle, it now appears that Eritrean peasants do not have any influence on the broad lines of their development (Tronuoll 1998).

ASSESSING THE FUTURE

The case study sketched here has a broader relevance. It reflects a history of state failure similar to the recent histories of other African states. It suggests the limitations – and risks – of efforts to alleviate grievances, generated by state failure, by recourse to problematic, officially imposed theories of ethnicity, self-determination and ethnic federalism, *or* by recourse to dogmatic, official doctrines prescribing national unity and centralised governance. It suggests the need to convert juridical states into organic social formations – and the need to rethink the fundamental tasks of states in the African context.

A significant report by UN Secretary-General Kofi Annan to the Security Council in 1998 discusses strategies to arrest the widespread conditions of repression, ethnic conflict, civil war, and other failures of states in Africa. The causes of these trends are said to derive from pathologies of state formation during both the colonial and post-colonial eras. The creation of institutions and processes of governance which effectively excluded the mass of people from meaningful political participation led to many wrongs, including state failures to pursue people-centred and equitable development. The remedy must centre on efforts to create states committed to human development and poverty alleviation, respect for *all* human rights, encouragement of civil society organisations, democratisation of governance at all levels, and a rule of law geared to these indivisible, interdependent ends and means of governance.[12]

This interesting analysis shows how far the rapid evolution of international human rights law, and other bodies of international law, are forcing a revision of anachronistic theories of state autonomy – and a reconception of the essential rationale for respecting state sovereignty. Indeed, some scholars have even questioned the wisdom of international attempts to preserve badly failed states in Africa. The case for preservation through reconstruction rests on the obvious need to establish sociopolitical formations which can provide security and other essential benefits to the long-suffering victims of past state failure.

The principles underlying Kofi Annan's prescription have been elaborated in other reports and prescribed by international instruments setting out a body of norms repeatedly affirmed by the international community. They call for adherence to the interrelated goals noted above and for the creation of an environment of law and policy to enable their implementation (Paul 1995).[13]

Articulation of these new legal environments is a challenging, but long ignored, task for scholars, jurists and activists. The implications for constitutional ordering are profound, but it would take another chapter to even sketch some lines of action. Nor is such a project an aspirational, academic exercise when it comes to Ethiopia and Eritrea. Directive principles and other provisions in both constitutions – and Ethiopia's promise to implement the human right to development – would seem to mandate this effort (EPLF 1994:15; Eritrean constitution, arts. 7 and 10; Ethiopian constitution, arts. 43, 44 and 89).

Unfortunately, both regimes seem to be moving in a different direction. Measured against the criteria for success suggested above, there are disturbing trends in both countries. The existing de facto systems of one-party rule may ensure a degree of political stability today, but future dangers are evident: usurpation of the powers of governance at all levels by party leaders, coupled with increasing political repression and corruption. Both the PFDJ and the EPRDF are essentially controlled by non-transparent, centralised structures in which military leaders appear to play significant roles. The security of the regime in power, rather than the constitution, seems to be a central concern.

In Ethiopia, domination of both the ruling party and the government by Tigrayans (a small minority of the population) creates further risks. Eventually, divide-and-rule strategies may no longer enable this kind of minority leadership to retain control over the state's resources. Further, the self-determination ideology previously preached seems to have fuelled creation of Afar and Somali irredentist 'liberation fronts'. The OLF (and other illegal Oromo groups drawn from Islamic communities) still press for an independent Oromia. Many respected Amhara resent the EPDRF's repressive tactics and its sometimes blatant revisions of Ethiopian history which ignore the many essential legacies of the historic, core Ethiopian polity, including its preservation of the independence of the peoples of Greater Ethiopia from European rule.

The failure of both the government and its opponents to practise civility and trust, let alone genuine participation, in politics hardly teaches the value of democracy. Nor is democracy likely to be nurtured if it is not seen to be linked to development of, for and by the people.

The human rights records of both regimes are deplorable: they portray insensitivity to the need to empower and invigorate civil society and to incorporate rights into all spheres of governance. These trends, and the risks of divisive federalism in Ethiopia and sabotage of the ratified constitution in Eritrea, could pave the way for a reappearance, in new legal and ideological garb, of the old kind of authoritarian state, sustained by force rather than by popular legitimacy.[14]

NOTES

Neelan Tiruchelvam, friend and inspiration, might not be happy with this chapter, but it is written with the memory of all he stood for very much in mind.

1 For a most useful commentary on both the theory and text of this instrument, see Nahum (1997).

2 Abbay (1997) discusses the different uses of this history, by Tigrayans in Ethiopia and Eritrea, to create new national identities.

3 See Paul and Clapham (1969:366–85).

4 For detailed analysis of the constitution of 1955, see Paul (1960); for the system of governance, see Clapham (1969) and Markakis (1974).

5 Sometimes spelt 'Dergue'; at the time (1973), a somewhat obscure Amharic word meaning a rather invisible group which controls events.

6 See Keller (1988, 1995) for further discussion of Oromo politics.

7 *National Regional Self-Government Proclamation*, No. 7, 1972, *Negarit Gazeta* (1992); Nahum (1997).

8 *Constitutional Establishment Commission Proclamation*, No. 24, 1992, *Negarit Gazeta* (1992).

9 Compare Brietzke (1995) with Haile (1997) and Hagos (1995).

10 See arts. 13(2) and 28 (dealing with criminal liability for crimes against humanity, including torture, false disappearances) which appear to incorporate international instruments 'ratified by Ethiopia'.

11 See art. 43 (right to development), and also art. 44, which creates a right to a healthy environment and guarantees redress for victims of development-induced displacement; see also art. 55, ss. 2(d) and 14, on federal obligations to protect constitutional rights in the states.

12 'The causes of conflict and the promotion of durable peace and sustainable development in Africa', Report of the Secretary General (A/52/9761 and S/1998/318), United Nations, 13 April 1998.

13 See Nahum (1997:151): 'This is a constitution that wants to operate with its hands on the business [of government] and begs to be employed to radically transform [Ethiopian] society'. See also Nahum's Chapter 10, discussing the 'National Policy Objectives' of the constitution.

14 For extraordinary, different (positive and negative) views of Ethiopia's present situation, see Harbeson (1998b); Henze (1998); Joseph (1998). Two of these authors are prominent scholars of Ethiopia (Harbeson and Henze), and one is a prominent scholar of 'transitions' in Africa (Joseph).

REFERENCES

Abbay, Alemseged 1997. 'The trans-Mareb past in the present', *Journal of Modern African Studies* 35(2):321–34.

Brietzke, Paul H. 1995. 'Ethiopia's "leap in the dark": federalism and self-determination in the new constitution', *Journal of African Law* 30(1):19–38.

Clapham, C. 1969. *Haile Selassie's Government.* New York: Frederick Prager.

—— 1988. *Transformation and Continuity in Revolutionary Ethiopia.* Cambridge: Cambridge University Press.

Clay, Jason W., Sandra Steingruber and Peter Niggli 1988. *The Spoils of Famine: Ethiopian Famine Policy and Peasant Agriculture.* Cambridge, MA: Cultural Survival Inc.

Cohen, John M. 1987. *Integrated Rural Development: The Ethiopian Case.* Uppsala: Scandinavian Institute for African Studies.

—— 1995. *Ethnic Federalism in Ethiopia.* Discussion Paper No. 519. Cambridge, MA: Harvard Institute for International Development, October.

Constitution of Eritrea 1997. Constitutional Commission of Eritrea.

Constitution of the Federal Democratic Republic of Ethiopia 1994. Addis Ababa, 8 December.

Constitutional Commission of Eritrea 1995. *Constitutional Proposals for Public Debate.* August.

EPLF (Eritrean Peoples Liberation Front) 1994. *National Charter of Eritrea.* Asmara: EPLF.

Giorgis, Dawit Wolde 1989. *Red Tears: War, Famine and Revolution in Ethiopia.* Trenton, NJ: Red Sea Press.

Hagos, Tecola W. 1995. *Democratization? Ethiopia 1991–1994: A Personal View.* Cambridge, MA: Khepera Publishers.

Haile, Minasse 1997. 'The new Ethiopian constitution: its impact upon unity, human rights and development', *Suffolk Transnational Law Review* 20(1):1–84.

Harbeson, John W. 1998a. *The Ethiopian Transformation: The Quest for the Post Imperial State.* Boulder, CO: Westview Press.

—— 1998b. 'A bureaucratic authoritarian regime', *Journal of Democracy* 9(4):62–9.

Hassen, Mohamed 1990. *The Oromo of Ethiopia: A History 1570–1860.* Cambridge: Cambridge University Press.

Henze, Paul B. 1998. 'A political success story', *Journal of Democracy* 9(4):46–54.

Iyob, Ruth 1995. *The Eritrean Struggle for Independence: Domination, Resistance and Nationalism 1941–1993.* African Studies Series No. 82. Cambridge: Cambridge University Press.

Joireman, Sandra Fullerton 1997. 'Opposition politics and ethnicity in Ethiopia: we will all go down together', *Journal of Modern African Studies* 35(3):387–407.

Joseph, Richard 1998. 'Oldspeak vs. newspeak', *Journal of Democracy* 9(4):55–61.

Keller, Edmond J. 1988. *Revolutionary Ethiopia: From Empire to Peoples Republic.* Bloomington: Indiana University Press.

—— 1995. 'The ethno-genesis of the Oromo nation', *Journal of Modern African Studies* 33(4):621–34.

Levine, Donald N. 1965. *Wax and Gold: Tradition and Innovation in Ethiopian Culture.* Chicago and London: University of Chicago Press.

—— 1974. *Greater Ethiopia: The Evolution of a Multi-Ethnic Society.* Chicago and London: University of Chicago Press.

Lewis, I.M. 1955. *Peoples of the Horn of Africa.* London: International African Institute.

Marcus, Harold G. 1975. *The Life and Times of Menelik II: Ethiopia 1844–1913.* Oxford: Clarendon Press.

Markakis, John 1974. *Ethiopia: Anatomy of a Traditional Polity.* Oxford Studies in African Affairs. Oxford: Clarendon Press.

Nahum, Fasil, 1997. *Constitution for a Nation of Nations: The Ethiopian Prospect.* Lawrenceville, NJ: Red Sea Press.

OAU (Organization of African Unity) 1963. *Charter of the Organization of African Unity* (1963) 479 UNTS 70.

Paul, James C.N. 1995. 'The United Nations and the creation of an international law of development', *Harvard International Law Journal* 36(2):307–28.

Paul, James C.N. and Christopher C. Clapham 1969. *Ethiopian Constitutional Development.* Addis Ababa: Haile Selassie University Press, vol. 1 [vol. 2, 1971].

Sellassie, Bereket Habte 1998. 'Creating a constitution for Eritrea', *Journal of Democracy* 9(2):164–74.

Tareke, Gebru 1991. *Ethiopia: Power and Protest: Peasant Revolts in the Twentieth Century.* African Studies Series No. 71. Cambridge: Cambridge University Press.

Thomson, Blair 1975. *Ethiopia: The Country That Cut Off Its Head: A Diary of the Revolution.* London: Robson Book Ltd.

Trevaskis, G.K.N. 1960. *Eritrea: A Colony in Transition.* London: Oxford University Press.

Tronuoll, Kjatil 1998. 'The process of nation-building in post-war Eritrea: created from below or directed from above?', *Journal of Modern African Studies* 36(3):461–82.

Young, John 1997. *Peasant Revolution in Ethiopia: The Tigray People's Liberation Front, 1975–1991.* African Studies Series No. 90. Cambridge: Cambridge University Press.

Zewde, Bahru 1991. *A History of Modern Ethiopia 1855–1974.* Athens: Ohio University Press/Addis Ababa: Addis Ababa University Press/London: James Currey.

CHAPTER 9

THE POLITICS OF FEDERALISM AND DIVERSITY IN SRI LANKA

NEELAN TIRUCHELVAM

Leonard Woolf, the literary critic and publisher, was a colonial civil servant in Ceylon from 1904 to 1911 and served in both Jaffna in the extreme north and Hambantota in the deep south. Many years later, advising the British Labour Party, he argued for a constitutional arrangement which ensured a large measure of devolution, on the Swiss federal model, saying that the canton system had proved 'extraordinarily successful under circumstances very similar to those in Ceylon, i.e. the co-existence in a single democratic state of communities of very different size, sharply distinguished from one another by race, language and religion' (Spotts 1989:417). As early as 1926, S.W.R.D. Bandaranaike advocated the idea of federalism as a constitutional response to Sri Lanka's diversity. He pointed out that 'a thousand and one objections could be raised against this system, but when objections were dissipated some form of Federal Government would be the only solution' (*Ceylon Morning Leader*, 17 July 1926; see also Tiruchelvam 1992; Uyangoda 1994:97). Despite the foresight of Woolf and Bandaranaike, Sri Lanka's failure to lay down the constitutional foundation of a multi-ethnic society based on equality, ethnic pluralism and the sharing of power has generated ethnic fratricide and political violence (Tambiah 1986; Wilson 1988).

Sri Lanka is a multi-ethnic and plural society consisting of two linguistic groups: the Sinhalese (mainly Buddhists) and Tamils (mainly Hindus), and the Muslim community (mainly Tamil-speaking, but with a substantial section that is bilingual). Within the Tamil community, estate or Indian Tamils (those brought into Sri Lanka from India in the nineteenth century to work on tea plantations) constitute a distinct component. There are other minorities, including Christians, Burghers (descendants of Dutch and Portuguese settlers), and Malays. The Sinhalese constitute 74 per cent of the island's population, Ceylon Tamils 12.6 per cent, Indian Tamils 5.5 per cent and Muslims 7.4 per cent, according to the most recent census (1981). Since then, there have been significant demographic changes arising out of displacement, internal migration and outward migration. In the north-eastern province, Tamils constitute 69 per cent of the population, while 17.7 per cent are Muslims and 13.3 per cent are Sinhalese. Almost 27.4 per cent of the Ceylon Tamil population in 1991 lived outside the province. Some 30 per cent of Tamil-speaking Muslims live in the northern and eastern provinces, while the rest are dispersed throughout other parts of the island, with significant concentrations in the Colombo, Kalutara and Galle districts (Wilson 1993:144; Wriggins 1960).

Throughout the troubled history of modern Sri Lanka, federal and quasi-federal solutions have been central to the constitutional debate on the resolution of the conflict in the north-east. This chapter examines the strengths and limitations of the existing scheme of devolution of powers against the backdrop of an ideological contestation on the nature of the state. An assessment of the rationale, objectives and operation of the existing constitutional arrangements for devolution enables us to understand the more recent efforts towards comprehensive reform. The constitutional reform proposals put forward by the government in August 1995, and incorporated in the draft constitution produced by the government in 1997,[1] represent the boldest effort to share power as a means of ethnic reconciliation. This chapter examines whether the proposals would result in a paradigm shift from a unitary state, and also reviews the consociational principles which have been grafted onto the power-sharing arrangements to safeguard minorities within minorities. There is also a specifically theoretical quality to the debate on how constitutionalism can accommodate the politics of recognition, as symbolic recognition of the distinct identity of ethnic groups may be more important than the specifics of power sharing for an enduring resolution of the conflict.

THE IDEOLOGY OF THE CENTRALISED STATE AND ETHNIC CONSCIOUSNESS

Although ethnic minorities in Sri Lanka were unreconciled to the constitutional arrangements at the time of transfer of political power in 1948 from Britain to Sri Lanka, few expected that majority rule would be so quickly followed by discriminatory legislative measures. The first of these were citizenship laws which effectively disenfranchised estate Tamils of recent Indian origin. This legislation led to the formation of ethnically based Tamil parties to resist such laws. They advocated parity with respect to the status of the national languages and urged the creation of a federal constitution.

The second measure related to the promulgation of Sinhala as the sole official language. In the early 1950s, ethnic communities were becoming increasingly polarised, and ethnic political discourse was becoming strident and volatile. Political and ethnic polarisation intensified during the run-up to the 1956 general election when the Sri Lanka Freedom Party was swept into power in all parts of the country except the north-east (Manor 1989). The party's success symbolised the resurgence of the forces of Sinhala-Buddhist nationalism, while the Federal Party's success in the north-east represented the emergence of a new form of Tamil linguistic nationalism. Unfortunately, these events ensured that the assertion of one form of nationalism was viewed as a denial of the other. Colvin R. de Silva, the leading left-wing politician, warned, during the legislative debates on the Official Language Act, that the policy of imposing the language of the majority would have dangerous political consequences. He cautioned: 'Two languages – one nation; one language – two nations' (*Parliamentary Hansard* 1956:column 1914), and accurately predicted that the failure to resolve the language question in a manner satisfactory to the minority would eventually lead to a separatist movement.

These two developments were the consequence of what Jayadeva Uyangoda (1994:88) describes as 'the presence in Sinhalese society of a very specific political culture, along with an ideology and idiom of a centralized State'. The ideology of the centralised state drew its legitimacy from two distinct sources. On the one hand, the Sinhala ideological construction of the state was linked to the idea that the land, which had certain cosmic characteristics, belonged to the Sinhalese. This was linked to the idea of the Dhamma Deepa, the land in which Theravada Buddhism had been preserved in its pristine purity. On the other hand, the dominant colonial constitutional discourse had conceptualised the modern democratic state as one based on the centralisation of political and administrative space. Consequently, Uyangoda (1994:95) argues, the sovereign state of Sri Lanka was viewed as having the following characteristics: territorial unity, with no political or administrative decentralisation; a centralised legislature, with no limitations on legislative competence and excluding any subordinate or parallel law-making body; and a state embodying Sinhala interests and defined in opposition to the interests of ethnic and religious minorities.

Another development which exacerbated ethnic relations and transformed Tamil ethnic consciousness was the incidents of collective violence to which Tamils were repeatedly subjected – in 1958, 1977, 1981 and 1983. There was a qualitative difference in the intensity, brutality and organised nature of the violence of July 1983. No other event is so deeply etched in the collective memories of the victims and the survivors. It was also widely believed that elements within the state or the ruling party had either orchestrated the violence or encouraged the perpetrators. No commission of inquiry was ever appointed to clear the state of these allegations or to investigate the causes of the violence. July 1983 – 'the dark night of the collective soul' (Spencer 1990:192; see also Manor 1984:192) – also contributed towards convulsive changes in the politics of the Tamil community and their methods of struggle. The political leaders committed to constitutional change became marginalised, while militancy and the armed struggle assumed centre stage. Rohan Edrisinha and Paikiasothy Saravanamuttu (1993:77) have noted that the government's response to these events was to blame the victims: 'In a move openly designed to placate Sinhala chauvinism it passed the Sixth amendment to the constitution which effectively outlawed the advocacy of secession.' Consequently, from 1983 to 1988, the north-east was effectively deprived of any Tamil representation in parliament, district councils or local bodies, for few were prepared to take the required oath abjuring secession.

DEVOLUTION THROUGH PROVINCIAL COUNCILS

During the 1980s, belated efforts were made to address some of the underlying grievances of the Tamils and the Muslims which had been acknowledged in the manifesto of the United National Party in the general elections of 1977. The residual issues relating to statelessness were addressed by the Grant of Citizenship to Stateless Persons Act No. 5 of 1986, and the Grant of Citizenship (Special Provisions) Act No. 39 of 1988 (see generally on the denial of citizenship and voting rights of estate Tamils, Manogaran 1987:38). Tamil was, progressively, made a national language in the Second Republican Constitution of 1978 and an official language in 1987, although many problems remain with regard to the effective implementation of bilingualism.[2]

However, the most significant measure towards redressing the ethnic imbalance was the Thirteenth Amendment to the Constitution (Bastian 1994; Edrisinha and Saravanamuttu 1993; ICES 1998). As we shall see, however, the provincial councils scheme which it set up, designed to devolve power to the provinces, failed to achieve this objective for a variety of reasons. Legislative and executive authority is devolved to eight provincial councils, elected on the basis of proportional representation. Each province has a governor who is appointed by the president and holds office during the pleasure of the latter, but who may be impeached by the council for intentional violation of the constitution, misconduct or corruption. The executive power in respect of the devolved subjects is vested in the governor who must act in accordance with the advice of the board of ministers unless he has been expressly required by the constitution to act on his own discretion (*Mahindasoma* v. *Maithripala Senanayake*

[1996] 1 SLR 180). The governor appoints the member who, in his opinion, is best able to command the support of the majority of the council to head the board of ministers.

The subjects and functions devolved on the provincial councils are listed in the 9th schedule to the constitution. They include police and public order, provincial planning, local government, provincial housing and construction, agriculture and agrarian services, rural development, health, indigenous medicine, cooperatives, and irrigation. In respect of subjects such as law and order, education and land, the scope of devolution is further defined in appendices 1, 2 and 3. There is also a Concurrent List of subjects. The Reserve List defines a sphere of exclusive authority for the centre and includes areas such as defence and national security, foreign affairs, post and telecommunications, broadcasting, television, justice, foreign trade and commerce, ports and harbours, aviation, national transport, minerals and mines, and elections. The residual powers are also vested in the centre.

An unusual feature of the Reserve List which has caused uncertainty is a provision that national policy on all subjects and functions shall belong to the centre. The majority in the *Thirteenth Amendment* case ([1987] 2 SLR 312) relied on this provision to hold that parliament would retain the authority to legislate on all subjects for any part of Sri Lanka and, therefore, the devolution scheme was within a unitary state. Three factors influenced the distribution of powers between the centre and the regions. The process of disaggregation of powers from the unitary state leaves the concentration of powers in the centre largely unaffected. Government lawyers and draftsmen made several amendments to ensure that the scheme would escape judicial scrutiny. Line ministers were apprehensive that a sweeping transfer of powers would result in a radical reorganisation of the governance structures at the centre, and the consequent closure of several ministries.

It was envisaged that the provincial councils would be financed through direct grants from the centre, a limited form of taxation, and revenue-sharing arrangements. A Finance Commission, consisting of five members, is empowered to make recommendations with regard to allocations from the annual budget of funds adequate to meet the needs of the provinces. It also has the power to make recommendations with regard to the apportionment of funds between the various provinces, having regard to the objectives of balanced regional development in the country. The two ex officio members are the secretary to the Ministry of Finance and the governor of the central bank, while it is provided that the other three members should represent the Sinhala, Tamil and Muslim communities.

The devolutionary scheme also envisages the establishment of a High Court in each province to exercise original, appellate and revisionary jurisdiction in criminal matters. In addition, it has jurisdiction to issue prerogative writs such as habeas corpus, certiorari and prohibition in respect of any matter in the Provincial Council List. (The more recent creation of a commercial High Court in Colombo, with jurisdiction in commercial disputes above a prescribed limit and the vesting of powers in the Chief Justice to transfer any case from a High Court in one province to the High Court in another province, has been criticised as a dilution of the devolution of judicial power.)

The political and constitutional contexts within which the provincial council scheme evolved has continued to constrain the effective working of the councils. The scheme was an integral part of the Indo-Sri Lanka Accord entered into on 29 July 1987 and signed by President J.R. Jayawardene of Sri Lanka and Prime Minister Rajiv Gandhi of India (see Tiruchelvam 1998:34–7). The accord endeavoured to provide a conceptual framework for the resolution of the ethnic conflict and to outline institutional arrangements for the sharing of power between the Sinhala and Tamil communities. It declared that Sri Lanka was 'a multi-ethnic and multi-lingual plural society', consisting primarily of four ethnic groups: the Sinhalese, Tamils, Muslims and Burghers.[3] It further recognised that the northern province and the eastern province 'had been areas of historical habitation of the Tamil speaking population'. Thus, without conceding the claim that the north-east constituted part of the traditional homelands of the Tamils, the accord provided cautious acknowledgement of the distinct character of this region. Both of these statements had important ideological significance in framing the policy of bilingualism, the provincial council scheme, and the temporary merger of the northern and eastern provinces as the unit of devolution. The unit of devolution remains the most contentious issue in the political discourse on the resolution of the national question. The merger of the northern and eastern provinces was envisaged in the Provincial Councils Act of 1987 and was to be subject to a referendum in the eastern province, but the referendum was postponed by a presidential order and has not yet been held.

The framers of the accord had hoped that they would present political groups in the north-east and the south of Sri Lanka with a fait accompli and that they would progressively build a consensus around the main concepts and ideas embodied in the accord. But both the LTTE (the dominant politico-military formation in the north-east) and the JVP (the radical youth movement in the south) repudiated the accord. The controversy surrounding it ultimately led to an armed confrontation between the LTTE and the Indian Peacekeeping Force and to an insurgency in the south of Sri Lanka. These developments cast a dark shadow over the working of the provincial council system. Elections to the provincial councils were held in April and June 1988, but the Sri Lanka Freedom Party, the main opposition party, did not participate. Similarly, the elections to the North-East Provincial Council in November 1988 lacked legitimacy because of LTTE opposition and the difficulties in conducting a free and fair election. The devolutionary experiment in the north-east was shortlived, lasting from November 1988 to mid-March 1990. It is a cruel irony that the North-East Provincial Council is dissolved and all legislative and executive power remains vested in the governor of that province. (The dissolution was the sequel to a bizarre turn of events. In 1990, the council inexplicably adopted a resolution which threatened a unilateral declaration of independence, and the chief minister and his board of ministers ceased to function. The government, by an ordinary amendment to the Provincial Councils Act, empowered the governor to disqualify the members who contravened their oath or ceased to function and stipulated that, in either of these events, the council would stand dissolved.)

The constitutional framework was also limiting. Article 2 of the Second Republican Constitution states that the Republic of Sri Lanka is a unitary state. Although the majority of the Supreme Court in the *Thirteenth Amendment* case did not hold that the provincial council scheme was inconsistent with art. 2, they nonetheless interpreted the concept of 'unitary state' strictly:

> The essence of unitary state is that the sovereignty is undivided – in other words, that the powers of the central government are unrestricted. The two essential qualities of a Unitary State are 1) the supremacy of the central Parliament, and 2) the absence of subsidiary sovereign bodies. It does not mean the absence of subsidiary law making bodies, but it does mean that they may exist and can be abolished at the discretion of the central authority.

The majority took the view that 'no exclusive or independent power' is vested in the provincial council, and that parliament and the president have ultimate control over them. This approach to and definition of a unitary state influences the outlook of the bureaucracy and the judiciary in interpreting the powers of the provincial councils.[4]

There were other ambiguities and inconsistencies in the scheme. Article 154G provides that any law passed by parliament in respect of a subject in the Concurrent List shall prevail over any contrary provision in a statute made by a provincial council with regard to the subject. The effect of this provision was to subordinate the legislative powers of the provincial council in respect of the subjects in the Concurrent List to that of parliament.

The provisions giving the centre the power to make policy on all subjects undermined and eroded both the legislative power and the executive authority of the provinces. This provision in the Reserve List was invoked by parliament to enact the amendment to the Agrarian Services Act No. 4 of 1991 and the National Transport Commission Act No. 37 of 1991. Provinces were clearly empowered to legislate on the regulation of surface transport. The bill envisaged the establishment of a National Transport Commission to frame and implement policy in respect of passenger transportation by omnibus. It stated the policy of the government that bus transport should be vested wholly in the private sector and sought to prohibit any state institution, including provincial councils, providing bus services. The National Transport Commission was also empowered to regulate all aspects of bus services, including the issue of route licences and the determination of tariffs. These provisions were in conflict with powers vested in the provinces.

Another unfortunate feature is the provision in art. 155(3A) for the president, during a state of public emergency, to enact emergency regulations in respect of any matter in the Provincial Council List or the Concurrent List, with the effect of overriding or suspending the operation of a provincial statute. Edrisinha and Saravanamuttu (1993) have cautioned that, since emergency rule has been more the norm than the exception, the article could be invoked to 'substantially undermine the autonomy of Provincial Councils'.

The Provincial Councils Act No. 42 of 1987 has further diluted the scheme of devolution by vesting the financial powers of the provincial council in the governor. The governor is empowered under s. 19(5) to frame rules in respect of the custody and payment of money into provincial funds. Similarly, under s. 24, no statute relating to financial matters shall be passed by the provincial council unless the governor has recommended the consideration of that statute. Under s. 26(3), no demand for a grant to a provincial council may be made except on the recommendation of the governor. Similarly, s. 28 empowered the governor to submit supplementary estimates to the council. Quite contrary to the spirit and intent of the Thirteenth Amendment, these provisions effectively equated the governor to a minister of finance of the province. The governor is also empowered under s. 25(1) to submit to the council annual financial estimates. Edrisinha and Saravanamuttu (1993) add that 'the general position of the Governor under the 13th Amendment is a major impediment to substantial devolution'.

Even in respect of the powers and functions which were less ambiguously vested in the provinces, there has been no effective transfer of powers. The Provincial Council List under the Thirteenth Amendment provided that police powers and public order to the extent envisaged in appendix 1 were to be devolved to the councils. The scheme also envisaged the establishment of a provincial division of the police force within each province, and a provincial police commission to exercise disciplinary control over police officers. Nothing has been done to implement these provisions.

Further inroads into the scheme of devolution were effected in 1992 by the Transfer of Powers, Divisional Secretaries Act No. 58 of 1992. A new tier in public administration was created for each division within an administrative district, and the powers vested in government agents by any written law were transferred to the divisional secretary of each division. These secretaries, representing an extension of presidential power, perform administrative functions within the geographical limits of a province, but no provincial authority can exercise any direct control or supervision over them.

THE JUDICIARY, PLURALISM AND THE ADJUDICATION OF DISPUTES RELATING TO DEVOLUTION

Although the courts have been regarded as the custodians of pluralistic values and the protectors of minorities, the role of the judiciary in Sri Lanka has been more complex (see de Silva 1987:79–106). The first four decades revealed a reluctance on the part of the apex judiciary to evolve judicial concepts and techniques of analysis which would protect the interests and rights of minorities. In recent years, however, the courts have made an effort to uphold provincial autonomy, principles of democracy, and minority rights.

A few years after the transfer of power, the courts were called upon to adjudicate on the constitutionality of denying citizenship to estate Tamils of recent Indian origin. Section 29, a centrepiece of the Soulbury (Independence) Constitution, provided guarantees of equal protection and non-discrimination. Both the Supreme Court and the Privy Council failed to examine the social and political effects of the impugned citizenship legislation or the motives for its enactment. They were therefore unable to reach a determination on the constitutional issues within a broader concern of the objects and purposes of the constitution.[5] Similarly, when the Official Language legislation was challenged by a Tamil public servant in the mid-1950s, the Supreme Court evaded the constitutional issues and disposed of the case on the ground that a public servant did not have a legally enforceable contract.[6] These judgments reduced s. 29 to a 'pathetically inefficient sentinel of ethnic crisis' (de Silva 1987).

Under the Second Republican Constitution, the Supreme Court is expressly vested with a constitutional jurisdiction and is constituted 'protector and guarantor of fundamental rights'. A case of constitutional importance relating to inter-group equity involved admission to universities according to a formula which provided that only 30 per cent of admissions were to be based exclusively on merit. It was weighted in favour of educationally backward areas and effectively reduced the intake of Tamil students from the north into universities. The formula was upheld by the Supreme Court, invoking the principle of state policy relating to the removal of regional disparities. While the constitution envisaged that incursions into the principles of equality should only be permissible under legislation, the Supreme Court appears to have permitted such incursions even through executive action seeking to implement the principles of state policy.[7]

The *Thirteenth Amendment* case reflects judicial ambivalence: five of the Supreme Court judges upheld the constitutionality of the devolution scheme, while four were of the view that it violated the unitary character of the state. There was also a sharp difference in the judicial approach to constitutional adjudication. The majority judgment was based on a self-conception of the judiciary as a body with a liberal outlook and the capacity to approach highly emotive issues with objective detachment. It invoked neutral principles relating to definitions of a unitary state in the context of contemporary constitutional discourse and endeavoured to apply those principles to an evaluation of the proposed constitutional amendment. On the other hand, the approach of the dissenting judges seems to embody explicitly the historical and political sensitivities of a popular discourse on ethnicity. The judgments combined a very positivist conception of a sovereign state with a dominant, majoritarian ideological construction of the Sri Lankan state as one inextricably linked to Sinhala-Buddhist ideology. These sharply contrasting approaches to the resolution of conflicts in power-sharing arrangements have led constitutional lawyers to argue that, in the context of Sri Lanka's plural society, the judiciary is not the ideal forum for the resolution of ethnic conflict, particularly those relating to fundamental structural questions (Coomaraswamy 1994:121–42).

One of the early disputes, in 1989, related to the failure of the governor to assent to a statute of the North-East Provincial Council to transfer to the council the assets and liabilities, contracts and obligations connected with the transport services of two public sector bodies, the Northern Regional Transport Board and the Eastern Regional Transport Board, respectively. In addition, the statute sought to transfer to the provincial minister in charge of transport the duties and powers exercised by the National Minister for Transport. The governor referred the statute back for reconsideration; the council, exercising its power under 154H(3) re-passed the resolution and submitted it again for the governor's assent. The statute was referred to the Supreme Court under 154H(4) for a determination of its constitutionality. Under the Thirteenth Amendment, neither the governor nor the president could veto statutes of the council and could only refer statutes to the Supreme Court for determination on grounds of constitutionality.

The Supreme Court pointed out that the centre's power under the Reserve List in relation to transport included carriage of passengers and goods by land and held that, while a provincial council had the power to regulate road transport services within a province, it did not have the power to deprive the centre of its powers of providing road transport services.[8] The court noted that the acquisition and requisition of property was a Concurrent List subject, but, while it could include the acquisition of land, vehicles and buildings, it could not include the take-over of entire business undertakings. An important aspect, however, was the emphasis in the judgment of Justice Mark Fernando on the need to develop a process for the resolution of centre–province disputes. He pointed out that consultation between the centre and the province was mandatory on matters relating to the Concurrent List and only through such consultation could the proliferation of disputes be averted (Coomaraswamy 1994).

A bill to amend the Agrarian Services Act No. 58 of 1979 was challenged in 1991 on the ground that agrarian service was a devolved subject. The Provincial List included 'agriculture, including agriculture extension, promotion and education for provincial purposes and agricultural services'. On the other hand, the state contended that the bill was referable to an entry in the Concurrent List: 'establishment and promotion of agro-linked industries, the establishment and maintenance of farms, and supervision of private nurseries.' The bill sought to regulate, inter alia, issues relating to the eviction of tenant cultivators, the sale of paddy land and tenancy rights, the cultivation of lands in dispute, the establishment of a board of review, the regulation of the Agrarian Services Committee and the establishment of farmers' organisations. The Supreme Court rejected the contentions of both the petitioner and the state, and took the view that the bill was in fact referable to the Reserve List since it substantially dealt with the rights of appeal of tenant cultivators and the determination of disputes. Here again, the courts were willing to adopt a more extreme position than that canvassed by the state, to uphold the centre's legislative powers in respect of a subject which had been ordinarily considered to have been clearly devolved.[9]

One of the most disturbing efforts to weaken the devolution scheme was legislation, introduced in 1990, to provide for the dissolution of a provincial council by an ordinary amendment to the Provincial Councils Amendment Act No. 27 of 1990. The powers of dissolution of a provincial council are set out in art. 154B(8)(c), where the governor was empowered to dissolve a council, which decision had to be on the advice of the chief minister. Article 154L also provided for the president to issue a proclamation to assume the administration of a province when a council is unable to carry on administration in accordance with the provisions of the constitution. The North-East Provincial Council had precipitated a crisis by adopting a resolution in which the members of the council threatened to proclaim a unilateral declaration of independence. The government introduced an amendment to enable a governor to inform the president that more than half of the total membership of the council had acted in contravention of their oath or that the council has ceased to function. The president could then dissolve the council from the dates specified in such communication. Clearly, vesting such sweeping powers of dissolution in the president on the mere report of a governor had serious consequences for the scheme of devolution envisaged by the Thirteenth Amendment. No such amendment, however difficult the situation that was unexpectedly presented to the state, should have been effected without a constitutional amendment; nonetheless, the Supreme Court upheld the validity of this amendment.[10]

The Provincial Governor's case seems to show something of a change of approach on the part of the Supreme Court.[11] The court was called upon to interpret the scope of the governor's discretion, under art. 154F(4) of the constitution, to appoint a chief minister. The United National Party, the Democratic United National Party and the Podujana Eksath Peramuna contested the north-western and the southern provincial council elections held in May 1993. No party gained an absolute majority. In the north-western elections, the UNP won 25 seats, the PEP 18 and the DUNF 9. In the southern province, the UNP won 27 seats, the PEP 22 and the DUNF 6. There were rival claims for appointment as chief minister in both provinces: in the north-western province, G.M. Premachandra of the DUNF and Gamini Jayewickrema Perera of the UNP; and, in the southern province, A.G.H. Dodangoda of the PEP, and M.S. Amarasiri of the UNP. The governors of the two provinces appointed the UNP contenders as chief ministers.

These appointments were challenged before the Court of Appeal, which referred the cases to the Supreme Court under art. 125 of the constitution. Although the court held that there was no proper reference, it set out several guidelines with regard to the interpretation of the governor's discretion with regard to this matter: (a) the discretion of the governor to select as chief minister the person best able to command the confidence of the council is a discretion to give effect to the wishes of the people of the province and not for any other purpose, personal or political; (b) the exercise of the powers vested in the governor of a province under art. 145(4) (excluding the provision) is not a matter solely for his subjective assessment and judgment, but is subject to judicial review by the Court of Appeal; (c) the governor's choice may require the consideration of political factors, but it is not an act which is purely political in nature, for it involves the determination of legal rights concerning the allocation and exercise of powers by elected representatives of the people of a province; and (d) the governor's decision involves a constitutional power and duty and consequently implies a constitutional right in the members of the council to the proper exercise of such power.

In developing these principles of judicial review on the exercise of the discretion of the governor, the court reaffirmed certain basic principles of constitutional adjudication. The court pointed out 'that the Constitution and the system of government are founded on the Rule of Law; and to prevent the erosion of that foundation is the primary function of an independent judiciary'. The court therefore, in a significant departure from the previous judicial trend, asserted the supremacy of the constitution and the need to interpret the chapter on devolution so as to reaffirm that provincial councils are an integral part of Sri Lanka's representative democracy.

In 1996, the Court of Appeal was called upon to define the powers of the governor to dissolve a provincial council under art. 154B(8)(c).[12] On representations made by the general public and on information gathered by them on the alleged maladministration of the north-central province and the Sabaragamuwa province, the respective governors of these provinces sought the advice of their chief ministers on whether the said councils should be dissolved. Each chief minister commanded the support of the majority of the members of his council and advised against dissolution. So the governors sought the advice of the president, who directed them to dissolve the councils, which they did by orders published in the *Gazette*.

The Court of Appeal pointed out that the central question was whether the governor had a discretion to exercise the power of dissolution or whether he was bound by the advice of the chief minister (so long as the board of ministers commands the confidence of the council). The court stated that art. 154B(8)(d), specifying that the governor shall exercise his powers in accordance with the advice of the chief minister, is unambiguous and applies to all the powers of the governor under paragraph 8 of art. 154B. There is no express provision in the constitution empowering the president to dissolve a provincial council. The governors had therefore acted contrary to art. 154B(8)(c) by seeking the advice of the president in a matter over which they had no discretion and by dissolving the councils. Accordingly, the dissolutions were declared null and void.

In 1998, the Supreme Court considered the constitutionality of the failure to hold elections to five provincial councils.[13] The five-year terms of these councils had come to an end in June 1998. Notices had been duly published by the Commissioner of Elections of the intention to hold elections, nomination periods had been prescribed for each council and the nomination process had been completed. On 4 August, the president had issued a proclamation under the Public Securities Ordinance, declaring a state of public emergency throughout the island and issuing an emergency regulation which stated that the decision setting the date of elections to these provincial councils was deemed to be of no effect. The petitioners complained that the failure to hold elections was an infringement of their fundamental rights to equality before the law, the equal protection of the law and to the freedom of speech and expression.

While the case was before the Supreme Court, the term of the North-Western Provincial Council came to an end and an election date was fixed. The court therefore took the view that 'citizens, residents in the five provinces are thus being less favourably treated than those of the north-western province in respect of their right to vote'. It also held that the right to vote is one form of speech and expression which art. 14(1)(a) of the constitution protects. The court therefore upheld the contention that the emergency regulation violated arts. 12(1) and 14(1), but it failed to make a pronouncement on the validity of the proclamation of the emergency by the president. It also pointed out that chap. XVIIA, and especially art. 154A, contemplate 'the continued existence of the elected provincial councils'. The court could therefore not give an interpretation to s. 22.6 of the Provincial Council Act, which would in effect result in there being no election and therefore no elected provincial council.

When it came to examining the constitutionality of legislation to enable the Commissioner of Elections to fix new dates for elections to the five provincial councils which had been postponed, the Supreme Court asserted that the right to franchise in art. 4(1) of the constitution must include elections to provincial councils. It also pointed out that, while art. 154E provides for the automatic dissolution of a provincial council at the expiry of its five-year term of office, no provision is made for a 'caretaker' administration. The court therefore concluded that 'the constitution requires prompt elections: to hold otherwise would be to devalue the devolution of power'.[14]

THE DRAFT CONSTITUTION: DOES IT REPRESENT A PARADIGM SHIFT?

Edrisinha (1998:24) has correctly observed of the Thirteenth Amendment that 'the constitutional provisions are fundamentally flawed. They permit the Centre both to retain so much power and also undermine devolved powers so easily, that they cannot result in substantial devolution of power.' The concept of the unitary state also became embedded in the consciousness of the bureaucracy and, until more recently, the judiciary. It influenced the approach of both to the resolution of centre–province disputes. They did not often perceive themselves as neutral arbiters but as an integral part of the centralised state.

The proposals for constitutional reform released on 3 August 1995 redefined the nature of the state as a 'union of regions'; drawing on the language of the Indian constitution, Sri Lanka was further described as a 'united and sovereign Republic'. In the most recent legal text, published in 1996, there is a reworking of the language without any significant deviation from the original intent and impact of the provision in the August proposals. The Republic of Sri Lanka is now described as an 'indissoluble Union of Regions', thereby interpolating an archaic phrase drawn from the Australian constitution. Article 3, which relates to sovereignty and its exercise, also ensures that legislative and executive power will be directly vested in the regional council and its political executive in respect of the subjects devolved.

Most of the subjects and functions which were previously in the Concurrent List were transferred to the Regional List. This would significantly strengthen the capacity of the devolved authorities to adopt an integrated approach to the social and economic development of the region and thereby seek to redress regional disparities in development. A contentious issue has been the devolution of powers in relation to land. The draft text makes it clear that state land shall vest in the region and the regional administration shall be entitled to transfer or alienate land and engage in land use and land settlement schemes. The centre may, however, for the purpose of a reserved subject, request a regional administration to transfer state land to the centre. There is an obligation in the part of the centre to consult the region with regard to such requirements. The legal text also provides that interregional irrigation projects, where the command area falls within two or more regions, will be the responsibility of the centre. This provision is also found in the Provincial Council Scheme, although the selection of allottees and the alienation of land under such schemes were within the powers of the provincial council. This is a potential area of conflict and may require further clarification. Law and order, including the maintenance of public order, have been clearly devolved on the region, although there will be disputes as to whether the investigation of offences relating to the reserved list of subjects should be vested with the regional or national police service.

The issue arises as to whether the draft constitutional proposals would result in the establishment of a federal political system. Ronald Watts (1996:7) has pointed out that the term 'federal political system' 'refers to a broad category of political systems in which, by contrast to the single source of authority in a unitary system, there are two (or more) levels of government which combine elements of shared rule through a common institution and regional self rule for the governments of the constituent units'. Having regard to the structural characteristics of the proposed power-sharing arrangements, we can reach the following conclusions.

First, there are two orders of government at the national and regional level, each acting directly on their citizens. Second, there is a constitutional distribution of legislative and executive authority and allocation of revenue resources between the national and the regional orders of government, providing for areas of exclusivity and autonomy for each order.

Third, the proposed written constitution will not be unilaterally alterable, in that no bill for the amendment or repeal of the provisions of the chapter relating to devolution or relating to the distribution of subjects and functions between the centre and the region shall come into operation in respect of a region unless such act or provision has been approved by a resolution of a regional council established for that region.[15] Edrisinha (1998:13–37) has pointed out, however, that the draft proposals do not adequately and effectively establish the supremacy of the constitution. There is reference in the preamble to the constitution as the supreme law of the land, but there is no substantive provision which emphasises that all organs of government, all institutions and all citizens are subordinate to it.

Fourth, an umpire to rule on disputes between the centre and the region is an important feature of these arrangements. The draft provides for an arbitral tribunal to be established in the case of a dispute between a regional administration and the central government. Each party to the dispute shall be entitled to nominate a member and the members so appointed may nominate a chairman. Where there is no agreement between the members, the chairman shall be nominated by a constitutional council. An award or a determination made by a tribunal shall be binding on the parties to the dispute. Critics have contended, however, that the arbitral arrangement is no substitute for the judicial resolution of disputes between the centre and the region. Edrisinha (1998:20) has argued that 'what is tragic, but perhaps not surprising in Sri Lanka today is that no political party in the country is committed to what is the cornerstone of a constitutional democracy'.

Fifth, there are processes and institutions to facilitate collaboration between the centre and the region in respect of areas where governmental responsibilities are shared or overlap. The proposed Chief Ministers Conference is an important innovation in this regard.[16] It provides for the conference chair to be elected by the chief ministers in rotation, so that each will chair for a period of three months. It is further provided that the prime minister must meet with the conference and that a period of three months should not lapse between such meetings. The conference has the authority to ensure full compliance with the constitutional provision relating to devolution in accordance with the spirit and intention of the constitution, and to inquire into subjects where more than one region has a common interest or to make recommendations on

policy coordination. It can make representations to the Finance Commission and also address matters relating to financial administration and
accountability. In addition to the arbitral arrangement referred to above,
the conference may also settle disputes by mediation or conciliation.

One of the significant shortcomings in the proposals is the absence of
a second chamber providing for the representation of distinct regional
views. A proposal to establish such a chamber was made before the Select
Committee but was subsequently withdrawn by the government, ostensibly on the grounds of expense. However, the expenditure on a second
chamber could be minimised by a reduction in the size of the House of
Representatives and by ensuring that physical infrastructure and support
services are shared by both houses.

In Sri Lanka, progress on political arrangements to secure minority
rights has often been incremental. There have been no dramatic leaps of
faith in its recent history resulting in fundamental transformation of constitutional arrangements. Nonetheless, we must conclude that the draft
constitution, in moving away from an entrenched unitary state, has
brought about a paradigm shift vital to a meaningful sharing of power
between regions and communities.

CONSOCIATIONALISM AND MINORITIES WITHIN A REGION

There was no conscious attempt to emulate the Lijphartian consociational principles of grand coalition, mutual veto, proportionality and segmental autonomy (Lijphart 1977:25) in the framing of the first and
second constitutions. However, in the present constitution exercise, there
was a growing concern that institutions of representative democracy were
being crippled by the excesses of party politics. Both at the national and
provincial level, the Westminster model had contributed to an adversarial
form of democracy where the political response to almost every issue was
influenced by narrow considerations of political partisanship. The failure
to develop even a minimum consensus on common political and economic goals had severely handicapped the capacity to resolve pressing
problems. In the provincial councils, the intensity of party rivalry in the
allocation of resources and the determination of developmental priorities
had reduced their effectiveness as engines of development. There was
also a further concern that minorities within a region, unless they were
part of political coalitions which had been installed in power, remained
excluded from the benefits of development.

These considerations contributed to the framers of the draft constitution agreeing to one of the most radical departures from the Westminster model: a proposal that the system of proportional representation be
also extended to the political executive of the region. This would mean

that while the governor would call upon the leader of the political party in the council who commands the confidence of the council to become the chief minister, the other positions in the board of ministers would be shared on the basis of proportionality. Political parties represented in the council would be entitled to a number of positions in the board of ministers, proportionate to the votes that they had received. After the number of positions was determined, the party leader could nominate persons to the board. The chief minister would determine the portfolios to be assigned to each member of the board but could do so only after consultation with the leaders of the political parties concerned. In addition, each member of the board of ministers would constitute an executive committee which would be representative of all of the political formations in the council. Each member of the council would thereby become a member of at least one executive committee and would share in the exercise of executive power and, where appropriate, in the framing of legislative proposals for consideration by the council. The executive committees would ordinarily take decisions on a collegial basis rather than on a majority vote (for an examination of the executive committee system, see Wickramaratne 1998:163–74).

There is some uncertainty as to whether such a consociational arrangement can work in a political culture which has been characterised as being confrontational and combative. Lijphart (1977) observed that these principles can become operational where 'the political elites of rival parties would have to cooperate, not compete'. The arrangement will, however, compel political parties to work together to develop the regions in an integrated manner. It has been observed that, where there is an emphasis on compromise through pluralities of decision making, notions of minority and majority become less significant. It is intended to facilitate a process of political socialisation of the political elites with the full awareness that a society, 'with ethnic, religious, linguistic and like diversities territorially cross-cutting, cannot simply afford the luxury of having winners and losers'. This arrangement will also ensure that political and ethnic minorities will have assured representation in the political executive of the region, and thereby facilitate multi-ethnic governments in most of the regions.

There have been doubts as to whether the conditions for a successful working of consociational arrangements exist in Sri Lanka. First, the social cleavages are both intense and cumulative. Most Sinhalese and Tamils are differentiated by both language and religion. With regard to the estate Tamils, there is a coincidence of class and ethnicity, as most were until recently denied citizenship rights and they constitute a distinct social and economic underclass. Second, there are no overarching political loyalties which cut across ethnic groups and create 'cross pressures which make for moderate positions and attitudes'. There are both Tamils and Sinhalese in the major political parties (the United National Party, and the Peoples Alliance), but the majority of the Tamils and the Muslims of the north-east support regional and ethnic parties and political formations. This fragmentation of political affiliations has been recently mitigated somewhat by loose political coalitions between some of the regional and ethnic parties and the party in government. Third, the intensity of the antagonism and hostility between the major political parties (which have consistently secured more than 90 per cent of the votes in the south) has been at times as intense as ethnic antagonisms. Fourth, although there were instances of accommodation and cooperation among the English-educated political elite during and after the transfer of power, there has been a change in the social composition of the political leadership and the linkages and contacts have weakened.

There is also concern that the new institutional arrangements, with their complex and consensual decision-making processes, will weaken the effectiveness of the devolved institutions. It has been argued that, if the commitment to consociational principles were serious, these principles should also be extended to the structures and decision-making processes at the national level. There has been opposition to the recourse to devolved institutions as a laboratory for radical political experimentation, without building the capacity for effective governance of the second-tier leadership.

POWER SHARING AND IDENTITY POLITICS

The constitutional reform proposals undoubtedly represent the boldest effort hitherto towards ethnic reconciliation, but are they adequate given the magnitude of the crisis facing Sri Lankan society? Critics have argued that they fall significantly short of the Thimpu principles advanced by all of the major Tamil formations at the political negotiations conducted in Thimpu, Bhutan (see Somasundram 1999:42–66). The four principles placed before the Sri Lankan government were as follows:

- Recognition of the Tamils of Sri Lanka as a distinct nationality.
- Recognition of an identified Tamil homeland and a guarantee of its territorial integrity.
- Based on the above, recognition of the inalienable right of self-determination of the Tamil nation.
- Recognition of the right to full citizenship and other fundamental democratic rights of all Tamils who look upon the island as their country.

It is an examination of these principles that has led some commentators to advocate the need for a new initiative based on 'the core aspirations of the Tamil People' (Edrisinha 1998:36). The Indo-Sri Lanka Accord, by its emphasis on the need to nurture and protect distinct identities and by acknowledging that the north-east province constitutes the traditional habitation of Tamils and Muslims, provides an implicit acknowledgement of some of the Thimpu concepts. However, the mere symbolic acknowledgement of the definition of the national problem and the nature of Tamil national identity does not per se lead to a resolution. At the core of the Thimpu principles are substantive political arrangements for the redefinition of the nature of the state and the sharing of sovereign legislative and executive powers between the regions. The quest for a political resolution within a united Sri Lanka must therefore relate to the substantive issues relating to the exercise of political power rather than the more abstract formulations of political identity.

The constitutional reform proposal introduced in 1995 represents the boldest effort hitherto to bring about ethnic reconciliation. It recognises that ethnic conflict continues to pose fundamental problems relating to human rights, social justice and constitutional ordering. It validates James Tully's (1995:9) point about the need to find new state forms to accommodate different forms of diversity. It seeks to put behind us the absurdity by which constitutional entrenchment was used not to protect minority rights but to privilege the interests of the majority. The constitutional proposals are based on the realisation that one of the central problems of modern constitutionalism is to reconcile the claims for recognition of cultural identity. There is a particularly theoretical quality to this debate in Sri Lanka, where it is argued that the symbolic recognition and acknowledgement of Tamil identity must precede negotiations on power-sharing arrangements. This poses its own difficulties since the assertion of one form of identity is viewed as the denial of the other. Can modern constitutionalism accommodate multiple and distinct forms of belonging to the community, the region and the nation?

NOTES

1 See Select Committee's Report on Constitutional Reforms Presented to Parliament on 24 October 1997. The text of this and many other documents can be found on LAcNet (Lanka Academic Network) at <http://www.lacnet.org/devolution/proposal.html#ITM2>. See also <http://www.lanka.net/lakehouse>.
2 On the language rights of Tamils under the constitution, see de Silva and Wriggins (1956–89:390).
3 The articulation of Sri Lanka as a multi-ethnic and plural society may appear as the confirmation of an obvious empirical reality; however, it ran counter to the dominant Sinhala-Buddhist ideological construction of the state and the nation.
4 Colvin R. de Silva, the author of the First Republican Constitution, has advocated a more flexible approach to the definition of a unitary state (see 'Uni-

tary constitutions and federal constitutions', *Ceylon Daily News* 22 October 1987:6).
5 See *G.S.N. Kodakan Pillai* v. *P.B. Mudanayake et al.* (1953) 54 NLR 350 (Supreme Court); *G.S.N. Kodakan Pillai* v. *P.B. Mudanayake et al.* (1953) 54 NLR 433 (Privy Council).
6 *C. Kodeeswaran* v. *The Attorney-General* (1970) 72 NLR 337. The Supreme Court judgment was reversed on the question relating to the rights of a public servant to sue in contract, and the constitutional issues were referred back to the Supreme Court. The case was not proceeded with, however, as it had been overtaken by the adoption of the First Republican Constitution in May 1972.
7 *Seneviratne and another* v. *University Grants Commission* [1980] 1 SLR 182. See also de Silva (1987).
8 *Northern and Eastern Provinces Transport Board* case, S.C. No. 7/89 (Special) (PPA/2/PC/19).
9 Supreme Court on the constitutionality of 'An Act to amend the Agrarian Services Act No. 58 of 1979', *Parliamentary Hansard* (1990:columns 192–5).
10 Judgment of the Supreme Court on the bill titled 'An Act to amend the Provincial Councils Act No. 42 of 1987', *Parliamentary Hansard* (1990:270–1).
11 *Premachandra* v. *Montague Jayewickrema and another* [1994] 2 SLR 90.
12 *Mahindasoma* v. *Maithripala Senanayake* [1996] 1 SLR 180.
13 *V.C. Karunaratilake and another* v. *The Dayananda Dissanayaka, Commissioner of Elections* [1999] 4 LRC 380.
14 *J.V.P. and others* v. *The Attorney-General* (S.C. Special Determination No. 9/98, SD).
15 See chap. XV, art. 141(4) and (5) of the Government's Proposals for Constitutional Reform, October 1997. Contrast chap. 6, arts. 146, 147 and 148 of the Constitution of the Republic of South Africa, as adopted by the Constitutional Assembly on 8 May 1996.
16 See chap. XV, art. 141 of the Government's Proposals for Constitutional Reform, October 1997.

REFERENCES

Bastian, Sunil (ed.) 1994. *Devolution and Development in Sri Lanka.* Colombo: ICES with Konark Publishers.
Coomaraswamy, Radhika 1994. 'Devolution, the law, and judicial construction', in Sunil Bastian (ed.) *Devolution and Development in Sri Lanka.* Colombo: ICES with Konark Publishers.
de Silva, H.L. 1987. 'Pluralism and the judiciary in Sri Lanka', in Neelan Tiruchelvam and Radhika Coomaraswamy (eds) *The Role of the Judiciary in Plural Societies.* London: Frances Pinter Publishers.
de Silva, K.M. and Howard Wriggins 1994. *J.R. Jayewardene of Sri Lanka, A Political Biography, Volume Two: 1956–1989.* London: Leo Copper.
Edrisinha, Rohan 1998. 'A critical overview: constitutionalism, conflict resolution and the limits of the draft constitution', in Dinusha Panditaratne and Pradeep Ratnam (eds) *The Draft Constitution of Sri Lanka: Critical Aspects.* Colombo: Law & Society Trust.
Edrisinha, Rohan and Paikiasothy Saravanamuttu 1993. 'The case for a federal Sri Lanka', in Rohan Edrisinha and Jayadeva Uyangoda (eds) *Essays on*

Constitutional Reform. Colombo: Centre for Policy Research Analysis, University of Colombo.

ICES (International Centre for Ethnic Studies) 1998. *Sri Lanka: The Devolution Debate*. 4th edn. Colombo: ICES.

Lijphart, Arend 1977. *Democracy in Plural Societies: A Comparative Exploration*. New Haven: Yale University Press.

Manogaran, Chelvadurai 1987. *Ethnic Conflict and Reconciliation in Sri Lanka*. Honolulu: University of Hawaii Press.

Manor, James (ed.) 1984. *Sri Lanka: In Change and Crisis*. London: Croom Helm.

Manor, James 1989. *The Expedient Utopian: Bandaranaike and Ceylon*. Cambridge: Cambridge University Press.

Somasundram, M. 1999. 'The Northern Ireland Agreement: Thimpu principles applied to a society with two mind sets?', in M. Somasundram (ed.) *Reimagining Sri Lanka: Northern Ireland Insights*. Colombo: ICES.

Spencer, Jonathan 1990. 'Introduction: the power of the past', in J. Spencer (ed.) *Sri Lanka: History and Roots of Conflict*. London: Routledge.

Spotts, F. (ed.) 1989. *Letters of Leonard Woolf*. London: Weidenfeld and Nicolson.

Tambiah, Stanley J. 1986. *Sri Lanka, Ethnic Fratricide and the Dismantling of Democracy*. Chicago: Chicago University Press.

Tiruchelvam, Neelan 1992. 'Bandaranaike ideology and social harmony', Bandaranaike Memorial Lecture, 26 September.

—— 1998. 'Devolution of power: the problems and challenges', in ICES *Sri Lanka: The Devolution Debate*. 4th edn. Colombo: ICES with Konark Publishers.

Tully, James 1995. *Strange Multiplicity: Constitutionalism in an Age of Diversity*. Cambridge: University of Cambridge.

Uyangoda, Jayadeva 1994. 'The state and the process of devolution in Sri Lanka', in Sunil Bastian (ed.) *Devolution and Development in Sri Lanka*. Colombo: ICES with Konark Publishers.

Watts, Ronald 1996. *Comparing Federal Systems in the 1990s*. Kingston: Institute of Intergovernmental Governmental Relations and Queens University, Canada.

Wickramaratne, Jayampathy 1998. 'The executive committee system and multiparty cabinets: power sharing in the regions', in Dinusha Panditaratne and Pradeep Ratnam (eds) *The Draft Constitution of Sri Lanka: Critical Aspects*. Colombo: Law & Society Trust.

Wilson, A. Jeyaratnam 1993. 'Ethnic strife in Sri Lanka: the politics of space', in John Coakley (ed.) *The Territorial Management of Ethnic Conflict*. London: Frank Cass.

—— 1988. *The Break-up of Sri Lanka: The Sinhalese–Tamil Conflict*. London: C. Hurst.

Wriggins, W. Howard 1960. *Ceylon: The Dilemmas of a New Nation*. Princeton: Princeton University Press.

CHAPTER 10

CYPRUS: FROM CORPORATE AUTONOMY TO THE SEARCH FOR TERRITORIAL FEDERALISM

REED COUGHLAN

THE RELEVANCE OF CYPRUS

For a comparative study of autonomy and ethnicity, Cyprus provides an interesting example of two distinct ways to manage ethnic tensions. First, the 1960 constitution which was handed to Cyprus on the occasion of her independence from Great Britain was an unusual experiment in consociational democracy. Under these arrangements the two ethnic communities, the Greek and Turkish Cypriots, who were interspersed throughout the island, were granted corporate autonomy in the form of an elaborate set of group rights which were enshrined in the constitution itself. I will examine this experiment in light of what we know about the conditions under which this form of government is likely to succeed. I will conclude that consociationalism, as proposed in the constitution, could not have been expected to succeed in Cyprus, not because the constitution was too rigid as the Greek Cypriots tend to claim, and not because the Greek Cypriots were unwilling to compromise as the Turkish Cypriots are inclined to argue, but rather because of the very structure of Cypriot society. Consociationalism is most likely to succeed in a society with three or more segments and where no single segment is dominant. However, Cyprus was (and is) comprised of two highly segmented elements which are demographically and economically unequal.

Second, after 1974 when an Athens-sponsored coup d'état toppled President Makarios to force 'Enosis' (unification of Cyprus with Greece) and Turkey intervened militarily, bringing about the partition of the island, it became possible to contemplate a different form of government, namely a territorially based federation, as the Greeks and Turks were now physically separated through an exchange of population. Roughly 45,000 Turkish Cypriots went to the North, and approximately

160,000 Greek Cypriots were forced to the South. Efforts sponsored by the Secretary-General of the United Nations to negotiate a bi-zonal, bicommunal federation have been ongoing for twenty-five years without success. I will argue that federalism is not an appropriate solution for Cyprus. The conditions which undermined the consociational experiment in the period 1960–63 are currently even less favourable to the establishment of a territorially based federation, because the socio-economic disparities between the two segments in the island have become much deeper.

The proximity and the importance of Cyprus to Greece and Turkey make a political solution to this conflict even more difficult. Greece came into being as a result of the war of independence against the Ottomans in the 1820s. Turkey took form a century later when Kemal Atatürk drove the invading Greek army out of Anatolia. The national political agenda in both countries is frequently defined by relations with the other, and Cyprus is often at the heart of the national debate. In spite of what many Greeks and Turks on Cyprus might say about the origins of this modern conflict, its roots go back more than a century.

The bicommunal nature of Cypriot society was established in the early years of Ottoman rule (1570s), when about 20,000 Turkish settlers came to the island. The first Ottoman census, taken to determine the taxable population, indicated that there were about 85,000 Greeks, Maronites and Armenians (Alastos 1955:262). Over the next 300 years, the size of the two communities fluctuated, but by 1878, when the administration of Cyprus was ceded to Great Britain, the population was approximately 73.4 per cent 'Greek Church' and 24.9 per cent 'Mahometan'. The first census under British rule, taken in 1881, broke the population down by religion, the primary anchor for peoples' identity at that time in Cyprus and in large parts of the Near East. The centrality of religion, however, began to shift, quite ironically, as a result of the spread of Greek nationalism which was spearheaded by the Orthodox Church. During the last half-century of Ottoman rule, the church spread Greek nationalist values through the proliferation of a network of schools throughout the Greek communities in Asia Minor, including Cyprus (Kitromilides 1990). This political socialisation was accompanied by an intentional effort to promote 'the linguistic homogenization of the Christian Orthodox populations of the East as the basis of their incorporation into the broader community of the Greek nation – language was replacing religion as the major unifying bond of nationality' (Kitromilides 1990:7).[1]

In Cyprus, the resurgence of Hellenism took the form of Greek irredentist nationalism, where agitation for Enosis gained rapid impetus under the relatively permissive British administration. From the very outset of British rule, the Greek Cypriots constantly agitated for the unification of Cyprus with Greece. This barrage of petitions and demonstrations was met by Turkish Cypriot counter demands that the administration of Cyprus continue unchanged.

In 1892 Greek Cypriot agitation for union with Greece led the British to offer Cyprus a constitution which provided for a legislative council. Cypriot representation on the council reflected the demographic ratio of the two communities on the island. There were eighteen members, of whom six were British officials appointed by the British High Commissioner, nine were elected from the Greek community, and three were elected from the Turkish community. While the Greek Cypriots were apparently satisfied with the arrangement, the Turkish community took exception. As one historian put it, 'the Moslems, however, saw in it an attack upon their status as the former ruling element in the island and protested accordingly. They expressed the fear that the Greek majority would pay no respects to their rights' (Alastos 1955:322). The Turkish Cypriots were concerned that the Greeks would use their majority rule to bring about Enosis. In a telegram to the British Secretary of State, the Turkish Cypriots pointed to the arrangements in Asia Minor where the Moslems were in a majority, but where the Christians had equal representation on administrative councils. Proportional representation was, as they put it, 'incompatible with local requirements, and, if enforced, will compel us all to leave the island for some other place'.[2]

The Greek community was also opposed to proportional representation, as it would deprive it of its demographic advantage. So, more than 100 years ago, both communities rejected the principles of proportional representation because these principles would get in the way of exercising what each took to be its legitimate prerogative to dominate the other. The lack of trust and mutual goodwill persists to this day.

In 1882 the British paid no attention to the Turkish Cypriot remonstrations and duly established the constitution under which Cyprus was to be governed until 1931. The riots that year, sparked by agitation for Enosis and discontent over supplemental taxes imposed by the government, led the British to impose martial law, to suspend the constitution and to abolish the legislative council. When proposals for a new constitution were forwarded by the British after World War II, they were met with the demand for 'Enosis, and only Enosis' by the Greek Cypriots.

Between 1878 and 1950 Greek Cypriots continually advocated Enosis; Turkish Cypriots consistently opposed it. Before World War I Cyprus officially still belonged to the Sultan, since the Cyprus convention only stipulated that the British would administer the island on behalf of the Sultan. The British response to Enosis between 1878 and 1914 was to point out that Cyprus still belonged to the Ottoman Empire and that it was not in their power to allow unification with Greece. Britain finally annexed Cyprus when Turkey joined the Axis powers in World War I. In October 1915 Britain offered Cyprus to Greece as an inducement to encourage Greece to join the war effort. King Constantine turned the offer down, much to the dismay of Enosis advocates on Cyprus. Thereafter, British responses to Enosis, though tempered at times with a certain philhellenic sympathy, was to turn a deaf ear to all appeals.

In 1950 the leader of the Greek Cypriot community, Archbishop Makarios, decided to hold a plebiscite to demonstrate the strength of support for Enosis. Ninety-six per cent of the Greek Cypriots voted in favour of Enosis. Finally, frustration on their part led to the formation of the National Organisation of Cypriot Fighters (EOKA) and to the decision to initiate a terrorist campaign against the British in an effort to secure their withdrawal from Cyprus so that Enosis could be achieved.

The alienation of the two communities was spawned by the Enosis movement, but it was also enhanced by their educational systems. Ethnic antagonism was spread through the two educational systems which were effectively transplanted from Turkey and Greece. Greek and Turkish Cypriots went to separate schools where they learned of the centuries of enmity and warfare between the two mainlands. The curricula ensured that students understood that 'their compatriots on the other side of the ethnic line were their traditional mortal enemies' (Markides 1977:23) and constantly reinforced the growing sense of distrust and antagonism between the two groups.

The rift between Greeks and Turks grew wider when the guerrilla war was launched by the Greek Cypriots in 1955. It was initially directed at the British, but, when EOKA began targeting Greek Cypriots in the security forces, intimidation triggered mass resignations and the British were forced to rely on Turkish Cypriots to replace them. It was not long before Turkish Cypriot policemen were murdered and this set in motion a series of revenge killings which soon escalated into full-scale intercommunal violence. Estimates of casualties are difficult to establish, especially of intercommunal violence, because many killings were motivated by efforts from within both communities to punish traitors to the cause. The Greek terrorist organisation targeted both Turks and Greeks who were judged to have been disloyal to Enosis. The Turkish Cypriot counterpart was the TMT, a terrorist organisation which advocated the partition of Cyprus as a solution to the intercommunal conflict. It went after Greek Cypriots to avenge earlier killings, as well as members of their own community who were seen to have betrayed the Turkish Cypriot cause. It was in this context that the movement to force Britain out of Cyprus as a prelude to unification with Greece gave birth to a conflict between two ethno-nationalist groups on Cyprus. When independence came to Cyprus in 1960, it was received with profound ambivalence. Greek Cypriots had been fighting for Enosis, not for independence. Turkish Cypriots had come to believe that partition was the preferred solution to the conflict.

THE ZURICH–LONDON ACCORDS AND THE 1960 CONSTITUTION

Following several years of terrorist violence (1955–59, the so-called emergency) amid efforts to negotiate a settlement, an agreement was eventually worked out among Greece, Turkey and Great Britain. While representatives of the Greek and Turkish Cypriots eventually signed the so-called Zurich–London Agreements, the Cypriots had not participated in negotiating their provisions. Further, the aspirations of the two communities, Enosis for the Greek Cypriots and partition for the Turkish Cypriots, were both explicitly prohibited in the Treaty of Guarantee, one of three constituent parts of the accords. Article 1 of the treaty specified that 'the Republic of Cyprus . . . undertakes not to participate, in whole or in part, in any political or economic union with any state whatsoever. With this intent it prohibits all activity tending to promote directly or indirectly either union or partition of the island' (Necategil 1989:151). The agreements stipulated the provisions of the constitution under which the newly independent Cyprus was to be governed; it was a constitution which was, in the words of one contemporary commentator, 'long, minutely detailed, precise, complicated and rigid to an unusual degree' (Baker 1959).

The Zurich–London accords provided a treaty of guarantee by which Britain, Greece and Turkey were to safeguard the constitutional integrity and independence of Cyprus, and a treaty of establishment which stipulated the retention by Britain of designated 'sovereign base areas'. The essentials of the constitution were spelled out in the document entitled 'Basic Structure of the Republic of Cyprus'. Cyprus was to be an independent and sovereign republic. The Cyprus constitution embodied all of the principles of consociational democracy, namely, 'grand coalition, proportionality, autonomy and veto' (Lijphart 1977). The president, a Greek, and the vice-president, a Turk, were to be elected by their respective communities and were to share prerogatives and executive power. The principles of grand coalition and proportionality were rounded out by the provisions that the council of ministers, the legislature and the public service were all to be apportioned in a ratio of 70 per cent Greek and 30 per cent Turkish. The army was to have a 60:40 ratio. The security forces, in the initial period, were to reflect a 60:40 proportion in recognition of the imbalance at the point of independence which had come about because recruits had only been drawn from the Turkish community during the years of the emergency. The supreme court was comprised of one Greek, one Turk and one external, neutral judge. Measures for autonomy included separately elected communal chambers as well as

223

provision for separate municipalities in the five main towns. The latter provision reflected the separation of the ethnic populations in urban areas which had occurred in the period of violence when the Greek Cypriot guerrilla war against the British spilled over into intercommunal violence and the Turkish Cypriots were forced into urban enclaves (Anderson and Killingray 1992; Patrick 1976).

The separate municipalities and the separately elected communal chambers went a long way towards the establishment of a federal structure, although without a territorial dimension. The interspersed demographic settlement of the population at that time precluded the establishment of ethnically separate regions under a federated system of government. On the other hand, these provisions, along with the deeply bicommunal nature of the constitution evident in the executive, legislative and judicial branches, lent an unmistakably federal character to the forms of governance dictated by the Zurich–London accords. Some analysts have argued that there are three forms of federalism: territorial federalism, consociationalism, also referred to as sociological federalism, and personal federalism. The distinction between the latter two forms hinges on the following: 'Personal federalism is a solution to the problem of the coexistence between different peoples, whereas consociational democracy is the solution to the problem of coexistence inside one single people between different tendencies (religious, social, etc.)' (Gagnon 1992:207). Whether we characterise the 1960 Cyprus constitution as consociational democracy or personal federalism probably does not matter, but the distinction raised is relevant because it points to one of the reasons that the experiment failed, namely that there was no overarching loyalty which united the two communities. The Cypriots were not a single people with different tendencies but, rather, two different peoples. Cypriot nationalism was virtually a figment of British imagination. Greeks and Turks on Cyprus thought of themselves as Greeks and Turks, not as Cypriots.

Although the federal arrangements embodied in the constitution of 1960 seemed uniquely suited to the highly segmented society on the island, intercommunal antagonism and conflict over its provisions undermined any prospects of success. In addition to the ambivalent commitment of the leadership to the unity of the country, the leaders of the two communities lacked another of the requisites of successful consociational democracy: they did not exhibit a spirit of moderation and compromise (Lijphart 1977:53). There were also several quite specific issues of friction. For example, the proportional representation in the legislature, the armed forces and the civil service was a major source of contention for the Greek Cypriots. Since the Turkish Cypriots comprised about 20 per cent of the population, the 70:30 ratio between the two communities in the legislature and civil service and the 60:40 ratio for the army and police were galling to the Greek Cypriots. They claimed that this provision was unfair, that it would cost their community jobs and promotion opportunities and that it would prevent the best-qualified candidates securing employment in the government. The Turkish Cypriots insisted that the ratio would ensure their legally entitled representation.

In addition, art. 173 of the constitution called for the establishment of separate municipalities. Control of their own municipalities was regarded as crucial by the Turkish Cypriots in order to compensate for the domination of the central government by the Greek Cypriots (Gowther 1993:71). Following independence, separate municipalities were extended for a time until 1963 when Makarios tried to abolish them by appointing centrally empowered municipal improvement boards. The local Greek authorities surrendered their powers but the Turkish Cypriots ignored the ruling and proceeded to set up their own municipalities. The Turkish Cypriots took the municipalities issue to the Supreme Court and the subsequent rulings demonstrated how deeply divided the society had become; even the supreme court broke down along communal lines (Salem 1992). In retaliation for the delay in implementation of the prescribed ratio and of the separate municipalities, the Turkish Cypriot representatives in the legislature refused to vote for the budget. Without tax legislation, the economy was crippled (Polyviou 1980).

The situation came to a head in November 1963, when President Makarios proposed thirteen amendments to the constitution which he offered as a set of solutions to the difficulties posed by the constitutional arrangements which, he claimed, 'threatened to paralyze the State machinery' (Adams 1966). These amendments included propositions to abandon the right of veto by the president and vice-president, to eliminate separate municipalities and to modify the proportional representation of the two communities in the public service and the armed forces to reflect their ratios in the population. The Turkish Cypriot leader, Vice-President Kutchuk, declared that the proposed amendments constituted 'a predetermined policy to abrogate the agreements which had brought about the Republic of Cyprus and to create an independent Greek state in which the Turks would be left at the complete mercy of the Greeks' (Kyriakides 1968). The Government of Turkey immediately rejected the proposals and intercommunal fighting broke out shortly thereafter. The threat of conflict between the two NATO allies, Greece and Turkey, led to the introduction of the United Nations Peacekeeping Force on Cyprus (UNFICYP). The third guarantor power, Great Britain, was shackled in the circumstances by the international post-colonial atmosphere. Britain could have intervened militarily with little difficulty since the Base Areas were already established, but, as one analyst put it, this would have required 'the sort of large-scale troop commitment it had sought to escape by granting independence in the first place. To have returned in strength would have carried with it the risk of inviting international repercussions by appearing to be re-occupying the island' (McDonald 1988:96).

The failure of the 1960 constitution has been attributed to a variety of causes. Some have argued that the experiment failed because the Greek Cypriots resented the disproportional Turkish representation (Lijphart 1977:159). Others have suggested that the rigidity of the constitution itself led to its demise, since the basic provisions were exempt from constitutional amendment. The Bureau of Intelligence and Research at the US State Department concluded that this rigidity was compounded by the dangers inherent in the 'detailed codification of community rights which will tend to perpetuate rather than eliminate the communal cleavages' (Vlanton and Alicia 1984). Indeed, the unique feature of a constitution built on the principles of consociational democracy is the recognition it accords to communal separatism, yet this was diagnosed by the US State Department as its greatest weakness (Doumas 1970).

Greek Cypriots are prone to blame the rigidity of the constitution for its failure. From their perspective, the constitution seemed to provide no inducements to cooperate and its design seemed to anticipate that the two communities would be incapable of making concessions. As one observer put it, 'government itself was conceived of not as a process based on compromise and mutual accommodation but as a static amalgamation of checks and balances, the underlying theory apparently being that only through neutralisation of the power of the larger group would there be security for the smaller' (Polyviou 1980:23). Conflict and confrontation became a self-fulfilling prophecy as the mutual veto gave rise to constitutional deadlock.

Turkish Cypriots had much more sympathy for the design of the independence constitution. They believe that it could have been made to work if the Greek Cypriots had not been determined to reject an arrangement under which the rights of Turkish Cypriots were guaranteed. Their view is that no constitution would have been acceptable to the Greek Cypriots unless it allowed them to dominate the minority.

However, an analysis of the Cypriot experiment in consociational democracy (or personal federalism) in light of the conditions which favour success in this form of governance shows that it was neither the rigidity of the constitution nor the intransigence of the Greek Cypriots that accounts for its failure. Rather, it was the structure of the society itself which proved inhospitable to consociationalism. Consociational democracy requires that the political leadership be committed to the maintenance of the unity of the country and that they exhibit a spirit of compromise and mediation (Lijphart 1977:53). The Cypriot leadership had never committed itself to the unity of the state; Greek Cypriots wanted Enosis, Turkish Cypriots wanted partition. The long history of antagonism and mutually exclusive political agendas had long ago ruled out moderation and compromise in intercommunal politics. In addition, Lijphart (1977:54) enumerates six conditions which enhance the prospect of overarching elite cooperation necessary for consociationalism to succeed: 'a multiple balance of power, small size of the country involved, overarching loyalties, segmental isolation, prior traditions of elite accommodation and . . . the presence of cross cutting cleavages'.[3] None of these conditions helped to nurture elite cooperation in Cyprus. A multiple balance of power implies two notions: that there are at least three segments in the society in question and that no single segment is dominant. In dual-segment societies, politics is seen as a zero-sum game where, as Jurg Steiner puts it, 'a gain for one is easily perceived as a loss for the other. With many subcultures, it is not very clear who loses if one of the subcultures improves its position. Bipolar arrangements tend to exacerbate intercommunal antagonisms. An imbalance of power between the segments tends to encourage the majority segment to dominate rather than cooperate' (Lijphart 1977:55–6). The Turkish Cypriots comprised only about 18 per cent of the population and they were economically disadvantaged as well. The dual imbalance of power on Cyprus was fatal.

The small size of a country is a favourable factor because vulnerability in the international context tends to encourage internal solidarity and to motivate communal segments to cooperate in the face of potential and real external threats. But such threats must be perceived to be equally dangerous to all segments. In the Cypriot context, the only external threats were Greece and Turkey and these dangers were evaluated quite differently by the two groups on the island. Further, small size is an advantage only to a point. Consociational democracy requires exceptional leadership and this may be more scarce in a very small society. Regarding the other factors conducive to consociationalism, we can observe that overarching loyalties, especially in support of Cypriot nationalism, were moribund. If Cypriot nationalism had emerged as a viable force on the island, it might have helped to counteract the destructive clash of Greek and Turkish nationalism which, in turn, was responsible for the fact that there was no tradition of elite accommodation on the island. Finally, segmental isolation was social and not yet territorial and cross-cutting cleavages were virtually absent. Why, then, are we surprised that the 1960 constitution collapsed in civil war? Conditions did not favour success. Even if all other conditions had been different, the experiment was programmed for failure by virtue of the fact that one of the segments, the dominant Greek Cypriots, were reluctant partners to an agreement which, in their view, had been forced upon them. As Lijphart (1977:160) puts it, 'consociationalism cannot be imposed against the wishes of one or more segments in a plural society and, in particular, against the resistance of a majority segment'.

Following the collapse of the constitution in December 1963, the governmental machinery of the Republic of Cyprus was operated by Greek Cypriots. Turkish Cypriots were confined to decisions affecting the administration of their own communities. It was during this period that a quarter of the Turkish Cypriot population became refugees and more than half of these gathered in armed enclaves occupying less than 2 per cent of the territory on the island. The intercommunal violence in 1963 and 1964 led the Turkish Cypriots to conclude that physical, geographical separation of the two communities was essential to their safety and security.

The crux of the dispute in the period 1963–74 was that the Greek Cypriots wanted a unitary government in which the rights of the minority were constitutionally guaranteed; the Turkish Cypriots insisted that the bicommunal constitution had established the republic on the federated principle of two separate communities with identical political rights.

The Greek Cypriots continued to openly advocate Enosis until 1968. Two events in the preceding year may be mentioned in connection with their decision to abandon the quest for Enosis, which was no longer regarded as a realistic goal. First, a coup in Athens brought a military junta to power and unification with Greece suddenly seemed less attractive. Second, and more importantly, an attack by Greek Cypriot forces on the Turkish Cypriot village of Kophinou brought Turkey to the brink of invasion. American intervention averted the crisis, but, from that point on, it was clear that Enosis would not be tolerated by Turkey. Shortly afterwards, intercommunal talks were initiated, with a view to restoration of a bicommunal constitution. These talks failed to restore any form of constitutional arrangement between 1968 and 1974, even though some progress was reported.

NEGOTIATIONS

The coup d'état against Makarios in the summer of 1974, sponsored by the pro-Enosis military dictatorship in Athens, and the subsequent intervention by the Turkish army, tragically shattered any progress that had been made in the negotiations. The partition of the island, the separation of the two populations and the continued presence of Turkish troops in the North radically altered the balance of power and changed the formula for a federal solution in Cyprus. The most significant change was that, for the first time, a federal solution could be contemplated in the context of territorially separated ethnic populations. In the years just before 1974, Turks and Greeks lived interspersed throughout the island. There were 110 Turkish villages and 444 Greek villages, but by this time there were very few mixed villages left (Patrick 1976:12). The five main towns had separate Greek and Turkish areas. After the Turkish army took control of about 37 per cent of the territory in the North, there was an exchange of populations. The UN troops, who had been sent to Cyprus to prevent further intercommunal violence in 1964, were now deployed along the 'Green Line' which separates the populations in two zones: North and South.

Over the next several years, negotiations were conducted under the auspices of the UN Secretary-General. The Greek and Turkish Cypriot leadership reached two 'high level agreements' which identified various principles for the development of a solution, although the modalities for implementation were left unspecified. The first high-level agreement in 1977 between the Greek and Turkish Cypriot leaders, Makarios and Denktash, specified that the two communities looked forward to the establishment of 'an independent, non-aligned, bicommunal, federal republic'. Although the agreement did not actually include wording to this effect, Makarios apparently agreed to a bi-zonal federation. As President Clerides later said in his memoirs, in February 1977 Makarios realised that international pressure was not going to force the withdrawal of Turkish troops and that he 'had to negotiate a settlement, and that the only settlement that had a chance to be accepted by the Turkish side was a bicommunal–bizonal federation'.[4]

Following the death of Makarios later that year, the foreign minister, Spyros Kyprianou, stepped into the presidency. In 1979 Denktash and Kyprianou reaffirmed the 1977 agreement and made a commitment to pursue negotiations in good faith. A year later, the Secretary-General stipulated that both sides had agreed, in principle, to a federal solution of the constitutional aspect and to a bi-zonal solution to the territorial aspect of the Cyprus problem.

Negotiations over the shape of a new federal constitution were held intermittently over the next decade. Prospects for a settlement were constantly undermined by the Greek Cypriot efforts to internationalise their cause, though that is not to say that these efforts were ineffective. On the contrary, the frequent resolutions issued by the United Nations and other international groups have been a source of irritation and annoyance to the Turkish Cypriots, who do not have access to these fora because the Greek Cypriot Republic is the only recognised government on the island. The Turkish Cypriot Declaration of Independence in 1983 was calculated to put the two sides on an equal footing in the negotiations, though the immediate consequence was opprobrium from all sides except mother Turkey. Nevertheless, proximity talks later that year raised hopes for the summit meeting in January 1985. The failure of these meetings was reflected in the modest efforts launched in the lower-level talks of 1986. Further efforts under the auspices of the UN Secretary-General were no more productive.

An agreement between Greek Cypriot President Kyprianou and Turkish Cypriot President Denktash was very nearly consummated in 1988, but Kyprianou backed out at the very last minute. He was roundly criticised for his intransigence by his own community. Intercommunal negotiations between Denktash and George Vasiliou, president of the republic between 1988 and February 1993, did not go well. Lack of respect and trust fundamentally undermined prospects for meaningful progress.

In 1992 the 'Set of Ideas', developed under the auspices of the UN Secretary-General, called for the design of a bi-zonal, bicommunal federation. The federal republic was to have encompassed two politically equal federated states which would have identical powers and functions. The Secretary-General proposed reducing the Turkish Cypriot region from the current 37 per cent to about 28 per cent of the island, which would have allowed about 150,000 Greek Cypriot refugees to return to their homes. His proposals called for a single sovereignty and political equality, although this was not to signify equal numerical participation in government. Under this scheme, the federal government would have been empowered to deal with foreign affairs, defence, federal judicial and law enforcement, customs and central banking, communications and the environment. The two federated states would have been charged with education, cultural affairs, and matters of security and justice within their respective borders (Gobbi 1993). The executive branch would have been structured like the constitution of 1960; in the legislature, the upper house would have been divided 50–50 and the lower house would have a 70 per cent Greek and 30 per cent Turkish representation. The overall package required concessions from the Greek Cypriots regarding the strength of the federal structure in exchange for Turkish Cypriot territorial concessions (*Economist* 1993).

The Turkish Cypriots indicated a preference for a sovereignty association rather than a federation, and they pressed for a rotating presidency. The Greek Cypriots, for their part, continued to push for the right of all Cypriots to movement, settlement and property ownership anywhere on the island, a set of demands which the Turkish Cypriots view with horror because of their fears of being overrun by the much richer and more numerous Greeks.

The inability of the two sides to reach agreement led to the introduction of confidence-building measures (CBMs) the next year. UN Secretary-General Boutros-Ghali had concluded that a 'deep crisis of confidence' militated against the prospects of an intercommunal agreement and therefore turned away from efforts to secure a comprehensive settlement towards a more modest plan to restore trust and intercommunal confidence. In 1993 the Secretary-General proposed the CBMs, which would have freed up the trade and communications embargo in the North. Turkish Cypriots had a great deal to gain from the measures. Opposition to them in the republic stemmed from the fear that the impetus to a larger settlement would be almost wholly undermined because the measures might lead to international recognition of the Turkish Republic of Northern Cyprus (TRNC) (Bolukbasi 1995). The CBMs also eventually faltered precisely because neither side trusted the motivations and intentions of the other.

More recently, UN Secretary-General Kofi Annan invited Clerides and Denktash to meetings in New York and Switzerland. No progress was reported. Denktash was accused of intransigence by the UN mediator because he had demanded, as a precondition to further negotiations, that the European Union discontinue plans to begin accession talks with the Greek Republic of Cyprus. The Greek Cypriots continue to internationalise the Cyprus issue and to bring the weight of the United Nations and other international bodies to bear on the Turkish Cypriots. At the same time, Denktash repeatedly introduces new arguments and objections to the negotiations. In 1990, for example, the negotiations had ground to a halt because of his insistence that the Greek Cypriots recognise the Turkish Cypriots' right to self-determination. He was subsequently chastised by the Secretary-General for his views on the Set of Ideas, because they were out of line with earlier agreements (Bolukbasi 1995:474). Again, in 1993, talks ran into difficulties when Denktash threatened to boycott negotiations unless the United Nations accepted TRNC sovereignty prior to a settlement, because 'it is impossible for a federation to be constructed by a state on one hand and a community on the other' (Dodd 1998).

POLITICAL DIFFERENCES

A review of the history of intercommunal negotiations does not encourage optimism.[5] The positions of the two sides have hardened, if they have changed at all in the last twenty years, and a clear pattern of intercommunal polarisation set in during the early 1990s. The first half of 1993, in particular, saw overtures to Greece and Turkey by their compatriots on Cyprus which deepened their respective relationships with the mother countries and damaged prospects for settlement on the island. The election to power of the Panhellenic Socialist Movement (PASOK) party in Athens in 1993 presaged a shift in Greek Cypriot approaches towards a more inflexible stance at the negotiating table. In the 1980s, when PASOK was in power, the Greek government took a strong nationalist position on Cyprus and helped to put together the aggressive armaments program which has contributed to the arms race on the island (*Economist* 1993:10). In March 1994 the Greek Cypriots secured a defence alliance with Greece which stipulated that, in the event of hostilities, Greece would provide air and naval support. Of course, the Turkish Cypriots immediately called for closer defence ties with Turkey. Towards the end of 1994 the Turkish Cypriots again declared that recognition of their sovereignty was a precondition to further negotiation. In a still more serious step, the Turkish Cypriot Assembly passed a resolution in which they stipulated that federation was not the only possible form for a settlement of the Cyprus problem, thereby calling into question its long-standing commitment to a federal settlement.

The Turkish Cypriots have responded to the Greek Cypriot application to the European Union by announcing a joint Turkey–TRNC agreement which anticipates further economic integration between them. Turkish Cypriots argue that the 1960 settlement precludes Cyprus from joining any association unless both Greece and Turkey are also members. They claim that, because Greece is a member of the EU and Turkey is not, if Cyprus joined the EU it would be tantamount to indirect Enosis because 'Cyprus would automatically integrate with Greece through the EU institutional machinery' (Bahcheli and Rizopoulos 1996:27–39).

The increasingly shrill political rhetoric is matched by an escalation of military hardware on the island. Far from the demilitarisation which the Greek Cypriots claim they advocate, they are aggressively enhancing their fighting capability. In 1995 they bought 100 French main battle tanks as well as Exocet missiles. Turkey promptly announced that its tank strength on the island was to be increased from 200 to 300 (*Economist* 1996).

The two communities on Cyprus seem to be moving still further apart. The Greek Cypriots would like to see a federation in which the central government reserves all powers except those specifically designated to the two regional governments. The Turkish Cypriots envision a loose federation in which the states keep all powers except those specifically allocated to the central government (Gobbi 1993:29). A recent study of the political and economic implications of federated government on Cyprus provides a convincing justification for the advantages of a loose federation. Greek Cypriot Andreas Theophanous (1996) concludes that the prospects for friction of the sort which led to the breakdown of the 1960 constitution would be minimised by a loose federation because there would be fewer issues on which bicommunal agreement would be necessary. It seems only logical that the prospects for rebuilding trust between the two communities would be enhanced under federal arrangements which would lodge most governmental decisions within the two communities.

Some Turkish Cypriots advocate an approach which they call 'federation by evolution'. They suggest that the federal government be assigned a quite limited mandate until such time as mutual trust and confidence is restored and both sides can agree to an increase in central powers. They point to two examples in which federation by evolution led to the gradual strengthening of a central, federal government: Switzerland and the United States. One of the principal legal advisers to President Denktash argued this position by analogy:

> The thirteen colonies, which originally formed the United States of America, after declaring their independence from Britain in 1776, wanted to join together as one State and were looking for the best means of doing so. As they were suspicious of each other, however, and could not merge completely, they first decided to form a confederation. The constitution of this confederation was proclaimed in 1781. When the smaller member states of the confederation realized that the larger and wealthier member states did not constitute a danger to them it was agreed that the constitutional links between the partners could be strengthened by forming a federation to the mutual benefit of all the members . . . Switzerland is another example of this process of strengthening federal links with the passage of time and the growth of mutual trust and confidence between the members of a federation. (Ertekun 1984)

These examples illustrate the principle of 'growth of federation by evolution' which, the Turkish Cypriots argue, ought to provide a useful framework. The parties concerned lacked the requisite trust and confidence to enter into a strong and binding federation at the outset. It was only after experience had shown that a strong central government did not threaten the interests of the individual states that such an arrangement was possible. The Turkish Cypriots say that their level of trust is insufficient to allow them to consider a strong federation.

Greek Cypriots, on the other hand, do not acknowledge Turkish Cypriot trepidation and they continue to agitate for a unitary federation. In fact, when asked, most Greek Cypriots will say that they have always been on friendly terms with Turkish Cypriots. For them, the essence of the Cyprus problem is one of invasion and occupation by Turkey. The two sides hold different views about the solution to the Cyprus impasse because they have different views of history, but what they share is a basic lack of trust and a deep-seated insecurity about the future. The conflict between Greek and Turkish Cypriots is fundamentally about the security or, rather, insecurity of both communities. The intercommunal negotiations have been organised around attempts to find a set of territorial and constitutional arrangements under which both communities can feel secure from the threat of being dominated and overrun by the other. The structures of the constitutional arrangements deal with the important questions of the distribution of power and the allocation of government resources, but, in the Cypriot context, the most important issues have to do with the arrangements under which both communities are to feel safe from the threat they believe the other poses to their independence and freedom.

Turkish Cypriot fears of domination derive from their sense of victimisation as a result of Greek Cypriot efforts to bring about Enosis. Memories of intercommunal violence during the guerrilla war against the British, especially 1955 to 1958, and then the violence and expulsions associated with the constitutional crisis of 1963–64, have embedded fundamental insecurities and intercommunal distrust. Turkish Cypriots believe that the Greek Cypriots want to restore the status quo ante and set up a unitary government in which they, as a minority, will be eventually overrun by the Greek majority. The Turkish Cypriots are adamant that the continued presence of Turkish troops is crucial to their security and safety.

Greek Cypriot fears, anchored in three centuries of Ottoman rule, are given current expression in the humiliation and suffering they experienced in 1974 when they were driven from their homes and forced out of the North. They also express anxiety and dread at the prospect that Turkey might finish what it started in 1974. Many Greek Cypriots are convinced that Turkey intends to take over the whole island. The continued presence of 30,000 mainland Turkish troops stationed in the North since 1974 reinforces their fears. The Greek Cypriots are fully determined to see these troops withdrawn from Cyprus as a precondition to any settlement.

The Greek Cypriots want a strong unitary state; the Turkish Cypriots might concede to a loose confederation. These mutually exclusive goals are born of different historical experiences which, in turn, have spawned divergent cultures of fear, mistrust and insecurity. History cannot be rewritten, nor can we expect that the mutual lack of confidence can be overcome through the exercise of diplomatic intervention or UN-mediated negotiation. Such efforts have yielded little progress over many years.

THE ROLE OF THIRD PARTIES IN THE DISPUTE

The United Nations has played an active, but ultimately futile, role on the island. The UNFICYP has been successful in maintaining peace on Cyprus since 1974, but before the separation of the two populations occurred it was tragically unsuccessful in its attempts to prevent intercommunal violence. The various secretaries-general have sought to bring the two sides together to negotiate a settlement but have been rebuffed by intransigence and distrust on both sides of the Green Line. The Greek Cypriots have been much more successful than the Turkish Cypriots in securing the support of the international community. Beginning in 1964, when the Turkish Cypriots were no longer involved with the government of the republic, the international community continued to treat the Greek government of the republic as the official administration on the island, in spite of the fact that one of the two ethnic communities was no longer represented. This is one of the principal grievances of the Turkish Cypriot community and it is a constant source of diplomatic frustration for them. Since 1964 there have been dozens of resolutions and communiqués passed by international bodies, calling for the withdrawal of Turkish troops and a settlement on the island. The UN Security Council, the General Assembly, the European Parliament, the Council of Europe, and the Commonwealth Heads of Government have passed multiple resolutions in support of the Government of the Republic, implicitly and sometimes explicitly condemning the Turkish Cypriots. International opprobrium was especially vitriolic when the Turkish Cypriots declared independence in 1983. Leaders in the Turkish Cypriot community point out that the Greek Cypriots' resort to international fora have pushed them to rely exclusively on mother Turkey for recognition, security, markets and financial assistance.[6] Further, the Turkish Cypriots' experience with the UN peacekeeping force in the period 1963–74 and the painfully slow and inadequate response by the international community to the tragedy in Bosnia did little to instil confidence in international security guarantees. This goes a long way towards explaining why the Turkish Cypriots insist upon the Turkish military guarantee for their security in any settlement.

The Greek Cypriots, for their part, welcome the active involvement of the United Nations, unless that involvement leads to proposals for a settlement to which they feel they cannot accede. This happened in the late 1980s when Kyprianou backed out of an agreement at the very last minute, and in 1994 when Clerides pulled out of the negotiations over the confidence-building measures. Current initiatives are many and varied. Some have worried that competing initiatives, reflecting divergent approaches advocated by the United States, France, Germany, Russia and the European Union, may impede progress towards a settlement.

The involvement of the United States on Cyprus is regarded with ambivalence by both communities. Greek Cypriots widely believe that the United States shares a good deal of responsibility for the tragic events of 1974. Many think that Kissinger knew about the Greek junta's intentions and did nothing to warn them off (Stern 1977). Turkish Cypriots, on the other hand, resent the continued lopsidedness of the American approach, which treats the republic in the South as the official government on the island. In fact, there is a schizophrenic side to American involvement. The behaviour of the executive branch, especially the State Department, is influenced by an awareness of the strategic importance of Turkey and by the critical significance attached to maintaining peace between NATO allies, Greece and Turkey. The US Congress, on the other hand, is heavily influenced by the powerful Greek lobby.

The interests of Great Britain, the third guarantor of the 1960 Cyprus constitution, are tied to the continuing strategic importance of the

Sovereign Base Areas. Britain has been reluctant to do anything which might jeopardise them. Their importance to Britain and to NATO, especially as demonstrated in the Gulf War, has tended to compromise Britain in its role as a guarantor because of the fear that any change in the status quo might put the bases at risk.

Greece and Turkey, as the other two guarantor powers, play the most significant role in shaping the tone of intercommunal politics on Cyprus. One of the most important contextual conditions which impacts on the prospects of a settlement is the relative political stability of the governments of Greece and Turkey. Over the last twenty-five years, rapprochement initiatives between the two communities on Cyprus have been associated with periods of political stability in the two mother countries (Costas 1990). The corollary to this observation also holds true, for when governments are weak, either because a coalition is fragile or because economic or other domestic conditions are undermining popular confidence in the government, there is a pronounced tendency among politicians and in the media in both Athens and Ankara to engage in 'inflammatory flag waving, not least to distract the attention of their publics from more pressing domestic issues' (Bahcheli and Rizopoulos 1996:33). Naturally, when tensions surface between Greece and Turkey over other areas in dispute – for example, the demarcation of continental shelves, or limits to territorial waters and to airspace in the Aegean – the climate of intercommunal relations on Cyprus is adversely affected. These external issues brought the two NATO allies close to the brink of war in 1976, 1987 and again in 1996.

For Greece and Turkey, Cyprus is very much an expression and extension of their centuries-long conflict, and it has become a matter of national prestige. Cyprus plays an important role in the electoral politics of both countries. In Turkey, for example, according to one observer, '*no* Turkish government (whatever its "ideological" composition) can *ever* afford to be seen as having "abandoned" its Cypriot brethren' (Bahcheli and Rizopoulos 1996:32).[7]

Another area of contention involving third-party actors includes the set of issues surrounding the application by the government of the republic to join the European Union. The very application itself is anathema to the Turkish Cypriots, who are furious that the Greeks in the South, once again, presume to speak for all Cypriots.

CONCLUSION

Given this long and difficult history of conflict between Greeks and Turks on Cyprus and the inability of third parties to resolve it, what are the prospects for bringing about a bicommunal, bi-zonal federation in the future? The conditions favourable to the establishment of a federation are not very different from those which are conducive to consociationalism. For example, John Stuart Mill identifies three conditions. There needs to be mutual sympathy between the populations, a degree of mutual need, and the assurance that one unit will not dominate the others. What he says about mutual sympathy is illuminating:

> A federation is advisable . . . [if there is] a sufficient amount of sympathy among the populations. The federation binds them always to fight on the same side; and if they have such feelings towards one another, or such diversity of feeling towards their neighbors, that they would generally prefer to fight on opposite sides, the federal tie is neither likely to be of long duration, nor to be well observed while it subsists. (Mill 1910:494–5)

Conflicts between Greece and Turkey have often polarised the two ethnic communities on Cyprus. Unless and until the two mother countries resolve their differences, the degree of mutual sympathy on Cyprus will never favour the establishment of a federation. Mill's discussion of the issue of mutual need focuses on the need to enter a federation for protection against 'foreign encroachment'. Indeed, according to Lijphart (1977:66), 'it is striking that in all consociational democracies the crucial steps towards this type of regime were usually taken during times of international crisis or specific threats to the country's existence'. But we are reminded of an important caveat to the notion that external threats are conducive to federation: namely, that the threat must be perceived as a common danger to all segments. In the case of Cyprus, the external threats have come from Greece and Turkey and these threats have tended to divide the two segments rather than unite them. The final condition that Mill (1910:496) mentions is that 'there not be a very marked inequality of strength among the several contracting states'. The dual imbalance of power was cited as one of the major reasons for the collapse of consociationalism in 1963. The dangers inherent in a federation between the Greeks and Turks of Cyprus are now compounded by the much more pronounced economic disparities which characterise the two communities, compared with the relatively more modest differences evident in the 1960s. The fear of being dominated and overrun by the much richer and more powerful Greeks is *the* reason the Turkish Cypriots resist a federal settlement. Cyprus, John Stuart Mill would conclude, is not a good candidate for federalism.[8]

Contemporary discussions of the conditions for successful federations are no more optimistic. Echoing Lijphart's analysis of the conditions conducive to consociational democracy, Maurice Vile asserts that no two-unit federation has ever survived:

It is indeed very unlikely that such a federation could survive, because federal systems operate on the basis of the bargaining between shifting coalitions of groups, bringing about compromises because no single group or
coalition of groups is in a continually dominant position. The danger of an
irreconcilable confrontation between the units in a two unit federation is
so great that sooner or later it would lead to civil war, secession, or both.
(Vile 1982:216–28)

This is all the more likely, says Vile, if one of the units in a two-unit federation is in a dominant position. The dominant member state will effectively run the show much like a unitary state. That was precisely what the
Turkish Cypriots maintain that Makarios tried to achieve when he proposed amendments to the constitution in 1963. Of course, it is not always
possible that the political theorists' wish for a balance of power will be
found in the real world. Where there is an imbalance, federalism may
continue to operate effectively so long as there is acceptance of a specific
pattern of power between the entities (Frognier 1982:211). However, as
we have seen, the Turkish Cypriot rejection of Greek Cypriot domination
has been a recurrent theme in the history of intercommunal relations
since the end of Ottoman rule.

The difficulties confronting bicommunal societies such as Northern
Ireland, Sri Lanka and Cyprus derive from the fact that they are bicommunal and that the majority segment had sought and achieved domination (Kellas 1991). It has been extremely difficult to find a form of
governance which can manage the tensions which run through such societies. This is not to suggest that such societies are impervious to some
form of political solution. However, Cyprus stands out even in this group
of classically intractable disputes because of the conflict between the two
mother countries, Greece and Turkey. The intercommunal hostility on
the island has been shaped by the history of this struggle in the eastern
Mediterranean and the current impasse is very much defined by the
larger antagonists and their perceived needs.

Another difficulty is embedded in the political psychology of power
reversal. The tables were turned on the Ottoman Turks when the British
took over the administration of Cyprus in 1878. The erstwhile rulers of
the island were suddenly in a minority role in the British-run legislative
council. Later, the Turkish Cypriots were able to achieve disproportional
representation in the 1960 constitution, only to have that denied to them
by Makarios in 1963. Finally, with the partition of the island in 1974 and
the declaration of independence by the TRNC in 1983, the Turkish
Cypriots have accomplished de facto, if not de jure, autonomy. As they
have enjoyed autonomy for several decades, it would be that much more
difficult for them to surrender it.[9]

It may be that Cyprus has lapsed into a form of diplomatic and political stasis from which two states will emerge with full international recognition. There are, after all, sixteen member states in the United Nations with populations smaller than the TRNC, and the disadvantages associated with small size are frequently overstated. In this era of ethnic unmixing associated with the disintegration of empires (Brubaker 1995), it may be fitting that the international community finally acknowledge that federation, like marriage, cannot be forced upon an unwilling partner.

In facilitating whatever the final solution might be, the international community would do well to recognise that political devices like federalism cannot easily overcome the difficulties of governance for territories situated on the civilisational fault lines of contemporary geopolitics.[10] Tensions between two grossly unequal groups in a bicommunal society, where both groups constantly refer to their mother countries which are themselves locked in conflict, cannot be contained by federalism. Continued international mediation designed to achieve that goal flies in the face of what we know about Cyprus and what we have learned about the conditions under which federalism is likely to succeed.

NOTES

1 Although this was a gradual process. As late as 1930 the British Annual Report for Cyprus stipulated that 'nationality in the Near East is somewhat difficult of definition and is inseparably linked up with religion'. It was not until 1950, when the process of ethnic differentiation was completed, that British documents no longer referred to religion but simply distinguished between Greeks and Turks on the island.

2 The text of the petition is laid out in full in Orr (1918:97–9).

3 It may be important to emphasise that Lijphart enters a caveat here to the effect that these conditions are neither necessary nor sufficient, further that even in their absence consociationalism is not impossible.

4 Quoted in Moran (1997:104).

5 The discussion here necessarily skirts over important differences within each community. There is, of course, a wide variety of political opinion in the North and the South. For a discussion of politics within each community, see McDonald (1988:96).

6 Multiple interviews by the author with President Denktash, Prime Minister Eroglu and others, 1990 to the present.

7 Emphasis in original.

8 Peter Loizos (1994) provides a different but no less pessimistic assessment of Mill's conditions as they apply to Cyprus.

9 That was surely a major difficulty that Milosevic should have anticipated when he revoked Kosovo's autonomy.

10 Huntington's (1993) notion is useful, even if his argument is flawed by the broad sweep of his generalisations.

REFERENCES

Adams, T.W. 1966. 'The first republic of Cyprus: a review of an unworkable constitution', *Western Political Quarterly* 19(3):475–90.

Alastos, D. 1955. *Cyprus in History*. London: Zeno.

Anderson, D. and D. Killingray (eds) 1992. *Policing and Decolonization. Politics, Nationalism and the Police, 1917–65*. Manchester: Manchester University Press.

Bahcheli, T. and N. Rizopoulos 1996. 'The Cyprus impasse: what next?', *World Policy Journal*, Winter.

Baker, E. 1959. 'The settlement in Cyprus', *Political Quarterly*, July–September.

Bolukbasi, S. 1995. 'Boutros-Ghali's Cyprus initiative in 1992: why did it fail?', *Middle East Journal* 31(3):460–82.

Brubaker, R. 1995. 'Aftermaths of empire and the unmixing of peoples: historical and comparative perspectives', *Ethnic and Racial Studies* 18(2):189–218.

Costas, D. (ed.) 1990. *The Greek–Turkish Conflict in the 1990s*. New York: St Martin's Press.

Dodd, C. 1998. *The Cyprus Embroglio*. Huntington: Eothen Press.

Doumas, C. 1970. 'The 1960 constitution of Cyprus: some observations', *Southern Quarterly* 9(1):67–86.

Economist 1993. *Cyprus and Malta (Country Report 1–4)*. London: Economist Intelligence Unit.

—— 1996. *Cyprus and Malta (Country Report 1–4)*. London: Economist Intelligence Unit.

Ertekun, N. 1984. *The Cyprus Dispute and the Birth of the Turkish Republic of Northern Cyprus*. 2nd edn. Oxford: K. Rustem & Brother.

Frognier, A.P. 1982. 'Federal and party federal systems, institutions and conflict management: some Western examples', in D. Rea (ed.) *Political Cooperation in Divided Societies*. Dublin: Gill and Macmillan Ltd.

Gagnon, A. 1992. 'Approaches to the study of comparative federalism: the dynamics of federalism', in N. Salem (ed.) *Cyprus: A Regional Conflict and Its Resolution*. New York: St Martin's Press.

Gobbi, D.H.J. 1993. *Rethinking Cyprus*. Tel Aviv: Aurora.

Gowther, R. 1993. 'Ethnic conflict and political accommodation in plural societies: Cyprus and other cases', *Journal of Commonwealth and Comparative Politics* 31(1).

Huntington, S. 1993. 'The clash of civilizations', *Foreign Affairs* 3:22–49.

Kellas, K. 1991. *The Politics of Nationalism and Ethnicity*. London: Macmillan.

Kitromilides, P. 1990. 'Greek irredentism in Asia Minor and Cyprus', *Middle Eastern Studies* 26(1):3–17.

Kyriakides, S. 1968. *Cyprus: Constitutionalism and Crisis Government*. Philadelphia: University of Pennsylvania Press.

Lijphart, A. 1977. *Democracy in Plural Societies*. New Haven: Yale University Press.

Loizos, P. 1994. 'Understanding 1974, understanding 1994', *Cyprus Review* 6(1):7–19.

Markides, K. 1977. *The Rise and Fall of the Cyprus Republic*. New Haven: Yale University Press.

McDonald, R. 1988. 'The problem of Cyprus', *Adelphi Papers* 234.

Mill, J.S. 1910. *Utilitarianism Liberty and Representative Government.* London: M. Dent.

Moran, M. (ed.) 1997. *Rauf Denktash at the United Nations: Speeches on Cyprus.* Huntington: Eothen Press.

Necategil, Z. 1989. *The Cyprus Question and the Turkish Position in International Law.* Oxford: Oxford University Press.

Orr, C.C.W. 1918. *Cyprus under British Rule.* London: Zeno.

Patrick, R.A. 1976. *Political Geography and the Cyprus Conflict: 1963–1971.* Waterloo, Ontario: Department of Geography, University of Waterloo.

Polyviou, P.G. 1980. *Cyprus: Conflict and Negotiation 1960–1980.* London: Gerald Duckworth & Co. Ltd.

Salem, N. 1992. 'The constitution of 1960 and its failure', in N. Salem (ed.) *Cyprus: A Regional Conflict and Its Resolution.* New York: St Martin's Press.

Stern, L. 1977. *The Wrong Horse: The Politics of Intervention and the Failure of American Diplomacy.* New York: Times Books.

Theophanous, A. 1996. *The Political Economy of a Federal Cyprus.* Nicosia: Intercollege Press.

Vile, M.J.C. 1982. 'Federation and confederation: the experience of the United States and the British Commonwealth', in D. Rea (ed.) *Political Cooperation in Divided Societies.* Dublin: Gill and Macmillan.

Vlanton, E. and D. Alicia 1984. 'The 1959 Cyprus Agreement: oracle of disaster', *Journal of the Hellenic Diaspora* 11(4):9–31.

CHAPTER 11

BOUGAINVILLE AND THE DIALECTICS OF ETHNICITY, AUTONOMY AND SEPARATION

YASH GHAI AND ANTHONY REGAN

Ever since Papua New Guinea's independence in 1975, its relationship with the province of Bougainville has been troubled, with more than one attempt at secession. The linguistically and culturally diverse Bougainvilleans are themselves a microcosm of the extreme linguistic and cultural diversity of Papua New Guinea. Less than 5 per cent of the population and distinct from other Papua New Guineans mainly in terms of dark skin colour, they are concentrated geographically in a remote island group, offering no threat to other ethnic groups and not threatened by such groups elsewhere in Papua New Guinea. Both Bougainvillean ethnic identity and separatism are recent phenomena. The former emerged in the context of colonialism, which began in 1884. The politicisation of ethnic identity – the mobilisation of wide support based on identity in pursuit of political goals such as autonomy, increased government revenue and separation – began in the 1960s, in the context of both decolonisation and grievances against the colonial regime over the imposition of a massive mining project.

Because contextual factors are crucial to understanding how any particular ethnic conflict develops or is resolved, it is difficult to generalise from a single case. Nevertheless, the development within a short and recent time span of a politicised but divided ethnic identity, attempts to accommodate it with semi-federal arrangements and the subsequent development of violent separatist conflict offer insights into the dynamics of such phenomena. How does ethnic identity become politicised into separatist demands? Are some circumstances more favourable than others for the concession of federal or autonomy arrangements? Is there inevitably a tendency away from asymmetric arrangements towards uniformity? Can semi-federal arrangements accommodate and reduce ethnic tensions, or do they tend to reinforce ethnic identity? Is rejection of semi-federal arrangements in favour of violent separatist struggle necessarily an indictment of the arrangements, or are factors external to the arrangements of more importance? More generally, what does the evidence on these issues say about the relationship between ethnic identity and conflict and the constitutional arrangements intended to accommodate them? Does the interaction tend to transform both ethnic identity and constitutional arrangements? In other words, is there evidence of dialectical relationships in change of ethnic identification and of semi-federal arrangements, or between such arrangements and secession?

HISTORICAL BACKGROUND

The boundaries of Papua New Guinea and Bougainville are products of the vagaries of the late colonial era, when the island of New Guinea (immediately to the north of Australia) and many smaller nearby island groups were divided among the Dutch, German and British. Bougainville was administered by Germany as part of New Guinea, having been separated by Britain from its closest neighbours (culturally as well as geographically), the islands of what is now Western Province of Solomon Islands. After World War II, Britain was given administration of New Guinea by the United Nations; it already had sovereignty over Papua (subsequently administered on its behalf by Australia). They became independent as the state of Papua New Guinea (PNG). At 1000 kilometres east of the mainland national capital, Port Moresby, Bougainville is the most remote of nineteen provinces. It consists of two adjoining large islands – Bougainville (8646 square kilometres) and Buka (598 square kilometres) – five main atoll groups and many smaller islands. Its 9438 square kilometres constitute about 2 per cent of the PNG land area.

Ethnic identities within Bougainville and Bougainvillean ethnic identity
Papua New Guinea's population of approximately four million comprises over 800 distinct languages, often divided into numerous small and semi-autonomous societies, with most groups still heavily reliant on subsistence agriculture. Bougainville, with a population of approximately 175,000 and eighteen distinct languages, fits the PNG pattern of diversity. Its language groups have never been political units, tiny societies within them being the main units. Cultural differences existed both between and within language groups (Ogan 1991:92–3).

Consciousness of ethnic identity associated with language groups probably emerged as colonial control ended group warfare and brought contact between diverse groups, initially through involvement of many young males in plantation labour. It was colonial administrators and

243

missionaries who vested groups with 'tribal' ethnic identities by empha-sising language differences. At the same time, they ranked Bougainvil-lean language groups into positive and negative stereotypes ('backward' and 'progressive') (Nash and Ogan 1990), no doubt reinforcing normal human tendencies to stereotype linguistic and cultural differences. These stereotypes continue to be significant, paradoxically contributing to divisions within Bougainville while reinforcing Bougainville identity vis-à-vis other Papua New Guineans.

Except that Bougainvilleans are darker, few characteristics distinguish them from other Papua New Guineans. But during the colonial period this minor distinction became a focus for Bougainvillean ethnic con-sciousness, as a result of government policies whereby Bougainvilleans, regarded as reliable with leadership qualities, were used as police, and people from the highlands of the mainland were employed on Bougain-ville expatriate plantations and on the copper mining project, leading to contempt for and resentment against mainlanders.

Bougainville's ethnic identity was also shaped by its distance from Port Moresby and proximity to Solomon Islands, as well as by the propensity of the Australian administration to leave it to missionaries to provide important services. This contributed to two related phenomena: griev-ances about the neglect of Bougainville's development by the colonial regime, and the emergence of a cohesive and educated elite unique in Papua New Guinea. The two main churches – Catholic, with about 75 per cent affiliation, and Methodist, with about 15 per cent – provided all edu-cation (until the first government school in 1960), and extensive health and other services. Both churches answered to authorities in the neigh-bouring British-administered Solomon Islands, thereby limiting links to Papua New Guinea (and reinforcing pre-existing cultural affinities?). The Catholic education system, in particular, developed a highly articu-late and cohesive elite through a hierarchy of schools that selected promising students at an early age for training as priests. In 1966, stu-dents at the Catholic seminary in Madang were producing a journal that presented the first broad critique of colonialism by Papua New Guineans (Ballard 1977). By the 1960s, many priests and ex-seminarians, and sub-sequently university students from almost all Bougainville language groups, knew one another well and shared a common training steeped in Catholic social teachings. They were instrumental in the politicisation of ethnic identity from the late 1960s.

Politicisation of ethnic identity
In addition to the emergence of a cohesive, critical and educated elite, a critical factor in the politicisation of ethnicity was the opening of the Panguna copper mine against the wishes of the people and leaders of

Bougainville. Other factors included widespread antagonism to the colonial regime; the expansion of political opportunities presented by decolonisation; and political conflict with the central government from 1967 to 1977 and from the late 1980s. Reflecting variations among Bougainvilleans in culture, ethnic identity and economic status, the impact and importance of these phenomena was far from uniform.

Australia's failure to maintain the extensive road system and other infrastructure constructed by the Germans in parts of coastal Bougainville may have contributed to the unfavourable comparisons between regimes and to grievances about Australian neglect.[1] Antipathy to Australia has also been ascribed to such grievances and to a loss of stature suffered through Australia's flight in the face of Japanese invaders in January 1942 (Griffin 1982:115). The massive scale of the United States' military operations and the relatively egalitarian treatment of Bougainvilleans by US soldiers also established models of development and behaviour that contrasted poorly with Australia.

From the 1950s, opposition by the colonial administration to the development of local government councils (Connell 1977) indicated increased, but still localised, resistance to colonial authorities (Griffin 1977:33–46; Mamak and Bedford 1974:6–7). There were some indications of broader political horizons developing after World War II. The 1962 request for US control was not isolated (Ogan 1972:10). Even earlier, in 1953, a UN visiting mission was told by a meeting in south Bougainville of the desire for unity with affines in Solomon Islands (Griffin 1977:50), an issue discussed between Bougainvilleans and Solomon Islanders at the South Pacific Conference in Lae in 1965 (Crocombe 1968:42).

It was only in the late 1960s that Bougainvillean concerns about their situation escalated to public demands for secession, and this was largely in response to a dramatic intensification of grievances against the colonial regime concerning the Panguna mine. It was significant that this occurred at a time when political possibilities in Papua and New Guinea were being transformed by the beginnings of decolonisation. The first universal adult suffrage elections for the colonial legislature, the House of Assembly, were held in 1964, and thereafter at four-year intervals (1968 and 1972). Education about voting and the role of government and the increasing debate on constitutional development and independence that occurred from the mid-1960s all exposed Bougainvilleans to new forms of political activity. As Ogan (1974:129) has noted, there was continuity between 'cults' and new forms of political activity, all directed at changing a 'distressful situation'. Debate on decolonisation established a context in which there were new possibilities for Bougainvilleans to define themselves in relation to the state. If independence for Papua and New Guinea was a possibility, then why not autonomy, independence for Bougainville or even union with Solomon Islands (Griffin 1973:322–3; Hannett 1969; Nelson 1968)? Elsewhere too, demands for autonomy or closer relations with Australia were articulated (May 1982).

A major reason for the emergence of such local autonomy movements was the lack of any form of unifying national politics similar to those that emerged from independence struggles in Africa and Asia. There were no strong political parties articulating regional or national concerns. As a result, the grievances of local groups against the colonial regime defined national politics from the late 1960s until well into the 1970s, giving them a great deal of influence in the pre-independence constitutional debate.

The Panguna mine, one of the world's largest, was developed without consultation in Bougainville, the administration making it clear that the mine was to ensure the economic viability of an independent Papua New Guinea rather than benefit Bougainville. Even before test drilling began in the rugged mountains of central Bougainville in 1964, it was opposed by local landowners (Bedford and Mamak 1977:7–11) with strong support from Catholic clergy (Downs 1980:343–52). Opposition escalated in the late 1960s as the acquisition of coastal land for a mining town and other facilities greatly expanded the numbers of people directly affected and precipitated a series of bitter disputes between the administration and landowners. The socially and ecologically disruptive effect of the mining operations, aggravated by the presence of miners and other workers recruited from the mainland, provided a fertile ground for the mobilisation grievances. While concessions of increased rent and compensation in 1969–70 reduced the intensity of opposition, the preceding disputes consolidated Bougainvillean identity. As some of these grievances were felt by Bougainvilleans well beyond the landowner groups directly affected by the mine, they tended to become generalised complaints expressed in many parts of Bougainville.

Separatist demands emerge, 1967–1972

There is no doubt that the opening of the mine in the 1970s changed the attitude of Bougainvilleans to Papua New Guinea. As the intensity of grievances increased, independence gradually became a more serious goal. From late 1968 there were demands for a referendum on secession. In an informal vote on the issue, organised in 1970 by a pro-independence group in central Bougainville, the independence proposal received strong support in areas closest to the mine but also prompted ambivalence and even opposition elsewhere, especially in northern parts of Bougainville island and Buka (Griffin 1982).

When the 1972 House of Assembly elections led to the formation of the first indigenous-led PNG government under nationalist leadership, the four Bougainville members supported the government, three of them taking important positions in it. Some observers believed that

Bougainville was on the road to integration and that secessionist senti-ment would recede (Griffin 1982:134–5). In June 1972 a committee of the House of Assembly was appointed to consider Papua New Guinea's independence constitution. The terms of reference of the Constitutional Planning Committee (CPC) included 'central–regional–local govern-ment relations and district administration', and it was expected to find acceptable ways for the integration of Bougainville and of other groups demanding autonomy. But support for secession did not die, continuing to be discussed sporadically at meetings in Bougainville.

The central importance of antipathy to 'red-skin' Papua New Guineans as a factor in Bougainville ethnic identity was demonstrated in December 1972 when two senior Bougainvillean public servants were vic-tims of 'payback' killings by villagers after a road accident in the New Guinea Highlands. With opinion inflamed against 'red-skins', support for independence consolidated dramatically in all areas of Bougainville. Within two months, a committee of leaders from councils and other groups from all over Bougainville – the Bougainville Special Political Committee (BSPC) – was set up to negotiate the future status of Bougainville with the Port Moresby government. The CPC and the BSPC, together with the first Papua New Guinean–led central government, now became key actors in the development of proposals for constitutionally entrenched decentralisation arrangements.

DEVELOPMENT OF DECENTRALISATION PROPOSALS, 1972–1977

From February 1973 to April 1977, when the Organic Law on Provincial Government came into effect, movement towards autonomy for Bougainville was remarkable, all the more so given the high degree of centralisation of the previous colonial district administration system and the reluctance of entrenched bureaucracy. At each step of the way, the ini-tiative was taken by Bougainville, albeit with CPC support at some crucial points. But, although there was little pressure for change from other dis-tricts, the three main sets of concessions made by the central government – November 1973, July 1974 and August 1976 – were extended to all dis-tricts (Ballard 1981:96–9; Conyers 1976; Ghai and Regan 1992:6–7).

These developments raise two main questions. First, how was a high degree of decentralisation achieved in such a short time against consid-erable opposition and yet without bloodshed? Second, why did the cen-tral government establish uniform decentralisation arrangements rather than the asymmetrical arrangements preferred by Bougainville?

Decolonisation and decentralisation
Decolonisation everywhere is a period both of anxiety and of opportu-nity. Some groups fear loss of power and opportunities, while others seek

to acquire power or to redefine relationships with the state to their advantage. In Papua New Guinea, some groups – such as parts of the New Guinea Highlands – opposed independence until they could 'catch up' with the more 'developed' people of coastal and island areas. On the other hand, Bougainvilleans were not alone in seeing decolonisation as a time of new opportunity (May 1982).

Having determined to move quickly towards decolonisation, Australia was content largely to stand back from decisions on future arrangements. As a result, the constitutional debate – including the debate on decentralisation – was essentially an internal one, although influenced by external ideas. At the time the CPC was established, there was consensus in the new nationalist government under Chief Minister Michael Somare that an independent Papua New Guinea should be dramatically different from the colonial regime.

Initially, almost every possible aspect of future arrangements was 'on the table'. However, the validity of the colonial boundaries was assumed, so the CPC's terms of reference on what came to be called 'decentralisation' were directed not towards consideration of the possible separation of Bougainville or any other dissident areas but, rather, towards arrangements that could accommodate local demands. Further, ministers in the new government soon became more conservative as they developed a stake in existing arrangements, and tensions developed with the CPC. However, in conducting widespread public education campaigns and consultative meetings, the CPC quickly built its own power base, and so was able both to maintain significant independence from the government and to develop support for its own proposals.

The CPC chose to give priority to a few issues, including 'central–regional–local relations and district administration', and as a result had already reached agreement on the need for decentralisation to district-level governments before the sudden escalation of secessionist sentiment in Bougainville at the end of 1972 (Ballard 1981:101–2). Although its de facto chairperson, Catholic priest Fr John Momis, was a Bougainvillean, the CPC was not simply acting in response to local pressure. Its views on decentralisation were part of a complex political and constitutional analysis that pushed it towards uniform decentralisation, rather than asymmetrical arrangements.

In the first place, the CPC view of the entire constitution-making exercise was influenced by a paradigm of development very different from that which dominated constitution making in decolonising and post-colonial Africa and Asia from the 1950s (Ghai and Regan 1992:2–6). Reflecting modernisation theory, this latter paradigm emphasised the need for a powerful centralised executive if economic development was to be initiated, scarce resources allocated rationally, and ethnically divided societies held together. Under the influence of its two key members, John Momis and John Kaputin, whose political origins lay with local groups seeking autonomy – Bougainville and the Mataungan Association of East New Britain, respectively (Regan 1997a:314–16) – the CPC was convinced of the need to build upon Papua New Guinea's diversity. It looked to develop a state more democratic, participatory, responsive and accountable than the colonial state had been. Its decentralisation proposals were part of a complex web of recommendations directed to these goals. The CPC had high hopes of decentralisation; it would increase participation, responsiveness and accountability of the state and release people's energy for development and self-government.

For the CPC, the most suitable units for the decentralisation of power were the existing districts, although they were to be renamed provinces to mark the break with the colonial era. They had the advantage of being large enough to be viable, they were already well known, and there was already political mobilisation occurring around district-level identity, especially in Bougainville. Despite strong demands from some leaders, the CPC rejected use of the four main regions (Papua coast, New Guinea coast, Highlands and islands) as the basic units. They were large enough to promote regionalism and associated tensions that could threaten national unity. Further, regions would be too large to take account of diversity.

Uniformity v. asymmetry, multilateralisation v. bilateralisation
From 1973 to 1976, Bougainville swung between demands for special arrangements suitable to it and acceptance of uniform arrangements applicable to all parts of the country. The CPC and the national government were agreed on uniformity but differed on the extent of decentralisation. Although in this period Bougainville was a major actor, there were, in a sense, multilateral negotiations on decentralisation, initially with the CPC arguing for all districts and later with other districts making moves to establish their own governments on the model of Bougainville. During the secession crisis of 1975–76, negotiations were conducted on a bilateral basis between Bougainville and the national government, but the agreed decentralisation arrangements were subsequently applied to all provinces.

Although eschewing violence, Bougainville was in a reasonably strong position to advance its agenda. There was clearly strong popular support for secession. The central government was already heavily dependent on revenue from the Panguna mine, a fact underlined by the much higher levels of profits than expected from the first six months of its operation (1972) and consequential calls for a renegotiation of the mining agreement to ensure greater returns to Papua New Guinea.

Bougainville's demands of July 1973 – essentially, confederal arrangements with a right to choose independence at a later date – were 'a deliberate overbid' (Ballard 1981:106). The real concern was to obtain both a reasonable share of the revenue flowing from the mine and the autonomy to use it as Bougainville determined. As a result, a compromise was possible in the tense negotiations for the November 1973 agreement on district government as well as in the 1974 negotiations about establishing an interim provincial government. There was also steadily increasing awareness of the immense practical difficulties involved in secession.

Although, in 1972–73, the national government was open to special government arrangements in an effort to respond to divisive autonomy demands from the Mataungan Association in East New Britain (Ballard 1981:100), the CPC never seriously considered asymmetrical arrangements for Bougainville or any other group with special concerns. It saw the solution to the concerns of all such groups in the transformation of the colonial state, advocating constitutionally guaranteed decentralisation for all districts, with sufficient flexibility to permit gradations in the degree of autonomy between districts. The national government also believed that special arrangements for Bougainville could be divisive and strengthen widespread resentment of what was seen as the greed of the Bougainvilleans in attempting to get a disproportionately large share of mining revenue.

In its final report of July 1974, the CPC recommended, in considerable detail, entrenched legislative, executive and financial powers for transfer to an elected body in each province, the basic principles and features of the main institutions at that level, the machinery for intergovernmental relations, and provision for the gradation of arrangements between provinces, with semi-federal elements. By this time, decentralisation had become a matter of considerable controversy, in part because of ongoing difficulties in negotiating suitable arrangements with Bougainville. The central government opposed key features of the proposals, particularly the entrenchment of arrangements and the supremacy of provincial laws over national laws in designated areas, arguing strongly for flexibility.

A compromise, reached in the House of Assembly, was to state key principles in the constitution, leaving details for an organic law, with a lesser degree of entrenchment. A 'follow-up committee' was established to decide what should be included in the proposed organic law on provincial government. At this stage, although the national government was ambivalent about decentralisation, various efforts were being made to explore how the new policy might best be developed in practice, given the immense variety among the provinces of enthusiasm and preparedness for provincial government. In the meantime, however, relations with Bougainville had broken down over the negotiations of financial arrangements for the Bougainville Interim Provincial Government. The core issue was the tension between uniform and special arrangements. Bougainville sought to extract a reasonable share of national government revenue from the mine, while the national government was concerned about the costs of generalising what Bougainville demanded. Negotiations collapsed in May 1975, followed by threats of secession at a meeting of Bougainville leaders (Ballard 1981:106).

Debate on the draft constitution began on 29 May 1975, with rejection of the recommendation on provincial legislative supremacy. The day before, the Bougainville Interim Provincial Government agreed on secession. Throughout June and July, unsuccessful efforts were made to resolve the situation. Thereupon the government persuaded the Constituent Assembly on 30 July to delete the part of the draft constitution dealing with provincial government. Bougainville leaders responded by announcing the intention to declare their own independence on 1 September, ahead of Papua New Guinea's scheduled independence on 16 September. Following a Unilateral Declaration of Independence of the Republic of North Solomons (the name to emphasise traditional links to neighbouring Solomon Islands), the national government suspended the Bougainville Interim Provincial Government in October and withheld grant payments. Otherwise, aware of its limited capacity to impose its will by force, and determined to avoid bloodshed that could both divide the new state and destroy international confidence in it, the national government was moderate and conciliatory. Bougainville leaders sought recognition at the United Nations and explored possibilities of union with Solomon Islands, but to no avail. Early in 1976, Bougainville agreed to accept PNG sovereignty and the national government undertook to restore the provincial government provisions to the constitution. Immediate moves were made to introduce the constitutional amendments, inclusive of the provision that provincial laws might prevail over national laws. Other matters, including details of the provisions of the proposed Organic Law on Provincial Government, were resolved in the Bougainville Agreement of August 1976 through arrangements building upon the work of both the 'follow-up committee' and the CPC.

The Bougainville Agreement paid lip-service to Bougainville's desire for a special relationship with the centre. But the agreement itself, and the substantial support that both it and the constitutional amendments achieved in the national parliament, were endorsements of final acceptance of the proposition, so strongly supported by the CPC, that the road to unity lay through the recognition of diversity. In addition, concerns about the divisiveness of special arrangements remained strong and, as moves towards establishing provincial governments had already begun in some provinces under the March 1975 guidelines, it was clear that it would have been difficult to persuade the parliament to pass the necessary implementing legislation had it been restricted to Bougainville. Accordingly, it is not surprising that what had been negotiated bilaterally was multilateralised by the constitutional provisions of general application but with sufficient flexibility to offer Bougainville the possibility of much greater autonomy than other provinces. By the end of 1978, provincial governments had been set up in all provinces.

DECENTRALISATION ARRANGEMENTS, 1977–1988

Accommodation and recognition of ethnic identity
Both the multi-stage development of the arrangements and the uniform application of what was negotiated between Bougainville and the national government militated against overt recognition of Bougainville's specific concerns or identity. But, in reality, ethnicity was still a new force in Bougainville, coexisting with many other ethnic identities within Bougainville, with little save skin colour and an imprecise sense of superiority to 'redskin' Papua New Guinea as defining characteristics. As a result, the scope for arrangements reflecting ethnicity was limited. Identity issues such as recognition of language, culture or religion, often important in situations of ethnic conflict, were not pertinent. Surprisingly, restrictions by Bougainville on the mobility or employment of non-Bougainvilleans were conceded as inconsistent with the human rights provisions of the new PNG constitution; resentment over a lack of capacity to control such matters was to become an important issue in later conflict.

Some aspects of the arrangements did reflect local identity. The name 'North Solomons Provincial Government' emphasised Bougainville's ethnic links to groups in a neighbouring state. Further, the great degree of freedom made available to provinces in relation to the contents of provincial constitutions – laws dealing mainly with provincial structures and their procedures – was intended to permit arrangements reflecting local identity. The North Solomons Provincial Government constitution contained restrictions on the right to vote and to stand for election to office in the provincial legislature, mainly directed to ensuring that 'redskins' could not vote or stand in provincial elections, provisions that probably breached the human rights provisions of the national constitution (Ghai and Regan 1992:89–92), at the same time as it proclaimed North Solomons 'sovereignty'.

The first priority for Bougainville's leaders, however, was a high degree of autonomy rather than the powers needed to assert a distinct identity. Hence, in negotiating the Bougainville Agreement, the North Solomons delegation focused on ensuring that the arrangements in the organic law would provide a sufficient balance between its needs and those of the centre. Of particular importance in this regard were the entrenchment of the arrangements, their marked federal characteristics and the great flexibility available in the provisions on powers and functions, funding and staffing that offered the possibility of asymmetry through variation between provinces. There were also aspects of the arrangements which, despite being generalised, were so directed to Bougainville's concerns as to be of little or no relevance elsewhere.

There were three aspects to entrenchment of the new arrangements. The principles of decentralisation inserted in the constitution could not be altered save by an amendment made by two separate votes, each supported by a two-thirds absolute majority and separated by at least two months (ss. 14 and 17). The details of the arrangements were contained in the Organic Law on Provincial Government, which was entrenched in much the same way as the constitutional provisions. Finally, the organic law provided for provincial constitutions, laws passed by provincial constituent assemblies and containing details of provincial government structures and procedures, to have the same status as organic laws, thereby protecting them from even indirect alteration by ordinary Act of the national parliament (Ghai and Regan 1992:ch. 4).

Turning to federal characteristics, federal systems involve constitutional entrenchment of a mixture of shared rule (through the federal government) and self-rule (through the governments of the federating units). Notwithstanding the entrenchment of 'self-rule' provisions, there is such a high degree of shared rule that Papua New Guinea can be regarded as a unitary system with marked federal features. Constitutional entrenchment of arrangements for sub-national government usually applies only in federal systems. The freedom of states or provinces to make their own constitutions is not found even in all federal systems. Perhaps most pertinent is the fact that the provincial governments had potentially exclusive areas of legislative and taxation powers, albeit over limited areas. There were also entrenched mechanisms and procedures for the handling of intergovernmental relations, including the Premiers Council and the National Fiscal Commission. They were expected to be forums for negotiations over the transfer of increasing levels of powers and resources to the provinces. The arrangements for staffing and funding the provincial governments also lay between unitary and federal models. The organic law effectively made both the national public service and national revenue into pools shared between the levels of government, according to prescribed and entrenched formulas or procedures.

Prospects for flexibility and attendant asymmetry lay not only in the freedom to choose structures and arrangements for the decentralisation of powers and functions and the transfer of resources necessary for their exercise, but also in the fact that there was room for provincial variations as provincial executive authority derived from provincial laws and delegations from the national government. The key to extensive provincial powers and functions lay in the delegations from the centre as well as the transfer of concurrent legislative subjects, both of which had to be negotiated by individual provinces with the centre, with an obligation on it to accede to requests in relation to concurrent subjects. The most significant aspects of the arrangements that were directed mainly to Bougainville's concerns included provision for the payment of mineral royalties (1.25 per cent of export value) to the provincial government of a province where a mining project operated. Until the late 1980s, Bougainville was the only province with a major mine and received around US$5 million per year in royalties, providing the North Solomons Provincial Government with far more funds to spend at its discretion than any other provincial government.

Impact on Bougainville–PNG relations and Bougainvillean nationalism

Many aspects of the decentralisation arrangements were implemented and operated much as planned. Democratic political systems were established in all nineteen provinces. Provincial consciousness and identity increased. Significant powers and resources were transferred to provincial governments enabling some to develop their own policies, while others remained content to work mainly within national policy frameworks. Further, in the circumstances of increasing growth of power of the central government, the entrenchment arrangements prevented an increasingly hostile parliament from abolishing or weakening the decentralisation arrangements, until 1995.

Many aspects of the arrangements did not work as expected, for complex reasons. Perhaps the central factor was the concentration of political and economic power in and around the state and its bureaucracy. Few provincial governments operated effectively and thus failed to mobilise strong popular support. Nor were they able to cooperate effectively through the intergovernmental mechanisms to apply pressure for the increasing transfer of powers and resources to provinces. More importantly, the capacity for policy and administration was weak in all levels of government (in large part due to the failure of the Australian colonial administration to develop an educated elite), especially as both central state structures and decentralisation arrangements were complex. The North Solomons Provincial Government was undoubtedly one of the most effective government units in Papua New Guinea, but it was fully occupied with maintaining basic services and managing its capital expenditure program.

Relations between the national government and the provincial governments were often strained. The national government paid little more than lip-service to aspects of the machinery that it could not ignore – for example, the Premiers Council, which the organic law specified had to meet annually – while ignoring other aspects (the National Fiscal Commission, which had responsibility for making recommendations on and resolving disputes about intergovernmental fiscal arrangements, did not meet after 1984). Arrangements for the suspension of provincial governments were amended in 1983, removing important procedural safeguards against abuse, and subsequently those powers were used extensively against provincial governments and often for purely political reasons. Mechanisms intended to divert intergovernmental disputes from the courts being moribund, disputes increasingly went to the courts. While there was some of the legalism that the CPC had hoped to avoid through alternative dispute mechanisms, on some occasions the courts played a useful role in maintaining the balance between the centre and the provinces underlying the constitutional arrangements, sometimes by interpreting and providing authoritative statements on constitutional provisions that were being ignored or misinterpreted by the national government, notably in cases challenging the exercise of the government's suspension powers (Ghai and Regan 1992:321–43, 408).

The potentially flexible arrangements for the transfer of powers, functions and resources to the provinces achieved neither increasing transfers to the provinces as a group nor asymmetry if the better-managed provinces had assumed more powers. The reasons lay both in the unchallenged power of the centre and in the very early decision by the national government to adopt uniformity in arrangements for the transfer of powers and resources, a decision made in 1977 on the basis of the advice of international management consultants, McKinsey and Co. (1977). While the main concern of their advice was the difficulties involved in managing the transfer process at the national level, an important precedent in favour of uniform arrangements was thereby established.

In fact, although more effective than other provinces (Griffin and Togolo 1997), the North Solomons Provincial Government was like the others in showing limited interest in operating outside the broad policy framework provided by national government laws (Ghai and Regan 1992:135–94). Consolidation of power at the national level emerged early as a factor discouraging the provincial government from pushing for increased functions and resources. Serious disputes with the national government in 1981 over demands for increased resources for Bougainville in the context of a periodic review of the agreement governing the Panguna mining project (Wesley-Smith 1991) made it clear that there was no interest at the national level in transferring further resources.

In the 1970s, the central priorities of the Bougainvillean leadership had been to achieve autonomy and a share of mining revenue.

The decentralisation arrangements and the economic opportunities available to them ensured that members of the elite were accommodated, and so the North Solomons Provincial Government was able to manage relations with the national government within the framework of the constitutional arrangements, admittedly with some tensions. However, the provincial government had limited power to respond to either the ongoing tensions associated with the unresolved grievances of ordinary people concerning the mine or the tensions associated with rapidly increasing economic inequality (due to both the mine and related economic activity and increased small-holder activity) (Regan 1998a). These tensions manifested themselves particularly in the closely related phenomena of growing resentment of outsiders and concerns about the undermining of traditional authority and culture, supposedly by outsiders. Resentment against outsiders was fuelled by competition for economic resources in a situation of growing inequality.

In relation to the first issue, Bougainville made a number of efforts (in the late 1970s, in 1982 and in the late 1980s) to remove residents of squatter settlements around the main urban areas, generally people from other parts of Papua New Guinea who were blamed for increasing crime in Bougainville. But, with very limited legal authority due to constitutional guarantees of equality and freedom of movement, and in the face of strong criticism from other provincial governments, such efforts were limited (Ghai and Regan 1992:186, 307). In relation to strengthening traditional authority and culture, policies included a local government system initially based on traditional authority and schools conducted in local languages for the first two years of education. In the second half of the 1980s, the provincial government was exploring legislation on the management of customary land as a way of dealing with problems caused by individual members of Bougainvillean customary clan ownership groups purporting to sell land to outsiders. These initiatives had little effect. The general direction of economic change – especially the growing economic inequality that was so much at odds with the relatively egalitarian nature of traditional society – was of itself undermining traditional society, and the concerns people expressed in this regard were merely symptomatic of the much deeper tensions involved.

BREAKDOWN OF DECENTRALISATION ARRANGEMENTS

Conflict in Bougainville, 1988–1997

The violent conflict that erupted in Bougainville from late 1988 (Regan 1998a) originally had little to do with ethnic divisions and, while ethnicity rapidly became a central issue, it was largely a surrogate for other tensions and forces that contributed to the conflict. Entangled in a complex web of grievances and tensions related mostly to economic change, the wrongs – real and imaginary – committed by outsiders offered an attractively simple explanation, and an easy basis for mobilising support by leaders pursuing a range of sometimes inconsistent goals.

The initial spark for the conflict was intergenerational conflict about the distribution of rent and compensation within landowning groups whose land had been taken for mining purposes. The inability of the leaders of the younger generation to make headway sparked off frustration about broader concerns arising from mining (loss of land, environmental damage, lack of opportunities for advancement within the mining company, and so on), which neither company nor government (national and provincial) understood or responded to adequately. Frustration boiled over into demands for massive compensation and, eventually, attacks on mine property. The police riot squads (and, from early 1989, army elements brought in to assist the police), almost entirely comprising 'red-skins', engaged in indiscriminate violence that made ethnic identity a central issue.[2] Several unrelated violent incidents between Bougainvilleans and 'red-skin' labourers or squatters occurring early in 1989 added to the intensity of feeling.

The landowner leaders were soon at the centre of loose coalitions of interests with diverse and sometimes contradictory goals, all seeing independence as a key to achieving them. They included aggrieved landowners who wanted the mine closed for good, economic nationalists who wanted the mine to continue but with far greater returns to Bougainville and more jobs for Bougainvilleans, and egalitarian traditionalists who sought the removal of all 'red-skins' and a return to customary ways and traditional authority in an independent Bougainville. Young men with limited education and few economic opportunities achieved instant power and status in the ranks of the Bougainville Revolutionary Army (BRA). Unable to contain the BRA, in March 1990 the PNG forces evacuated, supposedly to clear the way for political negotiations. Instead, the BRA took power. The North Solomons Provincial Government ceased to operate. The BRA leader, Francis Ona, made a unilateral declaration of independence in May 1990 and proceeded to establish a new government – the Bougainville Interim Government (BIG). The national government suspended the North Solomons Provincial Government in August 1990.

During 1989, the North Solomons Provincial Government had worked towards compromise solutions. These included a package of measures negotiated with the national government that would have provided dramatically increased funding for landowners and the provincial government, and proposals for special autonomy arrangements for Bougainville. But, by the time detailed proposals emerged in mid-1989, the escalating violence had ensured strong, though far from uniform, popular support for the BRA's secessionist agenda, and the moderate proposals were rejected outright by the BRA. A provincial government minister advocating autonomy was murdered by BRA elements late in 1989. Some senior provincial government officers and Bougainvilleans involved in business activities associated with the mine were targeted by the BRA once the PNG forces had withdrawn. While the immediate complaint usually concerned collaboration with the national government against the BRA, there was also a clear rejection of a system seen to be contrary to Bougainville's interests and of the Bougainvilleans who had supported and benefited from it. In a very brief time, a community-based and populist leadership, deriving much of their power from armed support, replaced the educated elite leadership of the previous twenty years.

The PNG withdrawal removed the main unifying, pan-Bougainville element, and BRA groups subsequently often became involved in localised conflict, some against groups supposedly sympathetic to Papua New Guinea but much of it having nothing to do with secession. Groups that were losing in local conflict or fearing the eruption of such conflict sought assistance from PNG forces, thereby facilitating their return to parts of Bougainville from September 1990. The army then exploited the divisions among Bougainvilleans as it tried to extend its control. Former BRA elements and other Bougainvilleans formed resistance forces that fought alongside the army. Bougainvilleans opposing the BRA also tended to oppose its goal of independence, though often more out of fear of independence under a BRA-dominated government than because of opposition to the goal of independence as such. At the same time, the increasingly bitter conflict contributed to a hardening of support for independence in BRA and BIG ranks (Regan 1998a).

Breakdown of decentralisation arrangements elsewhere

The effective demise of the decentralisation arrangements in Bougainville in 1990 was a major factor in the mid-1995 abolition of the arrangements elsewhere in Papua New Guinea and their replacement with arrangements under which democracy and autonomy for the provinces were dramatically reduced. The effectiveness of the North Solomons Provincial Government and the strong popular support there for at least a high degree of autonomy undoubtedly acted as major limitations on the increasingly strident opposition to the decentralisation arrangements that developed during the 1980s. A central dynamic in the reform movement was the interest by MPs in gaining control of the resources of the provincial government. Members of parliament opposed provincial government because of the transfer of resources away from the centre and the platform for political competition that provincial governments provided (Ghai and Regan 1992:285–91). Throughout the 1980s and 1990s, access to the state and its resources became ever more important as the basis for accumulation in Papua New Guinea. In large part because of the peculiar dynamics of Papua New Guinea's variant of the Westminster system (Ghai and Regan 1992:409–14; Ghai 1997), there was a rapid escalation in state resources brought under political control either explicitly or informally.

Members of parliament were sufficiently united in their opposition to provincial government that it was possible to muster enough votes to amend the constitution and adopt a new organic law. In fact, aspects of the entrenchment provisions were ignored by the parliament in repealing and replacing the old arrangements, but surprisingly, in a very weak majority decision, the Supreme Court was not willing to find against what the parliament had done (Regan 1997b:224–7, 1998b:302–9). The elected provincial government was abolished and replaced by a provincial assembly comprising MPs from the province and heads of local-level governments. One MP became governor of the province – both head of the executive and chair of the assembly – while the others became heads of the main committee controlling planning and expenditure in the national parliament constituencies that were now the basis for administrative and local government arrangements in all provinces except Bougainville. At the same time, the autonomy of provincial governments was severely reduced, in terms not only of the powers available to the province but also of the ability of the national government to intervene in the affairs of the province.

THE FUTURE: ASYMMETRICAL ARRANGEMENTS OR SEPARATION?

The demise of the original decentralisation arrangements in the rest of Papua New Guinea helped to consolidate support in Bougainville for the proposition that, whatever happens, radical change is required in the political status of Bougainville. Nevertheless, older arrangements continued to apply in Bougainville for three and a half years after they were replaced elsewhere. This was done to enable a coalition of 'moderate' Bougainville leaders – that unexpectedly emerged late in 1994 with a proposal to lift the suspension on the provincial government and establish the Bougainville Transitional Government – to negotiate a new formula for autonomy.

The transitional government's initiatives in establishing communications with the BIG and BRA leadership played a major role in the development of a peace process from mid-1997. Other factors included the virtual military defeat of the PNG forces by the BRA, war weariness on all sides and a change of government in Papua New Guinea following the mid-1997 national elections. The peace process was assisted by substantial regional intervention, in the form of facilitation of the talks by the

New Zealand government and in the provision of an unarmed group of civilian and military personnel from New Zealand, Vanuatu, Fiji and Australia that monitored first a truce and subsequently a cease-fire. A small UN observer mission was also involved.

Central to the process have been efforts to reconcile and unify the divided Bougainvilleans, a process originally expected to result in the establishment of an elected Bougainville Reconciliation Government (BRG) by the end of 1998 in order to negotiate with the national government over the political future of Bougainville. During the latter part of 1998, constitutional amendments were introduced to enable the BRG to operate temporarily under the original decentralisation arrangements. But, due to political conflict in the national parliament unconnected with Bougainville, the necessary amendments were not passed and, as a result, the provincial government reforms operating in the rest of Papua New Guinea came into operation in Bougainville. The national government then suspended the provincial government and permitted the Bougainvillean groups to take steps towards establishing a reconciliation government by electing an assembly – the Bougainville People's Congress (BPC) – on an informal basis. With that exercise completed by May 1999, the BPC developed proposals on Bougainville's future for negotiations with the national government.

A major question both in the negotiations in 1975–76 and in the national government response to the violence and conflict in Bougainville from 1988 was the central importance of the Bougainville mine to the PNG economy and government revenue. (In the 1980s, it was contributing 17 per cent of national budget revenue – K184 million in direct and indirect taxes in a K1.25 billion national budget – over 36 per cent of gross export earnings, and 11 per cent of GDP (Griffin and Togolo 1997:357).) By 1999, there were two main reasons why this was no longer a key issue. First, the mine had not operated for ten years, and the destruction of infrastructure, poor copper and gold prices and the prospect of continuing instability in both Papua New Guinea and Bougainville make the likelihood of resumption of operations remote in the extreme. Second, other major mines as well as oil and gas projects had been established elsewhere in Papua New Guinea, more than making up for what in 1989 had been the terrible blow of the loss of the Panguna mine. While the changed circumstances concerning the mine may provide the national government with more options in the negotiations, there is still lingering concern that the mine might reopen, in which case Bougainville should not be free to derive benefits on its own.

Negotiations began in a brief meeting with Prime Minister Skate on 30 June 1999. However, they were not resumed until December, because of the change of government a few days later. Both Skate and his successor,

Sir Mekere Morauta, ruled out the possibility of independence for Bougainville, although Skate left open the possibility of not only a high degree of autonomy but also a referendum on the question of independence. Initially, the Morauta government was strongly opposed to Bougainville independence and even to discussing the referendum issue. However, at the third round of negotiations on 23 March 2000, the national delegation agreed not only to key aspects of autonomy but also 'to address the referendum issue', on the understanding that the holding of the referendum 'may be deferred until after autonomy has been implemented and can be fairly and properly judged' (para 6 of the Loloata Understanding signed by the two parties). Bougainville will be free to set up its own government with extensive powers (to be defined in the national constitution after suitable amendments). A referendum now seems quite likely and will be almost unprecedented in international law or practice. Implicit also in the agreement is asymmetry in favour of Bougainville, for the government is unlikely to grant such wide powers to other provinces, although undoubtedly others will demand a similar status.

As was the case with provincial government, there is at this stage limited indication that the Bougainville leadership envisages the policies of an independent Bougainville government being dramatically different from existing PNG policies. The focus of policy discussion is on the exclusion of outsiders, Bougainvillean control of economic development and the strengthening of traditional culture and authority.

CONCLUSION

The general issues raised in the introduction to this chapter can now be considered in the light of the admittedly specific experience in Bougainville of efforts to accommodate ethnic conflict through constitutional arrangements for uniform decentralisation as well as proposals for more asymmetrical power-sharing arrangements.

Considering first the issue of how ethnic identity becomes politicised in terms of separatist demands, even the forging of a distinct identity for a group of people divided by many other more localised identities has been a complex process. Undoubtedly, the combination of distinct skin colour, geographical concentration and grievances against remote authorities has been crucial. The articulation of grievances by an educated elite was central to political mobilisation around the Bougainville identity. The commitment to secession by the elite in the 1960s and 1970s was at best ambivalent, most probably using secession demands as a tactic in support of their real goal of autonomy. But the articulation of the goal and the conflict around it raised expectations among supporters that independence really could provide answers to concerns more related to tensions caused by economic and social change. So, even in the early stages, ethnic identity was in part a surrogate for other tensions, something it has certainly been during the conflict since 1988. On the other hand, the violence of the conflict with the PNG forces has been a major new factor intensifying the ethnic consciousness of Bougainvilleans since 1988.

The circumstances most favourable to concession of federal or autonomy arrangements to contain ethnic conflict in Bougainville were those involved in decolonisation. There can be few situations where more fundamental changes in regime occur, and of course such changes offer special opportunities to groups with special concerns to stake claims on the state. The special circumstances of Papua New Guinea's decolonisation favoured particularistic demands, the complaints of local groups against the colonial administration being central to the development of national politics. In the lead-up to independence, the virtual absence of other forms of national politics meant that there were limited countervailing pressures. By contrast, in the 1990s, entrenched interests at the centre see little reason to make concessions to Bougainville. The perception that the decentralisation arrangements operating from 1977 failed to contain Bougainville separatism leads many to argue against fresh concessions that they fear might again be generalised.

Regional and international intervention in the peace process in Bougainville in the late 1990s is a circumstance that might create conditions more favourable to the concession of special arrangements for Bougainville, in the form of asymmetrical arrangements (perhaps even independence). Whereas the international community ignored Bougainville's independence demands in the 1970s, the reasons for the very different reaction in the 1990s require brief comment. The attitude of the international community to intervention in internal disputes has changed in the last ten years, due to numerous factors that include the freeing up of international relations with the end of the cold war and the slowly growing acceptance of international responsibilities to prevent human rights abuses in internal conflicts. Hence, the violence of the Bougainville conflict might not only consolidate ethnic identity but also contribute to conditions favourable to the concession of special autonomy arrangements for Bougainville.

The Bougainville experience supports the proposition that there is a tendency for asymmetric arrangements to be generalised into uniform arrangements. At each point when concessions were made to Bougainville in the 1970s, the fear that special arrangements would be divisive was a major factor in the national government extending the arrangements to all provinces. Once flexible decentralisation arrangements were in place, a number of pressures made them operate in a uniform manner rather than facilitate Bougainville taking on additional powers and resources.

Most important here was the centralisation of economic power in the central government and the limited agenda of the Bougainville elite.

There is limited evidence in the Bougainville case to support either of the opposing propositions that federal or autonomy arrangements accommodate and reduce ethnic tensions, or that such arrangements necessarily reinforce the politicisation of ethnic identity. From 1977, a degree of accommodation of ethnic identity was achieved. But decentralisation did not give Bougainville the power to deal with basic grievances or with economic and social developments that created ever-growing tensions. While it was not ethnic divisions that caused the conflict of 1988–97, once other events gave rise to conflict in Bougainville, ethnic divisions were a weak point around which other tensions could easily erupt, and around which leaders of varied interest groups could mobilise support.

On the other hand, the rejection of decentralisation in favour of violent separatist struggle is not of itself an indictment of the decentralisation arrangements in Bougainville. The arrangements were not capable of limiting the unfolding of powerful economic and social forces, and it was those forces, largely external to the decentralisation arrangements, that led to the demise of decentralisation.

In the light of these comments, Bougainville offers equivocal evidence about the relationships between ethnic identity and federalism or autonomy as mechanisms intended to deal with ethnic conflict. There is little evidence of ethnic identity being in any major way transformed by the operation of the decentralisation arrangements of 1977–90. While the relatively successful operation of a provincial government for Bougainville probably helped to contain ethnic tensions for a time, those arrangements were increasingly seen by those with limited stakes in them (landowners receiving few benefits, those failing to extract economic benefit from the mine or from cash cropping, and so on) as irrelevant to the needs of Bougainville. The inability of the arrangements to respond to deeper concerns flowing from rapid socio-economic change probably contributed to increased resentment of outsiders who were, to some degree, a convenient explanation for a multitude of problems. It might be argued that only an extremely inward-looking form of either asymmetric autonomy arrangements or independence could have contained the forces at work in Bougainville, and such arrangements would have created their own tensions and problems. On the other hand, the provincial government was operating well in many respects and was seeking ways of dealing with the sources of ethnic tension. More responsive government initiatives in 1988 and less resort to state violence could have produced very different outcomes than the subsequent nine-year conflict. It has been violence more than any other single factor that has intensified Bougainvillean ethnicity since 1988 and made it much less susceptible to either uniform or asymmetrical power-sharing arrangements.

At the same time, the conflict certainly intensified Bougainvillean ethnic identity and the depth of ethnic division, and, as a result, the degree of autonomy that might be acceptable to accommodate ethnic identity is now far greater than it was in the 1990s. There is little doubt that, unless Papua New Guinea concedes an extremely high degree of autonomy, at the very least, there is a serious risk of recurrence of the violence and of intensification of ethnic divisions. In this sense, then, there is a strong relationship between the intensity of ethnic division and the kind of autonomy arrangements that may be able to accommodate them.

NOTES
We are grateful to John Ballard and David Hegarty for comments on a draft of this chapter.
1 In fact, colonial development was uneven, some other districts being even less developed (see Conyers 1976:52).
2 The police tactics did not reflect specific anti-Bougainvillean feelings. They had been developed to quell tribal fighting in the New Guinea Highlands and, while deeply resented, had not caused problems of the kind that arose in Bougainville (Mapusia 1986).

REFERENCES
Ballard, J. 1977. 'Students and politics: PNG', *Journal of Commonwealth and Comparative Politics* 13:112–26.
—— 1981. 'Policy-making as trauma: the provincial government issue', in J.A. Ballard (ed.) *Policy Making in a New State: Papua New Guinea 1972–1977*. St Lucia: University of Queensland Press, 95–132.
Bedford, Richard and Alexander Mamak 1977. *Compensation for Development: The Bougainville Case*. Bougainville Special Publication No. 2. Christchurch: Department of Geography, University of Canterbury.
Connell, John (ed.) 1977. *Local Government Councils in Bougainville*. Bougainville Special Publication No. 3. Christchurch: Department of Geography, University of Canterbury.
Conyers, Diana 1976. *The Provincial Government Debate: Central Control Versus Local Participation in PNG*. IASER Monograph 2. Port Moresby: PNG Institute of Applied Social and Economic Research.
Crocombe, R.G. 1968. 'Bougainville! Copper, CRA and secessionism', *New Guinea and Australia, the Pacific and South-East Asia* 3(3).
Downs, Ian 1980. *The Australian Trusteeship: PNG 1945–75*. Canberra: Australian Government Publishing Service.
Ghai, Yash 1997. 'Establishing a liberal political order through a constitution: the PNG experience', *Development and Change* 28.
Ghai, Yash and Anthony Regan 1992. *The Law, Politics and Administration of Decentralisation in PNG*. Monograph 30. Port Moresby: National Research Institute.
Griffin, J. 1973. 'Papua New Guinea and the British Solomon Islands Protectorate: fusion or transfusion?', *Australian Outlook* 27(3):319–28.

—— 1977. 'Local government councils as instruments of political mobilisation in Bougainville', in Connell 1977:29–57.

—— 1982. 'Napidakoe navitu', in R.J. May (ed.) *Micronationalist Movements in Papua New Guinea*. Political and Social Change Monograph No. 1. Canberra: Australian National University, 113–38.

Griffin, James and Mel Togolo 1997. 'North Solomons Province, 1974–1990', in R.J. May and A.J. Regan (eds) *Political Decentralisation in a New State: The Experience of Provincial Government in PNG*. Bathurst: Crawford House Press.

Hannett, Leo 1969. 'Down Kieta way: independence for Bougainville?', *New Guinea and Australia, the Pacific and South-East Asia* 4.

Mamak, A. and R. Bedford 1974. *Bougainvillean Nationalism: Aspects of Unity and Discord*. Bougainville Special Publication No. 1. Christchurch: Department of Geography, University of Canterbury.

Mapusia, M. 1986. 'Police policy towards tribal fighting in the highlands', in L. Morauta (ed.) *Law and Order in a Changing Society*. Canberra: Department of Political and Social Change, Research School of Pacific and Asian Studies, Australian National University.

May, R.J. (ed.) 1982. *Micronationalist Movements in Papua New Guinea*. Monograph No. 1. Canberra: Department of Political and Social Change, Research School of Pacific and Asian Studies, Australian National University.

McKinsey and Co. 1977. 'Making decentralisation work', mimeo, Port Moresby.

Nash, Jill and Eugene Ogan 1990. 'The red and the black: Bougainville perceptions of other PNGns', *Pacific Studies* 13:2.

Nelson, Hank 1968. 'Bougainville breakaway', *Nation*, 12 October.

Ogan, Eugene 1965. 'An election in Bougainville', *Ethnology* IV(4):397–407.

—— 1972. *Business and Cargo: Socio-economic Change among the Nasioi of Bougainville*. Bulletin No. 44. Port Moresby: New Guinea Research Unit, Australian National University.

—— 1974. 'Cargoism and politics in Bougainville 1962–1972', *Journal of Pacific History* 9.

—— 1991. 'The cultural background to the Bougainville crisis', *Journal de la Société des Oceanistes* 92–93(1–2):61–7.

Regan, A.J. 1997a. 'East New Britain Province, 1976–1992', in R.J. May and A.J. Regan (eds) *Political Decentralisation in a New State: The Experience of Provincial Government in PNG*. Bathurst: Crawford House Press.

—— 1997b. 'PNG', in Cheryl Saunders and Graham Hassall (eds) *Asia–Pacific Constitutional Yearbook 1995*. Melbourne: Centre for Comparative Constitutional Studies, University of Melbourne.

—— 1998a. 'Causes and course of the Bougainville conflict', *Journal of Pacific History* 33(3):269.

—— 1998b. 'PNG', in Cheryl Saunders and Graham Hassall (eds) *Asia–Pacific Constitutional Yearbook 1996*. Melbourne: Centre for Comparative Constitutional Studies, University of Melbourne.

Wesley-Smith, T. 1991. 'The non-review of the Bougainville Copper Agreement', in M. Spriggs and D. Denoon (eds) *The Bougainville Crisis: 1991 Update*. Canberra: Department of Political and Social Change, Research School of Pacific and Asian Studies, Australian National University.

CHAPTER 12

THE IMPLICATIONS OF FEDERALISM FOR INDIGENOUS AUSTRALIANS

CHERYL SAUNDERS

Australian federalism is a by-product of the manner in which the Australian state was created in 1901, through the voluntary amalgamation of six self-governing British colonies, each with its own constitution, institutions and laws. For its critics, the federal system is kept in place largely by habit and entrenched interests. More objectively, however, a federal form of government still plays an important role in Australia. Decentralised government of some kind is dictated by geographic size. By offering a more local level of government, federalism thus contributes, at least potentially, to Australian democracy. In the absence of other significant constitutional constraints, including protection of rights, federalism provides a check on public power. Indeed, given Australia's adherence to the British constitutional tradition, had a normative constitution not been necessitated by the introduction of a federal system, it is doubtful that Australia would have had one at all.

Australian federalism plays no role in moderating competing ethnic demands. For the first fifty years after federation, the Australian population overwhelmingly, although not exclusively, was Anglo-Celtic in composition. Successive waves of migration following World War II, initially from Europe and more recently from Asia, have created a multi-ethnic people, but in a way that has no particular implications for the federal system. There is no concentration of discrete groups in different parts of Australia. Multicultural policies are disputed, but no one seeks to resolve the dispute through the application of federal principles, in the sense of providing forms of self-government for particular ethnic groups. The policy demands of new immigrant groups are limited to more effective protection against discrimination, to facilitation of the use of community languages and preservation of community cultures, and to immigration programs more conducive to family reunion. Immigrants have come to Australia voluntarily and, for the most part, they accept that any changes that they seek can be effected within the framework of the existing governance arrangements, which attracted them to Australia in the first place.

The position of the indigenous people of Australia is quite different. Despite the legal fiction of *terra nullius*, an estimated 700,000 indigenous people inhabited the Australian mainland and surrounding islands when the British claimed sovereignty from 1770 (Gardiner-Garden 1994:8). Their ancestors had inhabited Australia for an estimated 50,000 years. They spoke up to 300 different languages and lived in hundreds of tribal groupings. They had their own systems of law and custom and their own established authority structures. And each group had a special relationship with its own part of the land

> . . . which defies definition. It is best described as a continuing dynamic notion, not bounded by geographical limits of a surveyor. It is a living, breathing entity made up of earth, sky, clouds, rivers, trees, rocks and the spirits sent by the Big One above to create all these things. It is the place wherein the spirits of our forefathers roam. The place wherein our spirits will reside on our return to the golden Corroboree ground, the Dream Time. Earth is an extension of our very souls, it is our everything. I repeat, it is our everything. (Bonner 1994:viii)

The British claimed sovereignty over Australia as a settled colony. There was no act of acquiescence on the part of the indigenous people, and no acknowledgement of conquest at the time or later. British law was introduced to the exclusion of indigenous law, at least in theory. The indigenous peoples were decimated, through deliberate slaughter and disease. Those in the southern, more settled parts of the country were progressively dispossessed of their lands. As they moved towards the north and west, they intruded on to the lands of others, causing further confusion and conflict.

By the latter part of the twentieth century, indigenous Australians constituted approximately 1.5 per cent of the total Australian population. They were grievously disadvantaged, economically and socially. On the face of it, they were in no position to exercise political influence. But the context was changing. In the wake of the rights revolution and of the decolonisation that followed World War II came a new understanding of the nature of indigenous communities, the depth of their heritage and their relationship with the land. Indigenous groups organised; non-indigenous Australians became increasingly ashamed of past repressive policies and continuing cultural, economic and social deprivation; the international community brought pressure to bear. More enlightened policies fuelled demands for rights to land, culturally sensitive administration, and non-indigenous recognition of indigenous laws and customs. For the first time, Australia confronted the presence of a different ethnicity, claiming original occupation and demanding a right at least to share the country.

The Australian experience is relevant to the theme of this book for this reason. This chapter explores the extent to which Australian federalism has helped or hindered the resolution of differences between indigenous and non-indigenous Australians. The result throws some light on the circumstances in which federalism may assist with ethnic tension and helps to explain the dynamics of federalism itself.

The most obvious way in which federalism might assist to resolve ethnic issues of this kind is by offering indigenous peoples opportunities for self-governance as a constituent part of the federation, geographically defined. There is a partial precedent in Australia, in Norfolk Island. Under current legislation, the territory has substantial local autonomy and some immunity from Commonwealth law in recognition of the 'special relationship' of its inhabitants to the island and 'their desire to preserve their traditions and culture' (preamble to Norfolk Island Act 1979). Proposed changes to this regime, which would extend the right to vote to all Australian citizens resident on Norfolk Island, suggest that this example is unlikely to be used more widely (Norfolk Island Amendment Bill 1999). Even without such a structural solution, however, federalism might be expected to encourage greater tolerance of diversity of policies and law and greater understanding of the desire of communities to make their own decisions. Similarly, long-standing acceptance of different legal regimes in the different States might be acknowledged as a precedent for the use by indigenous groups of their own customary law.

Institutionally, federalism offers opportunities to deal constructively with ethnicity as well. A special relationship between a national government and the indigenous people, to the exclusion of sub-national governments, as in the United States, offers a means of recognising the unique status of indigenous peoples without jeopardising the integrity of the state as a whole (Kickingbird 1993:12). Alternatively, if indigenous people are subject to State laws, an opportunity arises to experiment with new approaches, in more receptive parts of the country, without a need to persuade the entire national polity. In another variation, bodies which are representative of the components of the federation, such as an upper chamber of the national legislature or the meeting of heads of government, might be extended to embrace representation of indigenous people as well.

With relatively minor exceptions, however, the Australian federal system has not contributed to the resolution of indigenous issues in these or other ways. While there is now a limited measure of indigenous self-administration and limited recognition of customary law, in neither case has the federal system played a significant role. To substantiate and help to explain this claim, the next two parts of this chapter examine the position of the indigenous people within the federal system, both generally and with particular reference to self-government or self-determination.

It shows that, despite the federal system, Australian constitutional culture is not hospitable to indigenous issues. Dominant competing influences are majoritarian decision making, formal equality and parliamentary sovereignty within the framework of a not particularly restrictive constitution. Australia is firmly in the Western liberal tradition in its adherence to individual rather than collective rights. Even individual rights, however, are not protected by the constitution but solely by the common law and occasional statutes. The practical consequences of this were brought home to the indigenous people in 1997 in *Kruger* v. *Commonwealth*, in which the High Court rejected all grounds of challenge to the forcible removal of Aboriginal children from their parents in the Northern Territory between 1925 and 1949.[1]

It may be that the potential of the federal system to deal with indigenous matters has not yet been realised. Opportunities for it to play a greater role were suggested by two separate developments in the approach to the centenary of federation in 2001. The first is projected statehood for the Northern Territory. The second is the movement for reconciliation. The final part of the chapter explores both of these.

THE FEDERAL DIVISION OF POWER

Australia became a federation in 1901. The constitution was written over the preceding decade. It drew on both the British and US constitutional models. From Britain came the parliamentary system with which the colonies were already familiar and the constitutional culture associated with it, hostile to limits on the power of parliament except to the minimum necessary extent. From the United States came federalism and its accoutrements of a written constitution representing fundamental law, enforced through independent courts. A powerful upper house of the Australian parliament, loosely modelled on the US Senate, comprised equal numbers of senators from each of the original States, directly elected by the voters of those States (s. 7). In time, the Senate would be elected on the basis of a system of proportional representation, producing a chamber in which minority parties generally hold the balance of power (Coonan 1999:107). The constitution could be amended only by referendum, which required approval by double majorities (s. 128), nationally and in the majority of States.

Australia also followed the United States in the manner of distributing powers between the new national level of government (the Commonwealth) and the sub-national units (the States). The constitution lists national powers (s. 51). Those not listed, by inference, remain with the

States. Most Commonwealth powers are concurrent, in the sense that the States can exercise them as well. In the event of a conflict, however, valid Commonwealth legislation prevails (s. 109). In a departure from the US system, the Australian constitution provided also for the establishment of a High Court, as the final court of appeal in matters of State as well as federal jurisdiction. This enabled the emergence of a common law that was uniform across the country.

The indigenous people unambiguously fell within the authority of the States in 1901. They were specifically excluded from Commonwealth power to legislate with respect to 'the people of any race . . . for whom it is deemed necessary to make special laws' (s. 51(26)). In addition, the constitution provided that 'in reckoning the numbers of the people of the Commonwealth or of a State . . . aboriginal natives shall not be counted' (s. 127). This latter provision excluded the indigenous people from calculations required under the constitution to determine State revenue redistribution and the allocation of seats between the States in the House of Representatives. It further reinforced their political insignificance and may be a factor that contributed to their historic economic disadvantage.

The first Commonwealth franchise enacted in 1902 reinforced the effects of exclusion from the constitution by denying the vote to indigenous people, unless already held under the law of a particular State when the constitution came into effect (s. 41). While State practice varied, Western Australia and Queensland, the States with the largest populations of indigenous people, did not recognise their right to vote, and there is some evidence that Aboriginals who held the vote under s. 41 of the constitution were struck off the roll by Commonwealth electoral officials (Chesterman and Galligan 1997:89). In other respects as well, indigenous Australians were denied rights enjoyed by the wider community (Gardiner-Garden 1994:10).

Most powers likely to impinge on the interests of indigenous people were left to the States by the constitution. These included education, housing, health, police and civil rights. Importantly, they also included land management and associated activities, including primary production and mining. The Crown in right of the several States held all land unless and until it was transferred to private ownership or acquired by the Commonwealth. Under the constitution, the Commonwealth could acquire property only on 'just terms', requiring fair compensation, with the courts as ultimate arbiter (s. 51(31)). The legal fiction that Australia was *terra nullius* was in place well before federation and left no room for the recognition of indigenous interests in land as a right,[2] although some pastoral leases made explicit reservations for traditional Aboriginal use.[3]

The balance of power between the Commonwealth and the States with respect to indigenous people and the influence of indigenous people in the Australian constitutional system changed substantially over the course of the twentieth century, for a variety of distinct but interrelated reasons.

In 1911, the Northern Territory of South Australia was transferred to the Commonwealth under s. 122 of the constitution, which gives the Commonwealth power to legislate for territories, unrestricted by the federal provisions of the constitution. The transfer of jurisdiction was not immediately significant. Ultimately destructive policies of assimilation, including the forcible removal of indigenous children from their parents, were implemented in the Northern Territory as well, under Commonwealth auspices. In the early 1960s, however, the Commonwealth began to take steps to remove legal discrimination against indigenous people, including restrictions on the franchise (Commonwealth Electoral Act 1962, s. 2). And in 1976, land rights legislation enacted by the Commonwealth came into force in the Northern Territory, enabling Aboriginal groups to secure freehold title to existing reserves and to claim vacant Crown land, where traditional attachment could be established (Aboriginal Land Rights (Northern Territory) Act 1976). Statutory land rights initiatives were taken in most of the States as well: they were, however, 'limited and somewhat token . . . one of the less noble facets of Australian parliamentary democracy' (Chesterman and Galligan 1997:205). National land rights legislation was not secured before the 1992 decision in *Mabo (No. 2)* recognised the survival of native title and forced legislation to manage the manner in which claims were made.[4] The Aboriginal Land Rights (Northern Territory) legislation was still new when self-government was conferred on the Northern Territory in 1978. In a climate of doubt about whether a more independent Territory could be entrusted with an issue of such central concern to its minority indigenous peoples, the land rights regime stayed within Commonwealth control.[5] This was and remains a point of distinction between the powers of the Territory and those of the States (Nicholson 1985:698, 706; see also Reeves 1998), and will be a contentious issue for decision if and when the Northern Territory achieves statehood.

The second major development was the referendum of 1967. The referendum changed the constitution to remove the prohibition against including indigenous people in population calculations and, in effect, to give the Commonwealth concurrent powers with the States with respect to indigenous people. It was passed in all States, with an overall national vote of 92 per cent. Commonwealth power was extended by excising the reference to Aboriginal people from the so-called 'races' power, leaving it as a power to legislate with respect to 'the people of any race for whom it is deemed necessary to make special laws'. This was, as Justice Gaudron pointed out in *Kartinyeri* v. *Commonwealth*, a 'minimalist' approach to conferring power on the Commonwealth to legislate with respect to the Aboriginal people, the meaning of which was inherently ambiguous. No doubt its purpose was generally benevolent, although it is difficult to establish that specifically.[6] The original head of power clearly had been intended to enable adverse discrimination, however, if the Commonwealth saw fit. There is nothing in the wording of the power, as amended, to suggest that it could not similarly be used in relation to the Aboriginal people as well.

This conflict was considered by the High Court in the *Kartinyeri* case. The case concerned the Aboriginal and Torres Strait Islander (Heritage Protection) Act 1984, which provided a measure of Commonwealth protection for areas or objects of special significance to indigenous people, where comparable State legislation failed to do so. After a protracted dispute over one such area, in the course of which a State Royal Commission found that the heritage claims were false, in the absence of evidence from the claimants, the Commonwealth parliament amended the legislation to exclude that claim from the operation of the Act. The claimants challenged the validity of the amending Act on the grounds that it was not for the benefit of Aboriginal people. The challenge was dismissed, principally on the ground that what parliament can enact it can repeal as long as, presumably, the law as changed could have been enacted under the power in the first place (Lindell 1998:273).

Although it was not necessary for the High Court to deal with the scope of the power itself, four of the six justices did so. One accepted that the power could not be used to enact laws that 'adversely and detrimentally' discriminate against people on the grounds of race (Kirby J:765, in *Kartinyeri*). Three others denied this limitation, while suggesting that there may nevertheless be outer limits on the use of the power, drawn from the requirement for parliament to deem it necessary to make special laws. Thus, Justices Gummow and Hayne suggested that a law might be invalid if there were a 'manifest abuse' of the judgment that it was necessary to make a special law or to make the particular special law under challenge, a criterion which one leading constitutional practitioner has equated with irrationality (Gageler 1998:270, 272). In similar vein, Justice Gaudron (736, in *Kartinyeri*) observed that it would be 'difficult to conceive of circumstances in which a law presently operating to the disadvantage of a racial minority would be valid'. One reference in the joint judgment of Gummow and Hayne JJ (743–4) also raised the possibility that the conception of the rule of law, in accordance with which the constitution is framed, might provide a further constraint on the exercise of the power (Lindell 1998:277). The implications of these vague but potentially significant limitations no doubt will be elaborated in the future, and even now offer a fertile field for the elaboration of theories about judicial method. On any view, however, they are likely to assist the subjects of Commonwealth legislation only in extreme circumstances.

The power conferred on the Commonwealth by the 1967 referendum is held concurrently with the States. The Commonwealth was slow to exercise it; and Commonwealth interest in taking a lead in indigenous affairs has fluctuated with successive governments. The States still retain primary responsibility for indigenous residents as members of State communities in areas of general State law, including health, housing, education and law enforcement. The number of indigenous residents is a factor taken into account by the Commonwealth Grants Commission in calculating fiscal equalisation entitlements, but the general revenue funds which States receive in consequence are not tied to purpose. The effects of these divided responsibilities have been criticised. In 1995, the Aboriginal and Torres Strait Islander Commission (ATSIC) highlighted the problems many indigenous people face with substandard housing, municipal infrastructure and services; health, as indicated by high rates of infant mortality, lower life expectancy and high rates of hospitalisation and disability; and education, for which they sought a curriculum which respects the values of both indigenous and non-indigenous Australians (ATSIC 1995:85–91). The report identified failures of intergovernmental cooperative programs as a major factor contributing to continuing social and economic disadvantage and proposed new national programs. Attention was also drawn to the still unresolved problems of the application of the criminal justice system to indigenous people. This had been the subject of a report by a Royal Commission into Aboriginal Deaths in Custody three years earlier, the recommendations of which still were not implemented, despite commitments by all Australian governments (ATSIC 1995:91–4).

A further major shift in the manner in which the Australian federal system relates to indigenous Australians came through the external affairs power.

At the time of federation, power to legislate with respect to 'external affairs' was conferred on the Commonwealth (s. 51(xxix)). Its significance was restricted by Australia's colonial status, which left the United Kingdom, as the imperial authority, to make international arrangements on behalf of Australia. In 1901, too, the scope of international law was more limited, particularly in relation to human rights and the environment. Australia gradually acquired the authority to make its own international treaties and ultimately achieved full independence by an evolutionary process, the precise culmination point of which is uncertain but was no later than 1942.[7]

The aftermath of World War II saw the implementation of international human rights instruments, to which Australia became a party, including the International Covenant on the Elimination of All Forms of Racial Discrimination. In 1975, relying largely on the external affairs power, the Commonwealth enacted a Racial Discrimination Act, making it 'unlawful to do any act involving a distinction based on race, which has the purpose or effect of nullifying or impairing the recognition, enjoyment or exercise on an equal footing, of any human right or fundamental freedom' (s. 9). Section 10 of the Act provided that

> if by reason of a provision of a law of the Commonwealth or of a State or Territory, persons of a particular race do not enjoy a right that is enjoyed by persons of another race, or enjoy that right to a more limited extent, then by force of this section, those persons of the first-mentioned race shall enjoy that right to the same extent as people of other races.

The validity of the legislation was confirmed by the High Court in 1982, in the context of discrimination by the Queensland government against an Aboriginal group.[8] The *Koowarta* case marked an important stage in the evolution of the interpretation of the external affairs power to the point where it authorises the Commonwealth parliament to legislate to implement any international treaty to which Australia is a party. This was a highly contentious development, because of its effect on the constitutional distribution of power between the Commonwealth and the States.

The Racial Discrimination Act played a key role in the litigation, which ultimately led the High Court to decide that, in some circumstances, native title had survived European settlement and would now be recognised by the common law.

The notion that Australia was *terra nullius* dated from the nineteenth century and, in particular, from a decision of the Privy Council confirming a long-standing assumption that Australia consisted of 'a tract of territory practically unoccupied without settled inhabitants'.[9] In the 1970s, encouraged by the more informed climate of understanding of indigenous culture and law in the latter half of the twentieth century, attempts were made to secure judicial recognition of indigenous rights to land, without success.[10] In 1982, however, plaintiffs from a group of islands in the Torres Strait, formerly part of the State of Queensland since annexation in 1879, commenced proceedings in the High Court claiming ownership. The action was well chosen, in the sense that there had been no general European settlement of the island, apart from a small number of leases, and the islanders had lived on and cultivated land in a manner consistent with concepts of individual ownership. By comparison with indigenous people on the mainland, at least, it was relatively more straightforward for the islanders to establish historic possession. Even so, the High Court remitted the task of determining the facts to the

Supreme Court of Queensland. This proved an elaborate proceeding and the substantive issues did not return to the High Court for determination until 1991. In the end, the tribunal in fact accepted some aspects of the claim, although not those of Eddie Mabo from whom the case takes its name.[11]

Meanwhile, in 1985, the Queensland parliament had enacted legislation retrospectively invalidating any native title that might still exist in relation to the island, with retrospective effect from the date of annexation, in 1879. The validity of this legislation was challenged in the High Court in 1988 in *Mabo (No. 1)*,[12] on the grounds of conflict with the Racial Discrimination Act. In upholding the challenge, the High Court accepted that the effect of the Queensland law was to give the islanders more limited rights than those of other Queenslanders, contrary to s. 10 of the Act. Henceforth, the Racial Discrimination Act was recognised as a significant constraint on State dealings with indigenous people. And while from the standpoint of the Commonwealth the Act has the formal status only of ordinary legislation, its significance is such that, de facto, it has become regarded as quasi-constitutional in character.

The substantive issues in the case ultimately were determined in 1992 in *Mabo (No. 2)*. In a statement of principle that applied to mainland Australia as well as to the Torres Strait Islands, the High Court determined

> that the common law of this country recognises a form of native title which, in the cases where it has not been extinguished, reflects the entitlements of the indigenous inhabitants in accordance with their laws and customs to their traditional land . . .[13]

Survival of title depended on a continuing traditional connection with the land by the clan or group concerned (Brennan J:59–60, in *Mabo*). It was not extinguished by European settlement itself, which conferred underlying or 'radical' title to land on the Crown. It would be extinguished, however, by a subsequent grant of interest in the land revealing 'a clear and plain intention to do so' (Brennan J:64). It followed that native title was clearly extinguished by grants of fee simple and leases that conferred exclusive possession, although there was some doubt about grants made after 1975, because of the operation of the Racial Discrimination Act. Other doubts, about whether pastoral leases conferred over vast tracts of land extinguished native title, were the subject of a later decision which confirmed that native title could continue on pastoral leases when it was capable of operating consistently with the terms of the lease.[14]

Mabo had a profound effect on the position of the indigenous people in the Australian constitutional system, including its federal arrangements. Recognition of native title, with its underlying recognition of Aboriginal society before European settlement, gave moral and psychological

impetus to indigenous demands for legal, economic and social equality. It
effected a change in State land law, which could not be reversed unless, at
least, reversal could be achieved consistently with the Racial Discrimination Act. In fact, the conditions laid down in *Mabo* for a successful native
title claim would be difficult to establish and almost impossible in the settled south of the country where 200 years of dispossession have broken
the continuity of the links of most, if not all, groups with the land. The fact
of the decision meant that claims would be made, however, whatever
the outcome. This would be prolonged and expensive for Aboriginal
claimants, if the ordinary courts were used. There would also be a period
of uncertainty for parts of the non-indigenous community, including the
powerful mining and pastoral industries, both in relation to grants of
interests in land by the States after the Racial Discrimination Act came
into effect and generally. These concerns ultimately spread to the community more widely, with exaggerated descriptions of the potential effects
of *Mabo*.[15] Meanwhile, indigenous groups who were not in a position to
claim title to traditional lands because of past dispossession sought
compensation on grounds of equity.

These various considerations caused the Commonwealth to enact legislation, following consultation with Aboriginal leaders. The Native Title
Act 1993 established a Native Title Tribunal as the primary forum for
native title claims. It facilitated confirmation of the validity of different
types of land grants between 1975 and 1993, which might otherwise have
been inconsistent with the Racial Discrimination Act. In the case of past
grants by the Commonwealth, the Act itself declared them valid. In the
case of past Acts by States, the Act authorised validation by the State, subject to a requirement to pay compensation. It provided a framework
within which future grants inconsistent with native title might be made,
subject, among other things, to equality of treatment with non-native title
holders. This generally involved compensation and, in some cases, a
right to negotiate for native title holders, leaving failure to reach agreement to decision by the tribunal. The framework was exclusive and over-
rode inconsistent State law. The Act purported to leave intact the Racial
Discrimination Act. To the extent to which it drew distinctions on the
ground of race, it could be justified as a special measure consistently with
the international covenant or characterised as a law that was not rele-
vantly discriminatory.[16] The Act also established a land fund to assist
indigenous people to acquire land. It was expressed to operate retrospectively from June 1993.

Shortly before the Commonwealth legislation was passed, Western
Australia enacted legislation of its own (Land (Titles and Traditional
Usage) Act 1993), eliminating native title in that State in favour of a statu-
tory 'right of traditional usage' and offering compensation for native title

extinguished between 1975 and 1993 inconsistently with the Racial Discrimination Act. The Western Australian Act admittedly was inconsistent with the Native Title Act, if the latter were valid. There was a possible argument that it was inconsistent with the Racial Discrimination Act as well, on the grounds that, for example, rights of traditional usage were more easily extinguished than other forms of title in Western Australia.

Two suits, respectively seeking a declaration of the invalidity of the Commonwealth and Western Australian native title measures, were combined in the High Court. With one relatively minor exception, the validity of the Commonwealth Act was upheld. The Western Australian Act was declared invalid on the grounds of inconsistency with both Commonwealth Acts. As far as Commonwealth power was concerned, the case established that the 'races' power could support legislation of this kind, at least. It thus paved the way for the later decision in *Kartinyeri* that, except perhaps in extreme circumstances, it is for parliament to determine whether a special law is deemed necessary. The court rejected an argument that the proportion of the State land mass affected by the Commonwealth Act made the Act a discriminatory measure against Western Australia which rendered it invalid in accordance with prevailing principles of intergovernmental immunity. In rejecting the latter argument, the court relied on the familiar if artificial doctrine that the immunities principles protect only States as 'bodies politic' rather than their powers, specifically or in general.[17] The outcome of this typical struggle over power and policy between the Commonwealth and the States was to preserve the rights of a small indigenous minority which cannot hope to secure sufficient political power to protect its own interests from the non-indigenous majority.

The Native Title Act assumed what *Mabo* did not decide: that leases, including pastoral leases, extinguished native title to land. In the *Wik* case, in the context of pastoral leases in Queensland, a majority of the High Court held that this was not so as long, at least, as particular native title rights were capable of being exercised consistently with the terms of a pastoral lease. The furore that followed this decision was equal to, if not greater than, that which accompanied *Mabo* itself. On this occasion, however, the incumbent Commonwealth government, representing the national majority, sought greater limitation of native title rights. This involved, in particular, enhanced authority for the States to impose their own native title regimes as long as these were consistent with prescribed national standards. The eventual form of the legislation was tempered in its passage through the Senate by concessions to Senator Harradine from Tasmania who held the balance of power. These broadened, to a degree, the right of indigenous groups to negotiate in relation to development on some native title lands and strengthened the criteria for State and

Territory native title regimes (ATSIC 1998a). Critically, they enabled either house of the parliament to disallow a determination by the Commonwealth minister, approving a State or Territory regime (Native Title Act 1993, ss. 43A, 214). This paved the way for action subsequently taken by the Senate, to disallow the first such determination, in relation to the Northern Territory (Commonwealth Parliament 1999:1609). The effect was to leave in place, for the moment, the provisions of the Commonwealth Act.

Courts have played a key role in the history of the evolution of the constitutional position of the indigenous peoples of Australia. Courts gave the imprimatur to the doctrine of *terra nullius* in the nineteenth century. Appropriately, in these circumstances, a court was instrumental in repudiating the doctrine, thus casting doubt on its legitimacy from the start. Given the controversial nature of the issue, it is unlikely that governments and parliaments could have been persuaded to act so definitively. The preparedness of the High Court to do so, when the rights of a small minority were at stake, is a tribute to the value of judicial independence. The cost has been a new political interest in the function and composition of the High Court, which may be felt for some time to come.

Neither *Mabo* nor *Wik* were constitutional cases. The longer-term effectiveness of both, however, has been closely interwoven with the constitution. While there are no constitutional restrictions on State power to resume lands that are subject to native title, States must act consistently with Commonwealth legislation, including, for this purpose, the Racial Discrimination Act 1975. The Commonwealth itself is unable to override native title without compensation, because one of the rare constitutional limits on Commonwealth power precludes legislation with respect to the acquisition of property other than on 'just terms' (s. 51(31)). The Commonwealth can, of course, repeal or amend the Racial Discrimination Act, freeing the way for the States to act, but is inhibited from doing so by international opinion.

The courts were not the sole actors in these developments, however. On the contrary, legislation was necessary after *Mabo* to provide an effective framework for the adjudication of claims. The legislation required amendment again after *Wik*. In this context also, the effect of federalism was felt, through the influence of the Senate on legislation that was passed and on the way in which it has operated since.

ASPECTS OF SELF-GOVERNMENT

Aboriginal people constitute less than 2 per cent of the Australian population. Even with the wider opportunities for representation that a federal system offers, they are unlikely to have a substantive impact on public policy through general democratic processes. In fact, it has been relatively rare for indigenous Australians to hold elected public office at all, in either the Commonwealth or the States. Nor has there ever been substantial support for specific indigenous representation, the example of New Zealand notwithstanding. With a few notable exceptions, therefore, at Commonwealth, State and Territory and even local levels of government, indigenous Australians are subject to policies and laws made and administered by non-indigenous Australians. The problem is compounded by significant differences in the interests and preferences of indigenous and non-indigenous peoples, not only in relation to land but also in matters of language, culture and law.

Various institutions have been established from time to time to provide indigenous people with a limited measure of control over their own affairs. These include land councils, created in association with land rights legislation to represent Aboriginal groups on land rights claims. More generally, some jurisdictions have facilitated Aboriginal self-governance at the local government level or on areas owned by Aboriginal communities.

The most substantial venture so far, however, was the establishment of ATSIC by the Aboriginal and Torres Strait Islander Commission Act 1989. The objects of the Act refer to 'maximum participation' of indigenous peoples 'in the formulation and implementation of government policies that affect them'; promotion of 'self-management and self-sufficiency'; and coordination of policies affecting indigenous peoples between the levels of government 'without detracting from the responsibilities' of each. To this end, the Act provides for thirty-five elected regional councils, organised within seventeen zones, each of which elects a commissioner to ATSIC itself. The functions of ATSIC range from the formulation and implementation of programs to advice to the government on indigenous affairs (s. 7). Its actual authority to design and implement programs, however, depends on a conferral of specific functions, by the prime minister in relation to Commonwealth matters or by individual State and Territory governments in relation to matters within their usual sphere of responsibility (ss. 8 and 9).

The Aboriginal and Torres Strait Islander Commission has been a controversial body since its establishment. Even within the indigenous community, it has encountered some resistance. While ATSIC commissioners are, for the most part, elected, they are not always or necessarily people who enjoy traditional respect within Aboriginal culture. Nor do ATSIC areas necessarily coincide with tribal boundaries. From the outset, there was some opposition to ATSIC from non-indigenous Australians, as a government body with responsibilities only to one community. In time, however, other difficulties emerged, reflecting the unusual character of ATSIC itself. It is an elected body which combines both policy-making and administrative functions. It is established as an independent statutory corporation but necessarily doubles also as a source of advice to the Commonwealth minister, in the manner of a department. The minister has some powers in relation to ATSIC, including a power to issue general directions (s. 12), but lacks the full authority generally wielded by a minister in relation to a department of state. With hindsight, insufficient thought was given to the way in which a body of this kind would fit within an otherwise typically Westminster style of parliamentary government and administration, particularly when indigenous policy issues became sensitive, from the standpoint of the government of the day.

The results have included a series of controversies involving ATSIC on grounds of actual or perceived waste and mismanagement; the development of a separate source of policy advice to government on indigenous affairs, in the Department of Prime Minister and Cabinet; and the removal from ATSIC of functions in key areas, including indigenous education and health. Nor has ATSIC been entirely successful in coordinating activities across levels of government (ATSIC 1998b), despite a 'national commitment' endorsed by the Council of Australian Governments in 1992,[18] and despite ATSIC participation in the intergovernmental ministerial council dealing with indigenous affairs.[19]

The future of ATSIC is not entirely clear. It is likely to be retained, however, and gradually to stabilise and to become more widely accepted. It would be a pity if it were otherwise. The concept of an indigenous structure for policy development and service delivery seems correct in principle. It would be unrealistic to have expected that such an innovative and challenging idea would be implemented without difficulty the first time around.

ATSIC alone has not stilled a wider debate on self-government or self-determination. The debate is conducted at two levels. The first concerns sovereignty or self-determination in the sense in which this term is used in article 1 of the International Covenant on Civil and Political Rights: the right of peoples to 'freely determine their political status and freely pursue their economic, social and cultural development'. It takes its character in Australia from the ambiguous nature of the original European settlement. It is reinforced by the treatment of indigenous Australians as inferior citizens for most of the history of federated Australia. Taken to its extreme, it has implications for the cohesion of Australia itself as a nation-state.

The second level of the debate is practical and concerns the degree of effective self-government that is available to indigenous people. This has been variously described as self-management (House of Representatives Standing Committee on Aboriginal Affairs 1990:4) and self-sufficiency (Aboriginal and Torres Strait Islander Commission Act 1989), as well as self-government (Gardiner-Garden 1994:36). It is complicated by the impossibility of a single, uniform solution, suiting the circumstances of both urban and traditional indigenous groups and of groups in both the settled south and more sparsely populated north of the country. ATSIC has made an important contribution to self-government in this sense and may have further potential still, if its operations are effectively decentralised. Its functions and jurisdiction are too limited, however, to fully meet the demand.

Part of the demand stems from a desire of some groups for the recognition, at least in part, of indigenous customary law. It is clear that an extensive range of customary laws existed at the time Australia was settled. It is also clear that customary law continues to apply in many indigenous communities, often in an uneasy relationship with the general law. The failure of general law to recognise and appropriately accommodate customary law contributes to the destabilisation of indigenous communities and is not conducive to respect for either law, on the part of indigenous people.

The result is clearly unsatisfactory; the solution in policy terms, however, is less obvious. Customary laws differ between indigenous groups. Not all indigenous people wish to be subject to customary law. Some customary laws may be inconsistent with norms that, for one reason or another, should be applicable to all Australians. It is at this point that the debate on customary law links with the question of self-government for particular communities. In theory, at least, it would be possible to devise self-government arrangements which included provision for the application of customary law, in defined subject areas or subject to overriding national and international standards. The Charlottetown Accord, put to referendum in Canada in 1992, provided a possible model for this purpose.[20]

While there has been some talk about these issues, so far there has been little action. In theory, opposition to indigenous self-government should be more muted in a federal system, which by definition involves divided sovereignty. Nevertheless, discussion of self-government, in the sense of greater autonomy, inevitably founders on concerns about sovereignty, whether real or feigned. The concept of self-government for indigenous Australian communities is unlikely to be taken seriously until the two levels of the debate on indigenous autonomy are clearly distinguished and better understood.

THE FUTURE

There are two particular developments that could beneficially affect the constitutional position of indigenous Australians in the future. Both have been focused on the constitutional centenary in 2001.

The Northern Territory
Indigenous people comprise approximately 25 per cent of the population of the Northern Territory. This is the largest indigenous proportion

of population in any Australian jurisdiction. At the time of federation, the Northern Territory was part of the State of South Australia. It was transferred to the Commonwealth in 1911. The Territory achieved self-government in 1978 along lines that mirrored the position of the States, while falling short of the degree of autonomy that the States enjoy as constituent units of the federation.

For some time, the Northern Territory has been seeking statehood. Symbolically, the constitutional centenary has been an appropriate target. A 1996 draft of a statehood constitution provided for the recognition of Aboriginal customary law, in two separate versions. Alternative 1 restricted the use of customary law to circumstances where it would be implemented and enforced as part of the common law or the practice of the courts. Alternative 2 would have gone further, to enable customary law to be implemented and enforced in respect of any person who considers that he or she is bound by the law. The Northern Territory constitutional committee noted that 'no Australian jurisdiction has ever legally recognised the system of customary law operating amongst its indigenous inhabitants'. It also noted, however, that it had encountered 'no significant opposition to some form of recognition'.[21] The draft also would have provided for a repatriated Aboriginal Lands Act, entrenched by organic law, and would have recognised (if this was necessary) that the Northern Territory legislature might provide for Aboriginal self-determination.

Political controversy over the constitutional convention held to consider the draft and over the terms of the subsequent referendum caused the latter to fail. Indigenous Territorians were among its opponents. One reason lay in the convention's attitude to recognition of Aboriginal customary law. The proposals in the original draft were reduced to a limited form which would have required the parliament of the new Territory to enact customary law within five years, an impracticable feat which in any event was unacceptable to indigenous Australians (Heatley and McNab 1998:155).

This is not necessarily the end of the drive for statehood. In separate constitutional conventions, held before and after the referendum vote, the indigenous people set out their demands for a statehood constitution.[22] These included recognition of Aboriginal law as a source of law, operating through Aboriginal structures of law and governance; protection of indigenous rights and development of a framework for self-government; and more general constitutional initiatives, such as protection of human rights, effective separation of powers, and, perhaps, an electoral system based on proportional representation. While these demands are unlikely to be satisfied in full, they offer a base on which further negotiations might proceed. These negotiations will be delicate: the referendum was defeated by a relatively small margin and another round, with a more sophisticated process, could see it passed without substantial improvement in its application to indigenous Territorians. Even then, all would not be lost. The terms of statehood for the Northern Territory must be acceptable to the Australian parliament, including the Senate, where senators holding the balance of power presently are sympathetic to indigenous interests.

Reconciliation

To further reconciliation, the Commonwealth established in 1991 a Council for Aboriginal Reconciliation. One of the functions conferred on the council was to consult indigenous communities and the Australian community as a whole 'on whether reconciliation would be advanced by a formal document or documents of reconciliation' (Council for Aboriginal Reconciliation Act 1991, s. 6). In 1999, the council released for public consultation a draft Document for Reconciliation and four supporting draft strategies. The document itself refers, inter alia, to respect for 'the right of Aboriginal and Torres Strait Islander peoples to determine their own destinies'. The draft strategies refer to the right of indigenous Australians 'to participate, as they choose, in all levels of decision-making on matters which affect them and their communities' and to their 'continuing aspirations for greater recognition and self-determination within the framework of the Australian Constitution'.[23] They also contemplate recognition and protection of the declaration in the constitutions of the Commonwealth and the States.[24]

There may be no substantive decision on the declaration and supporting strategies before the constitutional centenary in 2001. In any event, they would be likely to be no more than another small step in improving the actual and symbolic position of indigenous Australians within the polity as a whole. Meanwhile, the prospect of a link between the declaration and the Commonwealth constitution has been complicated further by the 1999 proposal to add a preamble to the constitution. The preamble would have included a statement 'honouring Aborigines and Torres Strait Islanders, the nation's first people, for their deep kinship with their lands and for their ancient and continuing cultures which enrich the life of our country' (Constitution Alteration (Preamble) 1999). The proposal was put to referendum on 6 November 1999, but rejected. While many Aboriginal groups were opposed to the wording and advocated a 'no' vote, the fact of rejection is discouraging to the extent that it is likely to deter other attempts at constitutional change in the future.

CONCLUSION

The accommodation of indigenous people in constitutional systems is an issue for the end of the twentieth century. At stake is the right of indigenous people to live in a way which is guided by their own cultural practices under their own leaders, albeit within a wider framework of norms applicable to the whole community.

In principle, federations have an advantage in dealing with this issue. Federations are based upon the concept of divided sovereignty. They accommodate diversity. They offer an opportunity for experimentation through competition between jurisdictions. They enable innovation in smaller jurisdictions by means of which the larger national majority may be persuaded.

Nevertheless, federations find it difficult to deal adequately with the needs of their indigenous people. For the most part, federations offer diversity only on a geographic basis, which may or may not coincide with ethnicity. It is rare for indigenous groups to be geographically concentrated, Nunavut notwithstanding. Liberal democratic values make even federations loath to cut across geographic divisions to single out a particular group. Significant differences between the cultures of indigenous peoples and that of the general community are likely to be an additional barrier in practice. And in these increasingly multicultural times, indigenous demands often are echoed by demands for distinctive treatment from other ethnic communities as well.

The adaptability of federal forms to deal with indigenous issues varies between federations. In many ways, the Australian federation has been particularly unreceptive. The original doctrine of *terra nullius* encouraged belief that Aboriginal law and culture was inferior. The colonies which later became States and which are responsible for many of the areas of governance relevant to indigenous people were late to recognise them as equal citizens. The Commonwealth acquired its authority in relation to indigenous Australians after federation was far advanced. The scope of Commonwealth power was ambiguous from the start. Indigenous Australians became the victims of the buck-passing and irresponsibility that often is associated with concurrent federal powers. Their cause became even more controversial through entanglement with other intergovernmental disputes, including the scope of the external affairs power and the degree of protection that the constitution gives one government from another.

The Commonwealth has been a relatively more enlightened level of government for indigenous Australians. Even here, however, voters and politicians have resisted claims for autonomy of the most limited kind. This is partly the result of assumptions entrenched by the apparent homogeneity of the Australian population since European settlement. It is partly because the political system is strongly majoritarian and uneasy with compromise and consensus. Despite its federal institutional structure, Australian federalism has suffered from the lack of a federal culture, receptive to power sharing. The capacity of the federal system to respond to the needs of indigenous people is hampered for this reason as well.

NOTES

1 *Kruger* v. *Commonwealth* (1997) 190 CLR 1.
2 *Cooper* v. *Stuart* (1889) 14 App. Cas 286.
3 For example, Land Act 1933 (WA), s. 106.
4 *Mabo (No. 2)* (1992) 175 CLR 1.
5 Aboriginal Land Rights (Northern Territory) Amendment Act (No. 3) 1978 (Commonwealth): Commonwealth Parliamentary Debates, House of Representatives 109, 31 May 1978, 2820 (Staley).
6 *Kartinyeri* v. *Commonwealth* (1998) 72 ALJR 722, 732 per Gaudron J, 760 per Kirby J.
7 Statute of Westminster Adoption Act 1942 (Commonwealth).
8 *Koowarta* v. *Bjelke-Petersen* (1982) 153 CLR 168.
9 *Cooper* v. *Stuart* (1889) 14 App. Cas 206.
10 *Milirrpum* v. *Nabalco Pty Ltd* (1971) 17 FLR 141.
11 The findings of Moynihan J are summarised in the judgment of Brennan J in *Mabo (No. 2)*:17–20.
12 *Mabo* v. *Queensland (No. 1)* (1988) 166 CLR 186.
13 *Mabo* v. *Queensland (No. 2)* (1992) 175 CLR 1, 15, Mason CJ and McHugh J.
14 *Wik* v. *Queensland* (1996) 187 CLR 1.
15 One lurid example: *Mabo* 'carried the seeds of the territorial dismemberment of the Australian continent and the end of the Australian nation as we have known it' (quoted in Gardiner-Garden 1994:143, 165).
16 *Western Australia* v. *Commonwealth* (1995) 183 CLR 373, 483.
17 Ibid., 479, 480.
18 National commitment to the improvement of outcomes in the delivery of services for Aboriginal people and Torres Strait Islanders.
19 Ministerial Council on Aboriginal and Torres Strait Islander Affairs (MCATSIA).
20 The Accord was rejected at referendum. Had it succeeded, it would have added new provisions to the Canadian Constitution Act 1982, recognising the 'inherent right of self-government' of the aboriginal peoples within Canada, including the possible application of aboriginal law.
21 Legislative Committee of the Northern Territory, Sessional Committee on Constitutional Development, *Foundations for a Common Future*, vol. 1, November 1995:5–6.
22 Combined Aboriginal Nations of Central Australia held a convention at Kalkaringi in August. The Northern Territory Aboriginal Nations held a convention in Batchelor in December.
23 Draft National Strategy to Promote Recognition of Aboriginal and Torres Strait Islander Rights.
24 Draft National Strategy to Sustain the Reconciliation Process.

REFERENCES

ATSIC (Aboriginal and Torres Strait Islander Commission) 1995. *Recognition Rights and Reform*. Canberra: ATSIC.
—— 1998a. 'Detailed analysis of Native Title Amendment Act 1998' (October), <http://www.atsic.gov.au/issues/native_title.htm>.

—— 1998b. *Annual Report 1997–98*. Canberra: ATSIC.

Bonner, Neville T. 1994. 'Introduction', in *Mabo Papers*. Parliamentary Research Service Subject Collection No. 1. Canberra: Australian Government Publishing Service.

Chesterman, John and Brian Galligan 1997. *Citizens without Rights*. Cambridge: Cambridge University Press.

Commonwealth Parliament 1999. *Senate Journal*. 31 August.

Coonan, Helen 1999. 'The Senate: safeguard or handbrake on democracy', *The Sydney Papers* 11(1), Summer.

Gageler, Stephen 1998. 'The races power problem: the case for validity, *Public Law Review* 9.

Gardiner-Garden, John 1994. 'Aboriginality and Aboriginal rights in Australia', in *Mabo Papers* Parliamentary Research Service Subject Collection No. 1. Canberra: Australian Government Publishing Service.

Heatley, Alastair and Peter McNab 1998. 'The Northern Territory Statehood Convention 1998', *Public Law Review* 9.

House of Representatives Standing Committee on Aboriginal Affairs 1990. *Our Future, Our Selves: Aboriginal and Torres Strait Islander Community Control, Management and Resources*. Parliamentary Paper No. 137.

Kickingbird, Kirke 1993. 'The constitutional settlement', in Council for Aboriginal Reconciliation, *The Position of Indigenous People in National Constitutions*. Canberra: Australian Government Publishing Service.

Lindell, Geoffrey 1998. 'The races power problem: other observations', *Public Law Review* 9.

Nicholson, G.R. 1985. 'The constitutional status of the self-governing Northern Territory', *Australian Law Journal* 59:698.

Reeves, John, QC 1998. *Building on Land Rights for the Next Generation: The Review of the Aboriginal Land Rights (Northern Territory) Act 1976*. 2nd edn. Canberra: Australian Government Publishing Service.

CASES

Australia

Cooper v. *Stuart* (1889) 14 App Cas 286   270, 274
Kartinyeri v. *Commonwealth* (1998) 72 ALJR 722   271, 272, 277
Koowarta v. *Bjelke-Petersen* (1982) 153 CLR 168   274
Kruger v. *Commonwealth* (1997) 190 CLR 1   269
Mabo v. *Queensland (No. 1)* (1988) 166 CLR 186   275
Mabo v. *Queensland (No.2)* (1992) 175 CLR 1   271, 275, 276, 277
Milirrpum v. *Nabalco Pty Ltd* (1971) 17 FLR 141   274
Western Australia v. *Commonwealth* (1995) 183 CLR 373   276
Wik v. *Queensland* (1996) 187 CLR 1   275, 277, 278,

Canada

Amendment of Constitution of Canada, Re [1981] 1 SCR 753 ('Patriation case')   46
Authority of Parliament in relation to the Upper House, Re [1980] 1 SCR 54 ('Second Amendment case')
Eskimos, Re [1939] SCR 104   37
Hodge v. *The Queen* (1883) 2 SCR 712
Liquidators of the Manitoba Bank v. *Receiver General of NB* [1892] AC 437   51
Objection by Quebec to Resolution to Amend the Constitution, Re [1982] 2 SCR 793 ('Quebec veto case')   46
Quebec v. *Ford* [1988] 2 SCR 712 ('Quebec language case')   47
Secession of Quebec, Re [1998] 161 DLR 4th 385   3, 46–7

China

Lau Kong Yung v. *Director of Immigration* [1999] 4 HKC 731   96
Ng Ka Ling v. *Director of Immigration* [1999] 1 HKLRD 315   96
The Interpretation of the Standing Committee of the National Peoples Congress of Articles 22(4) and 24(2)(3) of the Basic Law of the Hong Kong Special Administrative Region of the People's Republic of China (Gazette of the Hong Kong Special Administrative Region, Second Supplement, Legal Notice 167 of 1999 (28 June 1999)   96

India

Mohammed Ahmed Khan v. *Shah Bano Begum* AIR 1985 SC 945   56, 57, 71n5

South Africa

Chairperson of the Constitutional Assembly Ex Parte: In Re Certification of the Constitution of the Republic of South Africa, 1996, 1996 (4) SA 744 (CC) 111–12

Chairperson of the Constitutional Assembly Ex Parte: In Re Certification of the Amended Text of the Constitution of the Republic of South Africa, 1996, 1997 (2) SA 97 (CC) 112

Speaker of the National Assembly Ex Parte: In Re Dispute Concerning the Constitutionality of Certain Provisions of the National Education Policy Bill 83 of 1995, 1996 (3) SA 165 (CC)   109

Speaker of the KwaZulu-Natal Provincial Legislature Ex Parte: In Re KwaZulu-Natal Amakhosi and Iziphakanyiswa Amendment Bill of 1995; Ex Parte Speaker of the KwaZulu-Natal Provincial Legislature: In Re Payment of Salaries, Allowances and Other Privileges to the Ingonyama Bill of 1995, 1996 (4) SA 653 (CC) ('Amakhosi case')   110

Speaker of the KwaZulu-Natal Provincial Legislature Ex Parte: In Re Certification of the Constitution of the Province of KwaZulu-Natal, 1996, 1996 (4) SA 1098 (CC) 110–11

Sri Lanka

Constitutionality of an Act to amend the Agrarian Services Act No 58 of 1979 (Hansard 1990:192–5)   207

Constitutionality of an Act to amend the Provincial Councils Act No. 42 of 1987 (Hansard 1990: 270–1)   207–8

J.V.P. and others v. *Attorney-General* reported as *Peramuna* v. *Attorney General* [1999] 4 LRC 22   210

Karunathilaka and another v. *Dayananda Dissanayaka, Commissioner of Elections* [1999] 4 LRC 380   209–10

G.S.N. Kodakan Pillai v. *P.B. Mudanayake et al.* [1953] 54 NLR 350 (Supreme Court)   205

G.S.N. Kodakan Pillai v. *P.B. Mudanayake et al.* [1953] 54 NLR 433 (Privy Council)   205

C. Kodeeswaran v. *The Attorney-General* [1970] 72 NLR 337   205, 217

Mahindasoma v. *Maithripala Senanayake and another* [1996] 1 SLR 180   200–1, 209

Northern and Eastern Provinces Transport Board Reference (S.C. No. 7/89 (Special) (PPA/2/PC/19, unreported)   206–7

Premachandra v. *Montague Jayewickrema and another* (Provincial Governor's Case) [1994] 2 SLR 90, [1994] 4 LRC 95   208–9

Seneviratne and another v. *University Grants Commission and another* [1980] 1 SLR 182   205–6

The Thirteenth Amendment to the Constitution and the Provincial Councils Bill in Re [1987] 2 SLR 312, [1990] LRC (Const.)   201, 203, 206

United States

New York v. *United States* (1992) 505 US 144   110

LEGISLATION

INDEX

Note: When a political entity has clearly become independent of another, such as Eritrea from Ethiopia, it is indexed separately. Where regions or peoples are the subject of significant discussion but where they are still clearly part of another entity or their position is unresolved, they are indexed under that greater entity; thus, Quebec is indexed under Canada, and Tamils under Sri Lanka.

Province of, split (1867) 29
Royal Commission on the
	Aboriginal Peoples (1997) 37
Supreme Court 3, 21, 33, 37, 46–7
tolerance, tradition of 30
United States, relations with 32
Victoria Charter 38
cantons, proposed for Sri Lanka 197
caste 53, 54, 55, 56, 70
census 5, 50, 198, 220
Ceylon, *see* Sri Lanka
chauvinism
	Han 77, 91
	Hindu 73n20
	Sinhala 200
Chesterman, John 271
China 1, 2, 4, 5, 7, 8, 10, 15, 16, 22
	autonomous regions 83, 86
	autonomy
		ethnic, assessment of 91
		ethnic autonomous area,
			criteria for establishing
			83–4
		forms of 83
		institutions, limits on 85
	centralisation 77
	Chinese Communist Party 4, 16,
		21, 77, 79, 80, 82, 86, 90, 91,
		94, 96
		constitution 83
	Confucianism 77, 96
	constitution (1982) 4, 81, 83, 85,
		89, 96
	Cultural Revolution 81, 86, 88–9
	diversity 78, 79
	Great Leap Forward 81
	Greater, reunification 4, 77, 78, 83,
		93
	Guangxi 83
	Han 85
		cadres to learn local language
			84
		distinctions among obscured 82
		dominance 81, 92
		Hong Kong, Macau and Taiwan,
			perceived to inhabit 93
		migration, internal 79, 88, 91

	nationalism 80
	Xinjiang, in 90
	Hui 79, 81
	Inner Mongolia 83
	Kazakhs 79
	Kirghiz 79
	Kuomintang 79, 86, 89
	legal system, weakness of 78, 91, 96
	Manchu 82
	minorities 77, 81–2
	Mongols 79
	National People's Congress 20–1,
		86, 93, 196
	nationalities, classifying 81–2
	nationality townships 83
	Naxi 82
	Ningxia 83
	People's Liberation Army 87
	Special Economic Zones 83, 85
	State Council 83
	Tadjiks 79
	Tartars 79
	Tibet 16, 78, 86–9
		'Agreement on Measure for the
			Peaceful Liberation of
			Tibet' (1951) 87–9
		Autonomous Region
			established 87
		China accused of genocide 88
		China invades 86
		Chinese interpretation of
			extent 88
		declaration of independence
			(1959) 87, 89
		history 86–7
		leaders 83
		theocracy 86
	Tibetans 79
		rights 88
		violation of human rights 88–9
	Uygurs 79, 90
	Uzbeks 79
	Xinjiang 79, 83, 86, 89–90
	see also Hong Kong, Macau, Taiwan
Chinese, overseas 85
Christians
	India 53

295